CONFRONTING GENOCIDE

IUS GENTIUM

COMPARATIVE PERSPECTIVES ON LAW AND JUSTICE

VOLUME 7

CONFRONTING GENOCIDE

Edited by
RENÉ PROVOST
and
PAYAM AKHAVAN

Springer

Editors
René Provost
McGill University
Faculty of Law
Centre for Human Rights and
Legal Pluralism
Peel Street 3644
H3A 1W9 Montreal Québec
Canada
rene.provost@mcgill.ca

Payam Akhavan
McGill University
Faculty of Law
Centre for Human Rights and
Legal Pluralism
Peel Street 3644
H3A 1W9 Montreal Québec
Canada
payam.akhavan@mcgill.ca

ISBN 978-90-481-9839-9
e-ISBN 978-90-481-9840-5
DOI 10.1007/978-90-481-9840-5
Springer Dordrecht Heidelberg London New York

Library of Congress Control Number: 2010937279

Printed on acid-free paper

Springer is part of Springer Science+Business Media (www.springer.com)

This book is dedicated to anyone who takes a step, however small it may be, to try to prevent genocide.

Acknowledgements

This book is devoted to exploring this new approach to an age-old problem. The essays were written in the wake of the remarkably diverse and original presentations delivered at the Global Conference on the Prevention of Genocide held at McGill University in Montreal. This was a unique gathering devoted to the idea that intelligent foresight and moral commitment to take timely action has the potential to stop the deluge before millions are drowned. The Conference brought together hundreds of exceptional participants, including genocide survivors, Nobel prize laureates, Pulitzer prize winners, acclaimed scholars and authors, illustrious statesmen and diplomats, media personalities, and other prominent figures, as well as 36 young student leaders from 22 different countries around the world. All sessions of the conference may be viewed at www.efchr.mcgill.ca. The essays in this book, authored by some of the conference participants, represent a sample of the rich and extraordinary exchange that took place in an effort to share this cumulative knowledge and wisdom with an even wider audience. We wish to acknowledge the Echenberg Family Foundation and its founder Gordon Echenberg, whose commitment made possible this first in a series of global conferences on human rights at McGill University. We also wish to express our gratitude to Nandini Ramanujam, Mary Race, Kirk Shannon and Nour Dib for their contributions to the preparation of this volume.

Montreal, Québec
15 June 2010

René Provost
Payam Akhavan

Contents

Contributors

Payam Akhavan Faculty of Law, Centre for Human Rights and Legal Pluralism, McGill University, Montreal, QC H3A 1W9, Canada, payam.akhavan@mcgill.ca

Taner Akçam Associate Professor, Department of History, Clark University, Worcester, MA 01610-1477, USA, takcam@clarku.edu

Jobb Arnold PhD Candidate, Cultural Studies Program, Queen's University, Belfast, UK, jobbera@gmail.com

Wiebe Arts Public Information Officer, Dutch Veterans Institute, Doorn, Netherlands, W.S.Arts@veteraneninstituut.nl

Yehuda Bauer Avraham Harman Institute of Contemporary Jewry, Hebrew University, 91905 Mount Scopus, Jerusalem, Israel, yehudabauer@hotmail.com

Irwin Cotler Parliamentary Office, Ottawa, ON K1A 0A6, Canada, cotlei@parl.gc.ca

Francis M. Deng Special Adviser of the Secretary-General on the Prevention of Genocide, New York, NY 10017, USA, fdeng1@jhu.edu

Richard J. Goldstone International Bar Association's Human Rights Institute (IBAHRI), International Bar Association, W1T 1AT London, UK

Douglas Greenberg Executive Dean of Arts and Sciences, Rutgers, State University of New Jersey, New Brunswick, NJ 08901-1248, USA, execdean@sas.rutgers.edu

Rebecca J. Hamilton Princeton, NJ 08540, USA, bec.hamilton@gmail.com

Ben Kiernan Department of History, Yale University, New Haven, CT 06520-8324, USA, ben.kiernan@yale.edu

Mary Kimani United Nations, Office of the Special Advisor on Africa, New York, NY 10017, USA, kimanim@un.org

Krzysztof Kotarski Centre for Military & Strategic Studies, University of Calgary, Calgary, AB T2N 1N4, Canada, Kkotarski@gmail.com

Catherine Lu Department of Political Science, McGill University, Montréal, QC H3A 2T7, Canada, catherine.lu@mcgill.ca

Frédéric Mégret Faculty of Law, Centre for Human Rights & Legal Pluralism, McGill University, Montreal, QC H3A 1W9, Canada, frederic.megret@mcgill.ca

Luis Moreno-Ocampo International Criminal Court, Office of the Prosecutor, The Hague, Netherlands, luis.moreno-ocampo@icc-cpi.int

René Provost Faculty of Law, Centre for Human Rights and Legal Pluralism, McGill University, Montreal, QC H3A 1W9, Canada, rene.provost@mcgill.ca

Gérard Prunier Centre national de la recherche scientifique, 75794 Paris Cedex 16, France, gerard.prunier@wanadoo.fr

Mark Thompson Open Society Foundation, Media Program, W6 0LE London, UK, markthompson1@onetel.com

Samuel Walker LL.M. Law, The Old Schools, University of Cambridge, CB2 1TN Cambridge, UK, samgwalker@gmail.com

Noah Weisbord Duke University Law School, Durham, NC 27708, USA, weisbord@law.duke.edu

Binxin Zhang Renmin University of China Law School, 100872 Beijing, China, muteng@hotmail.com

Wenqi Zhu Renmin University of China Law School, 100872 Beijing, China, wenqizhu@hotmail.com

About the Contributors

Payam Akhavan, a professor of Law at McGill University, was the first Legal Advisor to the Prosecutor Office of the International Criminal Tribunals for Former Yugoslavia and Rwanda and played a key role in the development of its foundational jurisprudence. He also has considerable experience in post-conflict peace-building and international dispute settlement, having advised the UN on transitional justice, appearing as counsel before international courts and tribunals on behalf of sovereigns, and serving on the board of directors of human rights NGOs, including the Iran Human Rights Documentation Centre in New Haven, of which he is also the president and co-founder. His work has been featured in the New York Times and, in recognition of his contributions to promoting accountability for human rights violations, he was selected by the World Economic Forum as a Young Global Leader in 2005.

Taner Akçam, a sociologist, historian and writer, was born in Ardahan province, Turkey, in 1953. He was granted political asylum in Germany after receiving a 10-year prison sentence for his involvement in politics related to democracy and human rights, which resulted in his adoption in 1976 by Amnesty International as a prisoner of conscience. He is the author of ten scholarly works of history and sociology, as well as numerous articles in Turkish, German and English. His latest publication is *A Shameful Act: The Armenian Genocide and the Question of Turkish Responsibility* (Metropolitan Books, 2006). Professor Akçam was one of the first academics to openly discuss the Armenian genocide by the Turkish Ottoman government in 1915. He is currently holder of the Kaloosdian/Mugar Chair in Armenian Genocide Studies at Clark University.

Jobb Arnold completed his MA in Social Psychology at the University of British Columbia and is currently a PhD candidate in the Cultural Studies program at Queen's University in Kingston Ontario. His research focuses on the dynamics of rupture and re-articulation of social and individual meaning, and the micro-politics of identity in Rwanda and Northern Ireland. He has worked with the United Nations Development Programme as well as the

Canadian International Development Association in Rwanda, and as part of EU sponsored projects focused on community reconciliation in Belfast.

Wiebe Arts is a former Dutch Infantry NCO (1984–2000) and Historian, working as a Public Information Officer at the Dutch Veterans Institute. As a member of the Royal Netherlands Army, he served as a peacekeeper of the United Nations Protection Force for the Former Yugoslavia (UNPROFOR) in the east Bosnian town of Srebrenica, a UN 'safe area,' between January and April 1995.

Born in Prague in 1926, **Yehuda Bauer** is an historian and scholar of the Holocaust, and Honorary Chairman of the International Task Force for Holocaust Education, Remembrance and Research. He attended Cardiff University in Wales, interrupting his studies to fight in the 1948 Arab-Israeli War, after which he completed his degree. He received his doctorate in 1960 and began teaching at the Avraham Harman Institute of Contemporary Jewry at the Hebrew University. In 1998, he was the recipient of the Israel Prize, the highest civilian award in Israel. In 2001, he was elected a Member of the Israeli Academy of Science. Currently, he serves as Professor of Holocaust Studies, Yad Vashem and Hebrew University, and academic adviser to the International Task Force for Holocaust Education, Remembrance and Research.

Professor **Irwin Cotler** has taught constitutional law, international human rights law, law and poverty, Canadian Charter of Rights and Freedoms, discrimination and the law, civil liberties, and comparative and international protection of minorities' rights. His main research areas are freedom of expression and assaultive speech, equality law, peace and human rights, and comparative constitutional law. Professor Cotler was Chair of InterAmicus, the International Human Rights Advocacy Centre based at McGill Law Faculty; and Co-Chair of the Canadian Helsinki Watch Group. He has defended political prisoners in Peru, Tunisia, China (KunLun Zhang), Nigeria (Wole Soyinka), Indonesia, South Africa (Nelson Mandela) and Russia (Andrei Sakharov, Aleksandr Nikitin) and he has addressed major academic gatherings in Washington, Moscow and Jerusalem. He has argued before the Supreme Courts of both Canada and Israel and he has testified before parliamentary committees in Canada, the United States, Norway, Sweden, Russia, Israel and various Latin American countries. He is an Officer of the Order of Canada, a member of the Académie universelle des cultures, and was awarded the Justice Walter Tarnopolsky Memorial Medal, the Medal of the Bar of Montréal, and the Martin Luther King Jr Humanitarian Award. In 1999, Professor Cotler took a leave of absence from the Faculty of Law and was elected Member of Parliament for the federal constituency of Mount Royal. He served as Minister of Justice and Attorney General of Canada from 2003 to 2006. Professor Cotler's work in genocide prevention and persecution of criminals has received international attention. He has worked tirelessly to bring Nazi war criminals to justice and convey the magnitude of the Darfur crisis to the public. Most recently he is working to indict Iranian President Ahmadinejad for incitement to genocide under the UN Charter and the Genocide Convention.

In May 2007, **Francis M. Deng** was appointed Special Adviser of the Secretary-General on the Prevention of Genocide on a full time basis and at the level of Under-Secretary-General. Dr. Deng holds an LLB (Honors) from Khartoum University and an LLM and JSD from Yale Law School. He first joined the United Nations as Human Rights Officer in 1967. In 1992, he joined the Foreign Service of his country, the Sudan, and served as Ambassador to the United States, Canada, and the Scandinavian countries and as Minister of State for Foreign Affairs. After leaving his country's service, Dr. Deng joined the Brookings Institution in Washington DC as a Senior Fellow where he founded and directed the Africa Project for twelve years. He also served concurrently as the Representative of the Secretary-General on Internally Displaced Persons from 1992 to 2004. Dr. Deng also held an appointment as Research Professor of International Politics, Law and Society at the Johns Hopkins University School of Advanced International Studies, prior to which, he was a Distinguished Professor at the Graduate Center of the City University of New York. Dr. Deng has also held visiting professorships and research positions at New York University, Columbia Law School, Yale Law School, the Woodrow Wilson International Center for Scholars, the Rockefeller Brothers Fund, the United States Institute of Peace, the John W. Kluge Center of the Library of Congress and the Center for International Studies of the Massachusetts Institute of Technology. Among his numerous awards in his country and abroad, Dr. Deng was co-recipient with Roberta Cohen of the 2005 Grawemeyer Award for "Ideas Improving World Order." He is also the recipient of the 2007 Merage Foundation American Dream Leadership Award and the 2000 Rome Prize for Peace and Humanitarian Action. Dr. Deng has authored, co-authored, edited and co-edited over thirty books in the fields of law, conflict resolution, internal displacement, human rights, anthropology, history and politics, and has written two novels on the crisis of national identity in the Sudan.

Richard J. Goldstone, 1959 BA 1962 LLB (Wits) practised as an Advocate at the Johannesburg Bar. In 1980 was made Judge of the Transvaal Supreme Court. In 1989 he was appointed Judge of the Supreme Court of Appeal. From July 1994 to October 2003 he was a Justice of the Constitutional Court of South Africa. In recent years he has been a visiting professor of laws at Harvard, Fordham, Georgetown and NYU Schools of Law. He recently led the UN Fact Finding Mission on Gaza. From 15 August 1994 to September 1996 he served as the Chief Prosecutor of the United Nations International Criminal Tribunals for the former Yugoslavia and Rwanda. In December 2001 he was appointed as the co-chairperson of the International Task Force on Terrorism that was established by the International Bar Association. He is presently the co-chairperson of the Human Rights Institute of the International Bar Association. From 1999 to 2003 he served as a member of the International Group of Advisers of the International Committee of the Red Cross. He was a member of the committee, chaired by Paul A. Volcker, appointed by the Secretary-General of the United Nations to investigate allegations regarding the Iraq Oil for Food Program. He is an Honorary Bencher of the Inner Temple, London, an Honorary Fellow of St Johns College, Cambridge, and an Honorary Member of the Association of the Bar of New York. He is a Foreign Member of the American Academy of Arts and Sciences. He has recently received the John D. and Catherine T. MacArthur Award for International Justice.

Douglas Greenberg is Professor of History and Executive Dean of the School of Arts and Sciences (SAS), the largest academic unit of Rutgers, the State University of New Jersey. Previously, he was Professor of History and Executive Director of the Shoah Foundation Institute for Visual History and Education at the University of Southern California. Greenberg has also served as President and CEO of the Chicago Historical Society, Vice President of the American Council of Learned Societies, and Associate Dean of the Faculty at Princeton University. In 2009, he received Phi Beta Kappa's Triennial Award for Distinguished Service to the Humanities.

Rebecca J. Hamilton is the Special Correspondent in Sudan for the Washington Post, with support from the Pulitzer Center on Crisis Reporting. A graduate of Harvard Law School and the Kennedy School, she is a former Open Society fellow. She helped spearhead the campaign for Harvard University to divest from companies doing business with Sudan, and has worked with internally displaced populations in Sudan. In 2007 she was selected as a Global Young Leader on Genocide Prevention. After graduating from law school she worked for the Prosecution at the International Criminal Court in The Hague. Her writing on genocide and Sudan has appeared in *Leiden J. Int'l Law*, *Foreign Affairs* and *The New Republic* and her first book, *Fighting for Darfur*, will be published in 2011.

Professor **Ben Kiernan** obtained his Ph.D. from Monash University, Australia. In 1990 he joined the History Department at Yale University, and was appointed the A. Whitney Griswold Professor of History in 1999. In 1994 he became founding director of Yale's Cambodian Genocide Program, and in 1998 he founded the Genocide Studies Program, an interdisciplinary, inter-regional program that researches comparative and policy issues at the MacMillan Center for International and Area Studies at Yale. As director of the Cambodian Genocide Program, Kiernan was instrumental in unearthing and disclosing documents attesting to genocidal crimes of the Khmer Rouge regime. He is most recently the author of *Blood and Soil: A World History of Genocide and Extermination from Sparta to Darfur*

(2007), which won the 2008 gold medal for the best work of history awarded by the Independent Publishers association, and the U.S. German Studies Association's 2009 Sybil Halpern Milton Memorial Book Prize for the best book published in 2007–2008 dealing with Nazi Germany and the Holocaust in its broadest context. In June 2009, the book's German translation, *Erde und Blut: Völkermord und Vernichtung von der Antike bis heute*, won first place in Germany's Nonfiction Book of the Month Prize sponsored by *Süddeutsche Zeitung* and *NDR Kultur*. Kiernan is also the author of *Genocide and Resistance in Southeast Asia: Documentation, Denial and Justice in Cambodia and East Timor* (2007), *The Pol Pot Regime: Race, Power and Genocide in Cambodia under the Khmer Rouge, 1975–1979* (1996, 2002, 2008), and *How Pol Pot Came to Power: Colonialism, Nationalism, and Communism in Cambodia, 1930–1975* (1985, 2004). His edited collection, *Conflict and Change in Cambodia*, won the 2002 *Critical Asian Studies* Prize.

Mary Kimani worked as journalist at the International Criminal Tribunal for Rwanda, where she was based in Arusha, Tanzania covering the Rwanda genocide trials. She later moved to Rwanda to work on a documentary project aimed at raising awareness and improving dialogue in post-conflict Rwanda, particularly between the survivors and perpetrators of the Rwanda genocide. Mary has also covered the Burundi Peace process and the conflict in the Democratic Republic of Congo for Reuters and others, and has written articles for Time Magazine, El Mundo, and other publications. After six years with Internews she joined the not-for-profit Action Aid International overseeing communication programs for Africa, before joining the United Nations. She holds an MA in International Relations and Diplomacy as well as a second MA in communication psychology. The findings of her first thesis were published in *The Media and the Rwanda Genocide* (2007).

Krzysztof Kotarski grew up in Warsaw, Poland before immigrating to Canada in 1991. He holds a BA in International Relations and History, and a MSS (Strategic Studies) from the University of Calgary, where he researched arms control programs in the former Soviet Union at the Centre for Military and Strategic Studies. Kris also works as a journalist for the CanWest News chain in Canada, primarily for the *Calgary Herald* where he writes a regular column on human rights and international affairs. He also writes for the *The Guardian*, focusing on politics and human rights in Eastern Europe. In 2006, Kris was a research fellow at the Geneva-based United Nations Institute for Disarmament Research (UNIDIR) where he worked on projects that examine the dynamics of weapons transfers in Latin America, South Asia and West Africa. Starting in 2007, Kris continued his work on small arms at the Canada-based Armed Groups Project where he is a research associate.

Professor Catherine Lu teaches at McGill University in the areas of political theory and international relations, including courses on contemporary political theory, the history of international relations thought, international ethics, human rights, humanitarian intervention, and problems of post-conflict justice and reconciliation. She is the author of *Just and Unjust Interventions in World Politics: Public and Private* (UK: Palgrave Macmillan, 2006) and has published widely in journals such as *The Journal of Political Philosophy*, the *Journal of International Political Theory*, the *European Journal of Social Theory*, *International Studies Review*, and *Review of International Studies*. She was a faculty fellow at the Edmond J. Safra Foundation Center for Ethics at Harvard University (2004–2005) and a recipient of an Alexander von Humboldt Foundation Fellowship for Experienced Researchers (2010–2011).

Frédéric Mégret is an Assistant Professor of Law, the Canada Research Chair on the Law of Human Rights and Legal Pluralism and the Director of the McGill Clinic for the Sierra Leone Special Court. In the past, he has worked for the International Committee of the Red Cross, assisted the defence counsel of one of the accused before the International Criminal Tribunal for Rwanda, and was a member of the French delegation at the Rome conference that created the International Criminal Court. Professor Mégret has also advised the Liberian government on the design of a human rights vetting procedure for its armed forces. He is currently engaged in a major research project that aims to explore the tradition of resistance to oppression in the light of contemporary international law ("Resisting oppression: civil disobedience, armed rebellion and international law"). As of the summer of 2009, he will be involved in a 3-year research project entitled "International criminal justice v. transitional justice," which explores issues of hybridity, accountability and victim-orientation in the context of international criminal courts. He is the author of "Le Tribunal pénal international pour le Rwanda" (Pedone, 2002) and of many articles and chapters on international criminal justice.

Luis Moreno-Ocampo, the current Chief Prosecutor for the International Criminal Court, rose to prominence as the assistant prosecutor of the National Commission on the Disappearance of Persons in the 1984–1985 "Military Junta" in Argentina. He was the co-founder of Poder Ciudadano, a non-governmental organization that promotes citizen responsibility and participation. In his role as Chief Prosecutor for the ICC he has investigated the abuses in the Democratic Republic of Congo, the insurgency of the Uganda-based Lord's Resistance Army and the Darfur conflict of western Sudan. Mr. Moreno-Ocampo is an active member of the Advisory Committee of Transparency International. He continues to serve as Associate Professor of Criminal Law at the University of Buenos Aires.

René Provost is a professor of law at McGill University and Director of the Centre for Human Rights and Legal Pluralism. He holds an LLB from Université de Montréal, an LLM from UC Berkeley, and a DPhil from Oxford. He is the author of *International Human Rights and Humanitarian Law* (Cambridge University Press, 2002), editor of *State Responsibility in International Law* (Ashgate/Darthmout, 2002), and co-editor of *Public International Law Chiefly as Applied and Interpreted in Canada* (Emond Montgomery, 2006). He has acted as a consultant for DFAIT and CIDA on numerous occasions and has collaborated with the Sierra Leone Special Court and the Extraordinary Chamber of the Courts of Cambodia.

Gérard Prunier is a research fellow at the Centre national de la recherche scientifique (CNRS) in Paris and Director of the French Centre for Ethiopian Studies in Addis Ababa, Ethiopia. He received a PhD in African History in 1981 from the University of Paris and joined the CNRS in 1984. Prunier has done extensive research on Eastern Africa and the Horn of Africa, and he has published over 120 articles and five books. He was a key figure in the French Ministry of Defense's crisis unit in Rwanda, which oversaw France's intervention in Rwanda in Operation Turquoise.

Mark Thompson works for the Media Program of the Open Society Foundation. During the 1990s, he worked in the former Yugoslavia as a journalist, and for missions of the United Nations and the OSCE. He is the author of *A Paper House. The ending of Yugoslavia* (1992), *Forging War: the media in Serbia, Croatia, Bosnia & Herzegovina* (1994, 1999), *Forging Peace. Intervention, Human Rights and the Management of Media Space* (with Monroe E. Price, 2002), and *The White War. Life and death on the Italian front 1915–1919* (2008). He has a PhD in Social Sciences from the University of Cambridge.

Samuel Walker is from Montreal and is currently reading for an LL.M. at the University of Cambridge as a Gates Scholar. He holds a B.A. in History from Yale University and a B.C.L. and L.L.B. from McGill University's Faculty of Law. In 2011 he will be a Law Clerk to the Honourable Mr. Justice Morris J. Fish of the Supreme Court of Canada. Sam has worked on and studied human rights issues while living in Bosnia, Uganda and Israel & Palestine.

Professor Noah Weisbord is presently assistant professor of law at Florida International University College of Law and is completing his doctoral dissertation at Harvard Law School on the crime of aggression in international criminal law. He was law clerk to Chief Prosecutor Luis Moreno-Ocampo at the International Criminal Court in The Hague. Prior to working at the International Criminal Court, he traveled to Rwanda to study gacaca-community-based genocide trials inspired by an indigenous justice tradition. He is currently an expert delegate to the Special Working Group on the Crime of Aggression established by the Assembly of States Parties to the ICC. The working group is tasked with defining the crime in the lead-up to the ICC's first review conference in 2010.

Ms. Binxin Zhang obtained a PhD of international law from Renmin University of China. Her area of expertise covers International Criminal Law and International Humanitarian Law. As member of a monitoring group organized by the Asia International Justice Initiative, Ms. Zhang worked as a trial monitor for the Duch case before the Extraordinary Chambers in the Courts of Cambodia from March – August 2009, in Phnom Penh, Cambodia. Her book "War Crimes" (co-authored with Professor Wenqi Zhu and Doctor Xinyu Leng) is published by Law Press in Beijing, the most prestigious publishing house in legal field in China. Ms. Zhang has also wrote and published a number of journal articles on the subject of International Criminal Court and International Criminal Procedure Law.

Professor Wenqi Zhu is currently Professor of International Law at Renmin University of China, Beijing, as well as Director of its International Criminal Law Institute and its International Humanitarian Law Centre. He is also Member of the Board of the Chinese Society of International Law. Professor Zhu was previously a diplomat in the Chinese Ministry of Foreign Affairs from 1988–1995, in part acting as Deputy Director of their International Law Branch. From 1995–2002 he held positions as a Legal Assistant, a Legal Advisor and Appeals Counsel in the Office of the Prosecutor at the International Criminal Tribunal for the former Yugoslavia. He holds an LLM and a PhD in international law from the University of Paris, II.

Chapter 1
Moving From Repression to Prevention of Genocide

Payam Akhavan and René Provost

Much of history is a tale of humankind's capacity for organized cruelty and violence. Far from being an aberration, conquest and war have been defining features of our collective past, integral to our conceptions of triumph and heroism. Indeed, the infliction of suffering on others has rarely been considered as necessarily evil. Rather, mass violence is always justified by appealing to higher ideals, if not the sacred. In this somber tale of history, the modern era holds a place of distinction. It is an era in which ancient murderous instincts reached a new stage of perfection, in the ideological guise of progress and civilization. Beyond atavistic hatred, totalitarianism ushered in a new age of extremes that made the violence of the past pale in comparison. It inspired the word "genocide"; a word that captured the transformation of the once unthinkable into historical reality. The challenge in our times is to consider whether this scourge is inevitable, or whether it can be prevented.

In contemporary history, the harbinger of rationalized mass-murder was the extermination and enslavement of indigenous peoples in the Americas – and later in Africa and Asia – in the quest for colonial domination. But it was 20th century Europe itself that witnessed the worst excesses. This Century of Genocide opened in 1915 with the eradication of almost 1.5 million Armenians by the Ottoman Empire. It was followed in 1932 by the Ukrainian famine in which millions perished under Soviet rule. It reached its apotheosis with the extermination of 6 million Jews in the Nazi Holocaust. This was an unprecedented attempt to systematically eradicate entire peoples, rationalized through a pseudo-scientific theory of racial purity, and implemented on an extraordinary scale by the vast and efficient structures of the modern State. In the European imagination of the time, this cataclysm could not be dismissed as an expression of "Oriental despotism" or "native savagery" in distant lands. It occurred in the heart of a

---

P. Akhavan (✉)
Faculty of Law, Centre for Human Rights and Legal Pluralism, McGill University, Montreal, QC H3A 1W9, Canada
e-mail: payam.akhavan@mcgill.ca

R. Provost, P. Akhavan (eds.), *Confronting Genocide*, Ius Gentium: Comparative Perspectives on Law and Justice 7, DOI 10.1007/978-90-481-9840-5_1,

much vaunted "rational" and technologically advanced Western civilization and shattered the blind faith in modernity's promise of progress.

Such was the scale of this cataclysm, that at the trial of the Nazi leaders in Nuremberg, the French Prosecutor described it as a crime "undreamt of in history." It fell to the Polish jurist Raphaël Lemkin to name this "nameless crime." Himself a victim of the Holocaust, he coined the term "genocide" to describe the collective destruction of groups on grounds of their identity. His remarkable one-man campaign to outlaw this crime culminated in the adoption of the Convention on the Prevention and Punishment of the Crime of Genocide by the UN General Assembly on 9 December 1948. The following day, the UN General Assembly adopted the Universal Declaration of Human Rights. Thus, this seminal treaty enshrined the absolute evil of the Holocaust and presaged the emergence of human rights as the global ethos of the post-war order. Amidst the anticipation and euphoria of a new epoch, the Genocide Convention was hailed as a triumph for international law. But the vow to "never again" allow such horrors to happen soon became an empty mantra as millions more became the targets of genocide, victims of tyranny and cynicism. Mass-murder in Bangladesh's war of secession, Idi Amin's massacres in Uganda, the Khmer Rouge killing fields in Cambodia, Mengistu's "Red Terror" in Ethiopia, the slaughter of Mayans in Guatemala, Saddam Hussein's gassing of Iraqi Kurds, the mass-execution of Bosnian Muslims at Srebrenica, the extermination of Rwandan Tutsis, these are but sample sections in a sweeping epic of evil in the latter half of the 20th century, following the criminalization of genocide. These immeasurable tragedies speak to our repeated failure to give effect to righteous declarations and lofty utterances that create the illusion of progress. One step that has been taken has been to revive the international criminal law regime which had remained dormant since the days following the Second World War. The ad hoc criminal tribunals created for the former Yugoslavia, Rwanda, Sierra Leone, Cambodia, and the permanent International Criminal Court, all stand for one form of commitment to react to genocide by holding individual authors accountable for that crime. Yet while we remember, regret, and sometimes prosecute these past abominations of the 20th century, another genocide unfolds in the Darfur region of Sudan. In the opening years of the 21st century, the world appears to fail the victims once more. It seems that "never again" has become "ever again."

Considering its moral enormity, intervention against genocide has become a litmus test for the UN and more broadly a profound challenge to our global conscience. Much has been said and written, by political leaders and diplomats, scholars and experts, journalists and activists, about what could and should have been done to stop mass-murder as it unfolded. During the 1994 genocide in Rwanda for example, General Roméo Dallaire, commander of UN peacekeeping forces, called for the deployment of additional troops. Some credibly claim that this could have stopped the killings and saved hundreds of thousands of lives. Similarly, others have maintained that in 1995, Dutch UN peacekeepers could have protected the Bosnian Muslim population of the Srebrenica "safe-area" against mass-murder. Such was the political fallout of this revelation that it prompted the resignation of the Dutch cabinet in 2002. In all of these situations, intervention was possible, and opportunities were missed. But in confronting genocide, it is necessary to expand the focus of our inquiry beyond these notorious incidents of failure, beyond intervention at the last-minute when genocide is imminent. There is a need for a radically new approach.

The point of departure in preventing genocide is the realization that such extreme violence is not an inescapable reality. Unlike earthquakes, tsunamis, and other natural disasters, mass-murder is not a divinely ordained or spontaneous occurrence. It is not the inevitable expression of primordial hatred, or an irreversible clash of civilizations between peoples of differing identities. It may be true that violence is a part of human nature, at least in a perennial struggle with our more noble attributes. At its root however, the very scale of genocide invariably requires incitement, planning and aforethought. It is thus a deliberate and calculated political choice, instigated by ruthless leaders who use mass-murder as an instrument of power. As such, it is a preventable phenomenon, and it is this pliability of outcome that presents the most fundamental challenge in confronting the prophets of doom. While genocide cannot be predicted with mathematical exactitude, there are indicia, warning signs, that foretell its possibility, and which provide an opportunity to arrest hate-mongering and violence before it escalates into an all-consuming cataclysm. The urgent need for preemption of mass-violence through more subtle means is only magnified by the proliferation of weapons of mass destruction in an age of global terrorism and the manifest failures of hegemonic militant survivalism as a response.

The challenge before the international community therefore, is to move from a culture of reaction to a culture of prevention. By the time that atrocities become worthy of headline news, it is usually too late. At this stage in the progression of violence, the options become increasingly limited. Absent pressing interests by powerful nations, there is no willingness for military intervention, and a sense of urgency by a distraught public is soon reduced to compassion fatigue. The time to act is before tensions escalate into genocidal violence, when the cost of intervention through more modest measures is manageable and likely to produce far-better results. In countries such as Macedonia and Burundi, for instance, modest but timely commitment of resources – such as preventive diplomacy and peacekeeping – averted what could have been ethnic war and genocide. It was exactly because of their success that these interventions never made the headlines. Prevention is essentially measured by what does not happen. Its invisibility is not only a virtue but also an enormous challenge, in that it invites factual denials that there ever was a risk and offers few hooks on which to hang a claim for a share of available resources within the international community.

The 1994 genocide in Rwanda is an outstanding example of how a preventive policy could have resulted in a different outcome. Several months before the systematic mass-murder began in April of that year, UN officials such as General Dallaire had warned of the Hutu extremists' plan to exterminate the Tutsis. He had called for a more-robust mandate for peacekeepers under his command, so that they could disarm extremist militia, but was told to desist. Beyond such preemptive use of force however, what is truly remarkable is that the mere jamming of the notorious RTLM Radio could have seriously undermined the *génocidaires*' capacity to mobilize Rwanda's largely rural population. The radio was the sole source of information for the illiterate majority from which hundreds of thousands were incited to exterminate the Tutsi by machete and other crude weapons. The Hutus were subjected to a steady stream of fear and hate propaganda that conditioned them to enthusiastically kill their Tutsi neighbours. Once the genocide began, the radio even instructed militiamen about the identity and location of those targeted for murder. Both the United States and France possessed jamming equipment on the ground, but refused to use it. Never mind that more troops could have been sent to create protective enclaves for Tutsi civilians — it should be considered that the extremists could not have mobilized their army of thousands of killers merely if RTLM radio was not allowed to broadcast. That there could have been a different outcome in Rwanda through such a feasible and cost-effective intervention is a powerful illustration of the unrealized potential of prevention in confronting genocide. Every genocide unfolds in its own specific manner, and the recipe for Rwanda does not necessarily transfer to other situations. There is thus a need to systematically and comprehensively analyse the prevention of genocide, to identify a toolkit of measures which can be adapted to the ever changing circumstances in which genocidal tendencies can fester into mass violence. This collection is an attempt to start such a systematic and comprehensive analysis.

The book is divided into three sections. Section 1, "Reconceptualizing Genocide," considers that the first step in confronting genocide is an understanding of its anatomy. In finding a cure, we must first understand the disease. The contributions to this Section therefore provide original analysis of how genocides unfold, so that preventive strategies can be conceived. Section 2, "Un/prevented Genocide," moves from the problem to the solution by examining past failures and successes in preventing genocide. The authors take us from the Holocaust to Darfur, from Rwanda to Srebrenica, and consider the available tools for prevention, ranging from military interventions and international criminal trials to economic sanctions and diplomacy. Section 3, "Prevention Beyond the State," considers a relatively unexplored aspect of the solution beyond the conventional understanding of global governance. The broad range of options discussed range from civil society activism and the use of "peace media" to resistance by victims and use of mercenaries to protect civilians.

Section 1, "Reconceptualizing Genocide," begins with lessons learned from history on confronting injustice, not from the familiar example of the Holocaust and other contemporary genocides, but from two less-studied catastrophes of the late 19th and early 20th century that marked an important beginning for humanitarian activism against atrocities. Professor Ben Kiernan of Yale University re-analyzes the Irish Famine of 1845–1851 and the brutal exploitation of the Belgian Congo between 1885 and 1920, in light of contemporary developments in genocide studies. While he concludes that the genocide label does not easily apply to either instance, he demonstrates that those who pioneered civil society activism in response to these injustices presaged the modern human rights movement, being among the first to invoke concepts such as "crimes against humanity" and to demand an "international tribunal" to punish such atrocities.

In the following contribution, the acclaimed French historian and expert on African conflicts, Gérard Prunier, offers a provocative foundational analysis of genocide, criticizing what he perceives as the strict and formalist definition in the 1948 Genocide Convention. He identifies what he terms "ambiguous genocides" in history, questioning our compulsion with trying to assimilate all mass killings to a precise historical event – the 1941–1945 extermination of Jews in Europe. Drawing on his knowledge of African conflicts, Prunier then applies these insights to the slow-motion annihilation still unfolding in the Darfur region of Sudan, and explores possible solutions, making the controversial suggestion that absent intervention by the UN, military assistance to rebel groups may be the only feasible path to protecting victims against genocide.

Francis Deng's contribution provides valuable insights on the meaning of genocide, derived from his own unique experiences as the UN Secretary-General's Representative on Internally Displaced Persons from 1992 to 2004 and as Special Adviser to the UN Secretary-General on the Prevention of Genocide since 2007. Deng recounts how his work with internally displaced persons came to be guided by the principle of recasting State sovereignty as a responsibility, implying both accountability and international intervention for the failure of States to protect vulnerable populations. He then applies this framework to the definition and prevention of genocide, in light of his UN mandate.

University of Southern California Professor Douglas Greenberg's contribution focuses on one of the key ingredients of genocide: namely, the close relationship between exclusionary conceptions of citizenship and nationality and ideologies that sustain genocidal violence. He provides an illuminating analysis of the common patterns that can be traced from the Armenian genocide to the Holocaust, Cambodia, and Rwanda, demonstrating the contemporary relationship between the construction of national identity and group victimization.

Mark Thompson, drawing on his experience as a journalist in conflict zones, explores another theme common to all genocides: the use of the media as a conveyor of the ideology of ethnic hatred and violence that is an essential constitutive part of genocide. He provides an original approach by highlighting the tension between Western ideals of free speech and the terrifying potential of propaganda, pointing out that blind adherence to free speech principles was at least partly to blame for past failures to prevent incitement. He includes in particular the example of the refusal by Western policymakers to shut down the notorious RTLM radio station in Rwanda. Thompson advocates a new "ethics of communication" as opposed to an "ethics of self-expression," emphasizing the need for accountability in public speech and an awareness of the dangerous link between unrestricted expression and collective hatred with the potential to escalate into genocidal violence.

Section 2, "Un/prevented Genocide," moves us beyond the definitional characteristics and warning signs of genocide to the methodology of prevention. Both past and present examples of successful confrontations are examined, and potential solutions explored. Professor Yehuda Bauer of the Hebrew University in Jerusalem, a renowned historian and scholar of the Holocaust, begins this section with his own reflections on the prevention of genocide. He explores some of the obstacles to prevention, including the complex psychology of killing, the relative unpredictability of genocide, and the need for intervention to be multi-faceted and pragmatic. Throughout, he provides prescriptions for how various actors and organizations may succeed in prevention of genocide, focusing in particular on the current situation in the Darfur.

Wiebe Arts, who served as a Dutch UN peacekeeper in Srebrenica in 1995, has written an extremely valuable and unique soldier's point-of-view on the role of the military in confronting genocide. He explores the conditions necessary for peacekeeping or military missions to succeed in preventing genocide, using the Responsibility to Protect guidelines on military intervention as a benchmark. In particular, Arts identifies the need for sufficient resources, the ability to deal with unreliable parties to armed conflict, the need for appropriate training, and an element of media savvy, as critical to preventing a repetition of the tragic UN failures in Srebrenica and Rwanda.

Professor Irwin Cotler of McGill University, former Minister of Justice and Attorney-General of Canada, argues that beyond troops, the law itself can also be mobilized against genocide. Recalling the Canadian Supreme Court's admonition that "[t]he Holocaust did not begin in the gas chambers; it began with words," he focuses on the role of domestic and international law in prohibiting incitement to genocide. Cotler expresses particular concern with the call for the destruction of Israel by the President of the Islamic Republic of Iran, Mahmoud Ahmadinejad, arguing that he should be held to account for incitement to genocide.

Professor Taner Akçam, an acclaimed and courageous Turkish historian and sociologist, considers the persistent denial of the 1915 Armenian genocide in Turkey. Akçam was the one of the first Turkish academics to openly discuss this controversial issue. His contribution explores some of the motivations driving the Turkish government's refusal to face history, criticizing in particular its claims that doing so would compromise national security. He argues that defeating such claims and acknowledging historical injustices is critical both for prevention of future atrocities as well as the democratization process in Turkey.

The eminent South African Judge Richard Goldstone – the former Prosecutor of the International Criminal Tribunals for the former Yugoslavia and Rwanda – considers the topic of economic sanctions as a key instrument of the prevention "toolbox." He examines three particular case studies – South Africa, Iraq and Sudan – assessing the relative strengths and weaknesses of the use of sanctions in those situations. Goldstone makes a forceful argument for the potential impact of economic sanctions in preventing genocide, but conditions this on judicious use tailored to the specific case at hand.

The final contribution to this Section is a rare Chinese perspective on genocide by two Chinese scholars, Wenqi Zhu and Binxin Zhang from Renmin University. Zhu and Zhang summarize China's international obligations with respect to the prohibition of genocide, but note the conspicuous absence of any implementing domestic legislation in this regard. They propose the drafting of new legislation in China criminalizing genocide as an important step in consolidating the norms and structures required to increase awareness of mass crimes.

Section 3, "Prevention Beyond the State," also considers approaches to genocide prevention, but goes beyond conventional State or UN-centred conceptions of global governance to analyze the role of civil society. Professor Frédéric Mégret of McGill University makes a highly original and thought-provoking scholarly contribution, arguing that international law should do more to empower the victims of genocide to resist their oppressors. He points out that in the past, the vast majority of survivors owed their rescue not to the chimera of the "international community," but rather to themselves, the courage of strangers or resistance movements. He thus proposes that the best hope in confronting genocide lies in empowering victims, who are often dismissed, even in the law itself, as passive "lambs to the slaughter" incapable of devising their own salvation. Instead of focusing on ambitious and unrealistic solutions like humanitarian intervention, Mégret argues that international law should shift its focus to resistance by victims of genocide.

A related contribution is that of Krzysztof Kotarski and Samuel Walker, who examine a relatively unexplored topic: namely, the potential use of mercenaries in preventing genocide. Although they approach the issue cautiously, they argue that the use of private military companies should be given serious consideration and not be summarily dismissed insofar as it provides an alternative where there is no political will for UN military intervention. They contend that the potential use of mercenaries in such circumstances may be legal, cheaper, faster, more effective, and unburdened by the usual obstacles to political will of States arising from the sacrifice of national blood and treasure.

Rebecca Hamilton for her part explores the central issue of how political will can be generated through citizen advocacy. She argues that in order to be successful, the prevention of genocide cannot originate solely within established power structures but must also be driven by external, popular pressure. She analyzes as a case study the remarkable efforts of the Genocide Intervention Fund in the United States, exploring their innovative campaign to pressure the US Congress to take action on Darfur by establishing a 1-800-GENOCIDE telephone hotline and issuing "scorecards" evaluating each legislator's performance vis-à-vis Darfur. Noting that lack of caring or empathy cannot be the only reason for inaction, she proposes that anti-genocide citizen advocacy become much more sophisticated, strategic, and pragmatic.

The next contribution is that of Luis Moreno-Ocampo, the Prosecutor of the International Criminal Court. He makes a case for the critical role the ICC plays not just in sanctioning but also in preventing genocide. He considers not only the deterrent effect of criminal justice to future crimes but also explores the peace versus justice debate, contending that these imperatives are complementary rather than in competition with each other. He argues that ICC intervention has in fact mitigated atrocities in places like Uganda and the Sudan.

Professor Noah Weisbord of Duke University Law School then responds to Ocampo's defense of the ICC, with a macro-level analysis of whether international criminal justice is in fact the false dawn of a fictitious international morality or an unachievable utopian ideal. He concludes that the ICC and its supporters have in fact successfully begun to build a new global cosmopolitan morality, a universal code that was once seen as the privileged domain of aristocratic elites, but which has since been democratized with the proliferation of international norms, institutions and the strengthening of civil society. He offers the ICC and the cultural shift it has realized as a successful example of this emerging reality.

Professor Catherine Lu of McGill University also examines the role of the ICC in preventing genocide but from a different perspective. She focuses on the pitfalls of idealizing international criminal justice in an imperfect world. She argues that the ICC is an inherently political institution, one that while aspiring to political impartiality, nevertheless prioritizes consequentialist claims that it contributes to peace and reconciliation. Lu thus contends that as a political instrument, the ICC can cause unintended harms, and that sometimes the price of peace may indeed be impunity for mass-crimes. She concludes that the ICC cannot disregard a "world of defective domestic and international political agents and structures" and that the ideal of universal justice should not blind us to pragmatic constraints and realities.

Relying on his extensive field-work in Rwanda, Jobb Arnold's contribution provides insights from psychology on how local reconciliation efforts can contribute to building a lasting peace in the aftermath of violence. He explores the concept of post-traumatic growth by conducting the first known empirical research on how Rwandan genocide survivors look to the future despite past tragedy. Arnold's findings help better understand reconciliation efforts in transitional societies, and provide a welcome infusion of hope by demonstrating that even Rwandans exposed to the most unimaginable horrors have been able to re-construct a sense of community and develop a positive outlook on the future.

The final contribution by Mary Kimani, a journalist now working for the United Nations, provides an insightful examination of the role of media in genocide. Whereas Mark Thompson had earlier offered a study of the media as one of the building tools of genocide, Kimani shows how "peace media" can be used to further tolerance and dialogue, and thus ultimately prevent mass atrocities. She draws mainly from her extensive experience in the African context, arguing that media, historically the mouthpiece of powerful interests in the region, can be positively reshaped to serve the public interest, citing several successful examples of this growing trend. Kimani makes a persuasive plea of increased support for "peace media" initiatives in Africa, which suffer from an inherent lack of commercial profitability despite their critical role in battling exclusionary ideologies.

As much as a preventive approach opens new possibilities for confronting genocide, it leaves unanswered a vital question: will re-conceptualization of genocide make an appreciable difference to the plight of victims who have been abandoned time and again? This is a fundamental question because in Bosnia, in Rwanda, in Darfur, the world knew what was happening but decided not to act. It is true that early-warning and prevention are more cost-effective than intervention after the fact. This approach thus may be more likely to induce the will to act. Nonetheless, lack of knowledge, inadequate theoretical frameworks, or flawed methodologies, hardly explain the repeated failure to protect the victims of mass-murder. So beyond utilitarian justifications, will the promises of genocide prevention be realized or will they be relegated to yet another intellectual construction that makes no appreciable difference on the ground?

It is evident that where powerful actors link intervention to the pursuit of vital interests, there is a greater likelihood of action. Those advocating prevention of genocide may thus appeal to this calculation of interest to infuse a strategic element of pragmatism to the desirability of engagement. It may be argued that genocidal violence is invariably accompanied by instability and the spillover effects of violence. Thus, it would follow that the international community should act in order to avoid manageable conflicts from becoming a wider regional or global problem. This after all is the language of global governance: rational, pragmatic, and mindful of political realities, immune from naïve idealism. To the human conscience however, the moral imperative of acting against genocide does not require such elaborate justification or cost-benefit analysis. In the face of immense human suffering, we are instinctively moved to help those in distress, to make right the wrongs that shock our elementary sense of justice. This impulse, born of empathy, arises more from an emotional connection than it does from a re-conceptualization of a problem, no matter how brilliant and original the perspective. Reducing mass-murder to a distant abstraction or theoretical construct may itself be part of the reason why knowledge is not translated into action. In studying this rich and diverse collection of essays, the reader must not lose sight of the limitations of such discourse in awakening the sense of moral urgency without which we will continue to be spectators to radical evil.

This Preface began by recounting humankind's appalling history of cruelty and violence. Yet those gathered at the Global Conference on Prevention of Genocide, and the remarkable authors that have contributed to this book, point to a different potential for solidarity and engagement with the downtrodden. Encounters with survivors of genocide teaches us that in the midst of utter darkness, those that have witnessed unspeakable horrors, and suffered irredeemable loss, but who refuse to surrender their dignity and go on living, searching for answers, seeking justice, these are the most powerful proof of the resilience of the human spirit, of the indomitable hope without which true civilization and progress would be extinguished. It is befitting then to recall the stirring and fateful words of 13 year-old Anne Frank, before she and her sister were discovered by the Gestapo at their home in Amsterdam and murdered in the Bergen-Belsen concentration camp. She wrote in her diary: "I still believe, in spite of everything, that people are truly good at heart." In searching for solutions to this scourge then, we are also searching for transcendence, for faith that a different and better tomorrow is within the reach of those that act on their conscience.

Part I
Reconceptualizing Genocide

Chapter 2
From Irish Famine to Congo Reform: Nineteenth-Century Roots of International Human Rights Law and Activism

Ben Kiernan

Throughout the nineteenth century, colonial conquests visited mass death on colonized peoples. Invading armies killed thousands in military actions, but even more died from famines and diseases, often in the wake of wars. Between 1800 and 1900, European or US troops and settlers subjugated three almost entire continents: North America, Australia, and Africa. Tens of millions of people starved to death in India and China. In Java, two hundred thousand people died during the Dutch conquest of the island. Cambodia's population fell by possibly 195,000 during its French colonization.[1]

A major goal of this colonial expansion was the creation of overseas zones of metropolitan sovereignty and economic monopoly. Yet the same era also saw the rise of new transnational humanitarian movements, and the beginnings of international humanitarian law, which contested such sovereign powers and monopolies. As constitutionalism and citizen involvement spread in metropolitan Europe and North America, non-government activism and interventionism slowly rose to confront colonial policies of reciprocal non-intervention and economic *laissez-faire*. Protest movements in Britain and the United States secured laws banning the slave trade in both countries in 1807.[2] The Anti-Slavery Society was formed in Britain

B. Kiernan (✉)
Department of History, Yale University, New Haven, CT 06520-8324, USA
e-mail: ben.kiernan@yale.edu

[1]Ben Kiernan, *Blood and Soil: A World History of Genocide and Extermination from Sparta to Darfur* (New Haven: Yale University Press, 2007), chs. 7–9; Mike Davis, *Late Victorian Holocausts: El Niño Famines and the Making of the Third World* (London: Verso, 2001); Peter Carey, *The Power of Prophecy: Prince Dipanagara and the End of an Old Order in Java, 1785–1855* (Leiden: KITLV, 2007); Ben Kiernan, "Serial Colonialism and Genocide in Nineteenth-Century Cambodia," in *Empire, Colony, Genocide*, ed. A. Dirk Moses (New York: Berghahn, 2008), 223.

[2]Adam Hochschild, *Bury the Chains: Prophets and Rebels in the Fight to Free an Empire's Slaves* (Boston: Houghton Mifflin, 2005); Robin Blackburn, *The Overthrow of Colonial Slavery, 1776–1848* (New York: Verso, 1988).

R. Provost, P. Akhavan (eds.), *Confronting Genocide*, Ius Gentium: Comparative Perspectives on Law and Justice 7, DOI 10.1007/978-90-481-9840-5_2,

in 1823 and in the US in 1831. Britain passed the Slavery Abolition Act in 1833. It took the Civil War for the US to pass its Thirteenth Amendment in 1865.[3] In Britain, the damning "Report of the Parliamentary Select Committee on Aboriginal Tribes (British Settlements)" in 1837 quickly led to the foundation in the same year of the Aborigines' Protection Society. The establishment of the International Committee of the Red Cross in 1863 was also followed within a year by 16 European states' adoption of the first Geneva Convention, on wounded prisoners of war.

These new civil institutions, along with the international outcry, particularly among missionary organizations, against the Ottoman massacres of Armenians in 1894–1896, all set the stage for the formation of other targeted human rights campaigns.[4] This was the background to the formation in the early twentieth century of the Congo Reform Association (1904–1913). Meanwhile, the 1899 International Hague Convention of the Laws and Customs of War on Land specifically prohibited the shelling of undefended towns or cities while contracting parties pledged that "individual lives and private property, as well as religious convictions and liberty, must be respected."[5] The subsequent Hague Convention of 1907 codified the laws of war and the concept of "crimes against humanity." Then came the 1909 merger of the Aborigines' Protection Society with the Anti-Slavery Society, and the unprecedented international public protests against the Armenian Genocide of 1915–1918.[6,7] The latter catastrophe in turn moved the Polish Jewish jurist Raphael Lemkin to campaign in the 1930s for the worldwide criminalization of extermination and other crimes against humanity, which the United Nations eventually prohibited when it heeded Lemkin's call and adopted the Genocide Convention in 1948.[8]

Unlike the Nazi Holocaust of the Jews and indeed most genocides, one major nineteenth-century colonial famine occurred in peacetime: the Great Irish Famine. This calamity in a long-established British colony prefigured

---

[3]For different views, see Thomas Bender, ed., *The Antislavery Debate: Capitalism and Abolitionism as a Problem in Historical Interpretation* (Berkeley: University of California Press, 1992).

[4]Deborah Mayersen, "Intermittent Intervention: Europe and the Precipitation of the Armenian Massacres of 1894–1896," in *Terror, War, Tradition: Studies in European History*, ed. Bernard Mees and Samuel P. Koehne (Unley, SA: Australian Humanities Press, 2007), 247–270, esp. 265–269.

[5]Douglas Peifer, "Genocide and Air Power," *Strategic Studies Quarterly* 2, no. 2 (2008): 97.

[6]M. Chérif Bassiouni, "Crimes Against Humanity," Crimes of War Project, www.crimesofwar.org/thebook/crimes-against-humanity.html (Accessed May 13, 2008).

[7]The main events of the Armenian Genocide are recounted in Douglas Greenberg, Chapter 5 (below); an explanation of the Turkish government's stance towards the genocide is provided in Taner Akçam, Chapter 10 (below).

[8]An analysis of the legal effects of the Genocide Convention on States Parties is provided in Wenqi Zhu and Binxin Zhang, Chapter 12, Sections 12.2 and 12.4.1 to 12.4.6 (below).

several twentieth-century peacetime disasters. Its onset from 1845 initially elicited substantial British government aid, but at the height of the disaster in 1847, for ideological reasons the government cut off its aid. That provoked severe criticisms from prominent British and Irish commentators, some of whom leveled explicit charges of "extermination." These and other criticisms of the withholding of famine relief persisted and helped prepare the stage for major new movements of humanitarian intervention against extermination and genocide in the twentieth century. One lesson of the Famine was that imperial powers were sometimes to be pressured into timely intervention to end a catastrophe. Citizen protest movements eventually arose to apply such pressure. A founder of the Congo Reform Association was Roger Casement, who was born in Ireland in 1864 and grew up in the shadow of the Famine.[9] It may have taken him decades in Africa to connect the two catastrophes, but Casement eventually returned to Ireland ready to give up his life in the anti-colonial cause.

2.1 Famine in Ireland, 1845–1851

The Irish Potato Famine of 1846–1851 killed approximately one million of Ireland's 8.5 million people, while another million emigrated. Ó Gráda considers it "much more murderous, relatively speaking, than most historical and most modern famines."[10] Economist Amartya Sen concurs: "in no other famine in the world was the proportion of people killed as large as in the Irish famines in the 1840s."[11]

Before the famine, Ireland's annual potato production exceeded 12 million tons, and its potato exports fed two million people in Britain each year.[12] The 1841 census found that two-thirds of the Irish, or 972,000 families, were employed in agriculture, compared to only 31 percent in Britain. Yet two years later London's new weekly *The Economist* published an article that termed the landless Irish agricultural workforce food "consumers" rather than producers: "Of the families of Ireland, 68 per cent subsist by their own manual labour; have no capital, and nothing but labour to sell. . .The bulk of these people are rather consumers than sellers of agricultural produce." The article added that almost half of Irish rural families,

[9]Séamas Ó Síocháin, *Roger Casement: Imperialist, Rebel, Revolutionary* (Dublin: Lilliput, 2007), 8.

[10]Cormac Ó Gráda, *Black '47 and Beyond: The Great Irish Famine* (Princeton: Princeton University Press, 1999), 4, 7, 41, 87, 232.

[11]Colm Tóibín and Diarmaid Ferriter, *The Irish Famine: A Documentary* (New York: St. Martins, 2001), 16–17.

[12]Ó Gráda, *Black '47*, 124; Christine Kinealy, "Food Exports from Ireland 1846–1847," *History Ireland* 5, no. 1 (1997): 34.

and over a third of the urban, "have no other house accommodation than a mud cabin, consisting of only one room." With an average of 6.54 inhabitants per house, "nearly half the population of Ireland are crammed into mud cabins of a single room."[13]

After a potato blight caused the outbreak of the famine in 1845, the British government provided assistance until October 1847.[14] The first of the British governments in office during the famine, that of Conservative Prime Minister Sir Robert Peel, decided quickly to provide relief to Ireland and to stabilize food prices there. London committed £358,000 in State expenditure, and £495,000 more in loans. This aid included £78,000 in grants to Irish relief committees, and £453,000 for public works in Ireland, half of it to be repaid by the relevant Irish district, along with further loans of £134,000. And, ignoring pressure from British merchants and grain producers, Peel purchased £100,000 worth of Indian corn from America and shipped it to Ireland (at a cost of another £85,000) for sale in the spring and summer of 1846. Peel's intervention worked. No excess mortality occurred in 1845–1846.[15]

However Peel's government fell in mid-1846. Lord John Russell, his successor as British Prime Minister, was closer to the free-trade lobby. The new Whig cabinet immediately moved to reassure private merchants and grain producers by limiting the number of government food depots in Western Ireland. Russell also ended government imports of Indian corn into Ireland, leaving supply and pricing to market forces. His government decided to rely on public works to provide relief, but the wages paid were too low to enable workers to afford famine food prices.[16] Nevertheless the Assistant Secretary to the Treasury, Charles E. Trevelyan, wrote that "numerous persons who do not really stand in need of relief are employed on the works," and that "rates of wages are given exceeding what is required for providing subsistence."[17] He maintained, "It forms no part of the functions of government to provide supplies of food or to increase the productive powers of the land." The government's role, Trevelyan insisted, was "to protect the merchant and the agriculturist in the free exercise of their respective employments."[18]

The Whigs and their prevailing *laissez-faire* ideology now opposed any "interference" with natural functions of the economy, which they argued

[13]"Political: The Actual Condition of Ireland," *The Economist*, October 14, 1843, 107–108.

[14]Ó Gráda, *Black '47*, 77.

[15]"Ireland – Past Measures and Their Results," *The Economist*, January 16, 1847, 58.

[16]Kinealy, "Food Exports," 34–36.

[17]Trevelyan, letter to Under-Secretary Pennefather, June 26, 1846, Tóibín and Ferriter, *Irish Famine*, 79.

[18]Trevelyan, letter to Lord Monteagle, October 9, 1846, Tóibín and Ferriter, *Irish Famine*, 71.

should be left to its own devices free of state action. The *Economist* feared that "our interference to save *tens* from starvation in 1845–1846, has only exposed *hundreds* to the same fate in 1846–1847."[19] Prime Minister Russell outlined his thinking in October 1846: "The common delusion that government can convert a period of scarcity into a period of abundance is one of the most mischievous that can be entertained. But alas! The Irish have been taught many bad lessons and few good ones."[20] His goal now was to reduce government aid. A few months later Russell asserted that in famine-struck Western Ireland, "the poor people of Clare were never so well provided for as they have been this season." Also opposing public relief, the *Economist* warned that it had been too successful: "To convert a period of distress, arising from natural causes, into one of unusual comfort and ease, by the interference of government-money, or of private charity, is to paralyze the efforts of the people themselves."[21] Only hard work and private capital could be productive. The *Economist*'s inaccurate corollary that Irish agricultural laborers were unproductive, "rather consumers than sellers," also influenced policy.[22] Property had precedence. Listing the anti-famine measures of 1845–1846, the *Economist* denounced the "objectionable" principle of "everything to be done by the Government," for that might "end in the confiscation of landlords' rights, the utter demoralization of the peasantry, the destruction of property, and enormous losses to the British Exchequer."[23]

Along with economic ideology, ethnic sentiments also affected London's policymaking. Imperial concerns accorded Irish victims no priority. Russell complained in August 1846 that "the effect" of the public works programs in Ireland "was, that ordinary work was abandoned." For instance, he said, "The harvest operation[s] in the north of England and Scotland have been greatly deranged" without their normal input of Irish seasonal labor.[24] Concerning food supplies, too, Trevelyan argued in October that "a general scarcity over the whole of the United Kingdom" made it unwise "to buy up without restraint supplies intended for the English and Scotch markets." It was equally unacceptable to Trevelyan "that the English and Scotch labourer" should "have to support the Irish labourers (for it is always the mass of the population which pays the bulk of the taxes)." Thus it was also unacceptable that the prices of food items should rise "to a famine price" as a result of "an unrestrained eleemosynary [charitable] consumption of

[19] "Ireland – Past Measures and Their Results," *The Economist*, January 16, 1847, 58.

[20] Tóibín and Ferriter, *Irish Famine*, 13.

[21] "Ireland – Past Measures and Their Results," *The Economist*, January 16, 1847, 58.

[22] "Political: The Actual Condition of Ireland," *The Economist*, October 14, 1843, 107.

[23] "Ireland – Past Measures and Their Results," *The Economist*, January 16, 1847, 60.

[24] Russell addressing House of Commons, August 17, 1846, excerpt in "Ireland – Past Measures and Their Results," *The Economist*, January 16, 1847, 58.

them in Ireland."[25] Trevelyan apparently considered such proposals to aid the Irish as lacking "restraint."[26]

As the famine approached its height in January 1847, the Irish M.P. John O'Connell told a London meeting that "The people were dying at the rate of three hundred per day." He called on England "to do justice to Ireland."[27] The *Economist* reported: "Every market day continues to add to the price of food, and especially of all those descriptions, which, from their lowness of quality, are adapted for the consumption of Ireland."[28] Yet the *Economist* condemned the Irish as "an entire people, naturally prone rather to rely upon others than upon themselves," and later reiterated that they were "always prone, unhappily, to lean upon extraneous aid."[29] Addressing Parliament, Lord Russell again criticized public works employment in Ireland: "One of these evils is that it leads to a difficulty of obtaining a supply of labour elsewhere. (Hear, hear.) When the works commenced, it was generally reported to us, and most especially by persons travelling through the country, that the parties who had obtained employment on the public works were seen idling on the road, doing no work and talking to one another." Lord Lansdowne agreed, lamenting that "a bounty" had been "created for the indolent, the idle, and the profligate. . .something like a premium on idleness."[30]

Some leading organs of the British press were yet more outspoken, and even critical of the government's plan to continue aid at much reduced levels. The *Economist* led the way in January 1847 when it protested against burdening "the English tax-payers" by moving "one-half" of the debt "from the shoulders of the Irish proprietors to those of the tax-payers in England." Ireland, the paper argued, possessed its own natural resources. "But the turbulence of the people, the insecurity of life and property, have hitherto crushed every effort to establish means to render these resources available: and the people, rapidly increasing, have been reduced, by acts for which they are chiefly to blame, to a sole reliance on the precarious crop of potatoes." The *Economist* also opposed government loans for seed purchases: "The Irish. . .will seize the impression that they are to be provided

[25]Trevelyan, letter to Chairman of the Board of Works, October 5, 1846, Tóibín and Ferriter, *Irish Famine*, 99.

[26]Cf. Robin Haines, *Charles Trevelyan and the Great Irish Famine* (Dublin: Four Courts, 2004).

[27]"Ireland – Past Measures and Their Results," *The Economist*, January 16, 1847, 67.

[28]"The Political Economist: Three Measures for the First Day of the Session," *The Economist*, January 16, 1847, 1.

[29]"Ireland – Past Measures and Their Results," *The Economist*, January 16, 1847, 60; "The New Measures of the Government," *The Economist*, January 30, 1847, 115.

[30]Lords Russell and Lansdowne, quoted in "The Political Economist: Ireland," *The Economist*, January 30, 1847, 113.

with seed by the government." Such loans, "perfectly sound and legitimate among private individuals," were "pernicious" for government to advance:

> But here, again, the insecurity of property – the weakness of the executive – the impossibility to rely on the faithful fulfillment of contracts in Ireland, would be found a great, if not an insuperable difficulty, in this aid being made available. Wherever we turn in Ireland, this universal evil intercepts all attempts at permanent improvement.[31]

Two months later, at the famine's height in March 1847, debate raged in the House of Commons. On March 25th, the Conservative opposition leader Lord Bentinck attacked the government "for not having supplied seed to the farmers of Ireland," where "hundreds of thousands of persons...had died." The Chancellor of the Exchequer responded by undertaking henceforth to ignore "the assertions" of Bentinck, and he "implored the house not to allow itself to be dragged into a general discussion on the affairs of Ireland." Concurring, Lord Sandon noted "the great difficulty now experienced in removing Irish immigrants back to Ireland, whence they were daily coming in large crowds." Sixty thousand had reached Liverpool since early January. Prime Minister Russell, for his part, foreshadowed a "mendicancy and vagrancy bill," and he "called upon every gentleman in Ireland" to help "in maintaining the public tranquility" there.[32] Meanwhile, the Irish M.P. John O'Connell warned the government against "the sudden removal of the people from the public works" in Ireland, in anticipation of which "a general feeling of terror and dismay prevailed throughout that country." O'Connell "implored the Government...to take measures to stop that frightful annihilation of life."[33]

The next day, the London *Times* blamed both British aid and Irish victims. It denounced "the ruinous effect of Governmental assistance on a people whose natural temperament disinclines them to help themselves, as well as the cunning which they enlist in support of their deliberate and daring indolence." The *Times* condemned the Irish for "the moral disease of a vast population steeped in the congenial mire of voluntary indigence," and even for "speculating on the gains of a perpetuated famine." Britain had done enough, the paper argued:

> We have made no distinction between Celt and Saxon. We have confessed English and Irish misdeeds or omissions...We have taken to ourselves... more than our just burden. But we have never said that it ought to be wholly and only ours. We have called on our Irish fellow-subjects to bear some part in the cost and consequences of a calamity which we might have thrown almost entirely upon them.

---

[31] Ibid., and "The New Measures of the Government," *The Economist*, January 30, 1847, 113–116.

[32] *Times*, Friday, March 26, 1847, 4.

[33] John O'Connell, speech in the House of Commons, March 25, 1847, reported in the *Times*, Friday, March 26, 1847, 4.

But the *Times* lamented of the Irish: "They have tasted of public money, and they find it pleasanter to live on alms than on labour... Deep, indeed has the canker eaten... into the very hearts of the people, corrupting them with a fatal lethargy."[34] The *Times* went on to describe the Irish as "a people born and bred from time immemorial in inveterate indolence, improvidence, disorder and consequent destitution." Even lack of generosity was uniquely Irish: "The astounding apathy of the Irish themselves to the most horrible scenes under their eyes and capable of relief by the smallest exertion is something absolutely without a parallel in the history of civilized nations."[35]

The influential magazine *Punch*, too, preferred to paint "a very negative picture of Irish irresponsibility and dishonesty," according to Ó Gráda. He concludes: "From Spring 1847 on, most of the English print media conveyed an impression of the Irish poor as devious, violent, and ungrateful, and of famine relief as a bottomless black hole," while in Ireland the fiercest reluctance to aid the victims revealed what he called "a marked sectarian edge."[36] Before the famine, British historian Thomas Carlyle had written in *Chartism* (1839): "The time has come when the Irish population must either be improved a little, or exterminated." Now in 1848, Carlyle predicted that "if no beneficent hand will chain [the Irishman] into wholesome slavery, and, with whip on back... get some work out of him – Nature herself... has no resource but to exterminate him."[37]

However, in the absence of both direct violence and demonstrable official intent to destroy an ethnic group, most modern historians of the Irish Famine eschew the term "genocide." Besides the potato blight itself, the major factor contributing to the death toll was the ruling British economic policy of *laissez-faire*, which Ó Gráda terms a case of "doctrinaire neglect." Fostering the free market and largescale agriculture eventually attracted greater official priority than alleviating Irish starvation. This too distinguishes the Famine from most cases of genocide, where faith in smallholder agriculture is often a detectable component of the dominant ideology.[38] Yet expansionism, another common factor in genocides, of course influenced the British imperial mindset. Trevelyan's October 1846 statement

---

[34] *Times*, March 26, 1847, 4.

[35] Ó Gráda, *Black '47*, 251 n.96, citing *Times*, March 26, 1847; Val Noone, "Famine and Imperialism: Ireland 1845–1852" (paper presented at Colloquium on "Comparative Famine and Political Killings: causation, scale and state responsibility," History Department, Melbourne University, August 13 1999).

[36] Ó Gráda, *Black '47*, 43–44, 83.

[37] Quoted in Claude Rawson, *God, Gulliver and Genocide: Barbarism and the European Imagination, 1492–1945* (Oxford: Oxford University Press, 2001), 234.

[38] Timothy Guinnane, "Ireland's famine wasn't genocide," *Washington Post*, September 17, 1997; Ó Gráda, *Black '47*, 10; Kiernan, *Blood and Soil*.

highlights both Ireland's incorporation in the United Kingdom and the subject status that weakened its case to share the burden with England or Scotland.

In the winter of 1846–1847, according to the Irish Constabulary, 400,000 people died of hunger. In January 1847, Russell's Whig government abandoned public works in favor of more successful soup kitchens. Britain's Lord Lieutenant of Ireland, Bessborough, remarked: "I know all the difficulties that arise when you begin to interfere with trade, but it is difficult to persuade a starving population that one class should be permitted to make 50 per cent profit by the sale of provisions whilst they are dying in want of these."[39]

In March 1847, ten thousand Irish died in workhouses alone.[40] But as the famine escalated, British policy hardened. When Bessborough's successor, the Earl of Clarendon, assumed office in mid-1847, three million Irish people were still receiving free daily soup rations.[41] In the British political climate, however, this seemed a marginal achievement. Clarendon wrote to Prime Minister Russell in August 1847: "We shall be equally blamed for keeping [the Irish] alive or letting them die and we have only to select between the censure of the Economists or the Philanthropists – which do you prefer?" London made its choice. British government relief ended when the soup kitchens did, in October 1847.[42] Clarendon then challenged the Prime Minister to tell the House of Commons that "deaths by starvation are daily taking place but that the Gov[ernmen]t has no measure of relief to propose."[43] Several months later, Clarendon again wrote sharply to Russell: "No-one could now venture to dispute the fact that Ireland had been sacrificed to the London corn-dealers because you were a member [of Parliament] for the City."[44]

The British Treasury described its policies in terms that suggested, in part, an enforcement of collective ethnic responsibility, which has been called making "Irish property pay for Irish poverty."[45] A year earlier Assistant Secretary Trevelyan, who was not anti-Catholic and insisted that "the People cannot *under any circumstances* be allowed to starve," had nevertheless denounced what he called a "defective part of the national character" of the Irish, and had condemned, in Irish landlords, "[t]he

---

[39] Kinealy, "Food Exports," 34–36.

[40] Kinealy, "Food Exports," 36.

[41] Christine Kinealy, *The Great Irish Famine: Impact, Ideology and Rebellion* (Basingstoke: Palgrave, 2002), 43.

[42] Tóibín and Ferriter, *Irish Famine*, 13; Ó Gráda, *Black '47*, 251 n. 96, 77.

[43] Clarendon, letter to Russell, October 30, 1847, in Haines, *Charles Trevelyan*, 376.

[44] Kinealy, "Food Exports," 36.

[45] Christine Kinealy, *A Death-dealing Famine: The Great Hunger in Ireland* (London: Pluto, 1997), 98–99; in Ó Gráda's words, "the poor were being made to pay for the perceived sins of the rich." *Black '47*, 83.

deep & inveterate root of *social* evil," for which now, he said, "the cure has been applied by the direct stroke of an all-wise Providence."[46] (Such Christian providentialism was widespread; just five months before, a French newspaper in Algeria had discussed even the destruction of "a Human Race... by a Providential Decree.")[47] Trevelyan predicted in 1848 that "posterity will trace up to that famine the commencement of a salutary revolution in the habits of a nation long singularly unfortunate, and will acknowledge that on this, as on many other occasions, Supreme Wisdom has educed permanent good out of transient evil."[48]

Trevelyan did not, however, share the views of the Dublin banker Robert Murray, who had in September 1845 found "the alleged failure of the potato crop" to be "very greatly exaggerated," and had then stated in 1847: "The surplus population of Ireland... is an overwhelming incubus at home, whether to themselves or others. Remove them and you benefit in a degree that cannot be overestimated. Precisely as you do so, you raise the social condition of those who remain."[49] Ideology aside, government denial of aid materially benefited those private landowners who hoped to clear their property of "surplus population."

Under a June 1847 amendment to the Whig Poor Law, any tenant holding more than a quarter acre of land became ineligible for government relief, forcing many tenants to surrender their land to their landlords simply in order to qualify for food assistance. When an English member in the House of Commons warned that this amendment would lead to "a complete clearance of the small farmers in Ireland," its Tory sponsor, Dublin M.P. William H. Gregory, retorted that if it would indeed "destroy all the small farmers," then he "did not see of what use such small farmers could possibly be."[50] The amendment passed 117 to 7. Trevelyan wrote: "After the 1st November, 1847, no person is to be relieved either in or out of a workhouse, who is in the occupation of more than a quarter of an acre of land."[51] A year later

---

[46]Haines, *Charles Trevelyan*, 4–5, 401; Trevelyan to Monteagle, October 9, 1846, in Tóibín and Ferriter, *Irish Famine*, 72.

[47]Jennifer Pitts (ed.), in Alexis de Tocqueville, *Writings on Empire and Slavery* (Baltimore: Johns Hopkins University Press, 2001), 249 n.6, quoting an unidentified Algerian newspaper, dated May 2, 1846.

[48]Quoted in Tóibín and Ferriter, *Irish Famine*, 16.

[49]Robert Murray, Provincial Bank of Ireland, to Chancellor of the Exchequer Henry Goulburn, Sept. 25, 1845, quoted in Cecil Woodham-Smith, *The Great Hunger* (New York: Harper & Row, 1962), 41; Robert Murray, *Ireland, Its Present Condition and Future Prospects* (Dublin, 1847), 19, quoted in Christopher Morash, *Writing the Irish Famine* (Oxford: Clarendon, 1995), 67; Tóibín and Ferriter, *Irish Famine*, 190.

[50]*Hansard's Parliamentary Debates*, 3rd series, xci, cols. 588–590, quoted in James S. Donnelly, Jr., "Mass Eviction and the Great Famine," in *The Great Irish Famine*, ed. Cathal Póirtéir (Dublin: Mercier, 1995), 160, 275.

[51]Trevelyan, *The Irish Crisis*, 151–154, excerpt in Tóibín and Ferriter, *Irish Famine*, 112.

the *Illustrated London News* reported the clearance of landed estates: "It does not require any very large or difficult expenditure of capital to clear them of the cottier population, or convert small holdings into large farms, to be cultivated in the English and Scottish style of agriculture. It is the easiest mode of improvement, and therefore, poor landlords are compelled to resort to it."[52] The death toll rose. As Ó Gráda writes, "what shocks is the *size* of the excess mortality in 1848–1850. The continuing winter mortality-peaks point like accusing fingers at the official determination to declare the crisis over in the summer of 1847."[53] The famine was most prolonged in the west of Ireland.[54]

Once the British government declared an end to the famine and to official provision of relief, private donations had to bear the burden. The response was an outpouring of contributions that set a groundbreaking precedent for international voluntary aid to victims of disasters worldwide. The British Relief Association raised nearly £500,000 for Irish famine victims, and the Catholic Church in Ireland over £400,000. The Society of Friends spent £200,000 on Irish famine relief from 1845 to 1849. In distant Oklahoma, less than a decade after the United States had deported them from their homelands, Choctaw and Cherokee communities sent small collections to victims in Ireland and Scotland, as did Native Americans in Canada.[55]

By contrast, London's official response to the famine from 1847 revealed its harsh *laissez-faire* policy, a more immediate and extreme case of British distance from the extensive killings of Australian Aborigines in the same era.[56] *The Times* proclaimed that "something like harshness" was "the greatest humanity." The editor of *The Economist* argued that "it is no man's business to provide for another." Relief aid would only move food "from the more meritorious to the less."[57] Morality, the paper said, should cede precedence "to the natural law of distribution," whereby "those who deserved more would obtain it."[58] A leading economist welcomed the Irish Famine's "illustrations" as "valuable to a political economist." Whitehall, Ó Gráda

---

[52] *Illustrated London News*, December 16, 1848, in Tóibín and Ferriter, *Irish Famine*, 125 (see also pp. 16, 193).

[53] Cormac Ó Gráda, *The Great Irish Famine* (London: Macmillan, 1989), 48; Tóibín and Ferriter, *Irish Famine*, 16.

[54] Ciarán Ó Murchadha, *Sable Wings over the Land: Ennis, County Clare, and its Wider Community During the Great Famine* (Ennis, Clasp Press, 1998); Kathleen Villiers-Tuthill, *Patient Endurance: The Great Famine in Connemara* (Dublin: Connemara Girl Publications, 1997); Ó Gráda, *Black '47*, 86–89.

[55] Kinealy, *The Great Irish Famine*, 73, 83, 80–81; *Arkansas Intelligencer*, April 3 1847.

[56] In *The Destruction of Aboriginal Society* (Canberra, 1970), C.D. Rowley terms the policy "*laissez-faire* in practice" (54).

[57] Ó Gráda, *Black '47*, 6; Ó Gráda, *Great Irish Famine*, 52.

[58] "The Political Economist: Ireland," *The Economist*, January 30, 1847, 113–114.

concludes, displayed "dogma and meanness." In the end its £9.5 million in expenditure on Irish relief was limited to 1846–1847, had little impact on the British budget, and compared poorly with Tsarist Russia's spending during the "much less threatening" famine there in 1891–1892.[59]

Britain's aid policies provoked severe criticism even at the top levels of British and Irish opinion, including warnings of the systematic "extinction" and "extermination" of the Irish, though the causes were identified very differently. In January 1847, the *Economist* complained of Ireland that "the whole country abandons itself to public relief" provided by the British government; the paper predicted that any further aid, that is, "perseverance in the system hitherto pursued, if it were possible, would end equally in an extinction of the people."[60] By contrast, the Catholic Bishop of Derry, in a letter written on April 9th, 1847, denounced the famine, not the relief program, as "wholesale systems of extermination." Two years later the Earl of Clarendon, Britain's Lord Lieutenant of Ireland (1847–1852), blamed London more directly. Clarendon wrote to Prime Minister Russell in 1849 to denounce Westminster's refusal of aid: "I don't think there is another legislature in Europe that would disregard such sufferings as now exist in the west of Ireland or coldly persist in a policy of extermination."[61] The next month, however, Russell denied Ireland the £100,000 minimum considered necessary to prevent further possible starvation.[62]

The critics were proven right. The prevailing dogma against "interference" in the economy failed. The market provided no solution to the famine. According to Christine Kinealy, nearly four thousand ships carried food out of Ireland in 1847 alone. More than 3 million live animals were exported from 1846 to 1850.[63] Ó Gráda correctly points out that "food imports dwarfed food exports," but also that "exports of oats in the second half of 1846 were still significant," after what Kinealy terms a poor grain harvest, especially of oats.[64] Jim Donnelly dates significant grain imports only from the spring of 1847.[65] A temporary ban on grain exports, as imposed in previous food crises, might indeed have helped alleviate starvation.[66] The 430,000 tons of grain exported from Ireland in 1846–1847 would have "filled only one-seventh of the gap" in potato production, yet surely could

---

[59] Ó Gráda, *Black '47*, 6, 44, 77, 79, 83.

[60] "Ireland – Past Measures and Their Results," *The Economist*, January 16, 1847, 60.

[61] George Villiers, Earl of Clarendon, letter to Prime Minister Russell, April 26, 1849.

[62] Ó Gráda, *Black '47*, 44, 83.

[63] Kinealy, "Food Exports," 33, 35; Noone, "Famine and Imperialism," cites Kinealy, *A Death-dealing Famine*; Tóibín and Ferriter, *Irish Famine*, 183–184.

[64] Ó Gráda, *Black '47*, 123; Kinealy, "Food Exports," 33.

[65] Jim Donnelly, *History Ireland* 1, no 3, cited in Kinealy, "Food Exports," 33.

[66] Ó Gráda, *Black '47*, 123–124; Kinealy, "Food Exports," 34.

have saved many lives.[67] Famine continued throughout much of the west of Ireland in 1849–1850, "despite plentiful supplies of food." The charge that "Ireland died of political economy" has some merit.[68]

Some features of the dominant British political thinking even suggest an economic form of "ethnic cleansing." For instance, the *Economist* explained in 1853, in praise of emigration:

> It is consequent on the breaking down of the system of society founded on small holdings and potato cultivation... The departure of the redundant part of the population of Ireland and Scotland is an indispensable preliminary to every kind of improvement. Extensive as has been the emigration which has already taken place from Ireland, there is a remarkable proof that it has not been carried too far. There is still no regular demand for labour in the West of Ireland... The revenue of Ireland has not suffered in any degree from the famine of 1846–1847, or from the emigration that has since taken place... The truth is, that Ireland has gained by the diminution which has taken place in her population.[69]

The contempt for small farmers in British ruling circles combined easily with racism. Yet as Ó Gráda points out, "not even the most bigoted and racist commentators of the day sought the extermination of the Irish." He adds that "attitudes sometimes described as 'racist' were really as much about class as race."[70]

Despite its dimensions the Irish tragedy was not strictly a case of genocide, a crime requiring an "intent to destroy" and more likely to be committed by regimes trumpeting the virtues of yeoman farmers (which Russell's Whig government did not do), even when trampling on their rights (which it did). Yet British responsibility for the welfare of the victims was clear and unmet.[71] The Irish toll prefigured later massive famines in British colonial India, as well as in China, and in the 1940s, wartime famines in British colonial Bengal and Japanese-occupied China and Vietnam.[72] The Irish Famine also heralded twentieth-century peacetime famines aggravated by new forms of "political economy," as much or more preoccupied with class than race. The death of millions in Ukraine, Kazakhstan and

---

[67] Ó Gráda, *Black '47*, 124; Clarendon wrote to Russell in late 1847 that "no distress would have occurred if the exportation of Irish grain had been permitted." Kinealy, "Food Exports," 36.

[68] Ó Gráda, *Black '47*, 125, 6.

[69] *The Economist*, February 12, 1853, 168–169. See R. L. Rubinstein, "Genocide and Civilization," in *Genocide and the Modern Age*, ed. I. Wallimann and M. Dobkowski (Syracuse: Syracuse University Press, 2000), 287.

[70] Ó Gráda, *Black '47*; Cormac Ó Gráda, "The Great Famine and Today's Famines," in *The Great Irish Famine*, ed. Cathal Póirtéir (Dublin, Mercier, 1995), 252.

[71] An explanation of the "sovereignty as responsibility" concept is provided in Francis M. Deng, Chapter 4 (below).

[72] Davis, *Late Victorian Holocausts*; Sugata Bose, "Starvation Amidst Plenty: The Making of Famine in Bengal, Honan, and Tonkin, 1942–1945," *Modern Asian Studies* 24, no. 4 (1990).

elsewhere during the 1930s Soviet Famine was largely a result of Stalinist ideological insistence on forced urban industrialization; and the worst human disaster ever, the Chinese Great Leap Forward famine of the 1950s, resulted from Mao's imposition of rural communization.[73]

Meanwhile more familiar forms of genocide persisted as the colonial world was bound and dragged brutally into the twentieth century. But London's rigid response to the Irish Famine of 1845–1851 discredited the ideology of inaction in the face of catastrophe, and helped arouse the specter of international relief and protest movements. Human "interference" to alleviate misery was now on the agenda.

2.2 The Congo Free State, 1885–1908

Between 1876 and 1896, seven European metropolitan powers "swallowed up the world's second largest continent."[74] In the Congo, a rapidly expanding domain privately run by King Léopold II of Belgium (r. 1865–1909) and claiming suzerainty over twenty million Africans, became one of the largest colonial territories in history. Indeed Léopold found inspiration in historical models. As a young duke in 1860, he had offered Belgium's governmental leader a plaque of marble taken from the Agora in Athens, inscribed with the words "Il faut à la Belgique une colonie."[75] Two years later, Léopold visited Spain. Instead of sightseeing in Madrid, he went straight to Seville to research the exploits of the *conquistadores* in Mexico. Léopold wrote that he was "very busy [there] going through the Indies archives and calculating the profit which Spain made then and makes now out of her colonies." He also admired the Dutch exploitation of Java through the imposition of forced cultivation. Léopold saw ancient precedents too, later asking one of his ministers "if he found nothing exciting in the idea of becoming a Pharaoh." The king had "a weakness for tinselly historical comparisons, whether to Rameses or Godfrey de Bouillon."[76] His friend and US agent Henry Sanford would even market Léopold's Congo to Americans as a new "Canaan for our modern Israelites."[77]

---

[73]Kiernan, *Blood and Soil*, chs. 13–14.

[74]Mark Cocker, *Rivers of Blood, Rivers of Gold: Europe's Conflict with Tribal Peoples* (London: J. Cape, 1998), 284.

[75]Daniel Vangroenweghe, *Du sang sur les lianes: Léopold II et son Congo* (Bruxelles: Didier Hatier, 1986), 13.

[76]Neal Ascherson, *The King Incorporated: Leopold the Second and the Congo* (London: Granta, 1999), 46, 164–165; Vangroenweghe, *Du sang sur les lianes*, 13.

[77]Adam Hochschild, *King Leopold's Ghost: A Story of Greed, Terror and Heroism in Colonial Africa* (Boston: Mariner Books, 1998), 80.

Perpetrators of genocide have often displayed a fascination for antiquity and territorial expansion, along with an agrarian vision of the land. Léopold's agricultural interest was pragmatic. The young monarch's energies first went into his royal estate, palace grounds, parks, and "a vast string of greenhouses." Later, when asserting his ownership of the Congo in 1885, he drew in part on a typical colonial claim that its inhabitants failed to cultivate or otherwise use the land. Léopold founded his African colony with a decree that the state owned all its "vacant land," which remained undefined, suggesting an attempted legal justification for the claim to the whole territory that he pursued in practice. In the colony's early years, he considered founding "five big Chinese villages in the Congo" – "Two thousand Chinese to mark our frontiers" – but that was more a territorial gambit than an agricultural scheme, and nothing came of it. Unlike more ideological perpetrators of colonialism and genocide, Léopold never romanticized his Congo enterprise as a smallholder farming utopia. Historian Adam Hochschild writes: "Leopold did not care whether the wealth he wanted came from the precious metals sought by the Spaniards in South America, from agriculture, or – as would turn out to be the case, from a raw material [rubber] whose potential was as yet undreamed of. What mattered was the size of the profit." In the end, if preoccupations with market economics and large-scale agriculture had driven British economic policy towards Ireland, Léopold's plans for the Congo would require a private monopoly both of the ivory trade and of native labor for rubber plantations.[78]

The king's territorial expansionist drive was as frenetic as that of any genocide perpetrator. As Léopold put it in 1877, he wanted "a slice of this magnificent African cake." Four years later he instructed his agent, the British explorer Henry Morton Stanley, to buy "as much land as [he would] be able to obtain," and to successively bring under Léopold's "suzerainty... as soon as possible and without losing one minute, all the chiefs from the mouth of the Congo to the Stanley Falls." In Stanley's view, Léopold had the "enormous voracity to swallow a million of square miles with a gullet that will not take in a herring."[79] By the 1890s, Léopold's attempt to expand his kingdom into the Nile valley brought his Congo Free State into conflict with both France and Britain.[80]

Violent conquest of the Congo began even before Léopold first met Stanley in 1878. The Englishman had just completed an Anglo-American exploration of the Congo basin. When inhabitants of an island in Lake Victoria threatened his party without attacking, Stanley opened fire while

[78]Hochschild, *Leopold's Ghost*, 38–40, 117–118.

[79]Vangroenweghe, *Du sang sur les lianes*, 15; Hochschild, *Leopold's Ghost*, 58, 70, 74.

[80]William Roger Louis, "The Stokes Affair and the Origins of the Anti-Congo Campaign, 1895–1896," *Revue belge de philologie et d'histoire* 43, no. 2 (1965): 572–584; Vangroenweghe, *Du sang sur les lianes*, 77.

retreating, killing 14 Africans. Returning to punish the islanders, he instructed his men to "fire as if they were killing birds." They shot dead 33 people and wounded a hundred. At the end of his expedition, Stanley reported having "attacked and destroyed 28 large towns and three or four score villages." Another explorer, Richard Burton, charged that Stanley "shoots negroes as if they were monkeys."[81] In December 1878, Stanley signed a 5-year contract with King Léopold to establish their enterprises in the Congo.[82]

Léopold never visited the vast region that became his personal fief, the Congo Free State (1885–1908).[83] This territory created at the high tide of imperialism was soon "awash in corpses."[84] A major cause was what the historian Robert Harms has called "the wild rubber boom" that struck Africa around 1890.[85] Soon a "violent rush for raw rubber" caused the rapid decimation of Congo's population by mass murder, introduced diseases, and plunging birth rates.[86] European overseers often worked the survivors to death, echoing the impact of Spanish rule on sixteenth-century Hispaniola.

The Belgian scholar Daniel Vangroenweghe has documented the Free State's repression in the large Equator District of central Congo. The District Commissioner from 1890 to 1893, Belgian *Force Publique* officer Charles Lemaire, later wrote that when the government set out to extract wild rubber, he had advised it: "on devra couper des mains, des nez, et des oreilles" (we shall have to cut off hands, noses, and ears). In his 1891 diary, Lemaire named five of the villages he burned, plus "all but two of the villages of Irebu," while other colonial forces destroyed eleven more villages in the district. Besides many individual murders, Lemaire also recorded "15 blacks killed" on April 14th, 1891, and "20 natives killed; 13 women and children taken prisoner" on July 7th, 1892.[87] Troops led by Free State officer Peters slaughtered 34 Africans in April 1892. Lemaire's soldiers killed another 37 that August, and a third unit killed fifteen more in December 1892. After Africans killed Peters and an assistant in January

---

[81]Martin Ewans, *European Atrocity, African Catastrophe: Leopold II, the Congo Free State, and its Aftermath* (London: Routledge, 2002), 50–52; Hochschild, *Leopold's Ghost*, 50.

[82]Ewans, *European Atrocity*, 57.

[83]Peter Singleton-Gates and Maurice Girodias, *The Black Diaries: An Account of Roger Casement's Life and Times with a Collection of his Diaries and Public Writings* (New York: Grove, 1959), 87.

[84]Hochschild, *Leopold's Ghost*, 227.

[85]Robert Harms, "The End of Red Rubber: A Reassessment," *Journal of African History* 16, no.1 (1975): 73.

[86]Nancy Rose Hunt, "An Acoustic Register, Tenacious Images, and Congolese Scenes of Rape and Repetition," *Cultural Anthropology* 23, no. 2 (2008): 221, 227–228.

[87]Vangroenweghe, *Du sang sur les lianes*, 46, 30–36; Hochschild, *Leopold's Ghost*, 227–228.

1893, State troops, in two weeks of reprisals, killed 64 Mongo tribes people and "massacred numerous inhabitants" in other Mongo villages.[88]

Félix Fuchs, the Free State's *Gouverneur-Général*, feared that "Lemaire's hostile policy" had provoked the rebellion in Equator. Yet State violence escalated there. In 1894, a *Force Publique* officer quoted Lemaire's successor, Captain Léon Fiévez, as saying of recalcitrant villagers: "I made war against them. One example was enough: a hundred heads cut off, and there have been plenty of supplies at the station ever since. . . I killed a hundred people. . . but that allowed five hundred others to live." Early the next year a Swedish lieutenant in the Free State forces, Knut Svensson, wrote in his diary of killing 572 people around Bikoro in four months. Another *Force Publique* officer, Louis Leclerq, wrote in his diary on June 21st, 1895: "We sent several groups of soldiers to scour the area; they came back several hours later with 11 heads and 9 prisoners. A canoe sent out hunting in the evening also brought back several heads. 22 June 1895: They brought us three prisoners in the morning, three others towards evening, and three heads." A Swedish missionary in Equator district, Reverend E.V. Sjöblom, described a journey he made "through no fewer than 45 villages which had been totally burned and 28 villages entirely deserted, because of the rubber campaign."[89]

The "most notorious" rubber enterprise in Congo was the private company Abir, founded in Antwerp in 1892 when the Free State lacked the capital to develop the north of Equator district. Robert Harms writes that from 1893 the inhabitants of Abir's large exclusive concession area, in lieu of paying taxes to the State, had to collect wild rubber for the company, while the State supplied weapons and kept order through a network of military posts, in return for half the shares in Abir. Over seven years of "heavy fighting," the company took control of its concession area. The price of rubber doubled in the decade after 1894, and by 1899 Abir was reaping profits that Belgian commentators considered "perhaps without precedent in the annals of our industrial companies." Each military post comprised a rubber agent and "about eighty men armed with modern Albini rifles." The agent forced every adult male villager to collect four kilograms of liquid rubber per week. Sentries in the villages "flogged, imprisoned, or shot villagers who fell behind." Abir's extortionate quotas led to destruction of most of the area's wild rubber vines, including some that were "destroyed on purpose by people who believed that when the rubber was exhausted the company would go away."[90]

---

[88]Vangroenweghe, *Du sang sur les lianes*, 54, 42, 36, 38–39.

[89]Vangroenweghe, *Du sang sur les lianes*, 40, 55, 58–59, 65–66; Hochschild, *Leopold's Ghost*, 166, 228.

[90]Harms, "End of Red Rubber," 78–82, 87. For more on Abir, see Vangroenweghe, *Du sang sur les lianes*, chs. V, VI.

From his capital in Brussels, Léopold defended rule by violence. He wrote in 1897: "It is necessary to be at once firm and paternal," even if, "with a view to the necessary domination of civilization, it be permitted, in case of need, to have resort to forcible means." Another rationale was agrarian. The king deemed it necessary to occupy "those vast tracts, mostly uncultivated and many unproductive, where the natives hardly knew how to get their daily food." Now, he claimed, "the soil yields produce in exchange for our varied manufactured articles." Thus, "the Congo state [had] become a country with distinct frontiers, occupied and guarded at every point."[91] Yet Congolese resistance continued, and also, among outsiders there and abroad, an international movement eventually arose to document and publicize Belgian colonial crimes.

The first future human rights campaigner to arrive in the Congo was the young Irishman Roger Casement, son of an Ulster Protestant father and Catholic mother. During the Irish Famine, Casement's father had served as a British officer in India (1840–1849), then briefly joined the Hungarian patriots' uprising against Austrian imperial rule, displaying a "romantic dedication to the cause of small nations" and to what he called a "universal republicanism" that may have influenced his son Roger's view of the world.[92] From his Dublin birth in 1864 to his London execution for treason in 1916, Roger Casement was to spend "one third of his life in Africa."[93] But he grew up in Ireland during a tumultuous era. His biographer Séamas Ó Síocháin points out that Casement's father was moved to join Fenian rebels in the wake of their 1867 anti-British uprising, and that "Casement's teenage years coincided with the Irish Land War" of 1879–1882. Agricultural depression, poor weather, and two failed potato crops in the late 1870s threatened "a disaster on the scale of the Great Famine" of the 1840s. Irish historian T.W. Moody has termed the anti-landlord activism of the Irish National Land League, established in 1879, "the greatest mass movement of modern Ireland." At this time, the young Casement papered the walls of his attic room with "cartoons cut out of the *Weekly Freeman*, showing the various Irish Nationalists." In 1881, aged sixteen, he kept a copybook in which he pasted clippings about Land League activities.[94] The next year, in a poem about England's conquest of Ireland, Casement penned these lines on the themes of colonial catastrophe and distant exile that would characterize his later years: "Far thy children from this country are by Saxon hatred banned. None are left to mourn or weep

---

[91]King-Sovereign of the Congo Free State to the State agents, Brussels, June 16, 1897, in *La Belgique Coloniale*, August 14, 1898, text in Singleton-Gates and Girodias, *Black Diaries*, 83–84.

[92]Singleton-Gates and Girodias, *Black Diaries*, 38–39; Ó Síocháin, *Roger Casement*, 8.

[93]Singleton-Gates and Girodias, *Black Diaries*, 63.

[94]Ó Síocháin, *Roger Casement*, 8; Séamas Ó Síocháin, "Roger Casement's Vision of Freedom," in *Roger Casement in Irish and World History*, ed. Mary E. Daly (Dublin: Royal Irish Academy, 2005), 1–2.

thee, slaughter reddens all the land."[95] After a lifetime documenting colonial slaughter abroad, Casement would return home to end his days in nationalist opposition to British rule of Ireland.

At the age of twenty, Casement "went out to the Congo" in 1884. One of his first employers there found him "very good to the natives, too good, too generous."[96] In 1886, the year after the founding of the Congo Free State, Casement joined the exploratory expedition led by Léopold's American agent Henry Sanford. He witnessed a State agent, Lieutenant Francqui, order a native "so cruelly flogged... that he was literally cut to pieces." Casement had the victim "carried in my own hammock for over fifty miles when taking him to the State Doctor to have his wounds dressed and in order that I might lodge a complaint on his behalf." Yet the Irishman "was laughed at for [his] pains... Lieutenant Francqui was never punished."[97] During a riverboat journey in 1887, a Belgian *Force Publique* officer told Casement that he paid his African troops "5 brass rods (2½ d.) per human head they brought him during the course of any military operations he conducted."[98] In 1888, Casement left Sanford's expedition to go elephant-shooting, and then, "for some months I commanded the Congo Railway Company's advance expedition." After a brief visit home in 1889 "with all the love of Africa upon me," Casement returned there. "I organized the transport on the Lower Congo for the Belgian authorities."[99]

Now aged 25, Casement only slowly turned his attention to focus on colonialist outrages against Africans. He wrote Stanley in 1890 that he was "temporarily connected" with "a big Belgian company," and that he thought the Congo needed "a little more English or American practical knowledge." Casement concluded:

> On the whole one may say the Congo is improved from a State point of view – or rather from a Belgian point of view – but for outsiders, traders especially, I do not think the increased facilities of reaching the Upper Congo are compensation for the increased duties levied on trade, or the official impediments... I despair of the Congo as a future for Englishmen.[100]

---

[95] Roger Casement, "O'Rorke's Warning" (1882), excerpted in Margaret O'Callaghan, "'With the Eyes of Another Race, of a People Once Hunted Themselves': Casement, Colonialism, and a Remembered Past," in *Roger Casement in Irish and World History*, ed. Mary E. Daly (Dublin: Royal Irish Academy, 2005), 52.

[96] Casement, letter to E.D. Morel, June 27, 1904, in Singleton-Gates and Girodias, *Black Diaries*, 73; Hochschild, *Leopold's Ghost*, 195–196.

[97] PRO Foreign Office 10/807 (Roger Casement, memo to F.O., 14 January 1904), quoted in Ó Síocháin, "Roger Casement's Vision," 5.

[98] Hochschild, *Leopold's Ghost*, 196.

[99] Casement, letter to Morel, June 27, 1904, in Singleton-Gates and Girodias, *Black Diaries*, 73.

[100] Casement, letter to Stanley, June 28, 1890, excerpted in Marcel Luwel, "Roger Casement à Henry Morton Stanley: un rapport sur la situation au Congo en 1890," *Africa-Tervuren* 14, no. 4 (1968): 90–91.

He did not yet, in this report to Stanley, mention the experiences of its African inhabitants. But in 1892, Casement received an appointment with the British Colonial Office in Nigeria, where he did denounce "the atrocious conduct of the Germans" in their neighboring Kamerun colony. Casement wrote in 1894 that "we all on earth have a commission and a right to defend the weak against the strong, and to protest against brutality."[101] He would soon bring this conviction back to the Congo.

What drove Casement to do so is difficult to determine. After his youthful interest in Irish anti-colonial history and politics, the rise of cultural nationalism following the foundation of the Gaelic League in 1893 seems to have most influenced him, spurring his later praise for the "lovely, glorious language" of the Irish. Significantly, he was to assert that "it was only because I was an Irishman that I could understand *fully*, I think, the whole scheme of wrongdoing at work on the Congo."[102] He later wrote from Brazil: "Send me news of Congo and Ireland – nothing else counts."[103] The two colonial experiences intertwined: "In those lonely Congo forests where I found Leopold, I found also myself, the incorrigible Irishman." He went on: "I realized that I was looking at this tragedy with the eyes of another race, of a people once hunted themselves... And I said to myself then, far up the Sulanga River, that I would do my part as an Irishman and just because I was an Irishman, wherever it might lead me to."[104]

Something similar might be said of George Washington Williams, an African American lawyer and journalist who first visited the Congo in 1890, also fortified by the experience of "another race." Elected in 1879 as the first black member of the Ohio state legislature, Williams then wrote a two-volume book, *History of the Negro Race in America from 1619 to 1880. Negroes as Slaves, as Soldiers, and as Citizens, Together with a Preliminary Consideration of the Unity of the Human Family and Historical Sketch of Africa and an Account of the Negro Governments of Sierra Leone and Liberia*.[105] In the year his book appeared, Williams addressed the National Colored Convention, held at Louisville, Kentucky, in September 1883. The Convention also discussed the situation in Ireland and adopted a resolution stating, among other things: "As a race struggling and contending for our political and civil rights, we are not unmindful of the efforts of Ireland to gain her rights, and we extend to our Irish friends

[101] Casement, letter to H.R. Fox Bourne, July 2 1894, quoted in Hochschild, *Leopold's Ghost*, 197.

[102] Casement, letter to Cadbury, July 7, 1905, quoted in Hoschchild, *Leopold's Ghost*, 198.

[103] Casement, letter to Parry, October 9, 1906, quoted in Hochschild, *Leopold's Ghost*, 267–268.

[104] Casement, letter to Alice Stopford Green, April 30 1907, excerpted in O'Callaghan, "'With the Eyes of Another Race," esp. 49–56.

[105] (New York: G.P. Putnam's Sons, 1883).

profound sympathy and best wishes."[106] But Williams was also thinking of Africa. After US President Chester Arthur introduced him to Léopold's agent Sanford, Williams proposed to recruit African Americans to work in the Congo. He visited Léopold in Brussels, and then set out for the Congo Free State, where he spent six months in 1890.[107]

Williams was shocked by what he found. To describe it to the US Secretary of State, Williams coined the term "crimes against humanity," a concept destined to become a major breakthrough in international criminal law.[108] The Congo Free State, Williams decided, was in fact a new slave state built on stolen land, "the Siberia of the African Continent." From Stanley Falls in July 1890, Williams wrote a long *Open Letter* to Léopold, in which he proposed another new idea, "an International Commission" that would "attest the truth or falsity of these charges."[109] This *Open Letter*, Hochschild writes, was itself "the first comprehensive, systematic indictment of Leopold's colonial regime." Williams informed Léopold that his military bases on the Congo River were "piratical, buccaneering posts" whose troops extorted supplies "at the mouths of their muskets; and whenever the natives refuse... white officers come with an expeditionary force and burn away the homes of the natives." Worse, Léopold's State was "excessively cruel to its prisoners." Officials and traders, Williams wrote, were kidnapping African women and shooting villagers, terrorizing survivors to drive them into forced labor. "Your Majesty's Government is engaged in the slave-trade, wholesale and retail... The labour force at the stations of your Majesty's Government in the Upper River is composed of slaves of all ages and both sexes."[110] Three months later, Williams composed *A Report upon the Congo-State and Country to the President of the Republic of the United States of America*. He wrote that at Stanley Falls, "I discovered canoe loads of slaves, bound strongly together." The Free State, he said, was "an oppressive and cruel government."[111]

Williams's *Open Letter* was widely published in Europe and America. The Belgian paper *La Réforme* denounced Léopold's "absolute and uncontrolled regime" as one "fatally bound to produce the majority of grave deeds pointed out by the American traveler." Sadly, Williams contracted

---

106 "National Colored Convention," *Huntsville Gazette*, October 6, 1883, 1.

107 Hochschild, *Leopold's Ghost*, 102–107.

108 George Washington Williams. letter to US Secretary of State Blaine, September 15, 1890, quoted in Hochschild, *Leopold's Ghost*, 111–112. See also Williams, "A Report upon the Congo-State and Country to the President of the Republic of the United States of America," Luanda, October 14, 1890, Appendix 3 of John Hope Franklin, *George Washington Williams* (Durham: Duke University Press, 1998), 264–279.

109 George Washington Williams, "An Open Letter to His Serene Majesty Leopold II," Stanley Falls, July 18, 1890, Appendix 1 of Franklin, *George Washington Williams*, 244.

110 Williams, "Open Letter," 248–252.

111 Williams, "Report upon the Congo-State," 277, 279.

tuberculosis and in 1891 he died in England, aged forty-one. So far, of hundreds of European or American visitors to the Congo, Williams "was the only one to speak out fully and passionately and repeatedly about what others denied or ignored."[112]

But more witnesses were on the way. In 1890, as Williams sailed back down the Congo River to report his findings to the outside world, his steamboat had crossed paths with another, carrying a young Polish officer, the future novelist Joseph Conrad, heading upriver towards Stanley Pool. Conrad's 1898 novel *The Heart of Darkness* also served as an international exposé of colonialism and death in the Congo.

In addition, Williams had blazed a trail that another African American was already following. Eleven days ahead of Joseph Conrad on the Congo River in 1890 was the Reverend William H. Sheppard, a Presbyterian from Virginia, the first black American missionary in the Congo.[113] Sheppard was to spend twenty years in Africa. In 1892, he became the first American or European to reach the capital of the still independent interior kingdom of Kuba, then at the height of its prosperity. "The Bakuba are morally a splendid people," Sheppard wrote.[114]

However, Belgian colonial power was expanding, and intensifying its violence to monopolize Congolese resources. In 1895, a Free State officer hung the Irishman Charles Stokes, an ivory trader married to an African. That murder became "the first incident to attract widespread attention to the maladministration of the Congo State." The former French explorer Lionel Decle launched a personal campaign to expose it.[115] Noting that "[t]he British nation takes the liveliest interest in the affairs of the Armenians," whom the Ottoman Sultan was then subjecting to mass murder, Decle echoed Williams in calling for an "international tribunal," in this case to judge Stokes' murderer. The Congo Free State, he wrote, was run by "savage Europeans, whose route is marked by a line of skeletons," because "the natives are heavily taxed, and are slaughtered by the thousands... When I was at Ujiji, on Lake Tanganika, I heard from the Arabs innumerable tales of Belgian cruelty... I have even heard of over a thousand severed hands being brought in to a single officer."[116] Decle added that Africans "who would not sell their ivory to the State were killed," and Arabs "were exterminated."[117] The historian William Roger Louis sees a political flaw in

---

[112]Hochschild, *Leopold's Ghost*, 112–114.

[113]Hochschild, *Leopold's Ghost*, 140, 152–154.

[114]William H. Sheppard, *Presbyterian Pioneers in Congo* (Richmond, VA: Presbyterian Committee of Publication, 1917), 15, 124; William E. Phipps, *William Sheppard: Congo's African American Livingstone* (Louisville: Geneva Press, 2002) 76, 79, 83.

[115]Louis, "Stokes Affair," 574.

[116]Lionel Decle, "The Murder in Africa," *The New Review* 13 (December 1895): 586, 598, 590.

[117]Lionel Decle, *Pall Mall Gazette*, November 28, 1895, quoted in Louis, "Stokes Affair," 578.

Decle's approach, that he remained "intent on exposing atrocities for the sake of exposing atrocities." He did not yet link them to Léopold's political regime as "the inevitable result of the system of exploitation on which the Congo state was based." Decle's sensational campaign, Louis writes, was soon "snuffed out." Possibly for diplomatic reasons, Britain's Prime Minister Lord Salisbury wanted none of it, and seemed satisfied in 1896 when he commented on the Stokes hanging, "I think it is forgotten."[118]

However, authoritative reports of large massacres were now reaching Europe. The former Congo administrator E. J. Glave, whose diary was published posthumously in 1897, wrote in an entry dated January 18th, 1895: "Many villages refuse to bring rubber; then they are attacked, and killed, or taken prisoners. While I was at Bayongé an expedition sent by Manahutto, under the orders of Lemery, arrived after having a fight with natives on the other side of the Wazimba. Many natives are said to have been killed, and thirty prisoners taken, mostly women."[119] A week later at Riba-Riba, Glave found that "the natives are treated with the utmost severity," with hangings "now quite frequent." "When a village does not consent to make rubber," he wrote, the authorities may "kill and take prisoners, which is quite general." At Kasongo one commander had just conducted "a devastating exploit, burning, killing," and bringing in 200 prisoners. In February 1895, Glave passed through Stanley Falls: "twenty-one heads were brought to the falls." Denouncing "the harsh, cruel policy of the state, wringing rubber from these people without paying for it," Glave predicted more resistance. On the Congo's north bank, he found "all the villages deserted." He added the next month: "War has been waged all through the district of Equator, and thousands of people have been killed and homes destroyed. This forced commerce is depopulating the country." Indeed, "at each post one finds the natives deserting their homes... Hundreds of people are killed in the wars... The decrease in the native population is very marked at Bangala, Equator, Lukolela, and Bolobo." Glave heard convincing new reports of soldiers cutting off the hands of their victims, bringing in "bunches of hands signifying their kill," including severed hands of children. "Much of this sort of thing is going on at the Equator station." "Everywhere I hear the same news of the doings of the Congo Free State – rubber and murder, slavery in its worst form."[120]

Two months earlier, the Free State's Equator District commissioner Léon Fiévez had corroborated much of this in a confidential official dispatch from Equator station on January 11, 1895. Before it was sent to Bruxelles, a judge and state inspector in the Congo, Marcelin de Saegher, read this dispatch

[118] Louis, "Stokes Affair," 577, 582; William Roger Louis, "Roger Casement and the Congo," *Journal of African History* 5, no. 1 (1964): 99–120.

[119] "Cruelty in the Congo Free State: Concluding Extracts from the Journals of the Late E.J. Glave," *The Century Illustrated Monthly Magazine* 32 (May-October 1897): 699.

[120] Glave, "Cruelty in the Congo," 701–709, 714.

and copied part of it. Fiévez had written: "I left on November 18 [1894] to do what was necessary for the establishment of the Boussira private domain." In a letter to a fellow judge in Belgium on February 16th, 1895, de Saegher gave further details of the contents of Fiévez's dispatch:

> Here is what this gentleman means by doing what is needed. He killed on the first occasion 959 (nine hundred fifty-nine) natives and took 200 prisoners of whom half are children aged 4 to 10... To comprehend the kind of butchery, think that we had only three killed and 10 wounded. A few days later 145 natives killed – 1 soldier killed, 2 wounded. Then 59 natives killed.

In sum, Fiévez had reported that in less than two months his operation had killed 1,346 people, expending only "2,838 cartridges," and had "devastated 162 villages, burned the houses and cut down the crops to reduce the populations by hunger." As a result, "the chiefs have promised to supply each month 1,562 portions of 15 kilos of rubber." De Saegher concluded that "this is not an isolated fact, but the *system* applied in *all the districts*."[121]

Around the same time, the American missionary Reverend John Murphy gave Reuters confirmation of a number of similar accounts, and claimed that in one town, "on the authority of a state official, 1,890 people have been killed."[122] In 1896, "a highly esteemed Belgian" told a German newspaper that Equator District commissioner Léon Fiévez had taken delivery of 1,308 severed hands in a single day.[123]

A year later the Swedish missionary Sjöblom reported wholesale massacres, one involving fifty people. "If rubber does not reach the full amount required, the sentinels attack the natives. They kill some and bring the hands to the administrator. Others are brought in as prisoners and taken to the coast." A British Foreign Office official reported in 1897 that even among British West African laborers in the Congo, "the loss of life has been very great." Now Lord Salisbury commented, "It is very horrible."[124] The population of Ikoko and nearby villages fell from 3,500 in 1895 to 650 in 1899. In Bikoro, several thousand natives were killed.[125] Free State officer Simon Roi told the missionary Ellsworth Faris in 1899 about his responsibility for mass killing. Faris wrote: "Each time the corporal goes out to get

[121]Marcelin de Saegher, *une lettre à Emile Steyaert, président du tribunal de première instance de Gand, 16 février 1895* (italics original); citing Fiévez to Bruxelles from Equator, dispatch no. GG/212, 8 pp. An extract and facsimile of Saegher's letter is in Philippe Marechal, "La controverse sur Léopold II et le Congo dans la littérature et les medias: Réflexions critiques," in *La Mémoire du Congo: Le temps colonial*, ed. Jean-Luc Vellut (Tervuren: Musée Royal de l'Afrique Centrale/Gand, Snoeck, 2005) 44–46.

[122]London *Times*, November 18, 1895, quoted in Ewans, *European Atrocity*, 177.

[123]Vangroenweghe, *Du sang sur les lianes*, 64; Hochschild, *Leopold's Ghost*, 226.

[124]Louis, "Roger Casement and the Congo," 99–100; Ewans, *European Atrocity*, 177–178, 183.

[125]Vangroenweghe, *Du sang sur les lianes*, 65, 68.

rubber, cartridges are given to him. He must bring back all not used; and for every one used he must bring back a right hand!" Roi told Faris "that in six months they, the State, on the Momboyo River had used 6000 cartridges, which means that 6000 people are killed or mutilated. It means more than 6000, for the people have told me repeatedly that the soldiers kill children with the butt of their guns."[126]

In 1895, London promoted Roger Casement to British Consul for Portuguese East Africa, and three years later, to Consul for Portuguese West Africa. During that time he was receiving "terrible private letters from the Congo of the continued violence and barbarities practiced by the Congo State soldiery." In 1898 Casement revisited the Free State, and the next year he reported "atrocities" in Upper Congo, repeatedly requesting Foreign Office permission to go there. In April 1900, he urged Britain to help end "the reign of terror" in the Free State, and to improve "the welfare... of all natives of the Congo." Later that year, Casement returned to Congo as British Consul in Kinshasa.[127]

By then the Free State had expanded into the Kingdom of Kuba. A Belgian official ordered his commanders: "[F]rom 1 January 1899 you must succeed in furnishing four thousand kilos of rubber every month. To effect this I give you carte blanche." Commanders, he ordered, should "work your people" with "gentleness first," but if necessary, they must "employ the force of arms" to bring in the rubber.[128] Using brutal African mercenaries known as Zappo Zaps, Belgian power soon overwhelmed the Bakuba people. In September 1899, a runner seeking help reached the nearby home of the missionary William H. Sheppard, who had visited Kuba in 1892. The American Presbyterian Congo Mission now asked him to investigate. Sheppard marched into Kuba, finding one deserted village after another. A survivor said the Zappo Zaps chief Malumba had assembled villagers and demanded 2,500 balls of rubber. When they protested that this was impossible, Malumba had ordered his men to open fire on the crowd. Pushing on, Sheppard pretended to be a Belgian officer. He tracked down Malumba, who told him: "I think we have killed between eighty and ninety, and those in the other villages, I don't know." Malumba showed Sheppard 81 severed hands. Another Presbyterian missionary sent Sheppard's long report to the Free State government, which denied responsibility, and to

[126] Hochschild, *Leopold's Ghost*, 226–227. For further evidence of the continuing atrocities, see Hunt, "Acoustic Register," 231–237, 239.

[127] Roger Casement, letter to Henry Foley, 24 April 1900, and Sir Martin Gosselin, 30 April 1900, excerpted in Ó Síocháin, *Roger Casement*, 114, 91–94, 97–99; and Ó Síocháin, "Roger Casement's Vision of Freedom," 6; Singleton-Gates and Girodias, *Black Diaries*, 74, 78, 82.

[128] Phipps, *William Sheppard*, 139–140.

London, where the Aborigines Protection Society took up the issue. So did the future Congo Reform crusader, Edmund D. Morel (1873–1924).[129]

Morel worked for the West Africa shipping firm Elder Dempster, which he knew carried Belgian weaponry to Congo and brought back rubber. A member of the Liverpool Chamber of Commerce, Morel began systematic inquiries. In a few years, he published four books detailing atrocities in the Congo: *Affairs of West Africa* (1902); *The Congo Slave State* (1903); *King Leopold's Rule in Africa* (1904), and *Red Rubber* (1907).[130] In 1903, Morel also launched a newspaper, the *West African Mail*, which featured long reports on the Congo, and published a pamphlet, *The Scandal in the Congo: Britain's Duty* (1904). Hochschild calls Morel "the greatest British investigative journalist of his time."[131] Once he had linked up with Roger Casement, they successfully enlisted a Trans-Atlantic support network of international literary figures such as Joseph Conrad, Arthur Conan Doyle, and Mark Twain.[132]

In 1900, when Morel began working on the Congo case, and Casement arrived in Kinshasa as the British Consul in the Free State, Kuba was only one of Congo's hardest-hit regions. Belgian parliamentarians denounced the reported murder and mutilation of several hundred men, women and children, to which four Belgian agents had confessed. Meanwhile Belgian-led forces launched a campaign against the rebellious Budja tribe, who refused to carry out labor requirements and had killed thirty soldiers. After one of several punitive expeditions against the Budja, an American officer wrote, "we had undergone six weeks of painful marching and had killed over nine hundred natives, men, women, and children." They burned down "village after village" and massacred thirty prisoners in a single incident. Belgian newspapers estimated the total death toll at 1,300 Budjas. Summing up the slaughter and the death toll throughout the Congo, Hochschild adds that disease spread rapidly among weakened populations. Smallpox left

[129] Pagan Kennedy, *Black Livingstone: A True Tale of Adventure in the Nineteenth-Century Congo* (New York: Viking, 2002) 132–133, 139–144, 147–148.

[130] Edmund D. Morel, *Affairs of West Africa* (London: Heinemann, 1902); *The Congo Slave State. A Protest Against the New African Slavery; and an Appeal to the Public of Great Britain, of the United States, and of the Continent of Europe* (Liverpool: Richardson, 1903); *King Leopold's Rule in Africa* (London: Heinemann, 1904); *The Scandal of the Congo: Britain's Duty* (Liverpool, 1904); *Red Rubber: The Story of the Rubber Slave Trade Flourishing on the Congo in the Year of Grace 1906* (London: Unwin, 1907).

[131] Hochschild, *Leopold's Ghost*, 186–187.

[132] *E.D. Morel's History of the Congo Reform Movement*, ed. William Roger Louis and Jean Stengers (Oxford: Clarendon, 1968); Hunt Hawkins, "Joseph Conrad, Roger Casement, and the Congo Reform Movement," *Journal of Modern Literature* 9, no.1 (1981–1982): 65–80; Hunt Hawkins, "Mark Twain's Involvement with the Congo Reform Movement," *New England Quarterly* 51, no. 2 (1978): 147–175.

"village after village full of dead bodies." Sleeping sickness killed half a million people in 1901 alone.[133]

That same year, Belgian newspapers made the first revelations of the atrocities in the Abir rubber concession area, when they published reports by a former company agent. Abir alone was providing ten percent of the Congo Free State's revenue. Its rubber production peaked in 1903, as did that of its main stockholder, the Société Anversoise, which ran a large neighboring concession area. But, as Robert Harms shows, these companies' ecologically destructive extractive operations were rapidly depleting the wild rubber vines in the Congo forests. Abir rubber extraction fell by nearly two thirds in 1903–1905; Société Anversoise production plummeted from 526 to 90 tons. The companies responded with even more ruthless and more extractive methods. Harms writes: "The agents did not know what to do except become harsher; the people in the villages began to despair." Towards the end of 1904 an African headman told a British missionary: "If we must either be massacred or bring rubber, well, let them finish us off."[134]

In June 1903 Roger Casement, now in his third year as British Consul to the Congo, began his famous official 4-month journey into the interior to investigate the atrocities there, including those in the Abir concession. With two decades of experience in the country, he was under no illusions. "I'm after a snake and please God I'll scotch it."[135] From the interior he wrote in early August 1903: "In the lake district things are pretty bad... Whole villages and districts I knew well and visited as flourishing communities in 1887 are today without a human being; others are reduced to a handful of sick or harassed creatures." Three weeks later: "Bolongo quite dead. I remember it well in 1887, Nov., full of people then; now 14 adults all told. I should say people wretched, complained bitterly of rubber tax."[136] The next month Casement wrote to the British Foreign Secretary that he had "broken into the thieves' kitchen," and described himself as a self-appointed "Criminal Investigation Department."[137] He reported in writing to the Free State's *Gouverneur-Général* about "these unhappy people whose sufferings I have witnessed and whose wrongs have burnt into my heart." He charged that the colony's "system" was "entirely wrong," potentially even genocidal. "Instead of lifting up the native populations... it can, if persisted in, lead only to their final extinction." Unlike Lionel Decle eight

[133]Ewans, *European Atrocity*, 184; Hochschild, *Leopold's Ghost*, 192–193, 226–227, 230–231.

[134]Harms, "End of Red Rubber," 83, 79, 81, 82, 86–87, 85.

[135]Hochschild, *Leopold's Ghost*, 200.

[136]Louis, "Roger Casement and the Congo," 105; Singleton-Gates and Girodias, *Black Diaries*, 159.

[137]Louis, "Roger Casement and the Congo," 104, 107; Hochschild, *Leopold's Ghost*, 201.

years earlier, Casement concluded: "I do not accuse an individual, I accuse a system."[138]

On his return to London in December 1903, Casement produced a devastating 61-page printed report that was widely read in Europe. His work on the report brought a visit from the campaigner Edmund Morel, and that led to their collaboration, and the formation of the Congo Reform Association. Arthur Conan Doyle described the two men's meeting, on December 10th, 1903, as the most "dramatic scene in modern history." Morel recalled of Casement: "as I saw him at that memorable interview... [t]he daily agony of an entire people unrolled itself in all the repulsive terrifying details. I verily believe I saw those hunted women clutching their children and flying panic-stricken into the bush; the blood flowing from those quivering black bodies."[139] In his diary, Casement wrote of Morel: "first time I met him. The man is honest as day. Dined at Comedy together late and then to chat till 2 a.m. M. sleeping in study. *December 11th*. Morel off after breakfast, and then to hard work all day, worked like Trojan, practically finished report." Early in that New Year of 1904, Casement in turn visited Morel's home: "Talked all night nearly, wife a good woman."[140] Indeed, Morel's wife Mary persuaded her husband to adopt Casement's proposal for a new Association. The next step, Morel wrote, was a visit to Casement's home in Ireland: "I crossed the Irish Channel... to meet him... It was... on that Irish soil... fertilized by so many human tears, that Casement and I conspired further... and drew up a rough plan of campaign." Several weeks later, Morel founded the Congo Reform Association. He opened its first public meeting in Liverpool on March 23rd, 1904.[141] The CRA forged few if any links with rebels in the Congo itself, nor was it able to end the Free State's atrocities, but it brought them to unprecedented global attention and ushered in a new era in human rights campaigning.

Meanwhile the situation in the Congo became even worse. Harms describes the Abir concession as plunged "into chaos between 1904 and 1906."[142] In May 1904, sentries with Albini rifles murdered 83 men, women and children of the village of Wala. The next year a British investigator found that "villages had been abandoned all over the territory. The people were living in rude leaf shelters built in the thickest parts of the forest." Some were fighting back. Rebels killed or wounded 142 Abir sentries in the first half of 1905. In one region, "the company called in State forces. Three European officers with contingents of soldiers began to tour the area, stopping at each village and threatening to return and destroy it if the people

[138] Louis, "Roger Casement and the Congo," 106–107; Hochschild, *Leopold's Ghost*, 201.
[139] Louis, "Roger Casement and the Congo," 114.
[140] Singleton-Gates and Girodias, *Black Diaries*, 183–185, 189.
[141] Hochschild, *Leopold's Ghost*, 206–207.
[142] Harms, "End of Red Rubber," 85.

did not bring in rubber." In another Abir region, half the population had fled by February 1906.[143] As rubber production also fell elsewhere in the Congo, State officials grew more desperate. In 1905 a district commissioner, Jules Jacques, demanded "absolute submission... or complete extermination" of the Inongo people. He added: "Inform the natives that if they cut another single vine, I will exterminate them to the last man."[144] However the ruthless extraction policies of both State and concession companies had already largely destroyed the Congo's natural rubber resources. In late 1906 the Free State took over both the Abir and the Société Anversoise concessions. In the next 2 years, 12 European officers and 650 troops "fought in the Abir territory for fourteen months without bringing all of it under control." The rubber had virtually run out. In Europe, however, "serious debate on the Congo question was just beginning."[145] Neither the Belgian government's direct takeover of the Congo Free State from the King in 1908, nor Léopold's death the next year, ended the agony of the African inhabitants.

The population of the Congo fell by half, according to some estimates, between 1885 and 1920. This was a statistical loss of possibly five to ten million from murder, starvation, exhaustion, exposure, disease, and a plummeting birth rate that failed to compensate even for normal mortality.[146] Vangroenweghe blames "the pitiless exploitation of rubber" for the deaths of "hundreds of thousands of natives," including four-fifths of the populations of some tribes.[147] Hochschild comments that "although the killing in the Congo was of genocidal proportions, it was not, strictly speaking, genocide. The Congo state was not deliberately trying to eliminate one particular ethnic group from the face of the earth."[148] Yet much of what occurred is indeed covered by the 1948 UN Convention on Genocide. That crime includes deliberate killings, *for whatever motive*, of members of an ethnic group with the intent to destroy them as such, "in whole or in part."[149] The mass murder and slave labor took the Congo case even beyond the demographic calamity of the Irish Famine. In contrast to Ireland in 1846–1851, colonial officials and their agents in the Congo were directly culpable for

143 Vangroenweghe, *Du sang sur les lianes*, 123–125; Harms, "End of Red Rubber," 85–86.

144 *West African Mail*, March 16, 1906, p.1219, quoted in Hochschild, *Leopold's Ghost*, 228–229.

145 Harms, "End of Red Rubber," 87–88.

146 Marechal, "La controverse sur Léopold II et le Congo," 47–48, citing Daniel Vangroenweghe and Jan Antonissen, *Humo*, Novembre 24, 2002 and March 23, 1999, respectively; Hochschild, *Leopold's Ghost*, 225–233.

147 Vangroenweghe, *Du sang sur les lianes*, 18–19.

148 Hochschild, *Leopold's Ghost*, 225.

149 The difficulty in meeting Genocide Convention criteria particularly in relation to intent and protected groups is addressed in Gérard Prunier, Chapter 3, Section 3.1 (below) and Francis M. Deng, Chapter 4, Sections 4.2 and 4.3 (below).

appalling violence. The widespread killings distinguished the Congo from the famine deaths in Ireland.

Elsewhere in Africa, British colonial expansion came closer to genocide. In 1893, not far south of the Congo, colonists under the umbrella of the British South Africa Company seized land and cattle from the Mashona and Ndebele populations of what soon became Southern Rhodesia. The latter rebelled and British repression took thousands of lives in 1896–1897. But Cecil Rhodes prevented an escalation into genocide, a strategy that was widely discussed. His ally Lord Jarvis had written to his wife on March 29th, 1896 about the 5,500 Ndebele people of Gwelo district: "I hope the natives will be pretty well exterminated... Poor devils, one can't help being a bit sorry for them." Three weeks later, he added: "our plan of campaign will probably be to proceed against this lot and wipe them out, then move on towards Bulawayo wiping out every nigger...after these cold-blooded murders you may be sure there will be no quarter and everything black will have to die." Jarvis repeated in July that "the best thing to do is to wipe them all out as far as one can – everything black." Even a priest recommended in 1897, according to Lord Grey, that "the only chance for the future of the [Mashona] race is to exterminate the whole people, both male and female, over the age of 14!"[150] As a new century dawned, genocide was in the air, and a violent storm was coming in from the colonies.

But so was an international protest movement, one that contested metropolitan policies based on colonial monopoly, racial superiority, *laissez-faire* economics, or "Providence." This new movement had cut its teeth in opposition to the mass murder and slavery practiced by Léopold's Congo Free State. Trans-Atlantic critics had coined a new language of international human rights law, including terms such as "crime against humanity," "International Commission," and "international tribunal."

Some of the origins of this new activist movement also lay in the Irish experience, which Roger Casement continued to draw on as he set out again in 1910 on his next official investigation, into the ongoing atrocities against Putumayo Indians of the rubber-producing forests of Peru. While preparing another horrifying report on their fate, Casement wrote in his diary of meeting an Indian whose name is "Simon Pisango – a pure Indian name – but calls himself Simon Pizarro – because he wants to be 'civilised.'" Casement found this name change quite familiar: "Just like the Irish O's and [Mac's?] dropping their first names or prefixes to shew their respectability and then their ancient tongue itself to be completely Anglicized." Ireland stayed on his mind. One day on the Amazon, Casement not only collected "disgraceful" evidence of "murders of girls, beheading of Indians and shooting of them after they had rotted from flogging," but also, as he confided to his diary that evening, he "[d]reamed and planned a great Irish romance of the

[150]Terrence Ranger, *Revolt in Southern Rhodesia, 1896–1897* (London: Heineman, 1967) 3, 71, 131, 237.

future."[151] Back across the Atlantic in 1913, he would write of the Irish as "white Indians," and of Western Ireland's County Galway as the "Irish Putumayo."[152]

Three decades of international involvement had led Roger Casement home for his final anti-colonial campaign. In April 1916, he attempted to join in the planned Easter Rising against British rule in Dublin. Police arrested him soon after he had rowed ashore from a German submarine and landed on a deserted beach in the west of Ireland. The British government transported him to London, exposed him as a homosexual, and convicted him of treason. Casement died on the gallows in Pentonville Prison on August 3rd, 1916, aged 51.

The Congo Reform Association was far from the first non-government campaign for human rights, but it proved to be a historic organization with lasting effects. Its significance stemmed less from its role in ending the Congo catastrophe, which diminished only slowly and was also affected by other factors, including ecological exhaustion and Congolese resistance, than from the global attention it focused on a colonial humanitarian disaster and on the major international culprits, and from the institutional precedent it set for targeted human rights campaigns in an era of emerging international humanitarian law. Just as the American lawyer George Washington Williams had first exposed Belgian atrocities in the Congo Free State and coined the concept of "crimes against humanity," and the French explorer Lionel Decle had called for an "international tribunal," Roger Casement and Edmund Morel took up the Congo case and led the CRA's transnational protest network. Their joint efforts pioneered twentieth-century non-governmental human rights activism.

Roger Casement's youth had been colored by Ireland's subjection to imperial rule and inaction in the face of famine. As we have seen, Williams and Morel were also well aware of the Irish tragedy. In turn, their independent experiences and observations of African colonial exploitation and violence drove all three men to pursue a course of public pressure for intervention, tackling head-on the prevailing sovereignty of a metropolitan government over its colony and its subjects. In this sense they were precursors of the jurist Raphael Lemkin, and helped set the stage for his major legal achievement, the 1948 international proscription of genocide. Williams, Casement, and Morel played key roles in the birth of modern human rights law and activism by helping to guide their development, in the decades following Britain's failed response to the Irish Famine, towards a twentieth-century international consensus that mass death is unacceptable anywhere and that organized intervention is required to bring it to an end and hold those responsible to account.

---

[151] Casement's diary, September 17 and 22, 1910. Singleton-Gates and Girodias, *Black Diaries*, 241, 245.

[152] Hochschild, *Leopold's Ghost*, 270.

Chapter 3
Darfur: Genocidal Theory and Practical Atrocities

Gérard Prunier

Previous genocides in the history of mankind were carried out stealthily (Cambodia), or very quickly (Rwanda), or else in the midst of events of such magnitude that the genocide became a secondary, almost hidden event in the larger frame of things. This was the case of the Armenian Genocide, which for a long time was just a footnote to the history of the First World War,[1] and it is true even of the Jewish Holocaust which, in spite of looming very large today in global consciousness, was a secondary matter, largely ignored at the time. A remarkably courageous analysis by a modern European Jewish historian reads:

> The sad truth is that during World War II itself, many people did not know about the fate of the Jews or if they knew, they did not much care. There were only two groups of historical actors for whom World War II was above all a project to destroy the Jews: the Nazis and the Jews themselves. For practically everyone else the war had quite different meanings: they had troubles of their own.[2]

The situation in Darfur today poses a series of quite different problems:

- It takes place in slow motion, almost directly under the eyes of the television cameras.
- Although nobody doubts the existence of the violence, its nature has been hidden under the veil of "ethnic violence," "rebellion," "nomads versus settled peasants" or even "climate change."
- It has fluctuated between periods of genocidal ultra violence and periods of relatively "quieter" counterinsurgency campaigns.

G. Prunier (✉)
Centre national de la recherche scientifique, 75794 Paris Cedex 16, France
e-mail: gerard.prunier@wanadoo.fr

[1]The main events of the Armenian Genocide are recounted in Douglas Greenberg, Chapter 5 (below); an explanation of the Turkish government's stance towards the genocide is provided in Taner Akçam, Chapter 10 (below).

[2]Tony Judt, "The Problem of Evil in Postwar Europe," *The New York Review of Books*, February 14, 2008.

R. Provost, P. Akhavan (eds.), *Confronting Genocide*, Ius Gentium: Comparative Perspectives on Law and Justice 7, DOI 10.1007/978-90-481-9840-5_3,

- There was no general agreement on the question of "intent," which is deemed essential to prove genocide, if we go by the United Nations December 1948 Convention on the Prevention of Genocide.[3]

So we are left with an extremely paradoxical situation: although the unfolding violence is highly visible, its very nature is questioned, nobody can agree on its causes, the countermeasures are open to discussion and the net result is that, beyond the well-meaning humanitarian rhetoric, practically nothing is done beyond keeping the surviving victims precariously alive.

3.1 The Ambiguous Definition of Genocide

In many ways the December 1948 Convention on the Prevention of Genocide is a dated text. Why? Because it was almost entirely driven by a very precise historical event, the 1941–1945 genocide of the European populations of Jewish origin by the National Socialist regime then in power in Germany.

Given the shock felt at the Holocaust, the lack of intervention by the Allied Powers to try to stop it during the event itself and the vast political problems then posed by the creation of the State of Israel, which was conceived of as a kind of "anti-genocidal" state, the Convention aspired to universalism but was in fact powerfully rooted in a single mid-twentieth century European historical event. Additionally, the historians dealing with the Holocaust – particularly those from the State of Israel – kept emphasizing the uniqueness of what had happened in Europe between 1941 and 1945. This created a basic contradiction for a document which was aiming at universal relevance: if the *Shoah* was unique, how could a text based on its memory be used to prevent the repetition of a similar phenomenon, particularly in parts of the world where the parameters threatening a repeat of potentially similar genocides follow a completely different sequence of events? As Tony Judt observes: "Moral admonitions from Auschwitz that loom large on the memory screen of Europeans are quite invisible to Asians or Africans."[4] When the international community adheres strictly to the criteria defined by the December 1948 text, it runs the risk of falling into largely abstract formalism and of not *seeing* the realities on the ground because it insists on their being framed by pre-defined and inapplicable conditions.[5]

---

[3] An analysis of the difficulty in determining intent according to the terms of the Genocide Convention is provided in Francis M. Deng, Chapter 4, Section 3.2 (below).

[4] Ibid.

[5] The difficulties in meeting the Genocide Convention requirements and potential failure to capture certain situations are examined in Francis M. Deng, Chapter 4, Section 4.2 (below).

This brings us back to the present near obsession with what the journalists call "the Big G Word," genocide. The application of the word is itself ambiguous. For the sake of argument let us take an episode of the Ugandan civil war of the 1980s. In 1982 the regime of then President Milton Obote decided to undercut the support given to the National Resistance Army of then rebel leader Yoweri Museveni by persecuting the Rwandan Tutsi refugees who were living in the Western Ugandan Province of Ankole. Several hundreds were killed, their cattle were stolen and they were pushed over the border towards Rwanda which – then solidly in the hands of the Hutu-dominated regime of President Juvenal Habyarimana – refused to allow them in. As a result many died of diseases and starvation in a two-kilometer wide strip of borderland between the two countries. Was it genocide or not? Everybody knew the victims to have been racially targeted. But there was no clearly defined "intent." Did the Obote regime intend to destroy the Rwandan Tutsi "in whole or in part?" In part, definitely. In whole, probably not. In any case the regime always denied having targeted the refugees because of their ethnic origins, preferring to label them as "supporters of the rebellion" – which they were.

In the course of my experiences with African conflicts I have seen such situations arise time and time again. Here are some examples of "ambiguous genocides," largely forgotten by historians, which I have personally witnessed:

- The killings of the Langi and the Acholi by the Idi Amin Dada regime in Uganda, particularly in 1970–1972. Idi Amin has now become a kind of household name for evil and a precise analysis of what he did is often forgotten. His killings were far from always being random. Nevertheless he is never seen as "genocidal."
- What was known as *inkiza* (the catastrophe) in Burundi in 1972, i.e., the slaughter of approximately 200,000 Hutu (particularly schoolchildren) by the Tutsi dictatorship of President Micombero.
- The killings of the Majerteen and Issaq clans by the Siad Barre regime in Somalia from 1978 to 1991.
- The extensive massacres of the Baganda by the Obote regime in 1982–1985, when the slogan "A good Muganda is a dead Muganda" was used by the government's army[6] and up to 300,000 died.
- None of these were classified as "genocides," yet all of them could have been by simply sticking to the December 1948 definition. But what would have been the point if there had been no more reaction than there was at the time?[7]

---

[6] I saw these slogans still freshly scrawled on the walls with my own eyes in the weeks following the end of the war.

[7] None of these horrible violations of human rights led to any form of international action or even serious condemnation. As for the Idi Amin regime it was removed by the unilateral action of the Tanzanian Army in 1978–1979.

Part of the problem with the word "genocide" is the word itself. Is the definition supposed to be a kind of (negative) quality label or is it supposed to be a tool leading to action? Should action be restricted to circumstances properly labeled "genocide" even if the number of victims is limited, and should other victims, even those in much greater numbers, be left to their fate if they do not fit the label? Must the victims have a different ethnic origin from the perpetrators for the qualification to apply? What is it that we are talking about when we talk about genocide?

This ambiguity is very much with us in the case of Darfur, a province of the Sudan, populated partly by tribes who identify themselves as "Arabs"[8] and partly by "African" tribes. Both groups have suffered from political and administrative neglect and from economic marginalization. Starting in the mid 1980s, the "Arabs" were used both by foreigners (the Libyans) and by locally based political entrepreneurs to control the provincial politics to the detriment of their "African" neighbors. In February 2003, the "Africans" revolted against the Arab-controlled government in Khartoum and the government reacted with indiscriminate massacres of the "African" civilians. Was it "genocide" or not? If we go by the attitude of the killers who were boasting that they were killing *zurga* (Blacks) to "clear the land from slaves," there is no doubt that this was genocide. But the government claims that the *Janjaweed* militiamen who were committing these crimes were free agents and that they had nothing to do with the authorities.[9] Therefore the massacres would fall into the "less important" category of "ethnic violence."[10]

Does the classification really matter? Close to half a million people have died in Darfur during the last 5 years[11] and over 2.5 million are internally displaced. 150,000 have fled to Chad in spite of Chad not being a very hospitable land of asylum, particularly at present.[12] In the face of such protracted horror, is the name by which we call mass atrocities the most important part of the problem? Do the survivors care about whether their loved ones were slaughtered in genocide, ethnic cleansing or "ethnic

---

[8]This simply means tribes whose mother tongue is Arabic. Their racial appearance is often very close to that of the "African" tribes.

[9]These claims were completely spurious as the *Janjaweed* were armed, trained and paid by the government, operated jointly with regular army units and supported by vehicles and even aircraft of the government's army. For more details see my book, *Darfur: The Ambiguous Genocide.* (London/New York: Hurst/Cornell University Press, 2005).

[10]They would not even be labelled as "ethnic cleansing" because "ethnic cleansing" is supposed to be an organized crime, coordinated by authorities.

[11]The 200,000 casualty figure bandied around by the international community does not bear close scrutiny. For a realistic assessment of Darfur's human losses see the work of Sudan specialist Eric Reeves at www.sudanreeves.org (Accessed June 9, 2009).

[12]The situation in Darfur is examined in Catherine Lu, Chapter 18, Section 18.1 and 18.2 (below) and Luis Moreno-Ocampo, Chapter 16 (below).

massacres"? As each fact-finding mission realizes upon speaking to survivors in the Internally Displaced Persons (IDP) camps, nobody has the slightest doubt about the responsibility of the government in the killings.[13] Even today the so-called "police" who operate in and out of the IDP camps are comprised of former *Janjaweed*, and some women have experienced the shock of trying to file a complaint for rape only to be faced in the police station by the very men who had raped them.

Such experiences of course have little to do with the Jewish *Shoah*. They are neither better nor worse; they are completely different because everything from the historical context to the geography and from the culture to the political situation is different. As Tony Judt wrote very aptly in his searching examination of the historical legacy of the Jewish Holocaust for present world history: "When we ransack the past for political profit – selecting the bits that can serve our purposes and recruiting history to teach opportunistic moral lessons – we get bad morality and bad history."[14]

The December 1948 Convention on the Prevention of Genocide is a well-meaning but historically circumscribed text which responded to a specific historical moment with a deluded attempt at a universal proviso. It was trying to set up what had happened to the European Jews as a special and immutable experience. In fact, the Holocaust was neither and, since then, the Convention has tended to obscure rather than clarify the way in which we look at massive government violence against a segment of its population. On this problem of defining genocide one should, like the chairman and founder of International Crisis Group, former Australian Foreign Affairs Minister Gareth Evans, speak of "*atrocity crimes*."[15] Massive war crimes, crimes against humanity, ethnic cleansing and genocide all belong to the same category. Numbers are not criteria. An effort at redefining the December 1948 text is greatly needed, not in order to restrict it or broaden it, but to change the nature of the yardstick. The *modus operandi* should be the key: *who* is doing *what* to *whom*?[16] If Darfur has one lesson to teach us, it is that ambiguity is not acceptable and to see a government playing word parlor games with the lives of its citizens is not an acceptable practice for the world community.

---

[13] The experience of attending to the interests IDPs as part of a UN mandate is recounted in Francis M. Deng, Chapter 4, Section 4.1 (below).

[14] Judt, "The Problem of Evil," 2008.

[15] Gareth Evans, "Genocide or Crime? Action Speaks Louder than Words in Darfur," *European Voice*, February 18, 2005. See also David Scheffer, "How to Bring Atrocity Criminals to Justice," *Financial Times*. February 2, 2005.

[16] An argument for the use of the label "mass atrocities" is provided in Yehuda Bauer, Chapter 7, Section 7.1 (below).

3.2 The International Community's Impotence in Confronting the Genocide in Darfur

Darfur had been the locus of a low intensity conflict since the mid-1980s, one of these "little wars" of which there are so many on the African continent and which nobody takes seriously until they suddenly turn incredibly vicious.[17] Between 1985 and 2003 the violence had been constant, with repeated massacres of civilians by government-inspired Arab militias. The year 2003 marked a change in conflict structure, *not* the beginning of the conflict. As long as "small massacres went bubbling on,"[18] nobody cared, and the body count was acceptable. Then the conflict exploded with the guerilla attack on El-Fasher, when the victims had decided to strike back. The first few months of the Darfur genocide, however, were a period where the government was entirely free to repress, without fear of obstruction or international interference. Darfur had always been a backwater, and there were hardly any foreigners there when the large-scale war started in February 2003. There were no newspaper journalists and hardly any humanitarian workers. The massacres could take place for months without witnesses.

The world started to take notice when a number of advocacy NGOs published a series of scathing reports during 2004.[19] Action by the international community was a bit slower in coming and began to unfold only around September 2004 (i.e. 18 months after the violence had started and after perhaps 180,000 people had died). It was a confused mixture of NGO initiatives and UN efforts, mostly aimed at trying to mitigate the impact of the massacres, flight and food deprivation on the survivors. No military or police protection effort was attempted until 2005 when the African Union sent a first small group of monitors to Darfur. This limited involvement slowly grew into the *African Mission in the Sudan* (AMIS) which culminated at 7,000 men. The mandate of this Panafrican military force was to

[17]In early 1995, this author met many NGO and international workers in Rwanda who were talking of "*having been there as long as the war*," i.e., since the April 1994 genocide. They were completely unaware of the fact that there had been a war going on in Rwanda since October 1990. Similarly, practically nobody among the humanitarian workers who came into Darfur in late 2004 would have been able to date the beginning of the hostilities to 9 years before. See Africa Watch, *The Forgotten War in Darfur Flares up Again* (Africa Watch, London, April 6, 1990) and Gérard Prunier, "Ecologie, structures ethniques et conflits politiques au Dar Fur," in *Sudan: History, Ideology, Identity*, eds. Hervé Bleuchot, Christian Delmet and Derek Hopwood (Oxford: Ithaca Press, 1991), 85–103.

[18]These were the words used in an article entitled "Tutsis and Hutus: More Blood to Come" on Burundi in *The Economist*, July 22, 1995, 53, to describe still another one of these "low intensity" conflicts.

[19]See Amnesty International, Human Rights Watch Africa and the International Crisis Group reports for 2004.

protect the Darfur civilians. In fact, it never succeeded and seemed to spend most of its time: (1) surviving and ensuring its own security; (2) writing optimistic reports to justify its existence; and (3) traveling around in Darfur, monitoring the various violations of human rights. It never undertook one serious combat mission, it never fought anybody, and, if it saved any lives, it was inadvertently and indirectly.

The African troops were ill-equipped and poorly mandated to carry out their duties because the corruption of the African Union had reached incredible levels. The result was that the soldiers on the ground often did not see any money for 3 or 4 months at a time. Some of that money, supposed to be paid by the US and the EU, had never even been disbursed. Then large chunks were stolen, first in Addis-Ababa and also in El-Fasher. While salaries remained unpaid, fuel allowances were not given, resulting in patrol cancellations. Flights were reduced and many officers simply deserted the field, going back to Ethiopia or to their countries of origin. There was even often no money to hire interpreters and the AMIS men, who did not speak Arabic or any of the local languages, could not even speak with the people they were supposed to be "protecting."[20] This calamitous situation went a long way towards explaining Khartoum's attitude: when the Sudanese Islamists said that they were willing to keep the AMIS force, *only if it was not re-hatted and turned into a UN force*, it was because they knew that prolonging the status quo was a guarantee of international impotence. The AMIS force, as it stood, was almost useless. This is why in September 2006 the Khartoum government even went as far as offering to fund the AMIS budget in order to keep a useless symbol of international intervention close to its chest. By becoming the paying agent for this useless force it would have killed three birds with one stone:

- Gained control over the whole operation;
- Ensured continued international impotence; and
- Been able to pretend that "something was being done"

Then came the vote on August 31st, 2006, of Resolution 1706 which launched the principle of a "hybrid force" which would be both UN and African Union but which, according to the adamant proviso of the Khartoum authorities, had to remain "primarily African."[21] What did the Sudanese government mean by this statement? It was certainly not, as the government claimed, the result of the Islamist regime's love for Africa. It was based on a simple factual observation: the purely African force

---

[20]The adverse conditions surrounding peacekeeping missions and guidelines in line with the "responsbility to protect" are set forth in Wiebe Arts, Chapter 8, Section 8.1 and 7.2 (below).

[21]Sudan Tribune, *African Darfur troops must meet UN standards-joint envoy*, August 17, 2007.

deployed in Darfur for the past 2 years had achieved nothing and had not hindered in any way the political and strategic objectives of the Khartoum government. This impotence was due to a number of facts:

- African countries had no international weight: they could be manipulated and bullied, their soldiers could be killed and their international standing made light of, yet nothing would happen.
- African armies had no money or equipment; their command and administrative structures were often corrupt; they were very unlikely to have any ground efficiency.
- African governments could easily be hoodwinked into anti-Western attitudes when confronted with spurious "anti-colonialist" arguments.[22]

This "Africa first and only" proviso has worked wonderfully to keep the "hybrid force"[23] in absolute limbo. Today, over 2 years after the UNAMID process has been initiated, the force is still a paper construct only. On December 31st, 2007, UNAMID was born through the ridiculous artifice of the AMIS soldiers taking off their green berets and replacing them immediately with blue berets. Meanwhile, Khartoum-supported rebels have tried to overthrow the Chadian government, Darfur rebels have entered the Chadian civil war,[24] the Khartoum government has re-started its military campaigns against civilians suspected of supporting the rebellion and massive ground attacks and bombings have occurred. All this has been done right under the noses of the impotent UNAMID soldiers and the only reaction of the international community has been mild protests.

When one looks at this dismal track record, one is struck by the massive contradiction between the proffered lofty goals, policy announcements, warnings, objurgating, solemn declarations, and shocked protests on the one hand and the almost absolute absence not only of radical decisions but even of a serious follow-through on much milder ones on the other. The Khartoum regime is all the time allowed not only to get away with murder but even to manipulate, obfuscate, lie to, ridicule and deceive the international community. It can attribute the Darfur crisis to an "American-Zionist

[22]This was particularly conspicuous when looked at from the vantage point of Addis Ababa, where the African Union is based. Most senior African Union government representatives went along with the "anti-colonialist" rhetoric of the government of Sudan. This political line did not go down very well with junior diplomats for whom "anti-colonialism" was flogging a dead horse; it went down even less well with the African military men who were in Darfur and who, as Black Africans, had experienced the constant racism of the supposedly "anti-colonialist" Arabs.

[23]It is officially called United Nations African Mission in Darfur, or UNAMID.

[24]Gérard Prunier, "Chad: between Sudan's Blitzkrieg and Darfur's War," *OpenDemocracy.net* February 19, 2008, http://www.opendemocracy.net/article/democracy_power/africa/chad_sudan_darfur (Accessed June 9, 2009).

conspiracy,"[25] declare that the whole point of creating an international force for Darfur is "a campaign to re-colonize the Sudan,"[26] explain that the conflict is mostly about camel thefts, and bluntly deny it ever had anything to do with the invasion of Chad in February 2008, even as the Chadian rebels admit casually during radio interviews that they were armed and financed by the Sudanese government. Protected by the Chinese government which is Khartoum's main partner in producing and trading Sudan's oil production, the Islamist regime has ridiculed the world and turned all the declarations about protecting human rights into a compendium of grotesque lies and empty boasts.[27]

3.3 Can Atrocity Crimes such as Genocide Be Stopped, and, If So, How?

As the cases of Rwanda in 1994 and Darfur since 2003 have made amply clear, the international community is more of an archival deposit for pondering atrocity crimes than an operative structure for putting them to an end. If we look historically at how massive war crimes/human rights violations/genocides were brought to an end, it was always by direct armed action by a single group. We can easily compile a quick list of governmental crimes since World War II:

Atrocity	Terminating agent
The Jewish Holocaust	Allied Armies
Idi Amin's Ugandan dictatorship	The Tanzanian Army
The Khmer Rouge auto-genocide	The Vietnamese Army
The Obote II dictatorship	Ugandan NRA rebellion
The Ethiopian Menguistu dictatorship	Local TPLF rebellion
The Rwandan genocide	RPF armed action

None of these atrocities were ended by international collective action. And while it is difficult to discuss the record of armed action in the former Yugoslavia, the least that can be said is that the efforts at "classical" multilateral action (such as in Bosnia) were far from being undiluted successes.

---

[25] President Omar al-Bashir, "Sudan crisis focus of Al-Bashir Speech," http://www.webindia123.com, February 25, 2007, Accessed July 11, 2009, http://news.webindia123.com/news/ar_showdetails.asp?id=702250028&cat=&n_date=20070225

[26] Sudan Tribune, "Sudan's Bashir refuses to cooperate with the ICC," August 4th, 2008, Accessed July 11, 2009, http://www.sudantribune.com/spip.php?article28143.

[27] The possibility of using a modified Oil-for-Food program as a way to exert pressure on the Sudanese government while allowing oil exports to continue is advanced in Richard J. Goldstone, Chapter 11, Section 11.4 (below).

In cases where the local government was so powerful that rebellion was impossible and outside military action would have caused a massive international conflict,[28] the atrocities went on unabated, were never addressed by the international community and resulted in millions of deaths.

Where does that leave the case of Darfur today? The conventional wisdom on Darfur is that the rebels should be pressured to take part in some kind of "peace talks" which would lead the "non-signatories" to "join the peace agreement." Surely there must be a mistake in this line of argumentation because not one of its terms corresponds to a verifiable segment of reality.

First of all the "peace agreement" mentioned in such a discourse is the Darfur Peace Agreement (DPA), signed in Abuja in May 2006. Far from being a broadly agreed upon "peace agreement" which only a few spoilers and bad characters would have refused to join, the DPA was such a contentious document that only one of the rebel factions, the Minni Arkoy Minnawi-led faction of the Sudan Liberation Movement (SLM), signed the agreement. The SLM-MM represented at the time the most powerful military faction of the rebels, but it did not have the popular support that would have allowed it to translate this purely military capacity into a political settlement. As a result the SLM-MM withered away, its men left their leader to join the other non-signatory factions and the DPA never got off the ground. An additional reason for the DPA failure was the fact that its provisions, limited as they were,[29] were never even implemented. The investment fund never got any money and the regional administration was packed with Khartoum's cronies and deprived of any decisional powers. The whole thing was a (bad) joke. To think that, if it were signed, such a magic document would actually put an end to the Darfur violence is an act not of faith but of complete self-delusion.

Yet UN resolutions 1706 and 1733 are based on the belief that, as the charters of a "peace keeping operation," there is – or will be – some kind of a "peace" to keep. But at present there is no "peace" in Darfur, and UNAMID, already a ghost force, has no "peace" to keep. So if the only hope of a "peace" which would give a legal basis for UNAMID to operate is linked

[28]This was the case for the massive human rights violations committed by the Soviet regime in Russia up to the 1960s, by the Maoist regime in China up to the 1970s and by the Iranian regime up to the 1980s. Let us not even discuss the cases of the myriad of small dictatorships that proliferated in Latin America, Africa, Asia and the Middle East in the shadow of the Cold War and got away with murder in the name of either "Socialism" or "Freedom."

[29]There was a ridiculously underfunded compensation fund for the surviving victims of the massacres (each was supposed to receive about $18!), a $300 m (over 3 years!) investment fund for basic infrastructures and the creation of a regional administration.

to some vague adhesion of the rebels to a completely stillborn DPA, we are left with very little indeed. This means that, as is generally the case in the event of atrocity crimes, the only option remaining is the military option.[30]

The international community still deludes itself about the transforming powers of the January 9th 2005 so-called *Comprehensive Peace Agreement* (CPA) signed in Nairobi between the National Congress Party (NCP) and the Sudan Peoples Liberation Movement (SPLM). So far, the CPA has produced nothing except a breathing spell for the NCP and the creation of a largely inefficient administration in Southern Sudan where the problem of the 2008 census, 2009 elections and 2011 self-determination referendums are all left hanging. The former Khartoum Islamist regime in Sudan has very successfully bought time by renaming itself the Government of National Unity (GoNU), a legal construct devoid of political reality and in which the SPLM elements remain the eternal junior partners of something which perennially escapes their grasp. It is quite unlikely that the former government of Sudan – which is the real core of the paper-thin GoNU – would tolerate in 2011 a referendum leading to Southern Sudan's independence and cause it to lose its present oil revenues.

In the present situation there are only two options left: either the current Sudanese government is overthrown militarily by the people it oppresses or else it is removed by elections[31] and replaced with a democratic government with which it will be possible to negotiate. Unfortunately this last – and preferable – option might not be a possibility. On March 13th, 2008, the Khartoum government's Secretary of State for Information declared, while protesting the latest highly critical US Government Report on Human Rights in the Sudan: "We have proof that the US government wants to overthrow us. Before it wanted to overthrow us by force and now it wants to overthrow us by elections."[32] The concept of "overthrowing by elections" is, to say the least, paradoxical. But in a way, it is logical if we adopt the perspective of the regime. They always assumed that they had a God-given right to rule. As a result the very concept of losing an election is completely alien to their way of thinking. From their point of view they are entitled to rule. Forces that stand in their way can be negotiated with if they are strong, but if they are weak, they will be lied to and deceived,[33] destroyed

[30] An argument for resorting to mercenaries in genocidal conflicts is provided in Krzystof Kotarski and Samuel Walker, Chapter 14, Section 14.3 and 14.4 (below).

[31] The National Islamic Front received 7% of the vote in the last elections before it carried out its *coup d'état*. Its victory in a free and fair poll is quite unlikely.

[32] Sudanese Media Center communiqué, Khartoum, March 13, 2008.

[33] This is particularly clear in the case of another forgotten "Peace Agreement," the Eastern Peace Agreement or EPA, signed in October 2006, none of whose provisions were ever carried out.

by military might if they dare to fight[34] or manipulated into a fake electoral process, as it is now increasingly obvious that it is being arranged for next year's "elections."[35]

3.4 Conclusion

Atrocity crimes are committed by non-democratic governments. Therefore the notion that these governments:

(a) would accept a legal definition of their crimes;
(b) would accept remedial collective action to stop them from killing; or
(c) would negotiate in good faith about a solution to their atrocities
are all rather unrealistic. Atrocity crimes are extremely violent. They do not belong to the realm of polite democratic discourse. Trying to fit one into the other is like trying to accommodate the proverbial square peg into the round hole. In the face of force, counterforce is often the only solution. If for reasons of political expediency or financial miserliness the democratic world is not ready to shoulder this moral duty, then it should at least have the honesty to admit its delinquency rather than pretend that it is doing something when almost all it does is talk.

---

[34]This is the case of Darfur.

[35]The struggles around the contents of the electoral law and the pre-election census are cases in point.

Chapter 4
Sovereignty as Responsibility for the Prevention of Genocide

Francis M. Deng

For two decades, I have been involved in developing and applying the concept of Sovereignty as Responsibility through three interrelated capacities and experiences: First, through policy research and publications conducted by the African Studies Project of the Foreign Policy Studies Programme at the Brookings Institution in Washington, D.C, which I helped establish in 1988 and directed for 12 years; then, in my position as Secretary-General's Representative on Internally Displaced Persons, IDPs, for 12 years, (1992–2004); and in my present position as Special Advisor of the UN Secretary-General on the Prevention of Genocide. I intend to draw on these personal experiences to shed light on some of the challenges posed by the conceptualization and operationalization of "Sovereignty as Responsibility" which has since evolved into the better known, internationally recognized concept of "The Responsibility to Protect."

The Responsibility to Protect, commonly represented by the acronyms RtoP and R2P, is now widely recognized as having its origins in the concept of "Sovereignty as Responsibility" which I and my colleagues developed at the Brookings Institution as part of a project that investigated the implications of the end of the Cold War on conflict prevention, management and resolution in Africa. I used this concept as a basis for engaging governments in promoting assistance for internally displaced persons (IDPs) in my capacity as the Special Representative of the UN Secretary-General on IDPs from 1992 to 2004. RtoP, the latest formulation of the concept, has generated a rather paradoxical debate in the international community. When it was enshrined in the 2005 Summit *Outcome Document* in paragraphs 138 and 139, it was hailed as one of the most important accomplishments of the UN norm-setting agenda since the end of the Cold War. Recently, however, as the response to this achievement is being celebrated around the world, views are beginning to differ on whether the Responsibility to

F.M. Deng (✉)
Special Adviser of the Secretary-General on the Prevention of Genocide, New York, NY 10017, USA
e-mail: fdeng1@jhu.edu

R. Provost, P. Akhavan (eds.), *Confronting Genocide*, Ius Gentium: Comparative Perspectives on Law and Justice 7, DOI 10.1007/978-90-481-9840-5_4,

Protect was endorsed by the Summit or was adopted only as a framework to be further developed conceptually, to be subjected to wider consultations, and to be presented to the General Assembly for consideration and formal adoption. At the core of the controversy are such questions as: What is meant by the responsibility to protect? Who bears that responsibility, the state or the international community? If the latter, how is the international community to exercise that responsibility, through peaceful intercession or coercive intervention?

In linking Sovereignty as Responsibility to RtoP, my aim is to facilitate a point of entry into constructive dialogue and cooperation with governments in the shared responsibility to prevent genocide and the related crimes identified in the *Outcome Document* and to protect populations from those crimes. In this shared responsibility, the State is expected to assume the primary responsibility to protect its own citizens and all those under its jurisdiction, complemented by the international community to enhance the capacity of the State, to exercise its responsibility, and as a last resort, if the State is unwilling or unable to exercise that responsibility, the international community, however defined, is called upon to step in to fill the vacuum of national responsibility and provide the needed protection.

Although the *Outcome Document* stipulates the role of the state as the first layer of responsibility, supported by the international community as a second layer, a popular interpretation of RtoP has tended to lay emphasis on international military intervention.[1] This has generated a backlash from the global South who sees it as a potential tool for selective intervention by the more powerful states in their own national interest. The controversy on this threatens to re-write history and set back what has been recognized as a major accomplishment by the international community.

The Secretary-General, however, remains committed to the Responsibility to Protect and has appointed a renowned scholar of the United Nations system, Professor Edward Luck, Special Advisor to help with the conceptual and institutional development of the Responsibility to Protect, and to consult with member states toward broadening consensus on the issues involved and help operationalize R to P.

4.1 Reconciling Contradictions Within the International System

The international community operates within a system fraught with contradictions that need to be addressed and reconciled. At the core of these contradictions is the assumption that states discharge their responsibility

[1]Parameters for military intervention in line with the responsibility to protect are outlined in Wiebe Arts, Chapter 8, Section 8.2 (below).

for their citizens and all those under their jurisdiction. The reality is that countries experiencing internal strife are divided by acute national identity crises and cleavages based on race, ethnicity, religion, or political and economic ideology. The crisis is not so much a function of differences, but of gross inequalities in the shaping and sharing of power, wealth, services, employment, and development opportunities. While some enjoy a sense of belonging as citizens entitled to the rights of citizenship, others are excluded, marginalized, and denied the rights of citizenship and universal human rights. They become dispossessed and virtually stateless, with their citizenship diminished to paper value. Rather than protected and assisted, they are neglected and even persecuted as part of the enemy by association of racial, ethnic, religious or cultural affinity.[2] To whom do these dispossessed populations turn for help, protection and humanitarian assistance, but the international community? But when they do so, sovereignty, conceived narrowly and negatively as a shield against interference by outsiders in the affairs of a state is invoked to block international support for those suffering in the vacuum of state responsibility.

That was the challenge I confronted when I assumed the IDP mandate which dealt with an issue that was by definition internal and therefore fell under state sovereignty, but on which the international community had a subsidiary responsibility to protect and assist those dispossessed by their own governments. For the same reason, the IDP mandate was viewed with considerable suspicion by governments, as it was feared that it might provide grounds for international intervention in contravention of state sovereignty. Mindful of that sensitivity, the fundamental challenge that confronted me was how to gain access to the countries of concern and what to say to the authorities to engage them constructively on behalf of the internally displaced. Accordingly, the principle that guided me in my work was to positively recast sovereignty as responsibility. In significant part, this was related to post-Cold War developments. The plight of the internally displaced emerged into international consciousness in the late 1980s and the early 1990s for reasons connected to the end of the Cold War. Foremost among these reasons was the steady rise in the number of internally displaced persons associated with the increase in internal conflicts. In 1982, it was estimated that there were 1.2 million internally displaced persons. By 1992, the number had increased to between 20 to 25 million.[3] Concomitantly, as superpower rivalry came to an end, Western

---

[2]The way in which the abrogation of citizenship rights paves the way for genocide is illustrated in Douglas Greenberg, Chapter 5 (below).

[3]United Nations, Economic and Social Council, *Report of the Representative of the Secretary-General on Internally Displaced Persons, Mr. Francis M. Deng, submitted pursuant to Commission on Human Rights Resolution 2002/56*, E/CN.4/2003/86/Add.5, November 27, 2003, 7, http://daccessdds.un.org/doc/UNDOC/GEN/G02/156/70/PDF/G0215670.pdf?OpenElement (Accessed June 10, 2009. Today, the figure is higher

governments' geopolitical advantage in accepting refugees was diminished and their willingness to do so began to wane. This led to a desire to find a way to protect and assist displaced persons in their own countries so as to discourage them from seeking asylum abroad.[4] The end of the Cold War also marked a shift in the international attitude toward intervention in domestic affairs, particularly where states caused, or failed to react to, massive humanitarian crises within their own borders.[5] During the Cold War, most domestic and regional conflicts were in one way or another perceived as part of the proxy confrontation of the superpowers. Similarly, internal or regional crises and their humanitarian consequences used to be managed through the bipolar control mechanisms of the superpowers who offered effective support to their less capable ideological allies. The outcome of this was that such domestic crises as internal displacement were not visible to the outside world.

With the end of the Cold War, and the withdrawal of the strategic interests of the superpowers, these conflicts began to be seen in their proper national or regional contexts. Lack of support from major powers also left former allies with significantly reduced capacity for suppressing or managing conflicts and responding to their humanitarian consequences. Consequently, the post-Cold War era witnessed the proliferation of internal conflicts, which have tended to target civilians, including women, children, the elderly and the disabled. Without external support, governments were confronted with mounting crises they could hardly manage.

Human rights and humanitarian concerns began to replace strategic national interest as the driving force in international politics. By the same token, human rights, humanitarian, and development organizations became more active as the watchdogs of universal standards and whether these standards were being adhered to or violated within national borders. To reinforce their capacities, non-governmental organizations (NGOs) began to receive increased support from the donor community, which saw them as more transparent and credible than governments in meeting the humanitarian needs of the affected populations. With these new developments, the narrow view of sovereignty became increasingly challenged as the new media and NGOs exposed the plight of millions who fell victim to the new types of wars that were fought internally, with devastating loss of lives, egregious violations of human rights, and dehumanization of the civilian population perceived as enemies.

---

than ever, with an estimated 25 million internally displaced persons in 50 countries worldwide.

[4]Roberta Cohen and Francis M. Deng: *Masses in Flight:The Global Crisis of Internal Displacement* (Washington D.C., The Brookings Institution, 1996), 3–4.

[5]Ibid.

Speculating on the implications of the emerging new order for perceptions of national and regional conflicts, it was obvious that these conflicts would no longer be viewed in the context of the proxy confrontation between superpowers. But what new conceptual framework would influence response to these conflicts in the new era? Two initiatives helped shape my perspective on the emerging challenge. One was the development of an African Project in the Foreign Policy Studies Program at the Brookings Institution. The other was participating in the initiative of the Africa Leadership Forum founded and headed by former President of Nigeria, who was later elected twice, President Olusegun Obasanjo. President Obasanjo initiated a process toward a Helsinki-like Conference on Security, Stability, Development, and Cooperation in Africa (CSSDCA).

Our Brookings Africa Project made an initial assessment of conflicts in Africa and the challenges of the post-Cold War era.[6] Next, we undertook national and regional case studies to deepen our understanding of the issues involved. A synthesis of these case studies led to the main conclusion that as conflicts were now being properly perceived as internal, they also primarily became the responsibility of governments to prevent, manage, and resolve. Governance became perceived primarily as conflict management. Within the framework of regional and international cooperation, state sovereignty was then postulated positively as entailing the responsibility of conflict management and not negatively as a barrier against outside involvement in internal affairs.[7] The envisaged responsibility involved managing diversity, ensuring equitable distribution of wealth, services, and development opportunities, and participating effectively in regional and international cooperation for peace, security, and stability. In subsequent work, we tried to put more flesh on the skeleton of the responsibilities of sovereignty, building largely on human rights and humanitarian norms and international accountability.[8] Since internal conflicts often spill over across international borders, their consequences also spread across borders, threatening regional security and stability. In the apportionment of responsibilities in the post-Cold War era, sub-regional and regional organizations provide the second layer of the needed response. And yet, the international community remains the residual guarantor of universal human rights and humanitarian standards in the quest for global peace and security. We thus formulated sovereignty as responsibility with implicit accountability to the regional and international communities.

[6]Francis M. Deng and I. William Zartman, eds., *Conflict Resolution in Africa* (Washington, DC: Brookings Institution Press, 1991).

[7]Francis M. Deng, Sadikiel Kimaro, Terrence Lyons, Donald Rothchild and I. William Zartman, eds., *Sovereignty as Responsibility: Conflict Management in Africa* (Washington, DC: Brookings Institution Press, 1996).

[8]Francis M. Deng and Terrence Lyons, eds., *African Reckoning: A Quest for Good* (Washington, DC: Brookings Institution Press, 1998).

The development of the Helsinki-process for Africa was motivated by the concern that the post-Cold War global order was likely to result in the withdrawal of the major powers and the marginalization of Africa. It was, therefore, imperative for Africa to take charge of its destiny and observe principles that would appeal to outside potential partners, especially in the West, and thereby provide a sound foundation for a mutually agreeable partnership. This was found in the Helsinki framework of the Economic and Security Cooperation in Europe (ESCE), which subsequently became the Organization for Security and Cooperation in Europe (OSCE). A series of meetings culminated in the 1991 Conference in Kampala, Uganda, which was attended by some 500 people, including several heads of state and representatives from all walks of life. The conference produced the Kampala Document, which elaborated the four "calabashes," so termed to distinguish them from the OSCE "baskets," and give them an African orientation. The calabashes are: security, stability, development, and cooperation. The adoption of the CSSDCA by the Organization of African Unity (OAU) was initially blocked by a few governments that felt threatened by its normative principles. However, when Obasanjo was incarcerated by the dictator Sani Abacha and asked me to assume the role of Acting Chairman of the Africa Leadership Forum, in collaboration with several scholars, we continued to expand on the principles of the Kampala Document in the Brookings Africa Project and produced a book, *A Strategic Vision for Africa: The Kampala Movement*.[9] When Obasanjo returned to power as the elected president of Nigeria, he was able to push successfully for the incorporation of CSSDCA into the OAU mechanism for conflict prevention, management, and resolution.

In connection with these initiatives, we began to focus attention on promoting the need to balance conventional notions of sovereignty with the responsibility of the state to provide protection and general welfare to citizens and all those under state jurisdiction. Building on the findings and conclusions of the Africa Project in my work on IDPs, I decided that given the sensitivity of the mandate, the only way to bridge the gap between the need for international protection and assistance for the internally displaced and the barricades of the negative approach to sovereignty was to invoke sovereignty as a positive concept of state responsibility toward its citizens and those under its jurisdiction. I argued that most states discharged this responsibility under normal circumstances, but in the exceptional cases where states failed to do so, the international community could assume that responsibility by stepping in to fill the vacuum of state failure. Given the threat of international action in the event of the state's failure to protect its own population, I argued further that the best way to protect

[9]Francis M. Deng and I. William Zartman, *A Strategic Vision for Africa: The Kampala Movement* (Washington, DC: Brookings Institution Press, 2002).

sovereignty was for the state to discharge its responsibility and to be seen to do so, and if need be, request the support of the international community. This approach was well received and proved effective in the dialogue with governments.[10]

The principle of sovereignty as responsibility was subsequently promoted, strengthened and mainstreamed by the Canadian-sponsored International Commission on Intervention and State Sovereignty whose main principle, "the Responsibility to Protect" was endorsed by the Secretary-General's High Level Panel on Threats, Challenges and Changes in its 2004 report, *A More Secure World: Our Shared Responsibility*.[11] As the UN prepared for its 60th anniversary celebration, the Secretary-General pleaded that "we must embrace the responsibility to protect."[12] The World Summit of Heads of State and Government which convened in New York in September 2005 "stressed the need for the General Assembly to continue consideration of the responsibility to protect populations from genocide, war crimes, ethnic cleansing, and crimes against humanity."[13]

The challenge that postulating sovereignty as responsibility or the responsibility to protect poses for the international community is that it implies accountability. Obviously, the internally displaced themselves

---

[10] For my various contributions to the normative theme of the responsibility of sovereignty, see the following books, chapters and articles: Terrence Lyons and Francis M. Deng, eds., *African Reckoning: A Quest for Good Governance* (Washington, DC: Brookings Institution Press, 1998); Francis M. Deng, "Sovereignty and Humanitarian Responsibility: A Challenge for NGOs in Africa and the Sudan," in *Vigilance and Vengeance*, ed. Robert I. Rotberg (Washington, DC: Brookings Institution Press and The World Peace Foundation, 1996); Francis M. Deng, Sadikiel Kimaro, Terrence Lyons, Donald Rothchild and I. William Zartman, eds., *Sovereignty as Responsibility: Conflict Management in Africa* (Washington, DC: Brookings Institution Press, 1996); Francis M. Deng, "Reconciling Sovereignty with Responsibility: A Basis for Humanitarian Action," in *Africa World Politics*, eds. John Harbeson and Donald Rothchild (Boulder, CO: Westview Press, 1995); Francis M. Deng, "Frontiers of Sovereignty: A Framework of Protection, Assistance and Development for the Internally Displaced," in *Leiden Journal of International Law* 8, no. 2 (1995). The concept is also advanced in Roberta Cohen and Francis M. Deng, *Masses in Flight: The Global Crisis of Internal Displacement* (Washington, DC: Brookings Institution Press, 1996).

[11] The implementation of "responsibility to protect" principles for peacekeeping missions is presented in Wiebe Arts, Chapter 8, Section 8.2 (below).

[12] United Nations, *A More Secure World: Our Shared Responsibility*, Report of the Secretary-General's High Level Panel on Threats, Challenges and Changes (New York, NY: United Nations Publications, 2004) paras., 199–203; Kofi Annan, *In Larger Freedoms: Toward Development, Security and Human Rights for All*, Report of the Secretary-General of the United Nations. UN Doc. A/59/2005, March 21, 2005, para 135; and International Commission on Intervention and State Sovereignty, *The Responsibility to Protect*, Report of the International Commission on Intervention and State Sovereignty (Ottawa: International Development Research Centre, 2001).

[13] United Nations General Assembly. *2005 World Summit Outcome*, UN Doc. A/60/L1, September 15, 2005, paras. 138 and 139, http://daccessdds.un.org/doc/UNDOC/GEN/N05/487/60/PDF/N0548760.pdf?OpenElement (Accessed June 10, 2009).

and other victims of internal conflicts, trapped within international borders, marginalized, excluded, often persecuted, have little capacity to hold their national authorities accountable. Only the international community, including sub-regional, regional, and international organizations, has the leverage and clout to persuade or coerce governments and other concerned actors to discharge their responsibility or otherwise fill the vacuum of irresponsible or irresponsive sovereignty. A soft, but credible threat of consequences in case of failure to discharge the responsibility of sovereignty, combined with the promise of the benefits of international cooperation could be an effective inducement.

Governments of affected countries, even if willing to discharge the responsibility toward their populations, often lack resources and the capacity to do so. Offering them support in a way that links humanitarian assistance with protection in a holistic, integrated approach to human rights should make the case for international cooperation more compelling and persuasive. No government deserving any legitimacy can request material assistance from the outside world and reject concern for the security and the human rights of the people on whose behalf it requests assistance. Doing so would be like asking the international community to feed them without ensuring their safety and dignity, an implausible logic.

4.2 Anatomy of Genocide and Related Atrocities

The 1948 Convention on the Prevention and Punishment of the Crime of Genocide defines genocide in Article II as any "acts committed with intent to destroy, in whole or in part, a national, ethnical, racial or religious group." These acts include: killing members of the group; causing serious bodily or mental harm to members of the group; deliberately inflicting on the group conditions of life calculated to bring about its physical destruction in whole or in part; imposing measures intended to prevent births within the group; and forcefully transferring children of the group to another group.[14] The question will be what particular contribution the Special Adviser could offer to the efforts of others beyond general advocacy.

There has been intense debate on the Genocide Convention's focus on certain categories and exclusion of others, such as political groups, for protection. This essentially means that groups that are often the victims of genocidal acts are excluded.[15] Despite attempts to creatively interpret

[14]United Nations, *Human Rights Compilation of International Instruments*, Office of the High Commissioner for Human Rights, ST/HR/1/Rev. 6 (Vol. I/Part 2) (New York and Geneva, 1994), p. 673.

[15]The problematic consequences of applying the Genocide Convention terms in relation to targeted groups are explored in Gérard Prunier, Chapter 3, Section 3.1 (above).

the Convention, invoking both prior international norms, the General Assembly resolution that set the process of developing the Convention in motion, and the debates in the various fora in the process, to broaden the scope, this remains a controversial area.[16] As one observer put it, "One of the most contentious aspects of the genocide definition is the exclusion of political and social groups from the list of protected groups."[17] Frank Chalk stated the problem dramatically when he pointed out that the exclusion of these and other groups has serious consequences for the practical purposes of the Convention, as this means:

> ignoring the 15 to 20 million Soviet civilians liquidated as "class enemies" and "enemies of the people" between 1920 and 1939; ... neglecting the roughly 300,000 mentally impaired and mentally ill Germans and others murdered by the Nazis as "life unworthy of life"; ... overlooking the thousands of homosexuals killed by the Nazis because of their sexual orientation; ... disregarding the million or more Khmer murdered by the state and the Communist party of Kampuchea in the years from 1975 and 1978.[18]

The gravity of this omission becomes evident once it is realized that most, if not all, cases of genocide involve some aspect of political conflict, whatever the composition of the identities of the specific groups in conflict. It has been argued that politically motivated massacres are prohibited under other international instruments, but that the failure to protect political and social groups "constitutes the Genocide Convention's blind spot." That other international norms could obviate this blind spot is undercut by the fact that the jurisdiction of the *ad hoc* Tribunals and of the International Criminal Court is limited to the Convention-based definition of genocide, which restricts the scope of criminal responsibility.[19]

Article IV of the Convention includes in the category of persons criminally liable constitutionally responsible rulers, public officials and private individuals. However, proving intent to commit acts of genocide where large numbers of victim members of a group and victimizers are involved is obviously a formidable and an almost impossible task.[20] Genocidal *mens rea* or criminal intent is another area in which the Convention has been a

---

[16]See Beth Van Shaack, "The Crime of Political Genocide: Repairing the Genocide Convention's Blind Spot," in *The Yale Law Journal*, 106, No. 7 (May, 1997), 2259–2291; Guglichmo Veridrama, "The Genocide Definition in the Jurisprudence of the ad hoc Tribunals," in *The International and Comparative Law Quarterly*, 49, No. 3 (July, 2000), 578–595; and Ervin Staub, "Genocide and Mass Killing: Origins, Prevention, Healing and Reconciliation," in *Political Psychology*, 21, No. 2, (June, 2000) 367–382.

[17]Verdirama, "The Genocide Definition," 2000, 581.

[18]Frank Chalk, "Re-defining Genocide," in *Genocide: Conceptual and Historical Dimensions*, ed. George J. Andreopoulos (Philadelphia: University of Pennsylvania Press, 1997), quoted in Verdirama, "The Genocide Definition," 2000, 581.

[19]Ibid, 582.

[20]The difficulty in meeting the intent requirement of the Genocide Convention is highlighted in Gérard Prunier, Chapter 3, Section 3.1 (above).

subject of intense debate. As one authority has noted, "Despite the fact that the Convention is now 50 years old, the question 'What is genocide?' remains difficult to answer."[21] With respect to the specific issue of intent, "the prevailing interpretation assumes that genocide is a crime of specific or special intent, involving a perpetrator who specifically targets victims on the basis of their group identity with a deliberate desire to inflict destruction on the group itself."[22] Arguments have been made toward broadening the scope of intent. One suggests including "cases where a perpetrator acted in furtherance of a campaign targeting members of a protected group and knew that the goal or manifest effect of the campaign was the destruction of the group in whole or in part."[23] The international criminal tribunals for the former Yugoslavia and Rwanda are credited with having clarified and broadened the scope of intent.[24] In the *Akayesu* case, the Trial Chamber of the Rwandan Tribunal considered among the circumstances that can be indicative of genocidal intent:

> [t]he scale and the general nature of the atrocities; the fact of deliberately or systematically targeting victims of a group, while excluding the members of other groups; the general political doctrine of the perpetrators of the crime; the repetition of discriminatory and destructive acts; speeches or projects preparing the ground for the massacres. Applying these considerations to the facts of the case, the Trial Chamber found that it was possible to infer Akayesu's genocidal intention "inter alia, from all acts and utterances of the accused, or from the general context in which other culpable acts were perpetrated systematically against the same group, regardless of whether such other acts were committed by the same perpetrator or even by other perpetrators."[25]

Despite this progress, the problem of criminal intent remains elusive and unresolved. Some scholars have argued that intentionality be removed from the definition of genocide, as it is increasingly difficult to locate responsibility, given the anonymous and structural forces at work. While they do not dismiss the importance of individuals, these scholars consider it more productive to probe into the social structures that are prone to generating or preventing genocide.[26] As one observer put it, "A genocidal society exists when a government and its citizens persistently pursue policies which they know [or should know] will lead to the annihilation of the aboriginal

---

[21]Alexander K.A. Greenawalt, "Rethinking Genocidal Intent: The Case for Knowledge-Based Interpretation," in *Columbia Law Review*, 99, No. 8 (1999), 2259, 2263.

[22]Ibid, 2264.

[23]Ibid.

[24]The ICTR case law on intent, particularly *Akayesu*, is examined in Irwin Cotler, Chapter 9, Section 9.2 (below).

[25]Verdirama, "The Genocide Definition," 2000, 585.

[26]George J. Andreopoulos, "Introduction," in *Genocide: Conceptual and Historical Dimensions, ed. George J. Andreopoulos* (Philadelphia: University of Pennsylvania Press, 1997), 9.

inhabitants [or members of other groups] of their country. Intentionality is demonstrated by persistence in such policies, whether or not the intent to destroy the ... groups is verbalized"[27] Under such circumstances, "the emphasis on intentionality almost appears anachronistic...."[28,29]

With these problematic criteria, genocide is usually proven after the crime has been committed and well documented. Although prevention is prominent in the title of the Convention, undertaking preventive measures is constrained by both the difficulty of proving intent and lack of clear enforcement mechanisms. It is, of course, in the nature of prevention that it is not easily verifiable. Success essentially means that the prevented crime and the method of preventing it are invisible, unless those responsible for success expose the details of what has happened, which would be distastefully self-serving. Contemporary experience indicates that even when abundant evidence reveals that genocide may be in the making, the record of action to stop it is dismally poor. Not only are the perpetrators in denial but those who would then be expected to intervene also avoid that responsibility by not recognizing that genocide is being committed. That was the case in Germany until the outbreak of the war became unavoidable. That was also the case in Cambodia until Vietnam eventually intervened and overthrew the Pol Pot regime of the Khmer Rouge, and that was also the case with Rwanda where human rights observers warned the world that genocide was coming.[30]

The Rwandan tragedy poses a series of questions from which lessons can be drawn. Despite the Radio Mille Collines campaign and public statements calling for the extermination of the demonized Tutsi population, these questions persist: Who in fact physically killed? Did those who killed intend to eliminate the group in whole or in part? And what about the rulers and officials ordering or condoning the killings, was their intention to eliminate the group or simply to force them to accept the status quo with Hutu dominance? Who then can be charged with the crime of genocide and be found guilty beyond a reasonable doubt, the standard test in criminal liability? And what enforcement mechanism is in place to bring charges and impose punishments on those responsible?

---

[27]Frank Chalk, "Re-defining Genocide," in *Genocide: Conceptual and Historical Dimensions*, ed. George J. Andreopoulos (Philadelphia: University of Pennsylvania Press, 1997). 53.

[28]Isidor Walliman and Michael Dobkowski, "Introduction," in *Genocide and the Modern Age: Etiology and Case Studies of Mass Death*, eds. Isidor Walliman and Michael Dobkowski (Syracuse, NY: Syracuse University Press, 2000), quoted in Andreopoulos, *Genocide*, 1997, 44.

[29]The role of systems as opposed to particular individuals in fostering genocidal acts is highlighted in Ben Kiernan, Chapter 2, Section 2.2 (above).

[30]For a general pattern of denial in these and other cases of genocide, see Samantha Power, *A Problem from Hell: America and the New Age of Genocide* (New York: Basic Books, 2002).

In the case of Sudan's Western region of Darfur, instead of seeing the situation as the latest in a series of proliferating regional conflicts that began in the South in the mid 1950s, extended to the Northern regions of the Nuba Mountains and the Ingassara Hills in the mid 1980s, and on to the Eastern Beja region, all symptomatic of a turbulent nation in search of itself, the crisis was taken out of context and debate ensued as to whether it was a case of genocide or not.[31] This occurred in the context of the 10th anniversary of the Rwandan genocide and reflected a sense of guilt over the failure to act. The United States declared the Darfur atrocities genocide but without implications for additional action. The United Nations did not declare them genocide, but concluded that crimes not less heinous than genocide were being committed.

Even the precise identification of the targeted group can be problematic. In Rwanda, as indeed in Darfur, the question of who is a Tutsi, a Hutu, an Arab, or an African can be quite problematic. Is it an issue of objective determination, subjective self-identification, or identification by others, or both? Given the situation of mixed marriages, often with a long history of interaction and mixing, there can be no clear-cut answers to these questions.

International law has vacillated between favoring objective criteria for determining group identity, to moving toward the subjective standard based on the perception of the perpetrators about their targeted group. Again, the two tribunals on the former Yugoslavia and Rwanda have played a crucial role in this shift.

> From an initial rigid and objective approach to collective identities, the two *ad hoc* Tribunals have ... progressively moved towards a subjective position, quietly setting aside some important precedents. It is a welcome shift that takes into account the mutable and contingent nature of social perceptions, and does not reinforce perilous claims to authenticity in the field of ethnic and racial identities. The perception of the perpetrator of the crime is after all more important for establishing individual criminal responsibility than the putative "authentic" ethnicity of the victim.[32]

When I visited Rwanda shortly after the genocide of 1994 in my capacity as Representative of the UN Secretary General on Internally Displaced Persons, I addressed audiences in which some looked clearly Tutsi and others Hutu according to the stereotypes, but many I could not tell. When I later asked the Foreign Minister whether it was always possible to tell a Tutsi from a Hutu, he answered with a sense of humor, "Yes, but with a margin of error of some 35%." Some people believe that the margin of error in the Sudan could be even greater.

---

[31]The misperception of the Darfur situation is addressed in Gérard Prunier, Chapter 3, Sections 3.2 and 3.3 (above).

[32]Verdirama, "The Genocide Definition," 594.

In Rwanda, as I discussed with international lawyers who were conducting preliminary investigation into the responsibility for the genocide, it was obvious to me that there would be a major discrepancy in number between those who must have committed acts of genocide and those who would be found responsible. My concern, shared by the investigators, was that too much faith was being placed in prosecuting and punishing individuals responsible for the genocide of close to a million members of the Tutsi ethnic group and the Hutu moderates associated with them. The result of the investigation, indictments, trials and convictions would almost certainly be disappointing to the Tutsi ethnic group, who expected justice to be done. The possible outcome of such disappointment might be that they would then take justice into their own hands and inflict vengeful "genocide" on the Hutus. In the end, a few individuals were symbolically held responsible for a genocide that must have involved thousands of perpetrators.

The reaction of the Tutsi-dominated government could be vengeance. Since then, abundant evidence tragically points to that direction, whether in terms of massacres of civilian populations or the numbers of detainees languishing in overcrowded prisons without trials.[33] The International Panel of Eminent Personalities mandated by the Organization of African Unity (OAU) to investigate the Rwanda genocide and the surrounding events noted in its report: "Film footage from Rwandan prisons in the first year or two after the genocide shows men crammed together with little sanitation in disgusting conditions, many of them with open wounds and paralyzed limbs, the results they claimed of beatings and torture by RPF [the victorious Rwandan Patriotic Front] soldiers."[34] The Special Representative of the UN Commission on Human Rights on the situation of human rights in Rwanda, Michel Moussalli, reported in 2000 that "scores" of the people he saw in detention centers "showed the wounds of mistreatment."[35] And according to the High Commissioner for Refugees, "During 1998 more than 3,300 prisoners died. Conditions in the cachots, the local detention centers, are even worse. . . . Cases of torture or ill-treatment were also reported, usually at the time of arrest and interrogation, during detention in the cachots and in the military detention centers."[36] Amnesty International in a 2000 report noted:

[33] The psychological dimension of the reconciliation process in Rwanda is examined in Jobb Arnold, Chapter 19 (below).

[34] Rachel Murray, "The Report of the OAU's International Panel of Eminent Personalities to Investigate the 1994 Genocide in Rwanda and Surrounding Events," in *Journal of African Law*, 45, (2001), 123–133, quoted in Jeremy Sarkin, "The Tension Between Justice and Reconciliation in Rwanda: Politics, Human Rights, Due Process and the Role of the Gacaca Courts in Dealing with Genocide," in *Journal of African Law*, 45, (2001) 143, 156.

[35] Quoted in Sarkin, Ibid.

[36] Ibid.

> Conditions in many prisons and detention centres in Rwanda still constitute cruel, inhuman or degrading treatment. Gross overcrowding, poor hygiene and medical care, and insufficient food continue to cause widespread disease and thousands of deaths ... Many detainees in the cachots communaux, in military detention centres and in some brigades have been subjected to torture of other forms of ill-treatment – most commonly beatings. Beatings – usually inflicted during arrest or in the initial period of detention – were considered virtually "normal" by detainees due to their frequency ... In some cases, the torture or ill-treatment was so severe that detainees have died.[37]

And in its Resolution 1999/20, the UN Commission on Human Rights reiterated

> its concern at the conditions of detention in many communal detention centres and some prisons in Rwanda, call[ed] on the Government of Rwanda to continue in its efforts to ensure that persons in detention [were] treated in a manner which respect[ed] their human rights and emphasize[e] the need for greater attention and resources to be directed to this problem, and again urge[d] the international community to assist the Government of Rwanda in this area.[38]

One of the criticisms against the Genocide Convention is the absence of an international enforcement mechanism in the form of a criminal tribunal that would punish the perpetrators. Although the establishment of the International Criminal Court now remedies that gap, there are still practical difficulties with enforcement. Part of the problem is compounded by the fact that the state, in most cases the perpetrator of or complicit in genocide, is charged with the primary responsibility to prosecute, which makes the Convention, in the view of one commentator, unenforceable.[39] As another commentator noted, despite the commonly-held belief that the determination of genocide imposes an obligation to act under Article 8,[40] which provides that any state party to the Convention "may call upon the competent organs of the United Nations to take such action under the Charter... as appropriate for the prevention and suppression of acts of genocide," in reality the Article

> places no clear legal obligation on contracting parties to do anything at all. States may call on the U.N., but, of course, just because the U.N. is "called upon," does not mean that it can or will. There are no formalized procedures for doing so. Nor is there any punishment for a contracting party that does not call on the U.N. in such a situation.[41]

---

[37]Ibid.

[38]Ibid.

[39]See Helen Fein, "Genocide, Terror, Life Integrity, and War Crimes, the Case for Discrimination," in *Genocide: Conceptual and Historical Dimensions*, ed. George J. Andreopoulos (Philadelphia: University of Pennsylvania Press, 1997).

[40]The fact that characterizing a situation as genocide does not necessarily lead to action is illustrated in Gérard Prunier, Chapter 3, Section 3.1 (above).

[41]Erin Patrick, "Intent to Destroy: The Genocidal Impact of Forced Migration in Darfur Sudan," in *Journal of Refugee Studies*, 18, No. 4, 2005, 410, 420.

Even if the UN is called upon to act, it has been observed that

> the resistance of the United Nations to charges of genocide is not simply a reaction to the trivializing abuse of the concept. A significant factor is that genocide is usually, though not exclusively, a crime committed by governments or with governments' condonation or complicity. The United Nations being an association of governments, is generally reluctant to undermine the authority of – and, by implication, all of – the member regimes.[42]

Furthermore, "being an international organization composed of sovereign states and committed to the principles of sovereignty and territorial integrity, it would be difficult for the UN to initiate proceedings against fellow member states."[43] Even if there were provisions for an international penal tribunal, it is highly unlikely that the system would be of much use as long as only governments could take cases to court.

Because of these conceptual and practical difficulties, this chapter adopts a broader perspective on the issue of genocide, with an emphasis on prevention. As one commentator observed,

> Debates over what constitutes "real genocide" versus "political mass murder" detract from a more important focus on causes, consequences, and international responses to systematic atrocities . . . While each ethnic conflict has its own unique history . . . they share a variable "incubation" period for "predisposing factors," followed, at some point, by a set of "triggering factors" that results in mass violence.[44]

This means that "the emotion laden word 'genocide' represents but the most horrific aspect of a much larger phenomenon of ethnic violence."[45]

4.3 The Identity Factor in Genocidal Conflicts

Considering the categories of targeted groups in the Genocide Convention, genocide is essentially a zero-sum conflict of identities. Among the bases of identity that generate genocidal conflicts are race, ethnicity, culture, language, and religion. Territory as a concept of identification usually overlaps with one or more of these factors and is therefore a complementary or an affirmative factor. Self-identification and identification by others imply

---

[42] Leo Kuper, "Theoretical Issues Relating to Genocide: Uses and Abuses," in *Genocide: Conceptual and Historical Dimensions*, ed. George J. Andreopoulos (Philadelphia: University of Pennsylvania Press, 1997), 36.

[43] Andreopoulos, *Genocide*, 1997, 3.

[44] William B. Wood, "Geographic Aspects of Genocide: A Comparison of Bosnia and Rwanda," in *Transactions of British Geographics*, New Series, 26, No. 1 (2001), 57, 58.

[45] Ibid. For a detailed analysis of the nature of genocide and the importance of prevention, including pillars and institutional arrangements for realizing it, see David Hamburg, *Preventing Genocide: Practical Steps Toward Early Detection and Effective Action* (Boulder and London: Paradigm Publishers, 2008).

elements of subjectivity and objectivity that raise complex issues of the relative emphasis to be placed on these dimensions for both analytical and policy purposes.

Two sets of discrepancies might arise. One has to do with the degree to which subjective factors of self-identification or identification by others match the objective elements of the claimed or imputed identity. Under normal circumstances, self-identification is a personal matter that should not concern others. The other set of discrepancies has to do with the degree to which an exclusive group identity is projected or represented in the definition of the collective national identity or recognizes other identities, but rather than treat them equitably, dominates them. The discrepancy between the exclusive identities and the collective national identity makes the issue of identity in both its subjectivities and objectivities critical to genocidal tendencies and a matter of public policy and scrutiny.

Guglielmo Verdirama has offered a detailed analysis of the subjective and objective factors in the determination of the identities of the victims and perpetrators of genocide. According to him, "There are two ways of determining who is a member of a group. First, objective criteria can be applied. Second, membership of a group can be decided on the basis of subjective identification, either by the victims themselves or by the perpetrators of the crime. This distinction is far from having only theoretical importance."[46] Whether the perpetrators of genocide would be found guilty of the crime would depend on the identity of the group targeted:

> In the case of the Holocaust, if objective criteria of membership and identity were applied, it would be concluded that genocide was perpetrated only to the extent that the victims were "really" Jewish. In other words, persons who were killed because they were perceived to be Jewish by the Nazis – and were considered Jewish under the Nuremberg laws – would not be considered victims of a genocide, but, presumably, of a crime against humanity and/or a war crime.[47]

There are, however, problems with objective criteria. "One ... is that rules on the membership of groups are nearly always disputed. For example, the question of who is a Jew is notoriously controversial. The *halachic* rules on matrilineal descent and on conversions have been contested at least since the 18th century by various streams of Conservative, Reformed or Progressive Judaism."[48]

As already noted, ethnic identification in Rwanda, as indeed in the Sudan, raises comparable complexities, "although Western observers have often failed to perceive such complexity, or have made the too common mistake of forcing a European reading of identities in the Rwandan context."[49] It was also noted earlier that the Rwandan and Yugoslav

[46]Verdirama, "The Genocide Definition," 2000, 588.
[47]Ibid.
[48]Ibid.
[49]Ibid., 589.

Tribunals have provided "groundbreaking law," which shows a progressive shift from objective to subjective criteria in determining identity. As Verdirama has observed:

> Initially, the Rwanda Tribunal was reluctant to adhere to the subjective positions, not least because of the existence of precedents in which both the Permanent Court of International Justice and the International Court of Justice had opted for objective criteria. In addition, reluctance to determine membership of a group on the basis of subjective criteria can also derive from criminal law. In fact, mistakes of fact can often be determinative of the qualification of the crime. ... In the context of the Rwandan genocide, the rape and killing of a woman believed to be a Tutsi on the basis of her physical appearance – while she was in "reality" of mixed origin with a Hutu father and a Tutsi mother – would be considered a crime against humanity and not a genocidal act, if this approach is taken.[50]

Building on precedents, Verdirama concluded that national identity is considered a "social fact" by the law:

> The ICJ disregarded two elements that would appear to be of greatest significance as far as national identity is concerned: the self-perception of the individual, and the view of the concerned State. The reason for disregarding these elements was essentially the belief that there is something more "objective" than them: the existence of an authentic and objectively verifiable link between the person and the country of his or her nationality.[51]

The Trial Chamber of the International Criminal Tribunal for Rwanda struggled with the objectivity-subjectivity determination of identity. Initially it defined the national group "as a collection of people who are perceived to share legal bonds based on a common citizenship, coupled with reciprocity of rights and duties." On the ethnic group the Chamber pointed out that the essential aspect was that its "members share a common language or culture." *Akayesu* also confirmed the objective approach to membership for the two remaining protected groups. A racial group was thus found to be "based on the hereditary physical traits often identified with a geographical region, irrespective of linguistic, cultural, national or religious factors," while a religious group was defined as one "whose members share the same religion, denomination or mode of worship." In no case was any reference made to subjective identification either in the form of self-identification or identification by others.

The complexity of the Hutu-Tutsi dichotomy soon proved problematic for the Tribunal:

> It was clear to the Trial Chamber in *Akayesu* that Tutsis did not closely match any of the four definitions. Indeed, although commonly described as an ethnic group, Tutsis do not share a different language or, arguably, a different culture: Kinyarwanda, a tonal Bantu language, is spoken by both Hutus and Tutsis, and there is no difference in the customary practices of the two groups.[52]

---

[50] Ibid.

[51] Ibid., 591.

[52] Ibid.

So, if identities are so overlapping, does it mean that establishing the intent to target a particular group has no foundation, that it would be based on an erroneous ground? Since this would be a pretext for the perpetrators to evade culpability, the answer both legally and morally has to be in the negative. Again here, the case of Rwanda has set a pioneering precedent:

> A "quiet" shift towards the subjective approach has taken place. The Tribunals are, in other words, beginning to acknowledge that collective identities, and in particular ethnicity, are by their very nature social constructs, "imagined" identities entirely dependent on variable and contingent perceptions, and not social facts, which are verifiable in the same manner as natural phenomena or physical facts.[53]

This is what makes the dynamics of identity both a cause and a cure in that while the subjective view of the perpetrator of identity crime is accepted, even if erroneous, constructed identities that become conflictual can be challenged on the basis of objective facts to reconstruct pluralistic identity frameworks that are more mutually accommodating, tolerant, and cooperative.

4.4 The Challenges of the Mandate on Genocide Prevention

Genocide is unquestionably among the most heinous crimes on which there should be no controversy as to prevention and punishment. Yet, for the same reason, it evokes strong feelings and denials by both perpetrators and those who should intervene to stop it. As a result, genocide is often proven after the fact and after its perpetrators are out of power or no longer in a position to resist. For that reason, prevention is the best solution. And indeed, both former Secretary-General Kofi Annan, and his successor, Ban Ki-moon, have emphasized prevention. In January of 2001, in reaction to failures of the past to prevent genocide or comparable crimes, Kofi Annan told the Stockholm International Forum that, "We should ... consider establishing a Special Rapporteur on the Prevention of Genocide." Later that year, the Security Council, in its resolution 1366 (2001), invited the Secretary-General to refer to the Council information and analyses from within the UN system on cases of serious violations of international law, including international humanitarian law and human rights law. On 7 April 2004, the tenth anniversary of the Rwandan genocide, Secretary-General Annan announced the creation of the position of a Special Adviser on the Prevention of Genocide. The creation of that position was part of a broader Action Plan to Prevent Genocide involving the whole United Nations summarized under five headings: preventing armed conflict, protection of civilians in armed conflict, ending impunity, early

[53]Ibid., 592.

and clear warning and swift as well as decisive action. In a subsequent letter (S/2004/567), the Secretary-General informed the President of the Security Council of his decision to create the position.

According to the outline of the mandate contained in the annex to the SG's letter, the Special Adviser's responsibilities would be:

(a) to collect information, in particular from within the UN system, on massive and serious violations of human rights and international humanitarian law of ethnic and racial origin, that, if not prevented or halted, might lead to genocide;
(b) to act as a mechanism of early warning to the Secretary-General, and through him to the Security Council, by bringing to their attention potential situations that could result in genocide;
(c) to make recommendations to the Council, through the Secretary-General, on actions to prevent or halt genocide; and
(d) to liaise with the UN system on activities for the prevention of genocide and to work to enhance the UN capacity to analyze and manage information related to genocide or related crimes.

The appointment of Juan Mendez as Special Adviser became effective on 1 August 2004. The universally binding legal obligation expressed in the 1948 Genocide Convention to not only punish genocide, but also to prevent it was reinforced in the *Outcome Document* of the September 2005 World Summit. In the Document, world leaders expressed a political and moral commitment accepting the responsibility to protect civilians from genocide, war crimes, ethnic cleansing and crimes against humanity. At the end of May 2007, Secretary-General Ban Ki-moon appointed me as the new Special Adviser for the Prevention of Genocide and Mass Atrocities, succeeding Mr. Juan Mendez. In a continuing effort to strengthen the United Nations' role in this area, the Secretary-General asked me to devote myself full-time to the position instead of Juan Mendez's part-time arrangement. The position was also upgraded from the level of Assistant Secretary-General to Under-Secretary-General. The Secretary-General later appointed Professor Edward Luck as Special Adviser on the Responsibility to Protect at the level of Assistant Secretary-General. The two Special Advisers were to work closely in a combined office.

4.5 Approach to the Genocide Mandate

Although there are obvious differences between my previous mandate on IDPs and my present mandate on the Prevention of Genocide, they share the element of sensitivity and the tendency to use sovereignty as a shield against international involvement. Ironically, the legal obligations of genocide by definition override sovereignty,[54] but for the same reason the tendency to deny it and resist international involvement where the perpetrator still wields control over domestic jurisdiction is greater than in the case of response to internal displacement. However, to the extent that the genocide mandate focuses on prevention, the invocation of sovereignty as responsibility or the first layer of the responsibility to protect, the two mandates call for a common approach. For a constructive engagement with governments concerned in the case of genocide, it is important to act early before positions harden and denial and defensiveness set in. The critical questions to be addressed for prevention purposes at an early stage are: how to gain access for constructive engagement with the states concerned, what message should be used as a basis for such an engagement, and what is needed to foster international cooperation to protect populations at risk. However, the international community must be better prepared than it is now to take remedial action, in cases where the States are unable and unwilling to protect their own populations at risk.

This early prevention action should focus on elements which the Secretary-General included in his Five Point Action Plan and which my predecessor restated in four interrelated areas:

(a) the protection of populations at risk against massive violations of human rights or humanitarian law;
(b) accountability for violations;
(c) humanitarian relief and access to basic economic, social and cultural rights; and
(d) the initiation and support of steps to address underlying causes of conflict through peace agreements and transition processes.

These in a sense correlate with the phases identified by the International Commission as the responsibility to prevent, to react, and to rebuild.

The best preventive action is the creation of a political, economic, social and cultural framework for peace, security, democracy, and respect for all human rights and fundamental freedoms.[55] Anticipation, detection, and adoption of early warning measures constitute elements in a continuum of prevention. Early warning is defined as "the collection, analysis and communication of information about escalatory developments in situations that could potentially lead to genocide, crimes against humanity or massive and

[54] The *jus cogens* nature of the norms in the Genocide Convention is examined in Wenqi Zhu and Binxin Zhang, Chapter 12, Section 12.2 (below).
[55] For a recent comprehensive study of prevention, see David Hamburg, *Preventing Genocide: Practical Steps Toward Early Detection and Effective Action* (Boulder and London: Paradigm Publishers, 2008).

serious war crimes far enough in advance for relevant UN organs to take timely and effective preventive measures."[56]

Reaction envisages action beyond early warning measures and entails taking steps to prevent the detected or predictable crisis before it actually erupts; and acting to protect the civilian population and provide humanitarian assistance, should the crisis erupt. In most cases, early-warning will be the main contribution for prevention, because the means of response by the Special Advisor are quite limited. Due to lack of independent operational capacity, the mandate needs to work closely with others, both within and outside the UN system, including regional organizations, academic and research institutions, non-governmental organizations, and civil society generally. Emphasis needs to be placed on preventive diplomacy and offering governments and other pertinent actors support to strengthen their capacity to prevent genocide and mass atrocities.

An integral aspect of reaction is the search for solutions which includes initiating a peace process aimed at halting the crisis, restoring peace and security, and promoting reconciliation and transitional justice. Again, this is a generic, system-wide challenge since it is quite unlikely that the Special Advisor will be able to initiate peace processes. The question will be what particular contribution the Special Advisor could offer to the efforts of others beyond general advocacy.

Rebuilding requires addressing the root causes of conflict and instability to ensure durable peace, protection of all human rights and enjoyment of the rights of citizenship on the basis of full equality. Again, this is not an area in which the Special Advisor is expected to play a specific role beyond the general advocacy mentioned above and close cooperation with the peacemaking and peace building mechanisms of the UN. As the Advisory Committee noted in its 2006 Report, although the best of all ways to deal with crimes against humanity is to prevent them from happening in the first place,

> [m]any different kinds of responses can advance that cause, including the application of soft power in equitable development and technical assistance strategies designed to improve the quality of governance leading toward democratic institutions and practices, to build more tolerant inter-ethnic and communal relations, and reduce the potential for economic grievance becoming explosive.[57]

[56] Laurence Woocher, "Developing a Strategy, Methods and Tools for Genocide Early Warning," Paper Prepared for the Office of the Special Adviser to the UN Secretary-General on the Prevention of Genocide, Center for International Conflict Resolution, Columbia University, September 26, 2006, 1.

[57] Report of the Advisory Committee, October 2006, 4.

4.6 Constructive Management of Diversity as a Tool for Prevention, Reaction and Rebuilding

Considering that most countries are characterized by diversity involving categories identified in the Genocide Convention, – national, ethnical, racial or religious groups – the potential for identity conflicts that can escalate to zero-sum genocidal magnitude is widespread and cannot be localized in particular regions or countries. That fact in itself offers an opportunity to discuss the problem and the need for prevention at large to raise the level of awareness without making particular regions and countries feel targeted and become negatively defensive; but without overlooking particular situations of concern. Constructive management of diversity therefore becomes a crucial preventive principle as well as a tool for resolving crises and attaining sustainable peace and stability. The mandate should therefore operate at two interrelated, but also distinct levels in raising awareness generically while also generating appropriate responses to specific situations. At the generic level, the mandate has begun to organize regional and sub-regional consultations in collaboration with the Special Advisor on R to P and with regional partners, academic institutions, policy research centers, and civil society organizations, with the participation of the governments in the region to raise awareness of the threat of genocide, and the need for effective prevention policies and institutional responses. Agreeing on contextualized normative principles, institutions and mechanisms for prevention is an important step in the preventive direction.

The other dimension of the mandate's agenda is to monitor developments in countries around the world with the objective of identifying both situations of concern and those in which diversities are being constructively managed, thereby providing models for emulation. The critical question then becomes one of identifying conditions that make countries slide down the path of genocidal conflict and failure, and those that ensure peace, security, stability, and prosperity – the path of success in nation-building.

With this comprehensive approach, countries should not feel selectively targeted for naming and shaming, but positively challenged to elevate their performance, invite recognition for their positive achievements and earn the respect and legitimacy of their citizens and the international community for living up to the principles of sovereignty as responsibility or the responsibility to protect.

The regional approach is particularly significant because problems internal to a country tend to spill over and affect the neighbours, whether in political or humanitarian terms. Being more closely identified with the problems in the regional context, a partnership between sub-regional and regional organizations, and the international community, based on complementing regional legitimacy with international capacity, could be forged to make for effective prevention, reaction, or rebuilding.

The ultimate objectives of the whole exercise must be not only to prevent genocide, and react to the humanitarian consequences of the atrocities and genocidal conflicts that might ensure, but to address the underlying problems in a way that becomes circularly preventive of further atrocities and potential genocidal conflicts. The root causes of genocidal conflicts relate to the crises of identity which not only differentiate people on national, ethnic, racial or religious grounds, but stratify and discriminate on those bases. Given worldwide increasing awareness of human rights and norms of non-discrimination, the inevitable result of gross inequalities and denial of human rights and the rights of citizenship is a reaction that may be political, but might be manifested in violent rebellion. But tragically, such a rebellion may be met with the superior power of those in control of the state apparatus and may result in unscrupulous use of genocidal force.

The challenge then becomes forging a state framework with which all citizens can identify with pride and dignity, including equal access to power, economic opportunities, social services, and the enjoyment of all the rights of citizenship on equal footing. In many ways, the mandate of the Special Adviser on the Prevention of Genocide is popularly viewed as the impossible one, and rightly so, if it were seen as the sole responsibility of the Special Adviser. As I always say, it is an impossible mandate that must be made possible through an inclusive collaborative approach within and outside the UN with the Special Adviser acting as a catalyst in much the same way I conducted the mandate on IDPs. The framework of Sovereignty as Responsibility, which is also the core of RtoP provides a common ground for such collaboration.

Chapter 5
Citizenship, National Identity, and Genocide

Douglas Greenberg

"You have no right to live among us as Jews. You have no right to live among us. You have no right to live."[1] That is how the first great historian of the Holocaust, Raul Hilberg, summarized the entire history of the Nazi attack on Europe's Jews. For Hilberg, the history of the Holocaust was the history of public policy; it could be documented through the official record of the Third Reich, and it could be summarized in three sentences. Hilberg's great book, *The Destruction of the European Jews*, was published in 1961. In the intervening 45 years, the field of Holocaust historiography has expanded. Few scholars would argue today that we can understand so vast and monstrous an event simply by studying documents left by the perpetrators. But Hilberg's aphoristic summary of the development of the Nazi program of extermination continues to have great power because it so succinctly captures the steps through which the Nazi regime moved from the abrogation of rights to mass murder.

One could, of course, re-frame Hilberg's three sentences, without losing their meaning, in the following way: "Your rights are limited. Your citizenship is terminated. We will kill you." There was, in other words, a close connection in Nazi Germany between the commencement of genocide and the denial of citizenship. What I would like to explore, therefore, is the extension of Hilberg's description of the German situation to a comparative analysis of other genocides, especially the Turkish genocide of the Armenians in 1915, the so-called Cambodian auto-genocide beginning in 1975, and the Rwandan genocide of 1994. To establish a common framework for such analysis, I will begin with narratives of the main features of the four genocides.

D. Greenberg (✉)
Executive Dean of Arts and Sciences, Rutgers, State University of New Jersey,
New Brunswick, NJ 08901-1248, USA
e-mail: execdean@sas.rutgers.edu

[1] Richard L. Rubenstein and John K. Roth, *Approaches to Auschwitz: The Holocaust and its Legacy* (Louisville, KY: Westminster John Knox Press, 2003), 9.

R. Provost, P. Akhavan (eds.), *Confronting Genocide*, Ius Gentium: Comparative Perspectives on Law and Justice 7, DOI 10.1007/978-90-481-9840-5_5,

The Holocaust is probably the most familiar of the four. The *Shoah*, as it is called in Hebrew, was undertaken by an elected government of the National Socialist Party led by Adolph Hitler, who founded the party in 1919. Opposition to Jewish citizenship was a central feature of the Nazi political program, and Hitler was a rabid anti-Semite from the beginning, as he demonstrated in 1925 in *Mein Kampf*, although no explicit plan for a genocide was formed until much later. Significantly for this discussion, *Mein Kampf* included chapters on topics like "Nation and Race," "Subjects and Citizens," and "Propaganda and Organization."[2]

Hitler became Chancellor in 1933, when the Nazis had the second largest number of votes in the elections. He gained control of the German government on the death of the President, Paul von Hindenburg, in the summer of 1934. A champion of a new kind of racial anti-Semitism, which Saul Friedlander calls "redemptive anti-Semitism,"[3] Hitler moved quickly not only to consolidate his power but also to turn his ideology into law, which he did over the course of the next year or so. In September of 1935, Hitler issued the Nuremberg Laws.[4] The first of these was, not surprisingly, the *Reich* Citizenship Law, which pungently said that only a German or someone who was racially German (whatever that meant) could be the "sole bearer of full political rights in accordance with the Law."[5] As Hitler had indicated in *Mein Kampf*, however, there were obviously other people living in Germany: subjects, he called them, rather than citizens.[6] Nazi ideology regarded Jews as obviously not being of German or kindred blood (to use the phrase in the law).[7] Therefore, the *Reich Citizenship Law* abrogated Jewish citizenship and reduced Jews to the status of subjects.

The second of the Nuremberg Laws, *Law for the Protection of German Blood and German Honor*, regulated the relationship between Jews and German, by forbidding marriages between members of the two groups and outlawing extramarital relations between them. The law contained other provisions too, but sex loomed large as an obvious threat to the purity of German citizenship. The Nuremberg Laws were clear enough, but since Hitler's entire political program hinged on who was a citizen, the Nazis cleared up any remaining confusion in November 1938, just after the November Pogrom (usually called *Kristallnacht*). Few people in Germany

---

[2]Adolph Hitler, *Mein Kampf*, trans. James Vincent Murphy (Reedy, West Virginia: Liberty Bell Publications, 2004).

[3]Saul Friedlander, *The Years of Extermination: Nazi Germany and the Jews, 1939–1945* (New York: HarperCollins, 2007).

[4]The ways in which citizens can resist genocidal laws are outlined in Frédéric Mégret, Chapter 13, Section 13.5 (below).

[5]Jeremy Noakes and Geoffrey Pridham, *Documents on Nazism 1919–1945* (New York: Viking Press, 1974), 463–467.

[6]Hitler, *Mein Kampf*.

[7]Noakes and Pridham, "Documents on Nazism," 463–467.

could doubt that Jews were no longer citizens, but the First Regulation to the *Reich Citizenship Law* stated in so many words that "no Jew can be a Reich citizen. He has no voting rights in political matters; he cannot occupy a public office."[8]

Over the next several years, the Nazis continued to move harshly against those Jews remaining in Germany, who constituted only about 5% of the population, and those it absorbed in the *anschluss*. They considered transporting them out of Europe to Palestine, Alaska, the Dominican Republic, Honduras, Australia, Madagascar, and Eastern Europe. By the middle of 1941, however, with war underway throughout Europe and Poland, and the Western Soviet Union occupied by German troops, which brought several million additional Jews within the Nazi orbit, the situation had dramatically changed. The modest attacks on Jewish citizenship incorporated in the Nuremburg Laws were inadequate in the face of these numbers. By mid-1941, Jews were being herded into ghettoes, along with German Jews taken from Germany, where they suffered horribly from hunger and disease. Still, no final decision had been taken to kill them all.

There is a vast literature on when precisely Hitler and Himmler decided that all the Jews should be killed. It may have been as early as July of 1941; it surely was no later than December of 1941, when the US entered the war. Mass murder commenced in earnest throughout the late summer and fall of 1941, when the *Einsatzgruppen* moved East, systematically murdering every Jew they could find. We now know that Hitler and Himmler had decided before the New Year that they would kill every Jew in Europe.[9] They called a conference at Wannsee outside Berlin to confirm their decision, but the first death camp, Belzec, was already in operation. Apart from the appalling clinical approach of the so-called Wannsee Protocol, it is chiefly significant for its labored and confusing attempt to define who was a Jew on the basis of parentage. If it was important to know who was a Jew in order to deprive Jews of citizenship, it was even more important to know whom precisely to kill. The *endlosung*, the Final Solution to the Jewish Problem, was now underway. Soon more death camps, Treblinka, Sobibor, Majdanek, Chelmno, and Auschwitz, were operating. The rest of the gruesome story is horribly familiar. By April 1945, when the war concluded, 2/3 of the Jews in Europe, half the Jews in the world, about 6 million people had been murdered.

Of course, the Holocaust was not the only genocide of the twentieth century, or even the first. The best known, though not the first genocide of the early twentieth century, of course, was the Armenian Genocide of 1915, an event that has received somewhat more attention recently, but

[8] Ibid.

[9] See, for example, Richard Breitman, "Plans for the Final Solution in Early 1941," *German Studies Review* 17, no. 3 (1994): 483–493.

one whose details are still being reconstructed.[10] For many years, the Armenian Genocide was ignored by everyone but the Armenians. Hitler himself famously asked: "Who now remembers the Armenians?"[11]

The fall of the Ottoman Empire was a long, slow process. By 1913, however, a group called the Young Turks or Ittihadists had engineered a coup in which three men, the so-called Three Pashas (Ahmet Cemal Pasha, Ismail Enver Pasha, and Mehmet Talât Pasha) not only ruled the country, but also undertook a genocide of vast proportions in which members of the Armenian minority, long a prosperous and cosmopolitan segment of the Turkish population, were first stripped of their rights, then murdered in great numbers in a series of massacres, and finally sent on forced marches with hardly any food and water to the deserts of Mesopotamia and Syria. By the end of 1915, as many as a million Armenians were dead.

The justification for this slaughter was that the Armenians living near the Russian border were secret allies of the Russians, with whom the Turks were at war. Even before the war, however, Armenian churches and homes were burned. The political rights of Armenians were terminated. Armenian shops were looted. What would be called pogroms in another context, in other words, became commonplace, including the widespread murder of entire communities and wholesale destruction of Armenian property. Arms were distributed to local Turkish residents, who served as paramilitaries in something called the Special Organization and were charged with terrorizing the Armenian population in every possible way.

By the spring of 1915, it was not safe to be an Armenian living within the boundaries of Turkey. Massacres were an everyday occurrence and, ominously, local governors began to order the deportation of Armenians to the desert in huge numbers. There were mass arrests, and Armenian businesses and newspapers were closed and raided in Constantinople and throughout the country. Armenians lost all rights at law, and the genocide began to move ahead very rapidly throughout the summer of 1915, including not only mass murder but vast deportations. Just as the Nazis would later do with the Jews, the Turks simultaneously degraded Armenians and blamed them for the degradation.

Leslie Davis, an American witness, who thought no more than 15% of the Armenians marched into the desert survived, wrote:

> A more pitiable sight cannot be imagined. They are almost without exception ragged, filthy, hungry, and sick. This is not surprising in view of the fact that they have been on the road for nearly two months without a change of clothing, no

---

[10]The main events of the Armenian Genocide are recounted in Douglas Greenberg, Chapter 5 (below); an explanation of the Turkish government's stance towards the genocide is provided in Taner Akçam, Chapter 10 (below).

[11]Mark Gerzon, *Leading Through Conflict: How Successful Leaders Transform Differences Into Opportunities* (Watertown, MA: Harvard Business Press, 2006), 29.

chance to wash, no shelter, and little to eat. . . . to watch them one could hardly believe that these people were human beings.[12]

The rape of Armenian women became a commonplace; neither that nor the murder of Armenian children nor the pillaging of Armenian communities nor the dreadful conditions in which now virtually all surviving Armenians lived were remediable by law or the rights of citizenship. Foreign observers, like Lord Bryce and American Ambassador Henry Morgenthau, reported the genocide with alarm to their governments and the *New York Times* reported it in detail. No one lifted a finger. By the winter of 1915, it was estimated 800,000 Armenians were dead, but the deportations and murders continued. Half-hearted efforts to assist the so-called "Starving Armenians" began in the West, but without real commitment or energy. Murders, rapes, and deportations continued until the end of the war. No one knows the final death toll; it certainly approached or even exceeded one million human beings. The historic vitality of Armenian life in Turkey was effectively brought to an end by the genocide. The Turkish government continues today to deny the genocide and regularly lobbies governments around the world to enlist them in this denial.[13] Among the governments that do not recognize the Armenian genocide are those of the United States and Israel.

Two more recent genocides merit our attention too: those in Cambodia and in Rwanda. The Cambodian genocide under Pol Pot and the Khmer Rouge beginning in mid-1975 involved the eventual murder of as many as 3 million people. Estimates of the number of murders vary widely, but even Pol Pot himself estimated that his regime murdered approximately 800,000 people. It began, as the Holocaust and the Armenian genocide had, with the abrogation of citizenship and forced transportation, in this case from the capital city of Phnom Penh and into the countryside. Anyone associated with the previous government of Lon Nol was murdered almost immediately, along with their spouses, children, and relatives.

Although the ideology of the regime in what was then called Kampuchea was to create a fully egalitarian society of authentic Khmers, the determination of who was really a Khmer was essential to the mass murder, just as it had been with Jews and Armenians. The Cambodian genocide is often said to have been an auto-genocide in which the Cambodians murdered themselves without regard to ethnicity. It has been referred to as a genocide without racism, in other words, but this is not precisely the case.

It is certainly true that the Khmer Rouge especially targeted those they took to be middle- or upper class, a determination they made on the basis

---

[12] Norman M. Naimark, *Fires of Hatred: Ethnic Cleansing in Twentieth-Century Europe* (Cambridge, MA: Harvard University Press, 2001), 33.

[13] Historical reasons for the Turkish government's stance towards the genocide are addressed in Taner Akçam, Chapter 10 (below).

of one's work (as a civil servant for example), one's education, one's house, one's clothing, and one's style of life. Even wearing glasses was enough to suggest that a person should be killed. The transportation out of Phnom Penh and into the countryside, in fact, had an almost Darwinian flavor to it: those who could deal with the rigors of rural life were authentic Khmer peasants; those who could not clearly deserved to die, either of starvation and disease or, in an echo of the Turkish treatment of the Armenians, they had to be killed because they were so prone to weakness and could not contribute to the new nation that was being built.

More than this, however, the Khmer Rouge also had an ethnic program which, in classic circular reasoning, they linked to their attack on the urban classes. They especially targeted Chams (Cambodian Muslims and their descendants) and the many Vietnamese living in Cambodia. The ideology of the Cambodian genocide aimed to create an authentic national community, whose social boundaries included some and excluded others. While it is true, as is commonly said, that the main targets were the urban upper and middle classes, the regime defended what it was doing in nation-building terms and tarred their victims with the racial brush of being Chams or Vietnamese.

The regime in Kampuchea was itself not religious but it targeted religious minorities (including Buddhists, who were 85% of the population) in racial terms because it recognized that religion commanded a loyalty that competed with the state. The constitution stated this clearly: "All reactionary religions that are detrimental to Democratic Kampuchea and the Kampuchean People are strictly forbidden" and, ominously, "There is one Kampuchea, one single nation and one national language. The various nationalities no longer exist."[14]

We might think of the Khmer Rouge as murderous utopians, animated by an ideology in which racism inevitably played a role, however submerged. They were serious students of French Marxism attempting to create, as they put it, a society of "new people." That could only be done by the full extirpation of the old, whether it was represented by the Chams and Vietnamese or by the urban classes. Either way, the genocide involved definitional issues about who could or could not be a member of the new community, the new nation that was being built. The rhetoric of this genocide, as in the others, was that the state was infected with a disease that could only be cured by killing the germs.[15] The mere deprivation of citizenship was necessary, but it was insufficient to protect the state from infection. First, the infection

---

[14]Eric D. Weitz, *A Century of Genocide: Utopias of Race and Nation* (Princeton, NJ: Princeton University Press, 2003), 170.

[15]Samuel Totten, Paul Robert Bartrop and Steven L. Jacobs, *Dictionary of Genocide* (London: Greenwood Publishing Group, 2008), 203.

had to be removed from the center of the political body by depriving people of the rights of citizenship and literally transporting them away from the heart of society. Then the infection could be eliminated entirely through mass murder.

Although Rwanda is a very small country, the story there is among the most complicated we must address. Rwanda was colonized by the Germans and then by the Belgians. There were three main groups in Rwanda: the Hutu, who were mainly farmers, the Tutsi, who were mainly cattle herders, and the Twa, a forest people referred to in the West as "pygmies." The Rwandan kings were Tutsi, although they were outnumbered by the Hutus. When the Belgians took control of Rwanda, they filled the civil service with Tutsis and generally favored them over the Hutu majority.

The Belgians claimed a racial difference between the two groups, asserting that the Tutsi were originally from Northern Africa and genetically superior to the Hutu because they were more like whites. The Belgians associated specific physical characteristics with each group as well, although there were no scientific grounds for doing so. Hutus and Tutsis to this day share a common language (Kinyrwanda), common religious traditions (mostly Catholic), common culture, and common customs. But the Belgians had reasons of their own to cobble together their race theory and, in 1933 they issued identity cards to every person in Rwanda, labelling them a Tutsi, Hutu, or Twa, began keeping careful marriage records, by law, and required every person to carry his or her identity card at all times. People continued to carry these cards even after independence. This was racism, pure and simple.

Rwanda became independent in 1962, at which time the Hutu majority took the reins of government. Almost immediately, Hutus began to attack the Tutsis who had been so closely associated with Belgian rule. Beginning in 1963, there were awful pogroms in Rwanda in which Tutsis were unceremoniously butchered or transported from the centers in Butare and Kigali to the especially inhospitable region of the Bugesera in Southwestern Rwanda. Perversely, this was done with the assistance of the very country that had helped to create the idea of citizenship, France. Many Tutsi fled to neighboring countries, especially Uganda. There they established a thriving diaspora. Their children grew up as exiles who had never seen the country of their origin. These communities grew by natural increase and by immigration for 30 years as successive massacres and pogroms sent Tutsis fleeing Rwanda for safe havens elsewhere.

Meanwhile, in Rwanda, Hutus controlled most of the arms of society and government with Juvenal Habyarimana serving as president beginning in 1973. The exile Tutsi community in Uganda hoped to return home and created the Rwandan Patriotic Front or RPF, which invaded Rwanda from Uganda in 1990. Habyarimana fought the RPF, and eventually sued for peace in the summer of 1993. An agreement was signed in Arusha, Tanzania ending the civil war.

But the Arusha Accords, which required power sharing with the RPF, never really worked. Habyarimana was attacked by Hutus who represented a radical idea of a different sort of Rwanda, a Rwanda that was free of cockroaches, the epithet these representatives of so-called Hutu Power coined to describe Tutsis. Hutu Power promulgated what they called the Hutu 10 Commandments, a bizarre series of propositions mostly concerning sexual and marital relations between Hutus and Tutsis, and arguing for the removal of the Tutsis from Rwandan society. They began broadcasting over the radio a violent ideology that called for the extermination of the Tutsis as an infection in the body politic. Although the Rwanda of that time lacked a decent phone system and still has hardly any television, radio was ubiquitous. In every village, no matter how small, Hutus heard calls for the murder of their Tutsi neighbors. There had actually been extensive intermarriage among Hutus and Tutsis, so calls for the murder of all Tutsis were sometimes calls to murder one's own family members. Tragically, these were calls that many Hutus eventually heeded, murdering their spouses, children, and grandchildren in the name of Hutu Power's idea of citizenship.

The leader of the UN forces in Rwanda, Roméo Dallaire, repeatedly warned that a dangerous situation was about to become extraordinarily violent and that the Tutsi minority was in danger being subject to wholesale attack. His warnings were ignored in New York and in Washington, just as similar warnings had been ignored in the same cities in 1915 and in the thirties. On April 6, 1994, Habyarimana was returning from Arusha with Tanzanian President Ntaryamira when their plane was blown up as it was about to land in the Rwandan capital, Kigali. No one knows precisely who was responsible for the assassination; accusations and counter-accusations are being made to this day. There can be little doubt, however, that the assassination of Habyarimana was inspired by his implicit recognition of Tutsi citizenship in his negotiations at Arusha with the leader of the RPF, Paul Kagame.

Within a few hours of the plane's destruction, the genocide began. Hutus sympathetic to the peace accords and every Tutsi in the country were now subject not merely to the abrogation of rights of citizenship, which had been continuing since independence, but to murder. Hutu Power Radio issued instructions to the local paramilitaries, the Interahamwe, and explained why the nation could not exist if Tutsis were part of it.[16] At every street corner in Kigali and at roadblocks throughout the country, a combination of government troops and the Interahamwe stopped everyone to check ID cards. Hutus were allowed to pass. Tutsis were murdered on the spot. The genocide was terrifyingly well-organized and proceeded very quickly. In the Bugesera, small groups of Hutus, who thought of killing as their work,

---

[16]The role played by the radio in the Rwandan Genocide and its impact in African countries is examined in Mary Kimani, Chapter 20, Section 20.2 and 19.3 (below).

went faithfully to their jobs every day. They invaded churches in Ntirama and Nyanza where Belgian priests abandoned their sanctuary-seeking Tutsi parishioners, they seized schools, they overran community centers, and they killed every single Tutsi they could find. Most of the nearly one million people who died in the 3-month slaughter were dead within the first 6 weeks.

The same thing continued in every corner of the country. This was not anarchy and it was not, in the parlance of the Western press, tribal warfare. Rwanda was one of the most well-organized and highly mobilized states in the world. This was state-sponsored violence, no different than in Turkey, Germany, or Kampuchea. Rwanda was divided into 12 Prefectures led by a Prefect, each divided into 15 communes each with a mayor; the communes were divided into 1600 sectors, each with a council and then thousands of cells or groups of households. Everyone was armed in advance, and all of it was managed centrally toward one end: the murder of every Tutsi. This structure, combined with effective communication, level to level, provided by Hutu Radio, was what permitted the genocide to succeed so rapidly – along, of course, with the tacit support of the French and the Belgians and the utter lack of interest shown by the United States.

By July, an RPF offensive had succeeded and the genocide came to an end. In its wake were perhaps a million bodies, most of them unburied or floating in the rivers, as well as millions of refugees, many of them Hutu *génocidaires* who fled across the border to Congo, where in the hideous conditions of refugee camps, they now appeared to be victims rather than perpetrators. Paul Kagame became president of the country, a post he still holds.

No Rwandan carries an identity card now; people know who is a Tutsi and who is a Hutu, but the subject of ethnic identity cannot be discussed as a matter of law. Everyone is a Rwandan; separate racial identities, however spurious, can only turn reconciliation to revenge. The theory is that maintaining Hutu and Tutsi identities can only turn victims into killers, as Mahmoud Mamdani so aptly put it.[17] Today, 12 years after the end of the genocide, trials of the main architects of the genocide continue in Arusha, as do *gacaca*, weekly local tribunals in every community and neighborhood where individual killers must face their neighbors and the families of those they butchered in the bloody spring and early summer of 1994.[18]

Apart from their pure wickedness, these four genocides have much in common. I am only too aware of the intellectual dangers of comparative

[17] Mahmoud Mamdani, *When Victims Become Killers: Colonialism, Nativism, and the Genocide in Rwanda Princeton*, MA: Princeton University Press, 2001).

[18] The psychological effects of the Rwandan Genocide and psychological dimension of reconciliation are discussed in Jobb Arnold, Chapter 19 (below).

history, to say nothing of the potential disrespect one might show to the victims and survivors of particular genocides by treating them as though the differences do not matter. They do matter, but my focus here is on similarities rather than differences. Genocide, Philip Gourevitch, reminds us, is "an exercise in community building."[19] All four of these genocides were part of a program to build national communities. Each, in its way, was utopian; all incorporated ideologies of inclusion as well as ideologies of exclusion. All of them depended fundamentally upon knowing who was and who was not a citizen.

For many in the world, the idea of citizenship is positive. Many of us regard citizenship as precious possession, and we think others should want it. We establish rules for acquiring citizenship, complicated and often inexplicable rules, sometimes rules with powerful racial and ethnic criteria attached to them. But whatever the rules, however good or bad they may be, we should recognize that for us, just as for Turks, Germans, Cambodians, and Rwandans, citizenship is about inclusion and exclusion – who can and who cannot count on the rights that citizenship confers. Citizenship always involves a legally codified definition that leaves someone out; without exclusion, you would not need a definition to begin with.

The political sociologist, Michael Mann, has suggested in fact that because democratic regimes shift social stratification away from economic or social status and toward other forms of identity, they necessarily imply new forms of social danger, what he calls the "dark side of democracy."[20] In a majoritarian regime, in other words, minorities are often at risk whether they are Armenians, Jews, Chams, Tutsis, American Indians, or Australian aborigines.

We know the citizenship guarantees of the Constitution have sometimes been empty promises for, among others, African American slaves – absurdly defined as 3/5 of a citizen in the Constitution and actually not treated as citizens at all until only about 40 or 50 years ago.

Despite the putative guarantees of the Constitution, the American idea of citizenship excludes, just as it includes. Like some other states that arose from the liberal impulses of the modern era, the United States has also had its genocide. The slaughter of American Indians – which clearly meets even the most stringent definitions of genocide – arose from their being placed outside the protective boundaries of American citizenship. And African Americans were at least, if not more, vulnerable to potentially genocidal violence, *after* the end of slavery than before it. And one of the other most

---

[19]Philip Gourevitch, *We Wish to Inform You That Tomorrow We Will Be Killed with Our Families: Stories from Rwanda* (New York: Picador, 1999).

[20]Michael Mann, *The Dark Side of Democracy: Explaining Ethnic Cleansing* (New York, NY: Cambridge University Press, 2005).

democratic countries in the world, Australia, has also been a perpetrator of genocide.

Just to be clear about this, here are some numbers: Mann says that the aboriginal population of Australia in 1788 was around 300,000. By 1901, it was 93,000 and by 1921, 72,000, a decrease of 80%.

In the United States, the best estimate is that there were about 9 million Indians when whites arrived. In the census of 1900, there were 237,000 Indians (a 95% decline). Take California only: the Spanish missions estimated there were 310,000 Indians in Spanish California in the late 18th century. By 1849 (the year of the Gold Rush), that number had halved. In 1860, after 10 years of democratic "settlement," the Indian population of California was 31,000. That is a decline of 80% in 11 years. In the 12 years of the Third Reich, the Germans only managed to kill about two-thirds of the European Jews.

Statistics can be repeated endlessly and numbingly, of course. There is ideology here too, as in the other genocides. Mann quotes Jefferson on this point: "If we are ever constrained to lift the hatchet against any tribe, we shall never lay it down till that tribe is exterminated...in war they will kill some of us; we shall destroy all of them." The political will to undertake systematic murder at this level must arise from a legally cognizable idea of citizenship that excludes someone from its benefits.

People who are actually citizens cannot be legally stripped even of their rights – no less of their lives – as long as they are still citizens; that is what modern democracy is supposed to be about. People who are not citizens, on the other hand, can be stripped of anything, including their lives. So citizenship is an incredibly powerful idea and deeply connected to the violence of the modern world – although it is also paradoxically one of the most important achievements of the modern world, beginning with the French Declaration of the Rights of Man and Citizen.

To this we must add that genocide is a government policy, not a private prejudice. Evil as they are, a pogrom or a lynching is not a genocide. Genocide is an opportunity to mobilize participation of the citizens in the generation of new national identity through murderous violence. That is what happened in Turkey, in Germany, in Cambodia, and in Rwanda.

Gender and sex and marriage are also connected to genocide and citizenship. The ability to marry, to have children, and to pass onto them the benefits of citizenship is itself an attribute of citizenship. Thus, rules about who can and cannot be married to whom are an essential legal structure for the destruction of citizenship. That was true of the Nuremberg Laws; it was true in Turkey, in Cambodia, and in the Hutu 10 Commandments. The Hutu *génocidaires* and the Khmer Rouge, in fact, were as obsessed with this issue as the Nazis were. Prohibitions on intergroup sex, in and out of marriage, are a necessary prerequisite, it would seem, for genocide.

Yet there is more to the gender question. Women are especially marked for targeting in all genocidal situations. The point of attacks on women and children is to interrupt reproduction. Of course, the logic is again circular: they are not citizens so they must be killed. They must be killed, so they must not be citizens. They certainly cannot be permitted to reproduce. Genocide particularly targets women because it is through them that the status of citizenship is inherited and the Young Turks, Nazis, Khmer Rouge, and Hutu Power, all attacked women as the carriers of citizenship. This was done through legal mechanisms of the state before and during the genocides.

Ironically, the intensity of these attacks tells us something about actual power of mothers in families as well as about biology. The interruption of reproduction and the prohibition of sexual relations between the tyrant and the tyrannized is an act of civic purification, and each of the genocides articulated it that way. Intergroup sex destroys the integrity of citizenship because it confuses the citizenship of the next generation. The superb historian of Eastern Europe, Norman Naimark has commented on this. He says: "The ideology of integral nationalism identifies women as the carriers, quite literally, of the next generation of the nation. Not only do women constitute the biological core of nationality, but they are often charged with the task of passing on the cultural and spiritual values of nationhood to their children."[21]

Another critical, and perhaps defining, aspect of genocide involves the projection of racialized views about citizenship. The center of the Hutu Power ideology was that the Tutsi are biological outsiders, racial invaders. The Turks said the same of the Armenians, the Germans of the Jews, the Khmer Rouge even of their own countrymen in Phnom Penh, to say nothing of the Vietnamese and the Chams. They were illegal immigrants to be excluded from the national community and defined as non-participants in civic life.[22]

Genocide not only depends upon the exclusion of the target group from citizenship, it also depends upon the popular mobilization of the nation's idea of itself. In each of the cases we have discussed, in fact, there were paramilitary organizations drawn from the citizenry to participate in genocide: the Secret Organization, the police battalions and Hitler Youth, the local cadres in Kampuchea, and the Interahamwe in Rwanda. Moreover, all of them had to be motivated by some larger set of ideologies and propaganda to participate not in killing in the abstract, but in killing for the nation, killing for the protection of their own citizenship. Genocidal

---

[21] Norman M. Naimark, *Fires of Hatred*, 2001, 195.

[22] The characterization of "out-groups" in situations leading to genocide is discussed in Yehuda Bauer, Chapter 7, Section 7.2 (below).

success depends on the mobilization of the apparatus of the state, but it also depends on the mobilization of institutions of local government and on motivating the citizens themselves by deepening their prejudices to violent fear and murderous rage.

That was true of the Young Turks and the Ittihadists, it was true of Hitler and Goebbels, it was true of Pol Pot, and it was dramatically true of Hutu Power and Hutu Power Radio. Mobilization of the citizenry in genocide makes the definition of citizenship real and enforces the majoritarian tyranny. In the Nazi case, Christopher Browning notes: "If Nazi propaganda had not succeeded in turning many Germans into rabid anti-Semites in Hitler's own image, Nazi policies had succeeded in isolating German Jewry from the rest of society. The Jews had increasingly become an abstract phenomenon to whose fate Germans could be indifferent, not fellow citizens and human beings. . . ."[23]

And what about religion? Religion does not seem to have much to do with it. It is true that the Armenians were Christians targeted by Muslims in Turkey. It is true that Jews were targeted by Christians in Germany. Chams were Muslims targeted by Khmers in Kampuchea. Hutus and Tutsis have the same religion, but Hutus never redefined Tutsis religiously. Just the reverse: the church was perceived as a refuge by the victims, but was frequently an ally of the *génocidaires*. Yet none of the regimes was religious, and none of them worried about the actual religious practices of those they murdered. All were aggressively secular. They were racist and territorial, ideologically utopian and deeply majoritarian. Indeed, they all represented numerical majorities and reflected what Arjun Appadurai calls the fear of small numbers: the majority group accused the minority group of planning mass murder and then responded by pursuing genocide itself. Each of these regimes, in fact, pretended to a democratic ethos and also used a lack of authentic citizenship on the part of the minority as the justification for genocide.

These genocides share a common method: target a minority, demonize it and its members by racializing them, accuse the members of the targeted group of introducing impurity into the dominant culture, accuse them of planning the extermination of the majority, exclude them from participation in the nation by abrogating their citizenship, remove them physically from the center of political life, kill them all.

What happens when genocide ends? Citizenship is part of the solution, just as it is part of the problem – at least for Rwandans and Jews. Rwanda and Israel are now both countries in which the diaspora has returned to

[23] Christopher R. Browning and Jürgen Matthäus, *The Origins of the Final Solution: The Evolution of Nazi Jewish Policy, September 1939-March 1942* (Lincoln, NE: University of Nebraska Press, 2007), 13.

participate in the life of the nation. The Tutsi émigrés to Uganda, the leaders of the RPF, are among the most important leaders of the country, just as in Israel the yishuv led the movement to create the state and welcomed Jews from all over the world to the new state beginning in 1948.

In Rwanda, the government has literally outlawed the legal racial identities which the Belgians created 80 years ago. It argues that tensions can only be eased by the self-conscious erasure of the distinction that animated the genocide to begin with. It is difficult to know whether this will work. Perhaps the official history of a people can be controlled, but individual memory cannot be. Each week, also under government sponsorship, in every Rwandan neighborhood and village, the *gacaca* meet and memories are resurrected. Some in the room are killers; some are victims. No one is a Tutsi or a Hutu. All are Rwandans. But Rwandans surely do remember who is Tutsi and who is Hutu, who is a survivor and who is a killer, who is a widow and who is an orphan, who walks the streets with machete scars and who does not. It remains to be seen whether this sort of self-conscious and structural attempt to form a new idea of citizenship can now override the idea of Rwandan society that people carry with them in their heads and hearts.[24]

In Germany and Austria, anti-Semitism and Holocaust denial are against the law but they are not gone. Jews are a smaller minority in Europe and in the world now than they were in 1933, which Appadurai argues puts them in even greater danger.[25] There are more protections against violations of Jewish citizenship in Europe, but there are no guarantees anywhere except in Israel, a country which has also forged an idea of citizenship that has been vexed from the moment of the state's creation. Israeli citizenship is conceptually a defense against genocide – after the fact. Indeed, the national definition of Israel is the guarantee of Jewish citizenship being inviolate *somewhere*, a guarantee no Jew had in modern history until 1948.

But the Israeli idea of citizenship also shares all the contradictions I have been trying to describe. Like every modern idea of citizenship, it contains its own negation and the potential to justify the abrogation of rights. Zionism *is* an ideology of citizenship. In its best version, like American citizenship, it is also a vision of a democracy and justice. In its worst version, also like the American idea, it can be the prop for hatred and oppression. Which it will be is not foreordained; it is a choice for the citizens of a democracy to make.

In the end, citizenship, whether in Rwanda and Israel or in Turkey and Cambodia or in the United States and Australia, depends on a complex

---

[24]The psychological dimension of the reconciliation process is discussed in Jobb Arnold, Chapter 19 (below).

[25]Arjun Appadurai, *Fear of Small Numbers: An Essay on the Geography of Anger* (Durham: Duke University Press, 2006).

interaction between popular sentiment and political leadership. Citizenship is a paradox, as I have tried to indicate. For good or for ill, it is the most essential component of modern constitutional democracy. Whether it will lead to liberty or to genocide is a question that lies finally in the hands of the very democracy it empowers.

Chapter 6
Incitement, Prevention and Media Rights

Mark Thompson

It is said that the first pogrom of Russian Jews in the twentieth century happened in Kishinev, now in Moldova, on Easter day, 1903. Fifty-one Jews were killed, 500 were wounded, and much Jewish property was destroyed.[1]

The background of the pogrom was a diffused anti-Semitic prejudice that was also reflected in Russian law. In the foreground was Kishinev's only daily newspaper, which happened to be published by an anti-Semitic entrepreneur who used his paper to express his views and opinions on the Jewish threat. He ran sensational allegations about Jewish "ritual murders" and generally encouraged fear and hatred towards the minority.[2] At the same time – and this is important – his newspaper encouraged Moldavian assimilation into the Russian state and Russian culture.

Before Easter in 1903, rumours circulated, apparently unchallenged, that the Czar himself wanted Christians to take strong action against the Jews and that attacks on the Jews, over the Easter period, would not be punished.[3] When the attacks began, the city authorities, police and army were all passive.

In several ways, the events in Kishinev presaged the incendiary role that media would play in twentieth-century genocides. The pattern of majority behaviour would also become familiar in later atrocities, as would the attitude taken by church leaders. The context of social and political anxiety

M. Thompson (✉)
Open Society Foundation, Media Program, W6 0LE London, UK
e-mail: markthompson1@onetel.com

[1] Herman Rosenthal and Max Rosenthal, "Kishinef (Kishinev)," JewishEncyclopedia.com, http://www.jewishencyclopedia.com/view.jsp?artid=247&letter=K&search=kishinef (Accessed June 9, 2009).

[2] Edward H. Judge, *Easter in Kishinev. Anatomy of a Pogrom* (New York: New York University Press, 1992), 30–31.

[3] Ibid., 137.

R. Provost, P. Akhavan (eds.), *Confronting Genocide*, Ius Gentium: Comparative Perspectives on Law and Justice 7, DOI 10.1007/978-90-481-9840-5_6,

over national identity has also been a standard feature of genocides, real and attempted.[4]

In another way, however, the Kishinev pogrom did not anticipate the genocides that followed; it was not instigated, as far as historians can judge, by the Russian government. In this respect it was a pre-modern massacre, categorically unlike the events that we have witnessed since 1948, meaning events in which the decisions of sovereign governments have been all-important both in organizing a genocide and in constructing the scaffold of propaganda which supports that decision and its implementation, usually by masking them.

The essential theorist of state propaganda *in extremis* is Joseph Goebbels, who was highly intelligent, keenly aware of media technology and its power, and wholly committed to making his work successful. "It is beside the point," Goebbels wrote, as early as 1928, "to say that your propaganda is too crude, too mean, or too unfair, for all this does not matter."[5]

A government that commits itself to genocidal politics, or politics that could become genocidal, is playing for the very highest stakes. If it fails, it dies. There is little if any room for compromise or negotiation. Such a government has put itself beyond reach of criticism of its methods. Hence *all that does not matter*, as Goebbels said, and it cannot be allowed to distract from the business in hand. Hence, too, he stated as an axiom that "news policy is a sovereign function of the state, which the state can never renounce. News policy is a cardinal political affair."[6]

It is easy to see why Goebbels takes this position and why he remains bound to believe, as he wrote elsewhere, that the principal purpose of news policy was "to instruct and direct public opinion, above all during wartime."[7] The value of these remarks lies in their clarity. The propagandists who collaborated in the perpetration of more recent genocides have known that they must not speak like this, that they should invoke, in however twisted a way, the media-related human rights which have been defined and enshrined since 1945. This does not mean that the purposes of more recent genocide-related propaganda are essentially different, simply that the propagandists have adapted to changing times.

Yet if I had to list the techniques that may typically be used by propaganda related to genocide and crimes against humanity, I would not put direct incitement at the top of the list, at least not hate speech as we think of it with Julius Streicher in Nazi Germany or Radio-Television Libre des Mille Collines (RTLM) in Rwanda. That sort of direct exhortation now looks

---

[4]The risks of majority rule and the characterization of genocidal acts as part of a process of nation-building are discussed in Douglas Greenberg, Chapter 5 (above).

[5]Roger Manvell and Heinrich Fraenkel, *Doctor Goebbels. His Life & Death* (London: Greenhill, 2008), 85.

[6]*Ibid*, 217.

[7]*Ibid*, 184.

anachronistic. Part of the fascination of RTLM, and part of the reason why it can be a misleading case for discussion, is that the incitement was so blatant. Effective hate speech techniques can be more oblique and insidious. Of course this will depend on the local media culture, but presumably, given the ever accelerating spread of new media technology, and the ever greater familiarity of peoples around the world with the customs, narratives and semiotics of globalized media communication, we should expect hate speech techniques, or genocide-related media communication, to become more, not less, sophisticated.

In other words, we may not see another open-and-shut case of genocidal incitement such as RTLM, and if we want to think preventively, we would be wise to expect more subtle techniques, such as were used in the former Yugoslavia, for the most part, in the 1990s. The war crimes tribunal in The Hague has issued no indictments against editors or journalists or professional propagandists, though various politicians have been indicted for "the dissemination of information" to engender hatred and fear of national groups.

Successive prosecutors in The Hague were right not to pursue the media, much as I would have personally liked to see certain journalists in the dock, because their activity fell below the accepted threshold of criminal incitement.[8] This is not to deny that the media in parts of the former Yugoslavia played a crucial part in the attack against Croatia, the genocidal war in Bosnia and the atrocities in Kosovo, abetting the so-called "joint criminal enterprise" that was led by Milosevic. They mobilized nationalist myths, created cults of military commanders, and demonised and denigrated other national groups, though very rarely with the extreme means that we saw guiding Nazi propaganda. They fostered a sense of beleaguered but heroic resistance to an unjust and bullying international community. They denied and ignored allegations of atrocities. They inculcated the necessity to trust the political leadership with the destiny of the nation at this crucial juncture. They mocked and discredited domestic critics of the regime. They spread a sort of chaff of wild rumours, gossip, astrology and red herrings, in order to distract the public from what was being done in its name. They gave space to a few independent voices in order to show the public and the wider world that the media were *not* controlled. They praised the patriotism and efficiency of whichever forces were perpetrating the crimes, or they simply denied the existence of those forces.

Perhaps above all, they helped to build a wall between the public and the battlefield. As seen on Serbian state television, which was the outlet in the region with the most influentially damaging output, war-torn Bosnia appeared as if seen the wrong way through a telescope. After the first 6 or 9 months of the war, the state television coverage of Bosnia was

[8]A discussion of what constitutes incitement is provided in Irwin Cotler, Chapter 9, Section 9.2 (below).

usually the opposite of incitement. It was more like a bromide, a desensitizer. Audiences in Serbia were lulled by panning shots of empty towns and wooded hills, and telephoto images of remote and apparently peaceful towns, while reporters chattered breathlessly about Serbs "fighting for freedom" against "mujahedin," "jihad warriors," "Islamic fundamentalists" and "Muslim extremists."[9] Overall, Serbian state TV "constructed a version of reality in which Serb forces never attacked Bosnia, never slaughtered scores of thousands of its people and displaced scores of thousands more, never besieged its cities and towns, and never laid waste its villages."[10]

This, then, was Serbian state TV from about 1989 to 1994–1995. What was the sum total of its effect? Eventually, it helped to produce a disoriented and exhausted public, deeply misled about the actions and intentions of its own government and armed forces, about neighbouring governments, and about the wider world. Did people become Milosevic's willing accomplices? I suppose they did, in so far as they decided to trust their leaders. Yet the public mood or mindset was not so much vengeful or vicious as it was *stoical*, driven by an appalling sense of necessity: the necessity, in short, that at this historic juncture, the Serbs must stand together and face down the multiple plots laid by Bosnian Muslims ("Turks"), Albanians, and the New World order.

On the topic of prevention, let me start by observing that the really striking thing about the international response to media abuse in Serbia in the nineties is that the alternatives proved to be so stark, so devoid of nuance. Despite early awareness of the problem – there was some criticism at the Conference on Security and Cooperation in Europe in 1992, admittedly not a forum that would make Belgrade tremble – nothing was done to try and limit the harm that was perpetrated by Serbian state television. It was not even deprived of its satellite frequencies until NATO bombed its headquarters in 1999, an operation that kept the screens dark for less than 24 hours and made the network more popular in Serbia than it had been in years.

The international repertory of preventive or suppressive means, available for use against this pillar of hate speech, was very narrow indeed. I wish to explore one reason why I think this was the case, not only in Serbia, but in other conflict and atrocity zones as well – Rwanda, most obviously. This reason, or line of explanation, may strike you as rather remote, for it leads us far from the scenes and sights of genocide. In fact, it leads back 150 years to an English philosopher named John Stuart Mill.

Before I sketch an argument that there is a blur or even a fallacy at the heart of liberal thinking about media freedom, and that this blur or

---

[9] Mark Thompson, *Forging War. The media in Serbia*, Croatia, *Bosnia and Herzegovina* (Luton and London: Article 19 & the University of Luton, 1999), 89.
[10] *Ibid*, 95–96.

fallacy has had unfortunate effects in the world's conflict zones, I will say a little more about the Rwandan radio station, RTLM, which played such a prominent part in preparing and organising the genocide in 1994. The key word in the name of that station was "*libre*." This was cunning, because it connected the station to the principle of free expression. In the months before the genocide, when Western diplomats asked Rwanda's President Habyarimana to stop RTLM's incendiary broadcasts, he replied that it was a private station, protected by the right to freedom of expression. This apparently silenced the diplomats.[11]

After the genocide began, US State Department officials agreed with non-governmental activists that the broadcasts had to be stopped. The Pentagon, however, opposed jamming RTLM, partly on the ground that this would not accord with international legal conventions. State Department lawyers then concurred "that jamming the hate broadcasts would violate international telecommunications law and international conventions protecting freedom of information and expression."[12] Although non-governmental pressure to act continued throughout the genocide, the US government would not budge. Clearly, this was a smokescreen for a political decision, already taken, not to intervene coercively in any way. In truth, no such legal protection was available for media outlets that incite hatred and violence, let alone genocide. For that matter, these specious scruples had not prevented the United States from jamming radio stations during the 1991 Gulf War, nor would they prevent it from doing the same in Haiti a few months later, in September 1994.

Among notorious abuses of media-related rights, the Western democracies' tolerance of RTLM on grounds of freedom of expression should rank alongside the Iranian *fatwa* against the novelist Salman Rushdie. Yet it is nothing like as infamous. Why so? Because, I would suggest, it was expressed in terms of freedom of expression.

According to our deepest assumptions about media-related rights, the best or even the only yardstick for measuring this freedom is the ability of the producers to disseminate as they wish. Media rights are interpreted as pertaining much more to the producer than to the receiver. To put the point slightly differently, it is assumed that the receiver's rights are fulfilled by *more production*. In part, this assumption reflects the fact that the right of a producer to produce a message can be upheld more easily than the right of a receiver to receive a message. The putative right of a receiver *not* to receive a certain message is harder still to uphold. Due

---

[11]Alison Des Forges, "Silencing the Voices of Hate in Rwanda," in *Forging Peace. Intervention, Human Rights and the Management of Media Space*, eds. Monroe Price and Mark Thompson, (Edinburgh: Edinburgh University Press, 2002), 242.

[12]*Ibid*, 248–249.

application of the harm principle, even in extreme cases, goes against the grain of this assumption.[13]

Yet there is more to our liberal assumption than sheer pragmatism. Our very conception of media freedom is founded on freedom of expression. This linkage can be traced back to Mill's great work, *On Liberty* (1859), where it is stated that, "Liberty of expressing and publishing opinions" is "practically inseparable" from "absolute freedom of opinion and sentiment."[14] Mill's equation has been built into the language of media-related rights, and what this has meant in practice is that liberties originally claimed for self-regarding speech, expressive speech, have been transferred to other-regarding speech, speech intended as communication to others. Consequently, "[f]reedom of the press is routinely viewed as a special case of freedom of expression."[15] This is surely mistaken, because freedom of the press means "freedom for other-directed institutional action" and as such, it "cannot be justified or derived from claims for individual freedom of expression."[16]

Historically, it is as if – having since 1948 established a principled basis for keeping media out of the grip of political power-holders, something that was an essential task in light of what happened before and during the Second World War – our civilization has been unable, or has not quite found the nerve, to take the next step in the *democratic* development of media-related rights, which would involve binding the media to standards derived from an ethics of communication, as distinct from an ethics of self-expression. Existing hate speech provisions, important as they are, are a poor compensation for the lack of such agreed upon standards.

What this all means is that media rights, as they are commonly understood and acted on, are inherently skewed in favour of the producer – as the party doing the expressing – *vis-à-vis* the receiver, or object of communication. In potentially genocidal situations, this imbalance is likely to benefit the wrong people. It made it easy for the international community to ignore Serbian state television in 1991 and 1992. And in Rwanda in early 1994, it made it hard to rebut those in Kigali and Washington, D.C. who argued that any attempt by the international community to suppress Radio Mille Collines would violate media freedom.

---

[13]The harm principle is addressed in Irwin Cotler, Chapter 9, Sections 9.1 and 9.2 (below).

[14]John Stuart Mill, *Utilitarianism. On Liberty. Essay on Bentham*, ed. Mary Warnock (Glasgow: Collins Fount, 1979), 183.

[15]Onara O'Neill, "Rethinking freedom of the press," transcript of an address given at the Royal Irish Academy, December 4, 2003, 4, www.ria.ie/reports/pdf/pressfreedom.pdf (Accessed June 10, 2009).

[16]I am indebted to the philosopher Onora O'Neill for this reading. As she says, "If we are to have democracy, the media must not only express views and opinions but must aim to communicate and to inform."

This line of explanation is the only one that I have yet encountered which makes sense of my experience working and living in the former Yugoslavia in the 1990s, the only one, too, that really explains the tenacious assumption, with which we are all familiar: that it is *necessarily* good for people to be exposed to repellent opinions and lies.[17] This is an assumption whose paradoxes may be enjoyed in secure democracies, but when assumptions are exported to the highly illiberal environments where genocides take place, they can do enormous harm. Lastly, this explanation makes sense of the bizarre confrontations that I witnessed in Bosnia and Kosovo, and which also took place in Rwanda, when media freedom organizations, Western NGOs, vigorously opposed measures against hate speech that were plainly in the interest of the local people who had to live with, and perhaps die on account of, the consequences of that hate speech.

It may seem wilful to argue that our conception of media rights should be rethought and rebalanced in an effort to prevent the most extreme and incendiary abuses of media, which very seldom occur, after all.[18] But that is not my argument. My contention is that all of us would benefit if the media today were accountable to an ethics of communication. This could lead to changes just as radical as the digital revolution that is transforming our societies.[19]

---

[17] Jeremy Waldron, "Boutique Faith," *London Review of Books*, July 20, 2006.

[18] What, you might ask, is the connection between the output of RTLM or Serbian state television in 1994, on one hand, and our daily diet of television or radio news?

[19] The peace-building potential of the media is examined in Mary Kimani, Chapter 20, Section 20.4 (below).

Part II
Un/Prevented Genocide

Chapter 7
Some Problems of Genocide Prevention

Yehuda Bauer

7.1 Naming Genocide

There has been a great deal of controversy in the relevant literature about the definition of genocide. There appears to be a general consensus that the 1948 Convention on the Prevention and Punishment of the Crime of Genocide (UNGC) provides an inadequate definition.[1] The endless debate over definition is also evidence that the reality is much more complicated than what our concepts can capture.[2] The debate over definitions is thus best avoided altogether, and we should satisfy ourselves by loosely saying, in the spirit of Raphael Lemkin,[3] who coined the term "genocide," that what we deal with is the attempted annihilation of groups as such, whether they are ethnic, national, religious, political, economic or other. This broad description embraces genocides as defined by the UNGC, politicide,[4] and

Y. Bauer (✉)
Avraham Harman Institute of Contemporary Jewry, Hebrew University,
91905 Mount Scopus, Jerusalem, Israel
e-mail: yehudabauer@hotmail.com

[1]Article 2 of the Convention states, "genocide means any of the following acts committed with intent to destroy, in whole or in part, a national, ethnical, racial or religious group, as such: (a) Killing members of the group; (b) Causing serious bodily or mental harm to members of the group; (c) Deliberately inflicting on the groups conditions of life calculated to bring about its physical destruction in whole or in part; (d) Imposing measures intended to prevent births within the group; (e) Forcibly transferring children of the group to another group." *Convention on the Prevention and Punishment of the Crime of Genocide*, Resolution 260 (III), UN General Assembly, 9 December 1948.

[2]The problematic exclusion of certain groups from protection in the Genocide Convention is discussed in Gérard Prunier, Chapter 3, Section 3.1 (above) and Francis M. Deng, Chapter 4, Section 4.2 (above).

[3]See Raphael Lemkin, *Axis Rule in Occupied Europe: Laws of Occupation, Analysis of Government, Proposals for Redress* (New York: Howard Fertig, 1973).

[4]Ted Gurr and Barbara Harff argue that "genocides and politicides are the promotion and execution of policies by a state or its agents which result in the deaths of a substantial

R. Provost, P. Akhavan (eds.), *Confronting Genocide*, Ius Gentium: Comparative Perspectives on Law and Justice 7, DOI 10.1007/978-90-481-9840-5_7,

global totalitarian ideologies that resort to mass violence in order to gain world control. While the boundaries between these and other forms of mass murder are fluid, insofar as these above categories of violence share a basic similarity, we will refer to them as genocidal events, or genocidal massacres (Helen Fein, Leo Kuper),[5] or mass atrocities (David Scheffer),[6] for the purposes of this paper.

I now go on to make a distinction between genocide and conflict. A conflict is a dispute between two or more social, economic, religious, or political entities, in which each such entity has enough power to challenge the other(s); while power may be unequally distributed between the contestants, each has enough of it to effectually counter attempts by the adversary to annihilate it. Today's conflicts in Sri Lanka and Kashmir, and those between the Israelis and the Palestinians, or between the Kosovars and the Serbs, may serve as examples. In contrast, genocidal events are characterized by a much more severe power imbalance; here, one side has near-absolute or absolute power, while the other side has little or none. The most extreme example from recent history is Hitler's annihilation of the Jews: the Jews in this instance were powerless, and the Germans – in relation to their victims – absolutely powerful.

Genocide can, however, sometimes occur in the context of a conflict, as it did in Rwanda. This is especially likely to happen when a conflict is marked by a severe imbalance of power, and even more importantly,

---

portion of a group." But they go on to differentiate between genocide and politicide in the following way: "In genocides, the victimized groups are defined primarily in terms of their communal characteristics, i.e. ethnicity, religion or nationality. In politicides, the victim groups are defined primarily in terms of their hierarchical position or political opposition to the regime and dominant groups." See Ted Robert Gurr and Barbara Harff, "Toward Empirical Theory of Genocides and Politicides: Identification and Measurement of Cases Since 1945," *International Studies Quarterly* 32, no. 3 (1988): 360.

[5]Helen Fein and Leo Kuper define "genocidal massacre" to describe acts of mass death in which the scale is relatively small, and the perpetrators do not intend to murder all the members of a group, but only a portion of them. See Helen Fein, "Defining Genocide as a Sociological Concept," *Current Sociology* 38, no. 8 (1990): 18–19; and Leo Kuper, *Genocide: Its Political Use in the Twentieth Century* (New Haven: Yale University Press, 1981): 60.

[6]David Scheffer, former US Ambassador at Large for War Crimes Issues, has argued that just as the term genocide will forever describe the Holocaust and what happened in Rwanda and Bosnia and Herzegovina during the last decade, we need a term that encompasses a wider range of mega-crimes. I propose that we begin by describing this cluster of heinous, barbaric acts, which include genocide as "atrocity crimes." See David Scheffer, "50th Anniversary of the Entering into Force of the Genocide Convention," (address to the United Nations, United Nations Headquarters, New York City, New York, June 13, 2001). See also David Scheffer, "Genocide and Atrocity Crimes" *Genocide Studies and Prevention* 1, no. 3 (2006); and "The Merits of Unifying Terms: 'Atrocity Crimes' and 'Atrocity Law'," *Genocide Studies and Prevention* 2, no. 1 (2007).

is not amenable to solution through compromise, negotiation, accommodation, or external intervention leading to these outcomes. The Israelis, for instance, have a powerful army, but they could not annihilate the Palestinians if they so desired, because the international community would weigh in against such a genocidal program. Nor could the Palestinians annihilate the Jewish state, and this is not just on account of Israel's greater military and economic power, but also of the international support Israel can muster.

External intervention in genocidal situations, however, becomes impossible when one or more of the five veto-wielding powers in the UN Security Council has what it considers major interests in the state in question. In the case of Darfur, for example, China's oil interests in Sudan outweighed all other considerations; the Chinese supported the Sudanese government even as the latter presided over the ethnic cleansing of Sudan's black population.[7] China's support arose from its need to secure oil, via the pipeline running from the oilfields of Southern Sudan to the Red Sea. This support, moreover, is likely to continue unless China finds its economic and political interests in the West threatened (its Western markets endangered, for instance), or a political coalition emerges, that creates political costs that outweigh the benefits of supporting Khartoum.[8]

7.2 Rationalizing Violence

Human beings often have contradictory instincts within them; a force for good and a force for evil may thus be at work within the same person. Thus, Oskar Schindler, member both of the Nazi Party and of the German Military Intelligence, a rapacious businessman, a drunkard, a cheat, a liar, an alcoholic, a womanizer – in short, a thoroughly "bad egg," rescued over a thousand Jews during the Holocaust. After the war though, Schindler could not explain why he had done this. Stories such as Schindler's show that we have contradictory possibilities within us, which is encouraging for those working to prevent genocide. For they may now see that part of their task consists in figuring out how to strengthen people's better instincts at the expense of their worst.

This task is, of course, complicated by the fact that the perpetrators of violence claim to abide by the same ethical principles as those who oppose them. They purport to defend the collectivity which they represent, protect

---

[7] Accounts of the situation in Darfur are provided in Gérard Prunier, Chapter 3, Sections 3.1 and 3.2 (above), Catherine Lu, Chapter 18, Sections 18.1 and 18.2 (below) and Luis Moreno-Ocampo, Chapter 16 (below).

[8] The possibility of exerting pressure by imposing economic sanctions is analyzed in Richard J. Goldstone, Chapter 11, Section 11.4 (below).

its rights, deliver social welfare to its recipients, and so on and so forth. They develop into perpetrators as their morality becomes exclusionary, but within their own group they use the same arguments and follow the same policies that their opponents advocate in the name of an inclusionary world. The Sudanese regime, for instance, is quite willing to fulfill its governmental duties so far as the Nilotic tribes are concerned, but is not so willing when it comes to the Southerners and the Darfurians.[9]

There are again instances where the genocidal instinct arises from, and is validated by, one's religious beliefs. Thus, those who kill others, and in the process, themselves, in the name of Islamic radical ideology do so in the subjective certainty that to kill the enemies of Islam, and to martyr oneself for the Islamic cause, is to gain eternal life. Such beliefs are not restricted to radical Muslims alone; Christians were promised eternal life in Paradise if they fought against infidels, too – which is why I included global genocidal ideologies in my description of what we are trying to prevent. The Nazis talked about eternal Aryan glory and Communists about the supreme sacrifice to be undertaken in the name of the proletariat, even though Paradise for them was, of course, a religious superstition. The invention of Paradise, and The Other Place, was thus driven not only by the human fear of death; it was also necessary in order to make people fight and kill each other.

We gain further insights into the moral universe of *génocidaires* if we consider the ways in which societies distinguish between murder and killing. Almost all societies have laws against murder, defined as a particular category of killing; they do not outlaw killing at large. The term "murder" applies to cases where members of the in-group are victims; where members of the out-group are annihilated, the term "killing" applies, making such annihilation permissible. The Ten Commandments, thus, contain a command not to murder, not a command not to kill. Islamic *shuhood* (martyrs), again, do not murder; they kill, with their opponents, of course, holding the opposite view. Whether it is the Nazis, or communist officials, or Pol Pot activists, or Hutu Power people, or the *Janjaweed* – it is the idea that there are gradations amongst humanity ("*lebensunwertes Leben*") and that members of the out group are less human, that drives and justifies the propensity to kill.[10] Some out groups, again, may be considered more human than others. For the Nazis, thus, the Poles were subhumans, whereas the Jews were not humans at all. There is also a tendency for *génocidaires* to resort to sanitation-centric metaphors that portray the out group as unclean (bacillae, cockroaches and rats), and therefore worthy

[9]The characterization of genocidal acts as part of a process of nation-building is discussed in Douglas Greenberg, Chapter 5 (above).

[10]The rationale for characterizing targeted individuals as an out-group is discussed in Douglas Greenberg, Chapter 5 (above).

of being cleaned out. The invocation of dirt and impurity helps the *génocidaires* exclude victims from their universe of moral obligation,[11] thereby enabling the act of genocide.

7.3 Prevention as a Multifaceted Endeavour

So far as our responsibility to avert genocidal massacres is concerned, it is important to differentiate between the following two aims: (1) preventing a genocide that has not yet happened; and (2) terminating or reducing to less murderous proportions a genocidal event that is already underway. Both goals are important, but require different strategies to be achieved. I first discuss the goal of prevention.

Two problems arise *vis-à-vis* the issue of prevention. The first is that the very unpredictability of human actions may play havoc with our assessment of risks, for despite the sophistication of our analytical and fact-gathering tools, we inevitably face, in any given situation, an infinite number of causal chains. This means that we cannot be certain that we have taken into account all possible factors capable of engendering genocide.[12] The second problem is one that is discussed more frequently, namely, once we have the information, and assuming it is more or less reliable, what do we do with it?

The disaster in Kenya serves as an example of the limits of our capability to predict. Kenya was not high on the list of sites where observers thought mass atrocities could possibly occur. But the failure with regard to Kenya is symptomatic of a larger failure, associated with the prediction that sub-national ethnic identities would die out, and identifications forged at the level of the nation-state would reign supreme. Those who made this prediction have been proved wrong. We live in a world in which the Scots and the Welsh, not to speak of the Basques, Corsicans, Kurds, Tamils, and Kosovar Albanians, are seeking to give their sub-state communal solidarities some form of political or cultural expression. In Africa and Asia, many independent countries are the artificial creations of the colonial powers of yesteryear, and their borders are oblivious to ethnic and cultural boundaries that had developed over hundreds of years. Academics tell us that ethnicities are "constructs." But ethnic identities have proved much less malleable than the constructivist school suggests; it is the persistence of ethnic solidarities that explains the failure of civic national consciousness to take root in many parts of the developing world. There is a real danger, therefore, that ethnic differences may at some point in time overwhelm

[11] See Helen Fein, *Accounting for Genocide: National Responses and Jewish Victimization during the Holocaust* (New York: The Free Press, 1979).

[12] Examples of prevention mechanisms are outlined in Francis M. Deng, Chapter 4, Section 4.5 (above).

political structures in Subsaharan Africa, in India, and so on and so forth. Being aware of this danger is important in that it will force us to think about how to face these realities.

Genocide prevention, I argue, has to be a multifaceted endeavor. We have to hone our analytical capacities, study closely the risk posed by ideologies and cultural backgrounds,[13] engage in reality rechecks of risk assessments[14] and both test and enhance the practical applicability of our theoretical frameworks.[15] We should, moreover, constantly correlate the insights gained from the above with global political analyses, for any effective preventive action must of necessity be "globalized."[16] This emphasis on globalized action also brings us face to face with the limits of prevention, for while we need to have the ear of the political actors in the concerned state, it is obvious that only politicians operating in democratic set-ups can be approached for help. There is no way that the Chinese and Russian leadership, for instance, can be persuaded or influenced by Western actors who care about preserving the lives of potential genocide victims. But even Western diplomats would not be willing to engage seriously with the issue of prevention, so long as there are genocides unfolding that need their present attention. Future dangers, in other words, would be low on their list of priorities. Further, moral considerations would often be trumped by the issue of national interest, leaving us with the question: how then does one influence the political world?

Academics are often more influential than they think. Most Western governments maintain think tanks to help them fashion policy; these institutions are staffed by people who have sound knowledge of the policy area in question. Then there is the world of NGOs, some of whom enjoy greater influence over, and access to decision-making bodies, than others. But NGOs frequently fight amongst themselves and consequently neutralize each other, each defending its own turf in a competition over scarce funds and political influence. Thus, common ground needs to be found between

---

[13]The role of ideologies and culture in triggering ethnic conflict, and consequently genocide, has been examined in Ted Robert Gurr and Barbara Harff, *Ethnic Conflict in World Politics* (Oxford: Westview, 1994).

[14]For the role of risk assessment in preventing genocide, see John L. Davies and Ted Robert Gurr, eds., *Preventive Measures: Building Risk Assessment and Crisis Early Warning Systems* (Lanham, MD: Rowman and Littefield, 1998); and Barbara Harff, "No Lessons Learned from the Holocaust? Assessing Risks of Genocide and Political Mass Murder since 1955," *American Political Science Review* 97, no.1 (2003).

[15]See Helen Fein, "Testing Theories Brutally: Armenia (1915), Bosnia (1992) and Rwanda (1994)" in *Studies in Comparative Genocide*, ed. Levon Chorbajian and George Shirinian (New York: St. Martin's Press, 1999); and Gregory Stanton, "The 8 Stages of Genocide," Genocide Watch: The International Campaign to End Genocide, 1998, http:///www.genocidewatch.org/8stages.htm.

[16]A characterization of the way in which prevention should take place is provided in Francis M. Deng, Chapter 4, Section 4.5 (above).

major NGOs dealing with humanitarian issues and mass atrocities, so as to create a united front linking the major democratic players on the international scene – North and South America, Europe, India, and a few other states.

Preventive efforts must moreover be realistic if they are to succeed. In the current context, this means that they must proceed on the basis of the understanding that the US is no longer the only superpower, and that its influence in Africa and elsewhere is not only limited, but slowly declining. Following the US engagement in Iraq, American military strength on the ground was, before the present Administration took over, more or less sapped. And the current budget deficits run into hundreds of billions a year. The US is still a superpower, no doubt, but it is one that is in increasing trouble, which suggests that genocide prevention measures cannot disproportionately rely on US engagement alone.

China's role in Darfur, again, draws attention to the importance of factoring in interests, and bringing sanctions into play, in genocide prevention.[17] China's is a fast-developing state capitalism, with the exploitation of labor within China resembling the conditions of early capitalism in England in the first half of the nineteenth century. The internal market in China is, in other words, limited because of the low purchasing power of the masses, so China must export, which makes it more vulnerable to external pressures in the longer run. The Darfur crisis has to be seen in this perspective. China has a vast amount of dollar assets, largely because of its lop-sided positive balance of trade with the US. Some observers tell us that Chinese interests own some 20 percent of the American national debt, which runs into trillions of dollars.[18] China must also establish access to sources of energy to fuel her growth, and is consequently investing in the oil sector in Africa. In Sudan specifically, the Chinese support the ideological-military junta of Omar al-Bashir, because it believes that this will guarantee it oil concessions in the South, on the border between the South and the North, and in Southern Darfur. China pays Khartoum not only in dollars, but also in arms, with Chinese money also being used by Khartoum to purchase more arms from Russia. Since China and Russia will not act against their perceived interests, it is up to the West to figure out what kind of action – diplomatic, economic, political – could be adopted to stall the genocide. Diplomatic pressure could be a first step; divestment could be another, possibly more powerful one; in this, political alliances with like-minded states are essential, as unilateral steps almost always end in failure.

[17] The use of a modified Oil-for-Food program as a way to exert pressure on the Sudanese government while allowing for China's economic interests to be taken into account is discussed in Richard J. Goldstone, Chapter 11, Section 11.4 (below).

[18] James Fallows, "The $1.4 Trillion Dollar Question," *The Atlantic*, January/February 2008, http://www.theatlantic.com/doc/200801/fallows-chinese-dollars.

We now consider the role of the UN. So long as the UNSC is structured as it presently is, the likelihood of determined, "robust" intervention is limited to areas and situations in which the major powers have no interests that are perceived by them as being vital. There is, therefore, a need to devise a strategy which, while trying to work through the UN, also attempts to use the platforms of regional and other organizations in parallel. The general idea is to look at reality dialectically, cast our net as wide as possible, but not leave out the local, national, and regional perspectives. Prevention of a genocidal situation in, let us say, Kosovo, will have to take into account the fact that, while the UNSC is the place where much of the argument will be presented by the contending parties, the UNSC itself will most probably not be able to unite on a policy supported by all the five veto-wielding powers. An analysis has to be made of who has interests there, and what they are. Ideally, NGOs should be persuaded to use their influence, hopefully in cooperation with each other, to press forth one particular plan of action. It would probably save some lives to maintain Kosovar independence; Serb opposition could then be channeled towards a compromise that will give Serbia some influence and some cultural presence there (contrary probably to the aspirations of the Kosovar Albanians), and of course, provide the Serb minority with full and equal rights. Persuasion alone may well not be sufficient; one would probably have to apply economic and political pressure through the EU in order to overcome Russian-Serb and Kosovar Albanian resistance to the plan. Such tools will have to be provided by applied academic research, or in other words, theory-driven practicality.[19]

It is not enough to issue declarations, exhortations and statements of good will. It was at the initiative of the International Crisis Group that the "Responsibility to Protect" (R2P) resolution was passed by the UN.[20] But can this resolution be translated into practice? Through the UNSC, and against the vetoes of some of the big powers? The danger is that the R2P resolution might serve as a sedative inhibiting the adoption of effective preventive measures.[21] To sum up, so long as there is no consensual international force to intervene in conflicts that turn genocidal – and the

[19]Barbara Harff, in a private communication within an informal group of scholars dealing with genocide prevention, which included Gregory H. Stanton, Helen Fein, Ted R. Gurr, and others.

[20]On 28 Apr 2006, the Security Council unanimously adopted Resolution 1674 on the Protection of Civilians in Armed Conflict, also known as the R2P Resolution. This resolution contains the first official Security Council reference to the responsibility to protect "populations from genocides, war crimes, ethnic cleansing and crimes against humanity," thus reaffirming the provisions of paragraphs 138 and 139 of the World Summit Outcome Document. See "References to RtoP in Security Council Open Debates on Protection of Civilians," Responsibility to Protect, http://www.responsibilitytoprotect.org/index.php/united_nations/794?theme=alt1.

[21]The concept of "responsibility to protect" is discussed in Francis M. Deng, Chapter 4 (above).

evolution of such a force may well take generations, if not longer – one has to work with what one has, namely, economic and political interests. The art of the possible then becomes an exercise in trying to play out such interests against each other in order to prevent human catastrophes.

We now come to the second of the two questions we started out with: how do we deal with genocides that are already under way? With regard to Darfur, Steven Spielberg's refusal to organize the Olympic ceremonies in Beijing in 2008 had quite an impact, at least for a limited period of time. Since the Chinese need the West, public pressure emanating from Western quarters does have some significance. The Olympics were thus rightly used as a platform for public expressions of concern about Chinese policies in Africa generally, and in Sudan in particular. But the failure of using the Olympics beyond that very limited achievement also shows the limits that such an approach will have. Diplomatic pressure can only be effective if Western states combine and present a united front. Some commentators have pointed to humanitarian military intervention as the solution to the Darfur crisis, and to others of the same kind. The R2P approach also talks of a military option to be exercised by the UN as the representative of the "international community."[22] This would, however, be possible only if there is a degree of agreement between the veto-wielding powers at the UNSC. China and Russia will certainly not agree to anything more robust than pious declarations *vis-à-vis* Sudan, and it is moreover not clear whether military protection of civilians would be possible in Darfur. However, if non-military pressure were to be applied by democratic and perhaps even semi-democratic regimes on a consensual basis, it might have the effect of protecting potential victims. In other words, in those situations where the great powers have little incentive to step into the breach, one needs to side-step the Security Council, and rather use the UN to recruit a sizable combination of states to decide on steps for which the Security Council's approval is not needed.

It is not certain that genocidal situations can either be prevented, or actual massacres stopped. But there is a chance, which makes it worthwhile to think of how to advance on this front. As a Jewish tradition puts it, one is not obliged to succeed; but one is obliged to try.

[22]The implementation of "responsibility to protect" principles for peacekeeping missions is illustrated in Wiebe Arts, Chapter 8, Section 8.2 (below).

Chapter 8
Preventing Genocide Through Military Intervention: Peacekeeping Troops in the "Responsibility to Protect" Era

Wiebe Arts

In March 1999, NATO's Operation Allied Force was launched in a bid to force the Serbian government to cease repression and intimidation in Kosovo. That intervention, without a clear mandate from the United Nations Security Council, violated the sovereignty of a country for the purpose of preventing a humanitarian catastrophe, perhaps even genocide. The international community had failed to take this type of action in the past when, in spite of the UN Convention on the Prevention and Punishment of the Crime of Genocide (1948), many millions of people were systematically murdered in the second half of the 20th century. The most infamous examples are Cambodia in 1975–1979 (1,700,000 dead),[1] Rwanda in 1994 (up to one million dead)[2] and Bosnia-Herzegovina in 1992–1995 (200,000 dead).[3]

The latter two cases are notable for the fact that a United Nations military force was present in the area at the time and that the genocide took place sometimes literally before their eyes. Too few military resources, too few troops, too restrictive a mandate, a lack of international support and a wide range of other reasons can explain why the perpetrators of genocide were allowed to proceed almost unchecked. These were highly shameful events, which led to a reappraisal of the appropriate response to flagrant violations of human rights. This in turn resulted in the 2001 report

W. Arts (✉)
Public Information Officer, Dutch Veterans Institute, Doorn, Netherlands
e-mail: W.S.Arts@veteraneninstituut.nl

[1]Cambodian Genocide Program, "The CGP, 1994–2008," Genocide Studies Program, Yale University, http://www.yale.edu/cgp/ (Accessed June 4, 2009).

[2]United Nations, "Discussion Topics," Lessons from Rwanda: The United Nations and the Prevention of Genocide, http://www.un.org/preventgenocide/rwanda/infokit.shtml (Accessed June 4, 2009).

[3]Genocide Intervention Network, "History of Genocide," Genocide Intervention Network, http://www.genocideintervention.net/educate/genocide#bosnia1 (Accessed June 4, 2009).

R. Provost, P. Akhavan (eds.), *Confronting Genocide*, Ius Gentium: Comparative Perspectives on Law and Justice 7, DOI 10.1007/978-90-481-9840-5_8,

entitled "The Responsibility to Protect," published by the International Commission on Intervention and State Sovereignty.[4,5]

The report states that the international duty to protect populations against serious harm takes precedence over the principle of non-intervention, which is a major shift in international policy. The protection is threefold: the responsibility to prevent, the responsibility to react and the responsibility to rebuild. The responsibility to react expressly includes the possibility, in extreme cases, of military intervention.[6] It is a logical step, following international sanctions and prosecution, but it is not one to be taken lightly. That is why the report names a number of just cause thresholds and explains how a resolution in support of intervention may be adopted.

I do not wish to go into detail here on the just cause thresholds and the criteria that military intervention must satisfy. I would, however, like to discuss how such intervention can best be carried out from the troops' perspective – after all, they have to put the resolution to protect into practice. I will first give a brief summary of the circumstances which restricted military personnel's opportunities to halt the atrocities in Rwanda and Bosnia-Herzegovina, in particular in the Muslim enclave of Srebrenica in which 8,000 Bosnian Muslim men were murdered by Bosnian Serbs in 1995. Next, within the context of the "Responsibility to Protect," I will list a number of ideas for preventing such restrictions from arising again in future.

8.1 Failures of UN Peacekeeping Forces

Whenever the international community, i.e. the United Nations, has decided to send troops to an area torn apart by civil war, it has been because of a crisis (or the threat of one) and a great desire to help. After all, it is no small step, following extensive political and diplomatic efforts, to reach the conclusion that a costly force is the last possible resort for re-establishing order. The process includes a resolution accepted by the leaders of the conflicting parties and passed by the Security Council. After any objections have been dealt with, countries that are willing to contribute still have to be found; in short, raising a UN peacekeeping force is a huge undertaking. In the case of Rwanda, Security Council Resolution 872, adopted on 5

---

[4]International Commission on Intervention and State Sovereignty (ICISS), *The Responsibility to Protect*, Report of the International Commission on Intervention and State Sovereignty. Ottawa: International Development Research Centre (2001).

[5]The concept of "responsibility to protect" is discussed in Francis M. Deng, Chapter 4 (above).

[6]Ibid, X.

October 1993, created the United Nations Assistance Mission for Rwanda (UNAMIR), whose main task was to contribute to security in the capital Kigali and to monitor the ceasefire and the security situation during the final phase of the transitional government, in the lead-up to elections.[7]

The United Nations Protection Force (UNPROFOR), in the first instance destined for deployment in Croatia, was established on 21 February 1992 by means of Security Council Resolution 743.[8] The spread of hostilities to neighbouring Bosnia-Herzegovina and the alarming security situation in the Eastern cities led the Security Council to proclaim on 16 April 1993 that the city of Srebrenica was a Safe Area. A Safe Area "should be free from any armed attack or any other hostile act."[9] In order to put this into effect, UNPROFOR's mandate was extended to allow military personnel on the spot to repel attacks on the area and to monitor the ceasefire.[10] Next, member states were asked to supply troops, to which the Netherlands responded with the deployment of an armoured air mobile infantry battalion, known as 1 UN (NL) Infantry Battalion or Dutchbat.

The situations in Rwanda and Srebrenica differed in many respects: the size of the area, the number of inhabitants, the number of combatants, the type of terrain, the mandate of the peacekeeping forces, their arms and equipment, their information position, etc. There was one major similarity, however; namely, that neither UNAMIR nor UNPROFOR's Dutchbat were able to prevent genocide. Viewed from that perspective, it is possible to name four circumstances which hindered military personnel's execution of their tasks in both Rwanda and Srebrenica.

1. The political and military situations which determined the appropriate composition and equipment of the peacekeeping forces and their ability to execute their task changed rapidly. As a result, at the crucial moment there were too few military personnel, they were in the wrong composition, and they had too little or inappropriate equipment. Commanders on the spot reported the shortcomings and sent requests and proposals for improvement, but these were complied with either too late or not at all. Canadian Major General Roméo Dallaire, commander of UNAMIR, states categorically in his book, *Shake Hands with the Devil*: "If UNAMIR had received the modest increase of troops and capabilities

[7]United Nations Security Council, Res. 872, 3288th meeting, October 5 1993, U.N. Doc. S/RES/872 (1993).

[8]United Nations Security Council, Res. 743, 47 UN SCOR at 42, 3055th meeting, February 2, 1992, U.N. Doc. S/RES/742 (1992).

[9]United Nations Security Council, Res. 819, 3199th meeting, April 16, 1993, U.N. Doc. S/RES/819 (1993), 2.

[10]United Nations Security Council, Res. 836, 3228th meeting, June 4, 1993, U.N. Doc. S/RES/836 (1993), 2–3.

we requested in the first week, could we have stopped the killings? Yes, absolutely."[11]

2. The conflicting parties did not adhere to agreements made on disarmament, the freedom of movement of the UN troops, the authority held by party representatives, borders, deadlines and other issues necessary to the success of a peacekeeping mission. When the conflicting parties unilaterally changed or simply ignored such agreements, the military personnel were confronted with *faits accomplis*, which they were largely powerless to alter, to say nothing of forcing an event. For example, the Dutch military personnel in the enclave of Srebrenica were fully dependent upon road supplies. On 18 April 1993, the Bosnian Serb Lieutenant General Mladić and the Bosnian Muslim General Halilović signed an agreement on the demilitarisation of Srebrenica. It provided, among other things, that "Neither side is to hinder freedom of movement."[12] However, the Bosnian Serbs systematically blocked the entrance to the enclave, which greatly weakened the situation of both the UN troops and the population.
3. Neither UNAMIR nor Dutchbat possessed standard opportunities and resources for gathering up-to-date intelligence. Neither did they receive sufficient information from their higher echelons. This lack of information had consequences for the commanders in the field: "in the spirit of openness and transparency, [they had] to be totally dependent on the goodwill of opposing sides to inform the mission command of problems and threats."[13] Thanks to its good contacts with the locals and its mobility, UNAMIR was in a better position to gather information, but not on a permanent basis. Dutchbat had neither the mobility nor the contacts with the locals, or only to a much lesser extent. "As little was received via other channels, Dutchbat's information position could be described as negligible,"[14] was the harsh conclusion drawn by the 2002 study conducted by the Netherlands Institute for War Documentation.
4. There is every justification for asking whether the peacekeeping troops in Rwanda and Srebrenica had sufficient training to be able to recognise and prevent or halt the genocide. The answer is "no," simply because no account was taken of this eventuality and no costly training days were

[11] Roméo Dallaire, *Shake Hands with the Devil* (Toronto: Vintage Canada Edition, 2003), 514.

[12] Lieutenant General Mladić and General Halilović, "Agreement for the Demilitarization of Srebrenica," article 7, signed agreement, Sarajevo, April 18, 1993, cited in Thom Karremans, *Srebrenica Who Cares* (Nieuwegein: Arko, 1998) 267.

[13] Dallaire, *Shake Hands with the Devil*, 90.

[14] Cees Wiebes, *Intelligence en de oorlog in Bosnië 1992–1995. De rol van de inlichtingen- en veiligheidsdiensten* (Intelligence and the War in Bosnia 1992–1995. The Role of the Intelligence and Security Services) (Amsterdam: LIT Verlag Berlin-Hamburg-Münster, 2002), 454.

devoted to it. It is true that UNAMIR in particular did its best when the situation took on genocidal proportions, but it was certainly not prepared for such an eventuality. Dutchbat, too, did what it could with its smaller resources but was unable to obtain an overall picture of events. Ultimately, it was the Dutch Minister for Development Cooperation at the time, Jan Pronk, who first uttered the word "genocide" out loud.[15] In the case of Rwanda, it was not the military personnel who drew that same conclusion, but the non-governmental organisation Oxfam.[16] Being able to recognise a genocidal situation in good time thanks to adequate training is a basic precondition for successful action by the international community and consequently also for the physical and moral support of military personnel.

Four similarities in the Rwanda and Srebrenica situations caused major obstacles for military personnel: a lack of resources to respond to changing situations; conflicting parties which proved to be unreliable; a lack of credible information; and insufficient knowledge to recognise genocide in good time. If military personnel wish to effectively prevent or halt genocide in future, these obstacles must not be allowed to recur. Can this be achieved by applying the "Responsibility to Protect" concept?

8.2 Applying "the Responsibility to Protect" Concept

8.2.1 Operational Principles

The "Responsibility to Protect" concept contains a number of principles which military intervention must respect. The six operational principles are:

1. Clear objectives; clear and unambiguous mandate at all times; and resources to match.
2. Common military approach among involved partners; unity of command; clear and unequivocal communications and chain of command.
3. Acceptance of limitations, incrementalism and gradualism in the application of force, the objective being protection of a population, not defeat of a state.

---

[15] Netherlands Institute for War Documentation, *Srebrenica, een "veilig" gebied. Reconstructie, achtergronden, gevolgen en analyses van de val van een Safe Area* III (Srebrenica, a "safe" area. Reconstruction, background information, consequences and analyses of the fall of a Safe Area III) (Amsterdam: Boom, 2002), 2839.

[16] Dallaire, *Shake Hands with the Devil*, 333.

4. Rules of engagement that fit the operational concept; are precise; reflect the principle of proportionality; and involve total adherence to international humanitarian law.
5. Acceptance that force protection cannot become the principal objective.
6. Maximum possible coordination with humanitarian organisations.[17]

These are excellent principles, which indicate clearly to the commanders what their responsibilities are and what they need to take into account. But are they sufficient to prevent the military personnel on the spot from encountering the above-mentioned obstacles?

8.2.2 Resources

The lack of resources is named in the first principle, but "resources to match" is a rather vague term. It allows the country or countries supplying the troops to opt for the minimum contribution. Cost considerations or excessive pressure on the armed forces may lie at the root of such a decision. The minimum contribution, however, allows little room for upgrading operations in the event that the situation changes. In their analyses, military advisors will always look at several scenarios, but it is ultimately the politicians who approve the composition of the military unit to be deployed. It is worth recommending that politicians look primarily at the assignment and then at the finances, just as military personnel do. If intervention fails due to a lack of resources, what started out as inexpensive becomes very costly indeed.

Another aspect of resources is the opportunity to actually deploy them. Figures about armoured vehicles, helicopters and field hospitals are meaningless if there are insufficient numbers of well-trained personnel to use them. This also applies to the *ad hoc* purchase of modern equipment: a lack of training and vision concerning its deployment will lead to it being a burden rather than an asset. Military personnel always need time to prepare for a mission, to become accustomed to their equipment and to form a close-knit team. Quickly cannibalising existing units in order to form a different type of unit is not always desirable; in fact, it demonstrates a lack of knowledge of the global security situation and also of modern military methods. If, in exceptional cases, this does appear to be the best option, it must be accepted that a long period is needed in order for the unit to achieve the required level of deployability. "Resources to match" must therefore comprise: (1) the correct numbers of personnel and corresponding equipment, (2) the correct equipment and (3) well-trained personnel. If one of

[17] ICISS, *The Responsibility to Protect*, XIII.

these three is sub-standard, then the sum of the parts can never reach one hundred percent.

For the sake of convenience, let us also consider accurate information as a resource. How and when should such information be obtained and what resources should be used to obtain it? A peacekeeping force actually needs a substantial amount of accurate information before departure. It must be remembered that this starts with training each UN soldier about the nature of the conflict: how it arose, what parties are involved, where they are located and how one distinguishes between them. One major advantage of this knowledge is that personnel can then set about gathering information in a focused manner. How else can a commander remain informed of developments? It is paramount that no member state ever hold back any information. For instance, due to historical ties with the country of deployment, it is possible that a country may receive information which is important to the peacekeeping operation. Withholding this information due to a misplaced sense of loyalty or political opportunism can only be described as criminal. Yet commanders must also be capable of gathering intelligence themselves. To this end, they must possess regular military intelligence gathering units, such as reconnaissance units or signals interceptors. These units gather the intelligence requested by the commander's intelligence cell. It may also be desirable to deploy additional intelligence personnel who can focus entirely on human intelligence.

The intelligence cell processes any information received into intelligence that the commander can use to take decisions and formulate new information requirements. This continuous and cyclical process must not take place in public. After all, as soon as the conflicting parties know what is known about them or their intentions, they may react by changing their plans (incidentally, there are cases in which it is desirable to demonstrate knowledge of their plans, but this aspect of psychological warfare is disregarded here). Confidentiality has the highest priority; openness and transparency are no longer applicable. This is reasonably easy to achieve within a military unit, but it is a different case altogether when intelligence is sent to international committees. In this case, it should be a rule that only a handful of members are privy to the intelligence, regardless of any political pressure.

8.2.3 Unreliable Parties

The operational principles do not explicitly state how to deal with conflicting parties who breach or ignore agreements. This may of course be due to the nature of intervention according to the "Responsibility to Protect" concept. An uncooperative or powerless state must simply accept intervention and the conflicting parties are then faced with a *fait accompli*, i.e.

intervention. Yet the peacekeeping force cannot completely avoid reaching agreements with the parties, for instance on disarmament, the exchange of prisoners, demilitarised zones and the removal of roadblocks. The breach of such agreements cannot and may not be accepted, but how can action against such breaches, instead of simple acceptance of them, be made the norm from an early stage? The fourth operational principle, regarding the Rules of Engagement (ROEs), offers some assistance on this.

The peacekeeping mission's objective, to protect the population, is central to the operational concept. Inclusion in the ROEs of what is meant by obstruction by third parties and how the peacekeeping force should respond, means that the military personnel on the spot are given a clear picture of how to act. It goes without saying that operations must offer a proportional response; negotiation and sanctions must precede any military intervention. In the case of acute operations, too, such as when civilians come under fire, the military force used must be effective and proportional. Clear-cut ROEs and the continual application of these during training can lead to untrustworthy party behaviour being neutralised. Moreover, this procedure offers the peacekeeping force the opportunity to maintain the initiative, one of the basic principles of military operations that also applies unreservedly to peacekeeping forces. Obviously, ROEs must be kept secret in order to prevent third parties from anticipating operations.

8.2.4 Training

You may have noticed that the term "training" is used a great deal in this article. This is no coincidence: military personnel are best deployable when they have been as well and as thoroughly trained to do their jobs as possible. Training takes time – in the Netherlands, officer training takes many years, while basic training for the other ranks lasts several months. Basic training is followed over time by specific job training, refresher courses, retraining, cyclical training and special training. The majority of training is aimed at military personnel functioning in traditional military roles; these are multifaceted military personnel, but they are not always the best option for deployment as peacekeeping personnel. Such operations require specific skills, which need to be learned and practised separately. What kind of skills are these and how can these be included in training?

To begin with, military personnel must know about the nature of peacekeeping missions, especially of missions intended to prevent or halt genocide. This means that they must be able to recognise the signs of (imminent) genocide[18] Military personnel must also learn how to cope with

[18]The importance of setting in place early warning mechanisms is highlighted in Francis M. Deng, Chapter 4, Section 4.5 (above).

groups of people who are fleeing from violence. They must learn to distinguish the perpetrators of genocide among the masses. They must learn to operate among large groups of people in built-up areas. They must develop diplomatic skills in order to be able to carry out negotiations. They must learn to conduct conversations via an interpreter. It is impossible to give an exhaustive list here, but military personnel need to learn – and in some cases forget – a huge number of things before they can function as peacekeeping troops. It is also clear that there are two sensible methods for achieving this, namely by receiving cyclical training throughout their military careers or one-off comprehensive training prior to deployment. My personal preference is for a third method: a combination of the two above-described methods, as agreed upon by all UN member states.

Basic knowledge of and skills for peacekeeping missions can best be learned by repetition. By basic knowledge and skills I mean, for instance, the theoretical knowledge of how the United Nations works, what a peacekeeping mission involves, what genocide is, negotiating and talking via an interpreter, what ROEs are and how to act in accordance with them. These elements can be taught in cycles lasting several months. The benefits of cyclical training include the power of repetition and the relatively small amount of costly time used. Specific knowledge and skills needed for a particular peacekeeping mission, on the other hand, is best taught during training prior to the mission. At this point the location and conditions are known, as are the mandate and the ROEs. The focus can then be on converting traditional skills into peacekeeping skills, and training can be given according to the mission composition and equipment. Incidentally, this conversion does not just apply to knowledge and skills: it must be remembered that procedures are an inherent part of each mission. Everyone, from the individual soldier right up to the force commander, must be trained in these procedures. For most military trainings, it is rather simple to plan the teaching of operational principles number 2 (common military approach among involved partners; unity of command; clear and unequivocal communications and chain of command), number 4 (acceptance of limitations, incrementalism and gradualism in the application of force, the objective being protection of a population, not defeat of a state), number 5 (acceptance that force protection cannot become the principal objective) and number 6 (maximum possible coordination with humanitarian organisations). It must be stressed that principle 5 is above all a matter of mentality, which should be propagated both from top to bottom and from bottom to top.

In order to enable peacekeeping missions to succeed, it is important for the Security Council to be able to rely on the quality and integrity of the troops. No trust can be placed in fine words alone: hard and fast guarantees of quality must be the norm. This is easier to achieve than might at first be thought. It is a simple enough task to draw up a list of the knowledge and skills which the future peacekeeping troops, classified according to rank, need to possess. The next step is to found a centrally-located UN school for training instructors from the member states. Following certification, they can return to their own countries to train an elite body of UN instructors, who will only receive their certification following testing by the UN school. They can then train and test the national armed forces in accordance with UN norms. The creation of a high-quality network of capable trainers will enable the deployment of high-quality peacekeeping forces to those regions where the need is greatest.

Finally, I would like to take a brief look at modern military personnel. The changed security situation following the fall of the Berlin Wall led to many countries reorganising their armed forces. Most Western countries no longer apply conscription and the place of conscripts has been taken by men and women who practise the military arts as a profession. Where we once had mixed regular and conscript armed forces, we now chiefly have units manned entirely by professionals. The reasons for becoming professional military personnel are various and highly individual. For some it is the job security, for others the excitement and for yet others the opportunity to study. Yet modern military personnel also feel the need to mean something to the world and to their fellow humans. They view the task of protecting people or even saving lives as an honourable one. This intrinsic need is often overlooked, but it is really too fundamental to be forgotten. Member states would do well to acknowledge and internalise this need. Governments should realise that it is not just honourable to protect or save people's lives, it is also a normal human need. Certification and clear quality standards will mean that peacekeeping troops will no longer feel as if they are not real military personnel; they will consider themselves one of the most important links in the chain protecting their fellow humans.

8.2.5 Media

One factor which has not yet been discussed is that of the media and its power. The differences in this regard between the situation in Rwanda and Srebrenica are so great that a useful comparison is impossible. In Srebrenica, no journalists were allowed in by the Bosnian Serbs. News about the region and the events which led up to the genocide hardly reached people's living rooms.[19] It was only a few days before the fall of the enclave and the subsequent genocide that the media started to display an interest. This lack of interest meant that it was easier for the perpetrators of the genocide to prepare for and ultimately commit the atrocities; global interest in the situation might have helped to prevent this. In Rwanda,

[19] The role of the media in Bosnia during the war is examined in Mark Thompson, Chapter 6 (above).

UNAMIR commander Dallaire fully comprehended the power of the media. In order to tell the world about the developing humanitarian catastrophe and what the international community needed to do, he struck a deal with BBC reporter Mark Doyle. "I called him into my office and made him an offer he could not refuse. He could live with us, be protected by us, be fed and sustained by us, and I would guarantee him a story a day and the means (my satellite phone) to get that story to the world. (...) The key was for him to become the voice of what was happening in Rwanda".[20]

That publicity can be a deterrent was experienced firsthand by Dutch Marine Corps Major General (Ret'd.) Patrick Cammaert. Until April 2007, Cammaert was commander of the United Nations Organization Mission in the Democratic Republic of the Congo (MONUC). With 15,000 UN troops at his disposal, he could not protect the entire region, which is two-and-a-half times the size of France. He therefore recommended the use of publicity; it helps if you can denounce the perpetrator and the act. "Leaders who are named in the papers alongside their acts do not like it. And it places pressure on the government to do something about them."[21] On the one hand, publicity can place pressure on (future) perpetrators, on the other it can spur the authorities into action. One aspect which should also not be forgotten is that publicity can also contribute to understanding what the peacekeeping troops have to do and the conditions in which they have to do it. This has a positive effect on society's appreciation of the UN forces, which in turn allows them to be proud of what they do.

Unfortunately, not all peacekeeping missions can expect to encounter journalists of the same calibre as Doyle. Moreover, one cannot expect journalists to remain in the region permanently. As soon as there are no longer any interesting items to report, they will turn their attention to other regions of the world. What you then get is "parachute journalism": someone is sent to the region only once there is something to report. A lack of journalists can easily be overcome, however. A peacekeeping force should take on competent freelancers from various media disciplines, give them basic military training and make them part of the peacekeeping mission. This enables journalists to enjoy protection and freedom of movement, and they can be deployed by the commander as and when he sees fit (obviously this requires close consultation). It is important that journalists are not hindered in gathering news stories, otherwise they will quickly suspect propaganda. The government of the country providing the troops needs to make deals with public media on the broadcast of reports and the publication of articles. This approach deviates from the current policy

---

[20]Dallaire, *Shake Hands with the Devil*, 332.

[21]Bas den Hond, "*Pers kan blauwhelmen helpen bij hun taak* (The media can help blue berets in their work)", *Trouw*, October 20, 2007, 12.

of "embedded journalism"; it is nearer to that employed by police forces, which send special camera teams to record riots and similar events. Military commanders ought to have so-called Combat Camera Teams at their disposal. It is understandable that the operational principles do not mention their association with the media. But the sixth principle (maximum possible coordination with humanitarian organisations), can accommodate this association: humanitarian organisations have a particular interest in gathering widespread attention on what is happening in the conflict area. If there is too little media attention, humanitarian organisations should insist on extra journalists under military protection.

8.3 Conclusion

Due to a lack of equipment and personnel, the impossibility of changing situations created by uncooperative parties, a lack of accurate information, and training that was not specific enough to deal properly with genocidal situations, the UNAMIR and UNPROFOR peacekeeping troops were unable to prevent genocide in Rwanda and Srebrenica. These obstacles were all the result of an underlying cause, namely that the concept of the classic peacekeeping mission in the post-Cold War era was no longer valid. In 2001, the "Responsibility to Protect" concept was published, a concept which offers the opportunity to actively intervene in countries in which populations are suffering harm as the result of a civil war, insurgency, oppression or a failing state. The concept includes military intervention, albeit as a last resort and under strict preconditions.[22]

Above I raised the question of whether the Responsibility to Protect operational principles were sufficient to preserve military personnel in the field from the same obstacles encountered by the UN peacekeepers in Rwanda and Srebrenica. These obstacles were lack of resources, unreliable parties, appropriate training and media attention. First, I concluded that the availability of resources to match the mission's objectives and mandate, as laid down in the first principle, consists of three aspects: (1) the correct numbers of personnel and corresponding equipment, (2) the correct equipment and (3) well-trained personnel. I emphasized the crucial requirement that peacekeepers have access to accurate information. Secondly, I concluded that Rules of Engagement fitting the operational concept (fourth principle) enable peacekeepers to deal more effectively with unreliable parties. Furthermore, I determined that four of the six Responsibility to Protect principles can be simply integrated into military training. Finally, I argued that although the operational principles do not

[22] An argument for having recourse to mercenaries in genocidal conflicts is presented in Krzystof Kotarski and Samuel Walker, Chapter 14, Sections 14.3 and 14.4 (below).

mention media attention, the sixth principle is broad enough to include this element especially in the presence of a request by humanitarian organisations.

The operational principles of the "Responsibility to Protect" concept offer many opportunities for preventing past mistakes. A sound starting point for achieving the potential of (relatively) rapidly deployable troops would be the foundation of a UN school. Well-trained, well-equipped UN forces, with a mandate that is up to the task and who are proud of what they do, must and can make a difference in future missions.

Chapter 9
Combating State-Sanctioned Incitement to Genocide: A Legal and Moral Imperative

Irwin Cotler

9.1 Introduction: Hate Speech and Freedom of Expression

The enduring lesson of the Holocaust and the genocides that followed, from Srebrenica to Rwanda, was that they occurred not only because of the machinery of death, but because of the state-sanctioned incitement to hate. It was this teaching of contempt, this demonizing of the other; this is where it all began.

The Supreme Court of Canada affirmed this insight when it quoted the words of the Special Committee on Hate Propaganda in its *Andrews* decision on the constitutionality of *Criminal Code* provisions targeting hate propaganda.[1] The Report of the Committee stated:

> I would have thought it sufficient to look back at the quintessence of evil manifested in the Third Reich and its hate propaganda to realize the destructive effects of the promotion of hatred. That dark history provides overwhelming evidence of the catastrophic results of expressions which promote hatred. The National Socialist Party was in the minority in the Weimar Republic when it attained power. The repetition of the loathsome messages of Nazi propaganda led in cruel and rapid succession from the breaking of the shop windows of Jewish merchants to the dispossession of the Jews from their property and their professions, to the establishment of concentration camps and gas chambers. The genocidal horrors of the Holocaust were made possible by the deliberate incitement of hatred against the Jewish and other minority peoples.
>
> It would be a mistake to assume that Canada today is necessarily immune to the effects of Nazi and other hate literature.[2]

I. Cotler (✉)
Parliamentary Office, Ottawa, ON K1A 0A6, Canada
e-mail: cotlei@parl.gc.ca

[1] *R. v. Andrews*, 3 S.C.R. 870 [1990], 881.

[2] Special Committee on Hate Propaganda in Canada, *Report of the Special Committee on Hate Propaganda in Canada*, Minister of Justice, Canada (Ottawa: Queen's Printer, 1966), 179–180.

R. Provost, P. Akhavan (eds.), *Confronting Genocide*, Ius Gentium: Comparative Perspectives on Law and Justice 7, DOI 10.1007/978-90-481-9840-5_9,

In brief, the Holocaust did not begin in the gas chambers; it began with words. These are the catastrophic effects of racism. These are the chilling facts of history.

The Court recognized the import of this lesson even for a constitutional democracy like Canada, itself characterized by a strong constitutional commitment to freedom of expression in the *Charter of Rights and Freedoms*.[3] Indeed, Canada's respect for freedom of expression has a distinct lineage identifiable well before the *Charter* was enacted, as compelling, pre-*Charter* precedents such as *Switzman v. Elbling* confirm.[4] For instance, in the 1957 *Switzman* case, the Supreme Court of Canada held the provincial *Act Respecting Communistic Propaganda* to be unconstitutional. In his concurring reasons, Rand J. wrote that "[l]iberty in [political expression] is little less vital to man's mind and spirit than breathing is to his physical existence."[5,6]

It was in this context of recognized free speech protections that the Supreme Court of Canada upheld the constitutionality of the federal government's legislated hate speech protections, both in the criminal and non-criminal spheres.[7] The *Keegstra*[8] trilogy (which also included the aforementioned *Andrews* decision and the *Taylor*[9] decision) affirmed that racist hate speech in general, and Holocaust-denying hate speech in particular, constituted an assault on the very values that constitute free speech;[10] an assault on the very values that underlie a free and democratic society, such as the inherent dignity and worth of the human person, and the equal dignity and worth of all persons;[11] an assault on the right of minorities, particularly vulnerable minorities, to protection against group-vilifying speech;[12] an assault on treaty obligations to exclude racist hate speech from the ambit of protected speech;[13] and an assault on the principle of equality.[14]

---

[3] *Constitution Act, 1982*, Part I, being Schedule B to the *Canada Act 1982* (U.K.), 1982, c. 11 [the "*Charter*" or the "*Charter of Rights and Freedoms*"].

[4] *Switzman v. Elbling*, S.C.R. 285 [1957].

[5] Ibid., 306.

[6] The recourse to "freedom of expression" arguments and the distinction between expressive speech and other-regarding speech are examined in Mark Thompson, Chapter 6 (above).

[7] The insufficiency of hate speech protections and the need to develop an ethics of communication are discussed in Mark Thompson, Chapter 6 (above).

[8] *R. v. Keegstra*, 3 S.C.R. 697 [1990].

[9] *Canada (Human rights commission) v. Taylor*, 3 S.C.R. 892 [1990].

[10] *Keegstra*, 762–765.

[11] Ibid., 746, 756 and 758.

[12] Ibid., 746–747, 756 and 758.

[13] Ibid., 754.

[14] Ibid., 755–758.

In the trilogy, the Court also spoke of a harms-based rationale for regulating hate speech.[15] This paradigm emphasizes the injury to the individual members of the target group, the injury to the target group as a whole, and the injury to multicultural society more broadly implied by hate propaganda. As Jackson J. of the United States Supreme Court noted, in a quote repeated by the Supreme Court of Canada,[16] "sinister abuses of our freedom of expression ... can tear apart a society, brutalize its dominant elements, and persecute, even to extermination, its minorities."[17]

As counsel for InterAmicus, a McGill-based international human rights advocacy centre, I appeared in the *Keegstra* trilogy before the Supreme Court of Canada to argue in favour of the Court upholding the anti-hate legislation. Just as the Court itself, through its later decision, would hold that the regulation of hate propaganda and the championing of freedom of expression are not mutually exclusive endeavours, I appeared as a strong exponent of free speech – one who had cited *Switzman v. Elbling* in previous cases – but who took the view that there is no such thing as absolute free speech. As the former Dean of Law at Yale Law School put it, freedom of expression "is not absolute, however much so many persist in talking as if it is."[18] In a word, racist hate speech gives free speech a bad name.

And yet, with the *Keegstra* trilogy affirmed in the annals of Supreme Court jurisprudence, there is something even more heinous and damaging to a society than hate speech. For even if one were to argue that, in a constitutional democracy, hate speech should be protected – even if one were to argue against the *Keegstra* trilogy and assert that the legislation at issue therein constitutes an impermissible regulation of hate speech in a constitutional democracy – there is a more sinister and assaultive form of speech that raises no such debate and that is state-sanctioned incitement to hatred. Indeed, there is a clear juridical appreciation that this type of speech is not only the vocalization of hatred *par excellence*, but that it is inherently criminal conduct, falling within the jurisdiction of the International Criminal Tribunal for the former Yugoslavia (ICTY), the International Criminal Tribunal for Rwanda (ICTR), and the International Criminal Court (ICC). It is this state-sanctioned genre of hate-mongering that took us down the road to genocide in the Holocaust, in the Balkans and in Rwanda.

[15]Ibid., 746–749 and 758.

[16]Ibid., 748.

[17]*Beauharnais v. Illinois*, 343 U.S. 250 (1952), 304 (Jackson J., dissenting).

[18]Abraham Goldstein, "Group Libel and Criminal Law: Walking on the Slippery Slope." (Paper presentation, International Legal Colloquium on Racial and Religious Hatred and Group Libel, Tel Aviv University, Israel, 1991) 3.

9.2 State-Sanctioned Incitement to Genocide in International Law

The legal basis for prohibiting and prosecuting incitement to genocide in international law is well-established. Direct and public incitement to genocide has formed the basis of criminal indictments at the ICTR, pursuant to Article 2(3)(c) and 6(1) of the ICTR Statute, and the tribunal's treatment of these cases is largely responsible for building the edifice of modern international legal jurisprudence on the subject.[19]

The ICTR's jurisprudence emphasizes the gravity with which the offence of incitement to genocide is to be treated, even if there is no evidence that the incitement in question led to any loss of life. The mere prospect of genocide, as intended by the inciter, suffices to confirm the dire nature of the crime: "[G]enocide clearly falls within the category of crimes so serious that direct and public incitement to commit such a crime must be punished as such, even where such incitement failed to produce the result expected by the perpetrator."[20]

The foundational trial decision in the *Akayesu* case[21] – the origin of the above quote – considered the charge of incitement to genocide alleged against Jean-Paul Akayesu, a commune bourgmestre (equivalent to a mayor) and former teacher in Rwanda. On April 19, 1994, Akayesu led a gathering of over 100 people assembled around the dead body of a young Hutu. He urged the population to unite in order to eliminate the Tutsi, which he referred to using a derogative term and calling them the sole enemy. Akayesu even read out a list of names of individuals, whom he identified as being accomplices of the Rwandan Patriotic Front (which defended the Tutsi).

In analyzing the crime of incitement to genocide, the Trial Chamber specifically noted the role that such speech plays in the genocide-fostering process:

> At the time the Convention on Genocide was adopted, the delegates agreed to expressly spell out direct and public incitement to commit genocide as a specific crime, in particular, *because of its critical role* in the planning of a genocide, with the delegate from the USSR stating in this regard that, "It was impossible that

[19]Note, however, that the concept of punishing those who engage in direct and public incitement to genocide pre-dates the ICTR significantly. See, e.g., *Julius Streicher Case*, Nuremberg Proceedings, Vol. 22 (September 30, 1946), 502.

[20]*Prosecutor v. Akayesu*, Case no. ICTR-96-4-T, Judgment (Trial Chamber) (2 September 1998), para. 562.

[21]The *Akayesu* trial judgment was affirmed on appeal, 1 June 2001. The Trial Chamber decision remains a cornerstone precedent in international incitement law: see, e.g., *Mugesera v. Canada (Minister of Citizenship and Immigration)*, 2 S.C.R. 100 [2005] paras. 84, 86 and 88; *Prosecutor v. Bikindi*, Case no. ICTR-01-72-T, Judgment (Trial Chambers) (December 2, 2008), para. 387.

hundreds of thousands of people should commit so many crimes unless they had been incited to do so and unless the crimes had been premeditated and carefully organized." [...][22]

The ICTR found Akayesu guilty of inciting to genocide and, in so doing, elaborated three important dimensions to the crime of incitement to genocide: the *mens rea* element, the "public" element, and the "directness" element. Hateful speech not satisfying these elements, though potentially heinous and inflammatory, is not considered illegal under international law.

The *mens rea* element of the crime immediately distinguishes it from protected speech. Indeed, the mental component of incitement to genocide alone suffices to ensure that legitimate expression will not be caught by the prohibition. The Trial Chamber explained that

> The *mens rea* required for the crime of direct and public incitement to commit genocide lies in the intent to directly prompt or provoke another to commit genocide. It implies a desire on the part of the perpetrator to create by his actions a particular state of mind necessary to commit such a crime in the minds of the person(s) he is so engaging. That is to say that *the person who is inciting to commit genocide must have himself the specific intent to commit genocide*, namely, to destroy, in whole or in part, a national, ethnic, racial or religious group, as such.[23]

The "public" element of the speech is deduced in large part from the forum in which the comments are aired. The Trial Chamber thus referred to a line of authority that interpreted "public" to refer to any comments spoken in a public place, as well as the International Law Commission characterization of "public incitement" as occurring where there is "a call for criminal action to a number of individuals in a public place or to members of the general public at large by such means as the mass media, for example, radio or television."[24]

Finally, the "directness" element is satisfied where the incitement "specifically provoke[s] another," as contrasted with "mere vague or indirect suggestion."[25] The Trial Chamber took care to emphasize that the incitement must be viewed "in the light of its cultural and linguistic content," and that it would determine this question by "focusing mainly on the issue of whether the persons for whom the message was intended immediately grasped the implication thereof."[26]

Later case law also stressed the need to understand the impugned comments in context in order to determine whether they constitute "incitement" or not. The ICTR has explained that context alone can define the line between hateful rhetoric and illegal incitement:

---

22 *Prosecutor v. Akayesu*, para. 551. Emphasis added.

23 Ibid., para. 560. Emphasis added.

24 Ibid., para. 556.

25 Ibid., para. 557.

26 Ibid., paras. 557–558.

> A statement of ethnic generalization provoking resentment against members of that ethnicity would have a heightened impact in the context of a genocidal environment. It would be more likely to lead to violence. At the same time the environment would be an indicator that incitement to violence was the intent of the statement.[27]

Accordingly, just as incitement contributes to the genocidal process, the existence of this larger process will inform the legal analysis of the incitement.

In the *Ruggiu* case,[28] context was analyzed for a slightly different purpose – not to understand its intended impact, but simply to understand its intended meaning. This inquiry was necessary because of the accused's use of euphemism. In rendering its decision after Georges Ruggiu pled guilty to incitement to genocide, the Trial Chamber explained not only how Ruggiu's phrases were spoken, but more importantly, how they were understood. Notably, the tribunal alluded to how the meaning of phrases could change over time:

> The accused acknowledges that the widespread use of the term "*Inyenzi*" conferred the de facto meaning of "persons to be killed." Within the context of the civil war in 1994, the term "*Inyenzi*" became synonymous with the term "*Tutsi*." The accused acknowledges that the word "*Inyenzi*," as used in a socio-political context, came to designate the Tutsis as "persons to be killed."
>
> [...]
>
> The accused admits that as part of the move to appeal for, or encourage, "civil defence," he made a public broadcast to the population on several occasions to "go to work." The phrase "go to work" is a literal translation of the Rwandan expression that Phocas Habimana, Manager of the RTLM, expressly instructed the accused to use during his broadcasts. With time, this expression came to clearly signify "go fight against members of the RPF and their accomplices." With the passage of time, the expression came to mean, "go kill the Tutsis and Hutu political opponents of the interim government."[29]

The principle that euphemism cannot exculpate a *génocidaire* was again affirmed through the Trial Chamber's reasoning in the *Media Case*, as it became known.[30] In this decision, the ICTR elaborated the analysis to pursue in determining whether hateful speech regarding race, ethnicity, and nationality, falls under the banner of legitimate expression or criminal advocacy. Professor Gregory Gordon has distilled from the tribunal's decision four specific elements useful in analyzing allegedly inciteful

---

[27] *Prosecutor v. Nahimana, Barayagwiza and Ngeze*, Case no. ICTR-99-62-T, Judgment and Sentence (December 3, 2003) [the "*Media Case*"], para. 1022. The Appeals Chamber affirmed the importance of context in evaluating incitement in its judgment in the same case on 28 November 2007, paras. 697, 701 and 703.

[28] *Prosecutor v. Ruggiu*, Case no. ICTR-97-21-I, Judgment and Sentence (June 1, 2000).

[29] Ibid., paras. 44(iii)–(iv).

[30] *Prosecutor v. Nahimana, Barayagwiza and Ngeze.*

content: purpose, text, context, and the relation of the speaker to the subject.[31,32]

With regard to purpose, the determining factor is whether the intent "in publicly transmitting the material was of a *bona fide* nature (e.g. historical research, the dissemination of news and information, the public accountability of government authorities)."[33] For instance, the tribunal reviewed case law to the effect that when an interviewer takes care to distance himself from the remarks of his interview subject, it operates as an indicator that the purpose in question was to disseminate news rather than to propagate racist views.[34]

With regard to text, the ICTR referred back to the *Faurisson* case,[35] a decision involving a Holocaust denier in which the United Nations Human Rights Committee considered the meaning of the term "incitement" at Article 20(2) of the *International Covenant on Civil and Political Rights*.[36] The ICTR noted how the Committee focused on the use of the term "magic gas chamber" in determining that Faurisson was motivated by anti-Semitism and not the pursuit of historical truth.[37]

Examination of context – the importance of which has already been discussed – involves analysis of how such language is used in the immediate as well as the historical context, operating to shed light on the words uttered. On this point, the tribunal referred to jurisprudence from the European Court of Human Rights emphasizing how a general statement about massacres needed to be understood in the context of the massacres taking place at that time. The ICTR quoted the European Court's statement that, understood as such, the speaker's words were "likely to exacerbate an already explosive situation..."[38]

Prof. Gordon's fourth factor – the relationship of the speaker to the subject – is based on the Trial Chamber's recognition that "special protections"

---

[31] See Gregory Gordon, "From Incitement to Indictment?: Prosecuting Iran's President for Advocating Israel's Destruction and Piecing Together Incitement Law's Emerging Analytical Framework," in *Journal of Criminal Law & Criminology* 98, No. 3 (March 2008): 874–878.

[32] The prevalence of subtle forms of incitement is addressed in Mark Thompson, Chapter 6 (above).

[33] *Prosecutor v. Nahimana, Barayagwiza and Ngeze*, para. 1001.

[34] Ibid. The case being referenced by the Trial Chamber is the *Jersild* case, decided by the European Court of Human Rights: *Jersild v. Denmark*, 19 Eur. Ct. H.R. 1 (1995).

[35] *Faurisson v. France*, CCPR/C/58/D/550/1993 (1996).

[36] United Nations General Assembly Resolution 2200A (XXI), *International Covenant on Civil and Political Rights*, 21 U.N. GAOR Supp. (No. 16) 52, U.N. Doc. A/6316 (1966), 999 U.N.T.S. 171, *entered into force* March 23, 1976.

[37] *Prosecutor v. Nahimana, Barayagwiza and Ngeze*, para. 1001.

[38] Ibid., para. 1004. The case being referenced by the Trial Chamber is the *Zana* case: *Zana v. Turkey*, ECHR, 1997-VII, no. 57.

have been developed in jurisprudence to take into account "the power dynamic inherent in the circumstances that make minority groups and political opposition vulnerable to the exercise of power by the majority or by the government."[39] While the Appeals Chamber appeared lukewarm to the formulation of a rule based on this principle as such,[40] it did ultimately agree with the Trial Chamber's overall analysis.[41]

Two final ICTR decisions on incitement to genocide are noteworthy in the context of the present review. The *Kambanda* case[42] implicated the leader of Rwanda's caretaker government during the genocide (Jean Kambanda) and stands as a testament to the principle that nobody, not even a head of State, is above the law against incitement to genocide. Indeed, Kambanda's conviction marked the first conviction in history of a head of State for this crime. Kambanda pled guilty to directly and publicly inciting genocide (among other crimes); the acts for which he was convicted on this charge included encouraging a radio station on-air to continue inciting violence and calling it an "indispensable weapon in the fight against the enemy," congratulating individuals who already killed victims, and speaking before different audiences encouraging massacre.

One judgment that is presently on appeal – the *Bikindi* decision[43] – marks a more recent application of incitement principles by the ICTR. Simon Bikindi was a popular singer in Rwanda and his charge of direct and public incitement to genocide was based both on his songs, which the prosecution argued in themselves satisfied the elements of the crime, and on two speeches he gave over a vehicle's loudspeaker while travelling. Applying the jurisprudential principles noted above, and on consideration of the evidence, the Trial Chamber determined that Bikindi's songs were not illegal incitement *per se*, but his two speeches were. Interestingly, the Trial Chamber elaborated how it was able to reach this conclusion despite Bikindi's positive personal relationships with Tutsi:

---

[39] *Prosecutor v. Nahimana, Barayagwiza and Ngeze*, para. 1008.

[40] "The Appeals Chamber has a certain difficulty with these paragraphs. It notes, on the one hand, that the relevant issue is not whether the author of the speech is from the majority ethnic group or supports the government's agenda (and by implication, whether it is necessary to apply a stricter standard), but rather whether the speech in question constitutes direct incitement to commit genocide. On the other hand, it recognises that the political or community affiliation of the author of a speech may be regarded as a contextual element which can assist in its interpretation:" *Prosecutor v. Nahimana, Barayagwiza and Ngeze*, para. 713.

[41] Ibid., para. 715.

[42] See *Prosecutor v. Kambanda*, Case no. ICTR 97-23-S, Judgment and Sentence (September 4, 1998).

[43] *Prosecutor v. Bikindi*, Case no. ICTR-01-72-T, Judgment (Trial Chambers) (December 2, 2008).

> In reaching its conclusion, the Chamber has considered the evidence that Bikindi's second wife was Tutsi, and that he lived and worked with Tutsi on good terms. It has also considered the evidence that Bikindi assisted some Tutsi during the genocide while in Nyundo and supported some Tutsi while in exile in Zaire. However, the Chamber is of the view that Bikindi's direct and public address on the Kivumu-Kayove road leaves no doubt as to his genocidal intent at the time. Bikindi could not have been unaware of the targeting of Tutsi throughout Rwanda, including Gisenyi préfecture, at the time, a targeting that he had encouraged in the past by exhorting people to kill Tutsi in 1993 in Kivumu. Likewise, he could not have been unaware of the impact that his words would have on the audience, the words of a well-known and popular artist, an authoritative figure for the *Interahamwe* and a man perceived as an influential member of the [National Revolutionary Movement for Development].[44]

The *Bikindi* case also raised explicitly a tension that underlies many judgments on incitement to genocide: the appropriate balance between freedom of expression and the criminalization of genocidal incitement. Recognizing the right to freedom of expression, the Trial Chamber explained:

> However, this right is not absolute. It is restricted by the very same conventions and international instruments that provide for it. For example, the [*Universal Declaration of Human Rights*] states that everyone should be free from incitement to discrimination. Similarly, the [*International Covenant on Civil and Political Rights*] prohibits war propaganda, as well as the advocacy of national, racial or religious hatred that constitutes incitement to discrimination, hostility, or violence, and the [*International Convention on the Elimination of All Forms of Racial Discrimination*] aims to outlaw all forms of expression that explicitly lead to discrimination. Each of the regional conventions mentioned above also restrict the freedom of expression: the [*European Convention on Human Rights*] recognises that there are "duties and responsibilities" that accompany the freedom of expression and thus limit its application; the [*American Convention on Human Rights*] allows for legal liability regarding acts that harm the rights or reputations of others, or that threaten the protection of national security, public order, or public health or morals and considers as offences punishable by law any propaganda for war and advocacy of national, racial or religious hatred that constitute incitements to lawless violence; and the [*African Charter on Human and People's Rights*] restricts the right to that which is "within the law." The Chamber notes that the restrictions on this right have been interpreted in the jurisprudence of the various adjudicating bodies created from the international and regional instruments above. The Chamber also notes that a large number of countries have banned the advocacy of discriminatory hate in their domestic legislation.[45]

In fact, among those countries banning the advocacy of discriminatory hate in their domestic legislation is Canada. As discussed, the Canadian laws on hate propaganda have passed scrutiny under the *Charter of Rights and Freedoms* by the Supreme Court of Canada.[46] And recently, the

---

[44] Ibid., para. 425.

[45] Ibid., para. 380.

[46] *R. v. Keegstra*; *R. v. Andrews*; and *Canada (Human rights commission) v. Taylor*.

Supreme Court had the opportunity to examine the offence of incitement to genocide directly.

In the watershed *Mugesera* decision (in which I was implicated in my former capacity as Minister of Justice and Attorney General of Canada),[47] the Supreme Court considered the validity of a deportation order issued against Léon Mugesera. Mugesera was a formerly active member of a hard-line Hutu political party who incited to murder, genocide and hatred in a speech to 1,000 people. After fleeing from Rwanda, Mugesera successfully applied for Canadian permanent residence. The Supreme Court upheld the deportation order that was issued against Mugesera when the government discovered his past incitement, holding that the content of Mugesera's speech rendered him inadmissible to Canada.

Basing itself substantially on international jurisprudence, the Court in *Mugesera* lent its support to the principles of incitement to genocide established by the ICTR, including the insight that it is not necessary to establish a causal link between the incitement and genocidal acts that followed (if any).[48] Indeed, confirmation of this point is crucial not only in the prosecution of past incidents of incitement to genocide, but equally in the prevention of future cases of genocide. The bottom line – echoed now in both Canadian and international legal jurisprudence – is that the world need not wait until genocide has occurred to take action against those who would perpetrate it. On the contrary, international law mandates immediate action.

Holding those who incite to genocide responsible for their crimes under international law, even before the genocides they preach have materialized, has the potential to be an effective juridical tool in combating genocide. This insight finds particular application in the case of contemporary Iran.

9.3 Iran: The Epicentre of Contemporary State-Sanctioned Incitement to Genocide

Despite the international consensus against incitement, and despite the precedents in domestic and international law confirming its heinous nature and criminality, incidents of incitement to hatred and incitement to genocide continue unabated. Nowhere is this phenomenon more evident than in Iran, where public, state-sanctioned incitement is not only pervasive, but is carried out with impunity.

We have been witnessing for some time this state-sanctioned incitement to genocide centred in President Mahmoud Ahmadinejad's Iran. In this

[47] *Mugesera v. Canada (Minister of Citizenship and Immigration)*, 2 S.C.R. 100 [2005].
[48] Ibid., paras. 84–85.

respect, it is important to distinguish Ahmadinejad's Iran from the peoples of Iran who are themselves increasingly the target of the Iranian regime's massive repression of human rights – a fact underscoring the principle that countries that violate the rights of their own citizens will surely violate those of other countries.

Today, in Ahmadinejad's Iran, one finds the toxic convergence of the advocacy of the most horrific of crimes, namely genocide, embedded in the most virulent of hatreds, namely anti-Semitism. It is dramatized by the parading in the streets of Teheran of a Shihab-3 missile draped in the words "Israel must be wiped off the map"[49] while the assembled thousands are exhorted to chants of "Death to Israel."[50]

Ahmadinejad's Iran is also increasingly resorting to incendiary and demonizing language, including epidemiological metaphors reminiscent of Nazi incitement. For example, President Ahmadinejad and other senior officials in the Iranian government characterize Israel as a "filthy germ,"[51] a "stain of disgrace"[52] and "a stinking corpse,"[53,54] while referring to Israelis as "the true manifestation of Satan"[55] and "blood-thirsty barbarians"[56] – the whole as prologue to, and justification for, a Mid-East genocide, while at the same time denying the Nazi one.

---

[49] See Benjamin Weinthal, "German official was at anti-Israel rally," *Jerusalem Post*, October 15, 2008, http://www.jpost.com/servlet/Satellite?pagename=JPost%2FJPArticle%2FShowFull&cid=1222017532585 (Accessed June 4, 2009).

[50] See, e.g., Middle East Media Research Institute, for video evidence of numerous "Death to Israel" chants, http://www.memritv.org/content/en/search.htm (Accessed June 4, 2009).

[51] President Mahmoud Ahmadinejad, (speech on February 20, 2008). See "UN Chief: Ahmadinejad's verbal attacks on Israel intolerable," *Ha'aretz*, February 21, 2008, http://www.haaretz.com/hasen/spages/956306.html (Accessed June 4, 2009).

[52] President Mahmoud Ahmadinejad, (speech, October 26, 2005). See Joshua Teitelbaum, "Analysis: Iran's talk of destroying Israel must not get lost in translation," *Jerusalem Post*, June 22, 2008, http://www.jpost.com/servlet/Satellite?pagename=JPost%2FJPArticle%2FShowFull&cid=1213794295236 (Accessed June 4, 2009).

[53] President Mahmoud Ahmadinejad, (speaking on the 60th anniversary of Israel's founding, May 8, 2008). See "Ahmadinejad calls Zionist regime a 'stinking corpse'," *Islamic Republic News Agency* (*IRNA*), May 8, 2008, http://newsgroups.derkeiler.com/pdf/Archive/Soc/soc.iranian/2008-07/msg00228.pdf.culture (Accessed June 4, 2009).

[54] The recourse to dehumanizing sanitary metaphors is examined in Yehuda Bauer, Chapter 7, Section 7.2 (above).

[55] President Mahmoud Ahmadinejad, (speech, March 1, 2007). See "Zionist regime offspring of Britain, nurtured by US – Ahmadinejad," *Islamic Republic News Agency* (*IRNA*), March 1, 2007. http://www2.irna.ir/en/news/view/menu-239/0703015352005938.htm (Accessed June 4, 2009).

[56] President Mahmoud Ahmadinejad, (speech, broadcast on the *Iranian News Channel* (*IRINN*), August 1, 2006).

Calls by the most senior figures in the Iranian leadership for the destruction of Israel are also frighteningly reminiscent of calls for the Rwandan extermination of Tutsis by the Hutu leadership. The crucial difference is that the Hutus were equipped with machetes, while Iran, in defiance of the world community, continues its pursuit of the most destructive of weaponry: nuclear arms.[57] Iran has already succeeded in developing and testing a long-range missile delivery system for that purpose, as former President Akbar Hashemi Rafsanjani explains that "the employment of even one atomic bomb inside Israel will wipe it off the face of the earth."[58]

In the face of this hateful and inciting context not only fostered but created by Ahmadinejad's Iran, the international community has responded with silence verging on active acquiescence. That President Ahmadinejad is invited to address the General Assembly of the United Nations, giving him an international stage to further spread his message of hatred, is a mockery of history, law, and the UN itself.[59] The precedents of the ICTR and the Supreme Court of Canada ought to be applied: an individual who incites to genocide, who pursues the most destructive of weaponry in violation of UN Security Council Resolutions, who is complicit in crimes against humanity through genocidal terrorist proxies, who warns Muslims who support Israel that they will "burn in the fire of the Islamic umma,"[60] who is engaged in a massive repression of human rights in Iran, and who assaults the basic tenet of the UN *Charter*, belongs in the dock of the accused, rather than the podium of the UN General Assembly.[61]

The failure to stop past genocides, as in the unspeakable, preventable genocide of Rwanda, caused the then-UN secretary general Kofi Annan to lament in 2004, on the 10th anniversary of the Rwandan genocide: "We must never forget our collective failure to protect at least 800,000 defenceless men, women and children who perished in Rwanda 10 years ago. Such crimes cannot be reversed. Such failures cannot be repaired.

---

[57] See, e.g., George Jahn, "IAEA info suggests Iran worked on nuclear missile," *Associated Press*, September 16, 2008. For UN Security Council Resolutions on Iran's nuclear program, see S/RES/1696 (2006); S/RES/1737 (2006); S/RES/1747 (2007); S/RES/1803 (2008); see also S/RES/1835 (2008).

[58] See Teitelbaum, "Analysis," 2008.

[59] President Mahmoud Ahmadinejad, (speech delivered at the United Nations General Assembly, September 23, 2008, trans. Presidency of the Islamic Republic of Iran News Service).

[60] President Mahmoud Ahmadinejad, (speech at the "World Without Zionism Conference," Tehran, October 27, 2005).

[61] See Petition, "Danger of a Genocidal and Nuclear Iran: The Responsibility to Prevent," (petition released by the author and signed by leading jurists, genocide experts and survivors). http://www.irwincotler.parl.gc.ca/documents/081209_petition.pdf (Accessed June 4, 2009) for evidence detailing these points.

The dead cannot be brought back to life. So what can we do?"[62,63] The answer is for the international community to pay heed to the precursors of genocide in Ahmadinejad's Iran, and to fulfill its responsibilities under international law, including the obligations to prevent genocide and to punish incitement to genocide, as announced in the Genocide Convention.[64] A comparative examination of *Mugesera* and the contemporary incitement in Ahmadinejad's Iran reveals that the aggregate of precursors of incitement in the Iranian case are even more threatening than were those in the Rwandan one.

9.4 Evidence of Iranian Incitement

In the matter of evidence, it is possible to distil seven precursors to genocide that reveal themselves in Ahmadinejad's Iran.[65] Though not exhaustive, the following sections substantiate the threat of genocide manifesting itself today.

9.4.1 Delegitimization

Genocide is a crime almost unfathomable in its cruelty and its scale. It is impossible to perpetrate against victims that appear, to the *génocidaires*, as *human*. As genocide scholar Helen Fein notes, potential victims must be seen in the minds of the *génocidaires* as beyond "the boundaries of the universe of obligation."[66] The first step is to classify the "other" – the targeted State and its people – as illegitimate and unworthy of that universe of obligation.

This delegitimating paradigm finds expression in the rhetoric treating Israel as a foreign and alien entity that has no rightful place in the Middle East. This exclusionary rhetoric finds expression in the words of Supreme Leader Ayatollah Ali Khamenei: "What are you? A forged government and a false nation. They gathered wicked people from all over the world and made something called the Israeli nation. Is that a nation? All the malevolent

---

62 Secretary-General Kofi Annan, (address to the Commission on Human Rights, 7 April 2004).

63 The establishment on this occasion of the Special Adviser for the Prevention of Genocide is discussed in Francis M. Deng, Chapter 4, Section 4.4 (above).

64 United Nations General Assembly Resolution 260 (III), *Convention on the Prevention and Punishment of the Crime of Genocide*, December 9, 1948.

65 Compare to, for e.g., Gregory Stanton, "The Eight Stages of Genocide," first Working Paper (GS 01), Yale Program in Genocide Studies, 1998, http://www.genocidewatch.org/8stages1996.htm (Accessed June 4, 2009).

66 Helen Fein, *Accounting for Genocide* (New York: Free Press, 1979), 33.

and evil Jews have gathered there... Those [Jews] who went to Israel were malevolent, evil, greedy thieves and murderers."[67]

9.4.2 Dehumanization

Against this context of the singling-out and delegitimization of the alien "other" Israel, the next genocidal precursor is the dehumanization of Israelis and Jews through the use of epidemiological metaphors reminiscent of Nazi-like dehumanization of the Jews. Indeed, in the genocide-fostering process, biological euphemisms are not just rhetorical tools; they seek to preclude the intended victims from even being considered human to begin with.[68] Thus, just as Jews were labelled as "vermin" by the Nazis and the Tutsi were labelled as "cockroaches" in Rwanda, so too have Israelis and Jews been dehumanized and labelled in Iran as:

(a) a "filthy germ" and "savage beast;"[69]
(b) a "cancerous tumour;"[70]
(c) a "stain of disgrace" on the "garment of the world of Islam;"[71]
(d) a "stinking corpse;"[72]
(e) a "cancerous bacterium;"[73]
(f) "like cattle – nay, more misguided;"[74]
(g) a "rotten, dried tree;"[75] and
(h) an "unclean regime."[76]

---

[67]Supreme Leader of Iran, Ayatollah Ali Khamenei, *Radio Iran*, July 20, 1994 (Foreign Broadcast Information Service Daily Reports [FBIS-DR]), quoted in Meir Litvak, "The Islamic Republic of Iran and the Holocaust: Anti-Semitism and Anti-Zionism," *The Journal of Israeli History* 25, no.1 (March 2006): 271.

[68]The impacts of a rhetoric of dehumanization are analyzed in Douglas Greenberg, Chapter 5 (above) and Yehuda Bauer, Chapter 7, Section 7.2 (above).

[69]President Mahmoud Ahmadinejad, (speech, February 20, 2008).

[70]Supreme Leader of Iran, Ayatollah Ali Khamenei, quoted in "Iran leader urges destruction of 'cancerous' Israel," *Reuters*, December 15, 2000, http://archives.cnn.com/2000/WORLD/meast/12/15/mideast.iran.reut/ (Accessed June 4, 2009).

[71]President Mahmoud Ahmadinejad, (speech, October 26, 2005).

[72]President Mahmoud Ahmadinejad, (speaking on the 60th anniversary of Israel's founding, May 8, 2008).

[73]General Mohammad-Ali Jaafari, Commander of the Islamic Revolutionary Guard Corps, letter, February 18, 2008. See Dudi Cohen, "Iran: Cancerous Israel to be destroyed by Hizbullah," *Ynetnews*, February 18, 2008, http://www.ynetnews.com/articles/0,7340,L-3508176,00.html (Accessed June 1, 2009).

[74]President Mahmoud Ahmadinejad,(speech, August 1, 2006).

[75]President Mahmoud Ahmadinejad, (speech, April 14, 2006). See "Iran: Israel Facing 'Annihilation,'" *Associated Press*, April 14, 2006.

[76]General Yahya Rahim Safavi, founder of the Islamic Revolutionary Guards Corps and advisor to Supreme Leader Ayatolla Ali Khamenei, (remarks made at memorial service

9.4.3 *Demonization*

Related to the dehumanization process is the demonizing process. Under this paradigm, the would-be victims of genocide are portrayed as inspirations of the devil. Dehumanization coupled with demonization accomplishes the dual purpose of making the would-be victim appear not only to be less than human (if not sub-human), but also to appear more threatening, thereby providing a warrant for genocide.

Indeed, demonization of Israel and Jews is frequent in Ahmadinejad's Iran. In this vein, President Ahmadinejad has stated that "Zionists are the true manifestation of Satan"[77] and that the "Zionist regime" is the "flag of Satan."[78]

9.4.4 *Holocaust Denial*

If these above precursors of genocide – delegitimization, dehumanization and demonization – act as prologue to and justification for a Mid-East genocide are not enough, President Ahmadinejad's vocabulary of hate also denies the Nazi genocide[79] while it incites to a new one. In fact, Holocaust denial is another particularly powerful tool in the quest to demonize Israel and the Jews.

9.4.5 *The False Accusation in the Mirror as Another Warrant for Genocide*

Holocaust denial in Iran, with its inherent conspiracy theory that Zionists used the Holocaust to usurp Muslim land in the Middle East,[80] fits neatly with the false paradigm of what genocide experts have called the "accusation in the mirror" principle. *Génocidaires* will invoke this strategy to convince the audience that if the diabolical and murderous "other" is not attacked, then the audience will fall victim to the "other" – thus "casting

for Imad Mughniyeh, February 23, 2008). See Joshua Teitelbaum, *What Iranian Leaders Really Say About Doing Away with Israel* (Jerusalem: Jerusalem Center for Public Affairs, 2008):14.

77 President Mahmoud Ahmadinejad, (speech, March 1, 2007).

78 President Mahmoud Ahmadinejad, (speech), quoted by the *Islamic Republic News Agency (IRNA)* in "Ahmadinejad: Israel is 'flag of Satan,' may face disintegration," *Reuters*, August 18, 2007. Available at: http://www.haaretz.com/hasen/spages/894744.html (Accessed June 1, 2009).

79 See, e.g., President Mahmoud Ahmadinejad, (speech, August 1, 2006).

80 Ibid.

aggression as self-defence." Indeed, this is a leitmotif used and abused by the Nazis and the *génocidaires* in the Balkans, Rwanda and Darfur.[81]

President Ahmadinejad has expressly called the "Zionist regime" a "permanent threat."[82] He stated: "This [Zionist regime] was established in order to swallow up the entire region."[83] He has also used demonic imagery and conspiracy theory to emphasize this threat: "They kill women and children, young and old. And, behind closed doors, they make plans for the advancement of their evil goals."[84]

The same hateful, inciting narrative was advanced by Yahya Raheem Safavi, Iranian Revolutionary Guards Commander: "There is a need to topple the phony Zionist regime, this cancerous growth [called] Israel, which was founded in order to plunder the Muslims' resources and wealth."[85]

9.4.6 *Satanic Jews as Enemies of Humanity*

Thus, when President Mahmoud Ahmadinejad calls Jews "bloodthirsty barbarians,"[86] he is not only demonizing and dehumanizing them, but he is also characterizing them as threats to the entire Muslim community. His comments that Israelis have "no boundaries, limits, or taboos when it comes to killing human beings,"[87] that Israel is "fighting a war against

[81]See Catherine MacKinnon, "International Decision: *Prosecutor v. Nahimana, Barayagwiza, & Ngeze*," in *American Journal of International Law* 98, No.2 (April, 2004): 325, 330. See also Gregory S. Gordon, "'A War of Media, Words, Newspapers and Radio Stations': The ICTR Media Trial Verdict and a New Chapter in the International Law of Hate Speech," in *Virginia Journal of International Law* 45 (2004): 186.

[82]President Mahmoud Ahmadinejad, (speech opening the "Support for the Palestinian Intifada" conference, April 14, 2006), quoted in "President Mahmoud Ahmadinejad in his Own Words: 2007," *Anti-Defamation League*, June 12, 2008, http://www.adl.org/main_International_Affairs/ahmadinejad_words.htm?Multi_page_sections=sHeading_4 (Accessed June 4, 2009).

[83]President Mahmoud Ahmadinejad, (trasnscript of a speech broadcast on *Jaam-e Jam 1 TV*, 20 October 2006), http://www.memritv.org/clip/en/1301.htm (Accessed June 4, 2009).

[84]President Mahmoud Ahmadinejad, *Khorasan Provincial TV*, August 6, 2006, quoted in "In His Own Words," *Anti-Defamation League*, August 6, 2006, http://www.adl.org/main_International_Affairs/ahmadinejad_words.htm?Multi_page_sections=sHeading_5 (Accessed June 4, 2009).

[85]Yahya Raheem, (speech before forces from the Revolutionary Guards and the Basij, Iran), *Fars* (Iranian news agency), July 30, 2006, quoted in "Iran and Syria Beat the Drums of War," *Middle East Media Research Institute*, Special Dispatch Series no. 1225, August 2, 2006. http://memri.org/bin/latestnews.cgi?ID=SD122506 (Accessed June 1, 2009).

[86]President Mahmoud Ahmadinejad, (speech, August 1, 2006).

[87]Ibid.

humanity,"[88] and that Zionism is the main cause of all corruption and wickedness in the contemporary era,[89] need to be understood in this context.

Ayatollah Hossein Nouri-Hamedani made this theme explicit by declaring: "One should fight the Jews and vanquish them so that the conditions for the advent of the Hidden Imam be met. [...] [A]t present the Jews' policies threaten us. One should explain in the clearest terms the danger the Jews pose to the [Iranian] people and to the Muslims."[90]

9.4.7 *Anti-Semitism as Prologue to and Justification for Genocide*

In addition to copying the genocidal plan that characterized the mass murders in Rwanda, the Balkans and Sudan, the current Iranian regime is also relying on one of the most long-standing and virulent hatreds: anti-Semitism. For all its sophistication and euphemism, the dehumanization and demonization of Jews and Israelis in contemporary Iran is no different than the anti-Semitic discourse that has reared its ugly head for thousands of years. This simple fact was made most explicit when President Ahmadinejad addressed the United Nations General Assembly in September 2008, using this opportunity to rile against a supposed Zionist conspiracy that was to be held responsible for the international financial crisis.[91]

9.4.8 *Iran Has Channelled this State-Sanctioned Hate into State-Sanctioned Incitement to Genocide*

Empowered by the culture of hate it has planted with impunity, Ahmadinejad's Iran has felt no need to leave its genocidal intentions as an unspoken conclusion. To the contrary, the calls for Israel's destruction by Iranian officials are explicit and without ambiguity. It is only when

---

88 Patrick Bishop and Sebastian Berger, "'Eliminate' Israel to solve the crisis, says Iranian president," *Daily Telegraph*, August 4, 2006.

89 President Mahmoud Ahmadinejad, "Ahmadinejad: Zionist regime to be dismantled soon," *Islamic Republic News Agency* (*IRNA*), August 20, 2008, http://www1.irna.ir/en/news/view/line-24/0808203080171319.htm (June 4, 2009).

90 Ayatollah Hossein Nouri-Hamedani, (speech on April 14, 2005. "Ayatollah Nouri-Hamedani: 'Fight the Jews and Vanquish Them so as to Hasten the Coming of the Hidden Imam," *MEMRI Special Dispatch Series*, no. 897, April 22, 2005). http://memri.org/bin/articles.cgi?Page=archives&Area=sd&ID=SP89705 (Accessed June 1, 2009).

91 President Mahmoud Ahmadinejad, (speech delivered at the United Nations General Assembly, September 25, 2008).

President Ahmadinejad reformulates his statements for a Western audience that any alleged dissonance arises.[92] Thus, President Ahmadinejad has publicly called for Israel to be "wiped off the map."[93] This repeated call for genocide has occurred many other times as well. To cite a few occasions:

> Israel's days are numbered... [T]he people of the region would not miss the narrowest opportunity to annihilate this false regime.[94]
>
> [T]he Zionist regime is heading toward annihilation.[95]
>
> We will witness [the] dismantling of the corrupt regime in [the] very near future.[96]
>
> The region and the world are prepared for great changes and for being cleansed of Satanic enemies.[97]
>
> God willing, in the near future we will witness the destruction of the corrupt occupier regime.[98]
>
> This [Zionist] regime is on the verge of death, and we advise you to start thinking about your long-term interest and long-term relations with the peoples of the region. At the end of the day, these are all ultimatums.[99]

---

[92]See, e.g., President Mahmoud Ahmadinejad, "'In Iran, freedom is absolute,'" interview, *Los Angeles Times*, September 23, 2008.

[93]Nazila Fathi, "Wipe Israel 'off the map' Iranian says," *International Herald Tribune*, October 27, 2005.

[94]President Mahmoud Ahmadinejad, (speech delivered in Gorgan, Northern Iran), quoted on *Press TV* and *Aftab*, May 14, 2008. See Y. Mansharof and A. Savyon, "Ahmadinejad: Israel Is a 'Dead Fish' and a 'Stinking Corpse'; 'The Zionist Regime Will Be Wiped Off'; 'The European Governments Do Not Want the Zionists Living in Europe,'" *Middle East Media Research Institute*, Inquiry and Analysis Series no. 447, June 6, 2008, http://memri.org/bin/articles.cgi?Page=countries&Area=iran&ID=IA44708 (Accessed June 4, 2009).

[95]President Mahmoud Ahmadinejad, (speech at the opening of a conference, April 14, 2006). See Iran: Israel Facing 'Annihilation'," *Associated Press*, April 14, 2006, http://www.cbsnews.com/stories/2006/04/14/world/main1499824.shtml (Accessed June 4, 2009).

[96]President Mahmoud Ahmadinejad, (speech at the "World Mosque Week" conference, August 20, 2008). See "Ahmadinejad: Zionist regime to be dismantled soon," *Islamic Republic News Agency* (*IRNA*), August 20, 2008.

[97]President Mahmoud Ahmadinejad, (speech at a military parade, April 17, 2008). See Alan Johnson, "Iran and Oran," *Progress Online*, http://www.progressonline.org.uk/columns/column.asp?c=120 (Accessed June 4, 2009).

[98]President Mahmoud Ahmadinejad, (speech to foreign guests marking the 18th anniversary of the death of Ayatollah Ruhollah Homeini, June 3, 2007). See "Ahmadinejad says destruction of Israel is close," *Associated Press*, June 3, 2007, http://chinadaily.com.cn/world/2007-06/03/content_886021.htm (Accessed June 4, 2009).

[99]President Mahmoud Ahmadinejad, (speech broadcast on *Jaam-e Jam 1 TV*, October 20, 2006), http://www.memritv.org/clip_transcript/en/1301.htm (Accessed June 4, 2009).

[T]oday, the occupier regime [Israel] – whose philosophy is based on threats, massacre and invasion – has reached its finishing line.[100]

[T]his fake regime [Israel] cannot logically continue to live.[101]

But it is not only President Ahmadinejad who calls for the annihilation of Israel. The Supreme Leader of Iran, Ayatollah Ali Khamenei, makes it clear that this is the basic premise upon which the State operates: "It is the mission of the Islamic Republic of Iran to erase Israel from the map of the region."[102]

9.5 Recourses Against Iranian Incitement

Such incitement should not be allowed to continue with impunity. Indeed, there is a moral and legal imperative to stop it. Among the many remedies available to the international community are the following:

- The criminal incitement to genocide by Ahmadinejad and other Iranian leaders should be referred to the appropriate UN agencies. For instance, such referral may be accomplished pursuant to the Secretary-General's authority under Article 99 of the *Charter of the United Nations* or by any state party to the Genocide Convention pursuant to its Article 8. It is astonishing that this criminal incitement has yet to be addressed by the UN Security Council, the UN General Assembly, or any other body of the UN, though it found fit to give Ahmadinejad a podium.
- The situation of genocidal incitement by Ahmadinejad and other Iranian leaders – including their complicity in crimes against humanity – should be referred by the UN Security Council to the Prosecutor

[100] President Mahmoud Ahmadinejad, (statement from July 23, 2006). See "Iran: Israel doomed to 'destruction'," *Jerusalem Post*, *Associated Press*, July 23, 2006, http://www.jpost.com/servlet/Satellite?cid=1153291976348&pagename=JPost%2FJPArticle%2FPrinter (Accessed June 4, 2009).

[101] President Mahmoud Ahmadinejad, (statement from April 24, 2006). See Angus McDowall, "Iranian President insists 'Israel cannot continue to live,'" *The Independent*, April 25, 2006, http://www.independent.co.uk/news/world/middle-east/iranian-president-insists-israel-cannot-continue-to-live-475496.html (Accessed June 4, 2009).

[102] Kasra Naji, *Ahmadinejad: The Secret History of Iran's Radical Leader* (Los Angeles: University of California Press, 2008), 144. This quote has also been translated as stating that "the perpetual subject of Iran is the elimination of Israel from the region:" See Teitelbaum, "Analysis," 2008.

of the International Criminal Court for investigation and prospective prosecution.[103]

- State parties to the Genocide Convention should initiate an inter-state complaint against Iran before the International Court of Justice for its "direct and public incitement to commit genocide" in violation of the Genocide Convention, to which Iran is also a state party.[104]
- Sanctions from the international community should be targeted not only against Iran's illegal nuclear program, but its illegal genocidal incitement as well. The nuclear program represents merely the means to carry out genocidal intentions; the international community ought to focus on the latter as well.

A group of prominent international jurists, genocide experts and survivors has already united to call attention to Iran's illegal genocidal incitement, and to call for action from state parties to the Genocide Convention, the United Nations, and the international community in general in response.[105] If genocide prevention is to have any meaning, the ubiquitous incitement to genocide of Ahmadinejad's Iran must not be allowed to continue with impunity.

[103] *Rome Statute of the International Criminal Court*, U.N. Doc. A/CONF.183/9, art. 13(b).

[104] *Convention on the Prevention and Punishment of the Crime of Genocide*, 1948, arts. 3(c) and 9.

[105] Petition, "The Responsibility to Prevent."

Chapter 10
Facing History: Denial and the Turkish National Security Concept

Taner Akçam

In September of 2005, Turkish intellectuals who questioned the Turkish state's policy of denial on the deportation and killings of Armenians during World War I gathered for a conference in Istanbul. Outside, in the streets, demonstrators also gathered in protest against the conference. One of the placards read: "Not Genocide, but Defense of the Fatherland." Two parallel convictions are at work here, one referring to the past and the other to the present. Both the genocidal events of 1915 and the denial policy nine decades later are framed in terms of Turkish self-defense.[1]

One may well ask why demands from inside and outside the country that Turkey come to terms with its past are so vehemently rejected. In Turkey today, any attempt to open a discussion of historic wrongs is denounced as a covert move in a master plan to partition the country. Why is facing history seen as a threat to Turkish national security?

Before answering this question, I have to add that this is not just the view of the political elite but also underpins legal decisions. In a recent judgment against journalists Arat Dink and Sarkis Seropyan, who each received a suspended sentence of a in prison for using the term "genocide," the Turkish court stated that: "Talk about genocide, both in Turkey and in other countries, unfavourably affects national security and the national interest. The claim of genocide...has become part of and the means of special plans aiming to change the geographic political boundaries of Turkey...and a campaign to demolish its physical and legal structure."[2] The ruling stated further that the Republic of Turkey is under "a hostile diplomatic siege

---

T. Akçam (✉)
Associate Professor, Department of History, Clark University, Worcester, MA 01610-1477, USA
e-mail: takcam@clarku.edu

[1]The characterization of genocidal events as acts of self-defense is discussed in Irwin Cotler, Chapter 9, Section 9.4 (above).

[2]Court Decree, 2nd Penal Court of First Instance for the District Of Şişli, File Number: 2006/1208, Decree Number: 2007/1106, Prosecution No.: 2006/8617.

R. Provost, P. Akhavan (eds.), *Confronting Genocide*, Ius Gentium: Comparative Perspectives on Law and Justice 7, DOI 10.1007/978-90-481-9840-5_10,

consisting of genocide resolutions...The acceptance of this claim may lead during future centuries to a questioning of the sovereignty rights of the Republic of Turkey over the lands on which it is claimed these events occurred." Due to these national security concerns, the court declared that the claim that genocide occurred in 1915 is not protected speech: "the use of these freedoms can be limited in accordance with aims such as the protection of national security, of public order, of public security."[3]

When one discusses Turkish history from a human rights perspective, most people in Turkey become very sensitive. This extraordinary self-defensiveness originates from the breakup of the Ottoman Empire into nation-states, a process that gave rise to divergent and mutually exclusive historical accounts. From late Ottoman times to the present, there has been a continuous tension between the state's concern for secure borders and society's need to come to terms with human rights abuses. To understand and resolve this tension, we need to examine the rise of two opposing historical narratives.

Until recently, the dominant narrative has been the story of the partition of the Ottoman Empire among the Great Powers, which ended with the Empire's total collapse and disintegration. The foundational works by Ottomanists and Turkish historians scarcely mention the Christian peoples of the Empire. Scant reference is made to Greeks, Armenians, Bulgarians, etc. as contributors to Ottoman social and political life, let alone as the victims of massacres and other gross violations of human rights. Instead, especially in Turkish historiography, Christian communities are painted as the seditious agents of the imperialist Great Powers, continually plotting against the state.[4]

The ethnic and religious minorities, for their part, center themselves within a narrative of persecutions, massacres and, especially in the case of the Armenians, wholesale annihilation by their Ottoman rulers. The overall theme of the history as told from the minority perspective is the community's maturation and national emergence, thanks in part to the intervention of the Great Powers.

In this light, Turkish reluctance to face national history, in particular its reluctance to acknowledge the Armenian Genocide, can be understood in part as stemming from the conflict of two, apparently contradictory, historical narratives. Whenever the proponents of genocide acknowledgment bring up the Turkish history of human rights abuses, they are confronted with an opposing narrative, that of the decline and breakup of the Ottoman Empire. Nevertheless, the evidence shows that these two narratives are not contradictory at all. They are two sides of the same coin,

---

[3]Ibid.

[4]The characterization of genocidal acts as part of a process of nation-building is discussed in Douglas Greenberg, Chapter 5 (above); the concept of deligimation is examined in Irwin Cotler, Chapter 9, Section 9.4.1 (above).

complementary perspectives on a single course of human events. Both must be sufficiently understood and appreciated in order to grasp the ambiguities and contradictions of Ottoman and Turkish history and their ramification today.

There have been certain moments in that history where national security and human rights became inseparably intertwined. One such moment came immediately after the First World War, between 1918 and 1923. While working out the terms of a peace settlement, the political decision makers were grappling with two distinct yet related issues, the answers to which determined their various relationships and alliances. The first was the territorial integrity of the Ottoman state. The second was the wartime atrocities committed by the ruling Union and Progress Party against Ottoman Armenian citizens.

The questions surrounding the first issue were: should the Ottoman state retain its independence? Should new states be permitted to arise on the territory of the Ottoman state? If so, how should the borders of these new states be defined? These questions led to the formation of two different viewpoints, where the Turkish nationalist movement, under the leadership of Mustafa Kemal, favored continued sovereignty within reduced borders as defined by the 1918 Moudros Ceasefire Treaty, while the Allied Powers and ethnic-religious groups such as Greeks, Armenians and, to some degree, the Kurds, argued for the establishment of new states on both occupied and unoccupied territory of the Ottoman Empire. The successive treaties of Sèvres and Lausanne reflected these divergent points of view.

In historical accounts, the immediate postwar period is generally portrayed as a time of territorial conflict among national groups. The general understanding in modern Turkey is that the Turks, who see themselves as the legitimate successors of the Ottoman Empire, defended their sole remaining territory against the Armenians, Greeks and some of the Kurds, who were trying to carve up Anatolia into nation-states with the help of the British, French and Italians. The 1920 Treaty of Sèvres resolved the question of territory in favor of the non-Turkish nationalities. For the Turks, therefore, Sèvres remains a black mark. For the other ethnic-religious groups, however, the significance of Sèvres is quite different. Although it did not fully reflect their demands for territory, the treaty represented an unprecedented historical opportunity to resolve the territorial issue in their favor. Conversely, the 1923 Treaty of Lausanne, which guaranteed Turkish dominance in Anatolia for the Turks, stands as a milestone and validation of the Turks continued national existence, while the other nationalities see it as a great historical injustice.

To portray the period between 1918 and 1923 solely in terms of territorial conflict does not, however, fully reflect the other major concern of the day: the wartime atrocities against Ottoman Christians, especially Armenian citizens, and the punishment of the perpetrators. Although everyone agreed that punishment was necessary, there was disagreement about its severity and scope. The victorious Entente powers took the position that "the Turks,"[5] so to speak, organized the massacres of other peoples, above all the Armenians, during the First World War. It was therefore necessary to punish "the Turks" collectively in order to rescue the subject peoples (Arabs, Greeks, Armenians, etc.) from Turkish domination.

Punishing "the Turks" was to be accomplished in two phases. First, the members of the Ottoman government and other officials were to be tried for crimes against the religious and ethnic communities. Second, "the Turks" were henceforth to inhabit a state that would be rendered as small and as weak as possible. A telegram sent to the Paris Peace Conference on April 3, 1919 by the Assistant High Commissioner at Istanbul, Webb, clearly illustrates this policy:

> In order to punish all of those persons who are guilty of the Armenian horrors, it is necessary to punish the Turks as a group. Therefore, I propose that the punishment be given on a national level through the partitioning up of the last Turkish Empire, and on a personal level by trying those high officials who are on the list in my possession, and in a manner that would serve as an example for their successors.[6]

In short, casting the net as widely as possible, the Allied powers advocated for the trials of individual suspects and for the punitive dismemberment of the Ottoman state into new states created on its territory. Thus, the main ostensible reason given for partitioning Anatolia among various national groups was the desire to punish "the Turks" for the atrocities they had committed. The dismemberment of the Ottoman Empire as a form of punishment against a state for the atrocities committed during the war years has led to the current situation in Turkey today, where every reference to human rights abuses in the past is perceived as a problem of national interest and as an issue of state security.

Recall that postwar Turkey was governed from two political centers. Istanbul was the seat of the Ottoman government, and Ankara served as the headquarters of the Turkish Nationalist movement, led by Mustafa Kemal. Both the Istanbul and Ankara governments acknowledged the massacres of Armenians and agreed with the Allies that the perpetrators should be tried, terming the trials "just and necessary." However, Ankara and Istanbul vehemently opposed the punitive partition of Anatolia.

The Ankara and Istanbul governments signed a protocol in October of 1919 calling for the election of an Ottoman Parliament according to the Constitution. Five protocols were signed. The first protocol declared: "1. Ittihadism (Party of Union and Progress) or any hint of its reawakening

---

[5]I place the term "Turks" within quotation marks. Although the term was used in the discussions of the time, it is clear that in explaining historical events general terms such as this are not only wrong to use, but also incorrect from the standpoint of attempting to write a history.

[6]Admiral Richard Webb, Assistant High Commissioner at Istanbul, telegram sent to the Paris Peace Conference April 3, 1919, FO 371/4173/53351, folios 192–193.

is politically very damaging... 4. It is judicially and politically necessary to punish those who committed crimes in connection with the deportation." In the third protocol both parties agreed that the fugitive members of "Ittihad" who were wanted in connection with atrocities, were not to participate in the elections, because, as they wrote, "it would be improper for individuals who are connected to the evil deeds of the Unionists, or persons who have been sullied by the nefarious acts of the deportation and massacre or other wicked actions that are contrary to the true interests of the nation" to participate in the national elections.[7]

The founder of Turkey, Mustafa Kemal, addressing the Parliament on April 24, 1920, called the atrocities a "shameful act." Now Mustafa Kemal was not a human rights activist or an altruist but a politician. What he believed was that the war crime trials were the price of national sovereignty. The punishment of perpetrators, he wrote, "should not stay only on paper...but should be carried out, since this would successfully impress the foreign elements." In exchange for this concession the Turkish leadership expected a more favorable peace settlement without the loss of territory.

The failure of this strategy was made clear by two events in April of 1920. First, the Sèvres provisions proposed to punish "the Turks" by partitioning the Ottoman territory. Second, the Istanbul Court Martial, which had been established in November 1918 to try the perpetrators of the Armenian atrocities, now, under Allied pressure, began trying almost the entire Turkish national leadership, Mustafa Kemal foremost among them, and sentenced them to death in absentia. When the Turkish nationalists realized that their support for the punishment of war criminals would not prevent the partition of Anatolia, their attitude changed.

As Mustafa Kemal wrote to Istanbul on August 20, 1920, "[t]he Ottoman Government... continues to hang the children of the homeland on accusations of [having perpetrated] deportation and massacres, which now became totally senseless."[8] Kemal meant that the policy whereby the Ottoman government punished Turks for what they had done to the Christian minorities would make sense only if Turkey received some positive result in return, such as a better treaty to secure the Ottoman territories. However, Sèvres had been signed, Ottoman sovereignty was not acknowledged, and Ottoman territories were distributed among different nations. Therefore, Kemal reasoned these "senseless" death sentences should be halted.

Today, the Court Martial in Istanbul remains a symbol of these two interwoven but distinct strands of Turkish history, "territory and borders" on the

---

[7] The impact of punishing individual perpetrators of genocidal acts on peace prospects is illustrated in Luis Moreno-Ocampo, Chapter 16 (below).

[8] Bilal Şimşir, *Malta Sürgünleri* (Ankara, 1985), 334. The letter was written to the first Grand Vizier of the Armistice period, Ahmet İzzet Paşa, with the aim of its contents being communicated to the British High Commission.

one side and "human rights" on the other. As national sovereignty concerns became paramount, "human rights" issues were consigned to oblivion. This is one major reason why, in modern Turkey, the human rights aspect of history, including the Armenian Genocide, has been suppressed and forgotten. Also for this reason, any questioning of the "official history" is perceived as a threat to national security. Had the Western forces agreed to territorial integrity in exchange for trials in cases of "crimes against humanity," Turkish history today might look very different.

Reintegrating human rights issues into Turkish history requires acknowledging three important new perspectives. First, Mustafa Kemal's condemnation of the Armenian massacres is diametrically opposed to the current official Turkish policy of denial. Kemal's position during the difficult war years could be a positive starting point for a resolution. To become a truly democratic member of the society of nations, Turkey must confront this "dark chapter" of its history, this "shameful act," as Mustafa Kemal called the Armenian genocide.[9]

Second, until now, the Turkish-Armenian problem has been perceived within the old paradigm which produced these conflicts, namely, the collapse of the Ottoman Empire and the clash of different ethnic or national groups over lands and boundaries. We have to change this understanding. We need to create a new paradigm and to rethink the Armenian-Turkish conflict. I suggest that we have to reposition the Armenian-Turkish conflict within the new paradigm of transitional justice, that is, as a part of the democratization effort within existing nation-states. The conflict should not be regarded as a territorial dispute, but rather as a human rights issue. Turkey and Armenia should deal with their pasts as part of their respective democratization processes and try to redefine themselves and their perception of the other's identity. This can be done only if we patiently disentangle the question of human rights from the question of territory or national security. The question of territory should be considered as resolved and should remain closed. The question of human rights remains unresolved and must be reopened.

Third, the concept of Turkish national security must be revised and changed. In the past, Armenians were considered as security threats and targeted for massacres and deportations. And so, for decades, any undiluted and positive approach towards facing Turkish history, any attempt to open a discussion of historic wrongs, has been treated as an attack on Turkey's national security. This is why Turkish authorities denounce intellectuals as traitors and prosecute them under the infamous Article 301.

Criminalizing historical inquiries for national security reasons is not only a major obstacle for democracy; ironically, enforcing this security

[9]Taner Akçam, *A Shameful Act: The Armenian Genocide and the Question of Turkish Responsibility* (New York: Metropolitan Books, 2006), 12.

concept could create a real security problem in itself. There is a clear parallel between the Armenian policy in the past and the Kurdish policy today. The same concept of national security underlines Turkey's denial of the 1915 genocide and Turkey's incapability of dealing with the current Kurdish question. Just as the Armenians were considered as a threat in the past, a democratic future for the Kurds today is considered threatening as well.

As long as Turkey continues considers facing up to its historic human rights abuses and protecting its national security as two opposing poles that are mutually exclusive – indeed, as long as Turkey's national security is defined in opposition to an honest historical reckoning–further problems will be created. Denying historical injustices delays democratization and destabilizes relationships in the volatile Middle East. For this reason, any regional security concept that excludes facing history is doomed to fail. Instead of denying the past, Turkish policy should re-integrate facing history into a policy of national interest.

Chapter 11
The Role of Economic Sanctions in Deterring Serious Human Rights Violations: South Africa, Iraq and Darfur

Richard J. Goldstone

11.1 Introduction

Economic sanctions have become increasingly prominent weapons in deterring serious human rights violations. Although arguably crafted in part as a response to communism, the use of sanctions has grown since the end of the Cold War. For example, in 1991, the United States imposed sanctions against Iraq after the first Gulf War. In 1996, the Organization of African Unity imposed economic sanctions against Burundi. And in 2002, the European Union and the US prohibited almost 100 Zimbabwe government officials from entering the EU and the US; these actions were followed by an asset freeze and an embargo on shipments of military supplies.

The role of sanctions must be considered in the context of the proscription at international law of the threat or use of military force save in self-defense or when authorized by the Security Council.[1] The partial or complete interruption of economic relations is one of the measures short of the use of force that is expressly mentioned in Article 41 of the *Charter of the United Nations*.[2] Although the use of sanctions stops short of the use of force, it can have serious consequences for the targeted nation or group.

R.J. Goldstone (✉)
International Bar Association's Human Rights Institute (IBAHRI), International Bar Association, W1T 1AT London, UK

The author wishes to thank Rachel Rebouche and Vanessa MacDonnell for their valuable comments in preparing this essay.

[1] *Charter of the United Nations*, Article 2(4) read with Article 51.

[2] *Charter of the United Nations*, Article 41: "The Security Council may decide what measures not involving the use of armed force are to be employed to give effect to its decisions, and it may call upon the Members of the United Nations to apply such measures. These may include complete or partial interruption of economic relations and of rail, sea, air, postal, telegraphic, radio, and other means of communication, and the severance of diplomatic relations."

R. Provost, P. Akhavan (eds.), *Confronting Genocide*, Ius Gentium: Comparative Perspectives on Law and Justice 7, DOI 10.1007/978-90-481-9840-5_11,

This article focuses on the effectiveness of the economic sanctions imposed on South Africa, Iraq and Sudan. In all three cases, sanctions were but one of many tools used to dismantle anti-democratic and violent regimes. I conclude that despite the potential pitfalls of economic sanctions, sanctions *can* play a role in deterring serious human rights violations. In particular, lessons learned from the Iraqi experience could be used to guide the implementation of a modified oil-for-food program in Sudan. To succeed, such a program would need to establish clear benchmarks and be accompanied by regular monitoring. The program would also require the support of a broad coalition of governments and civil society organizations.

Of course, the use of economic sanctions provides but one approach to addressing the humanitarian challenges posed by violent regimes. By adopting an innovative approach to sanctions, however, it is my view that humanitarian outcomes can be more readily achieved.

11.2 South Africa

I need hardly describe the racial oppression that black South Africans endured under the system of Apartheid. In 1973, a UN Convention declared Apartheid to be a crime against humanity, and universal jurisdiction was conferred on states that ratified the Convention to prosecute the crime of Apartheid.[3] Regrettably, the Western powers did not become parties to the Convention and its provisions were honored in the breach. As discussed below, by 1978 some Western nations did begin supporting international anti-Apartheid measures.

During the Cold War period, international opposition to Apartheid grew, and it was one of the very few issues upon which many Western leaders and leaders of the Soviet Union and China agreed. On November 6, 1962, the UN General Assembly condemned South Africa's Apartheid policies,[4] and on August 7, 1963, the Security Council called for a voluntary arms embargo against South Africa.[5] However, the ability to implement the embargo as well as more-widely advocated sanctions was stunted by the opposition of the US, the UK and France, the main trading partners of South Africa.

As the international community and various nations began to react against racial discrimination,[6] South Africa went inexorably in the opposite

---

[3]United Nations General Assembly, Res. 3068 (XXVIII), *International Convention on the Suppression and Punishment of the Crime of Apartheid*, adopted and opened for signature and ratification as of November 30, 1973. Entry into force July 18, 1976.

[4]United Nations General Assembly, Res. 1761 (XVII), U.N. Doc. A/1761 (November 6, 1962).

[5]Unites Nations Security Council, Res. 181, U.N. Doc. S/RES/181 (August 7, 1963).

[6]During the 1960s and 1970s, important international human rights covenants, such as the *International Convention on the Elimination of All Forms of Racial Discrimination*, 660 U.N.T.S. 195 (January 4, 1969), were drafted and gained ever-growing support.

direction.[7] In the wake of growing international awareness of civil rights and racial equality, the opposition to Apartheid grew and an international anti-Apartheid movement became more vocal. Many Western governments found it more difficult to ignore the calls for firmer action to bring Apartheid to an end. Eventually, in 1978, the Security Council imposed a mandatory arms embargo against South Africa.[8] There were some immediate consequences. France cancelled the sale of Aviso corvettes and Cuba cancelled the sale of Cuban Mig 23s. South Africa used all the means at its disposal to circumvent the embargo and in 1986 the Security Council passed another resolution in an attempt to tighten the loopholes.[9] The embargo was extended to spare parts and components of weapons and the definition of affected goods was expanded to include military and police vehicles and equipment.

Attempts to impose mandatory trade sanctions failed in the face of strong opposition from the governments of President Ronald Reagan[10] and Prime Minister Margaret Thatcher. However, growing numbers of large corporations in Western nations began to impose their own policies against South Africa with the result that they divested themselves of South African share holdings and withdrew their businesses from South Africa.[11]

For similar reasons, attempts to impose a Security Council mandatory oil embargo on South Africa failed. However, in 1973 the Arab States decided to impose such an embargo. The embargo was strengthened by the decision of Iran, in 1979, to sever diplomatic relations with South Africa. These were effective oil sanctions that South Africa was forced to evade at high financial cost.

The decision of the United States Supreme Court in *Brown v. Board of Education*, 347 U.S. 483 (1954), also reverberated around the world and encouraged anti-Apartheid campaigners.

[7] Racial discrimination and oppression of the black majority in South Africa that began in 1652 with the arrival of the Dutch at the Cape of Good Hope became significantly more egregious with the introduction of the system of Apartheid after 1948.

[8] United Nations Security Council, Res. 418, U.N. Doc. S/RES/418 (November 4, 1977).

[9] United Nations Security Council, Res. 591, U.N. Doc. S/RES/591 (November 28, 1986). Among other actions taken to circumvent sanctions, South Africa purchased large quantities of oil on the black market and developed a substantial home-based arms industry.

[10] In fact, President Reagan loaned South Africa $1.1 billion during the height of opposition to Apartheid by US civil society and members of Congress.

[11] For example, US civil society, lead by groups like TransAfrica and the Free South Africa Movement, succeeded in mobilizing popular opposition to Apartheid and applying pressure on businesses to abandon their ventures in South Africa. The so-called Sullivan Principles, designed by Reverend Leon Sullivan, resulted in a number of American corporations operating in South Africa changing their business practices by abolishing racial discrimination in their work force. The Sullivan Principles set out a number of rights for South African workers, such as better wages, training for workers, the right to join a union, and premised the decision to divest on whether or not a South African employer had implemented those rights.

In September 1986, the US Congress adopted sanctions legislation.[12] That same month, the legislation was vetoed by President Reagan[13] and California passed a law requiring the state to divest itself of $11 billion in South African related investments.[14] In October, Congress overwhelmingly overrode the Presidential veto and passed the *Comprehensive Anti-Apartheid Act*.[15] This legislation prohibited all loans to South Africa as well as the import of iron, steel, coal, uranium, textiles and agricultural products. Furthermore, it severed air links and prohibited United States banks from accepting South African government deposits. It authorized substantial sums in aid for disadvantaged South Africans.[16] Also in 1986, the European Community banned imports of iron, steel, and gold coins from South Africa, as well as new investments in South Africa.

In February 1987, the Security Council considered a mandatory embargo modeled on the US *Compulsory Anti-Apartheid Act*. This was vetoed by the US and the UK Germany also voted against the resolution. France and Japan abstained.

By the late 1980s, a growing number of corporations from other Western countries, including the UK, France, Germany and Scandinavia, were imposing sanctions against South Africa. The opposition by US and UK leaders, based on their countries' entrenched economic interests in South Africa, continued to stall progress in dismantling Apartheid. Sanctions imposed by the Commonwealth were always kept to a minimum because of the opposition to sanctions by the UK.[17]

---

[12]The work of the Black Political Caucus in the US was instrumental in putting the Apartheid issue before Congress. African American leaders saw the struggle against Apartheid as a part of the global struggle against racism.

[13]Ronald Reagan, "Message to the House of Representatives Returning Without Approval a Bill Concerning Apartheid in South Africa," *The Public Papers of President Ronald W. Reagan*, Ronald Reagan Presidential Library (September 26, 1986), http://www.reagan.utexas.edu/archives/speeches/1986/092686 h.htm (Accessed June 12, 2009).

[14]*New York Times*, September 27, 1986. Legislation signed by California Governor George Deukmejian.

[15]*Comprehensive Anti-Apartheid Act*, 22 U.S.C. § 5001 (1986) (repealed June 8, 1994, date on which President certified to Congress that interim government, elected on nonracial basis through free and fair elections, had taken office in South Africa).

[16]Moreover, civil society and some members of government worked together to draft the Sullivan Principles.

[17]However, as suggested before, even though UK government opposed sanctions, popular unrest in the UK and throughout the Commonwealth induced businesses and non-governmental actors to withdraw from the South African market. An example was shareholder pressure that forced Barclay's Bank to divest its considerable interests in South Africa.

The policy of the Conservative Party of Margaret Thatcher was at odds with the popular anti-Apartheid movement that organized mass demonstrations in London and other cities in the UK. Broad opposition to Apartheid was also growing in most of the member nations of the Commonwealth. In 1989, a Commonwealth summit ended with a resolution to maintain existing sanctions and threatening to impose additional sanctions if progress was not made in dismantling Apartheid within 6 months. However, Prime Minister Thatcher issued a statement critical of sanctions.

There were mixed feelings about the morality and efficacy of sanctions within South Africa. Because of repression and the proscription of black political parties during the latter Apartheid years, the view of the majority of black South Africans on sanctions was difficult to gauge. Some liberal leaders, the courageous anti-Apartheid politician, Helen Suzman, included, were vociferously against sanctions on the basis that they would result in further hardship for the victims of Apartheid and do little to bring the evil system to an end.

On the other hand, many of the most well-respected and popular black leaders strongly supported the imposition of sanctions. In this regard, Archbishop Desmond Tutu took the lead. In 1979 he told a Danish journalist that it was "rather disgraceful" that Denmark was buying South African coal: "Told that black workers would lose their jobs if coal exports were ended, Tutu said that the suffering would be temporary."[18] In 1986, he said that those "who opposed sanctions by arguing that they would hurt the people they were meant to help were hypocritical. Blacks were killed, mainly by the security forces almost as if they were flies: more than 1,200 since August 1984. He had hardly heard a word of protest from whites who claimed to be concerned about blacks' suffering....Recent polls showed that more than 70 percent of black South Africans supported sanctions of some sort."[19]

The role that economic sanctions played in the downfall of the Apartheid system is a matter of controversy. There can be no doubt that alone they would not have worked. But they were applied in combination with political events in South Africa, an almost total ban on international sporting ties, growing violent opposition, the increasing isolation of South Africa, and, not the least, the fall of the Soviet Union. When he announced the end of Apartheid and the end of white-minority rule, then-President F.W. de Klerk referred to the importance of the last-mentioned factor as one that, amongst others, made it possible to remove the ban on a key constituent of the African National Congress alliance, the South African Communist Party.

---

[18] John Allen, *Rabble Rousers for Peace: The Authorized Biography of Desmond Tutu* (Glencoe, IL: Free Press, 2006), 178.
[19] Ibid., 231.

South Africa is often cited as the best illustration of the success of economic sanctions in bringing about the end of racial oppression. That is an exaggeration. However, one should not minimize the substantial role that sanctions played in bringing home to the Apartheid leaders the fact that oppression of the majority of the people of South Africa was a failed policy that should be ended sooner rather than later.

11.3 Iraq

By the summer of 1990, war between Iraq and Iran had come to an end. Then, on August 2 of that year, Saddam Hussein's forces took control of Kuwait. The invasion was condemned by the global community and the Security Council responded with the harshest and most comprehensive economic sanctions ever applied by that body. Under Resolution 661,[20] the Council prohibited most forms of trade and financial transactions with Iraq. In February 1991, a UN force led by the US, liberated Kuwait. Iraq itself was not invaded and the Security Council renewed its economic sanctions in order to compel Iraq to disarm.[21] However, Saddam Hussein did not succumb and the effect of the sanctions was the steady decline of the Iraqi economy and the standard of living of its people. Iraq could not legally sell its oil, which had previously accounted for a substantial proportion of the country's gross domestic product.

Unlike the situation with regard to South Africa, the sanctions were not designed to assist the people of Iraq but rather to topple the government of Saddam Hussein. Their effect severely and negatively impacted the lives of millions of Iraqis. There were reports of the deaths of many hundreds of thousands of people as a result of the sanctions.[22] Supplies of food and medical equipment became chronically short. In 2000, the London School of Hygiene and Tropical Medicine reported that child mortality had risen alarmingly as a consequence of the sanctions.[23] Saddam Hussein relied on these reports and the publicity surrounding them to call for an end to the sanctions.

In the face of growing hostility to the sanctions, the Security Council embarked on the Oil-for-Food Program. According to the terms of the initial

---

[20] United Nations Security Council, Res. 661, U.N. Doc. S/RES/661 (August 6, 1990).

[21] United Nations Security Council, Res. 687, U.N. Doc. S/RES/687 (April 8, 1991).

[22] John Pilger, "Squeezed to Death," *The Guardian*, March 4, 2000. "When asked on US television if she [Madeline Albright, US Secretary of State] thought that the death of half a million Iraqi children [from sanctions in Iraq] was a price worth paying, Albright replied: "This is a very hard choice, but we think the price is worth it."

[23] Ali M. Shah, "Sanctions and Childhood Mortality in Iraq," *The Lancet* 355, No. 1851 (2000).

resolution,[24] Iraq was allowed to sell up to $1.6 million in oil on the world market for a period of 6 months, provided that it was prepared to have the proceeds from such sales deposited to a UN controlled escrow account and to be used solely for humanitarian needs.[25] The aim of the Program was to prevent Saddam Hussein from using oil revenues for military purchases. At the same time, it allowed the proceeds of the oil sales to be used for the purchase of medical equipment and supplies and other kinds of humanitarian goods.

The Oil-for-Food Program began to operate in October 1997. The amount of oil Iraq was permitted to sell was increased incrementally, and in December 1999 the Security Council lifted all limitations on the amount of oil Iraq could sell under the Program. Under the Program, over $64 billion was paid into the UN escrow account in New York, and a similar amount was spent on Iraqi purchases.

As is now well known, the Iraqi government manipulated the Oil-for-Food Program and it became tainted with gross criminality. Some $1.8 billion in kickbacks and bribes was paid to Saddam Hussein.[26] In addition, Saddam Hussein smuggled about $10 billion worth of oil through neighboring states.[27] There were also allegations of corruption against officials at the UN. One charge implicated the son of the UN Secretary-General, Kofi Annan. That led Annan to establish an independent inquiry into the allegations. I had the privilege of serving as one of the three members of the committee appointed to launch and control the investigation. It was chaired by Paul Volcker, the former head of the US Federal Reserve Bank.

The detailed findings of the inquiry are not germane to this article. Suffice it to say that the committee came to the conclusion that the Oil-for-Food Program did bring much-needed humanitarian assistance to the people of Iraq. The existence of large scale corruption at various levels, both inside and outside the UN, was also confirmed. We held that the allegations of impropriety on the part of the Secretary-General with regard to the unfortunate activities of his son had not been established.

One of the most important lessons from the imposition of economic sanctions on Iraq is that sanctions are considerably less effective when the regime being targeted is prepared to sacrifice the lives of its citizens rather than succumb to UN demands. The limitations of sanctions must therefore be acknowledged.

---

[24]United Nations Security Council, Res. 986, U.N. Doc. S/RES.986 (April 14, 1995).

[25]United Nations Security Council, Res. 706, U.N. Doc. S/RES/706 (August 15, 1991); United Nations Security Council, Res. 712, U.N. Doc. S/RES/712 (September 19, 1991).

[26]Independent Inquiry Committee, *The Management of the Oil-for Food Programme, Volume 2: Report of Investigation, Programme Background*, Independent Inquiry Committee into the United Nations Oil-for-Food Programme, September 7, 2005, http://www.iic-offp.org/documents/Sept05/Mgmt_V2.pdf (Accessed June 12, 2009).

[27]Ibid.

The second lesson is that the UN, at all levels, including the Security Council, failed to take adequate steps to prevent the corruption on the part of the Iraqi leadership and the general criminality that became so central a feature of the Oil-for-Food Program. From the outset, the Program lacked defined goals and leadership, which provided fertile ground for corruption and prevented the UN from reacting effectively when allegations of kick-backs surfaced.[28] In order for similar initiatives to be effective in the future, programs must be carefully designed to include greater accountability and more rigorous oversight.

The third lesson to be taken from the Oil-for-Program is more positive. Despite the corruption which infected the Program, it did ameliorate to some extent the plight of the Iraqi people. This suggests that the use of sanctions can be used to respond to humanitarian crises, provided that such sanctions are better managed and delivered than was the case in Iraq.

11.4 Sudan

For the past 5 years, the government of Sudan and its proxy military force, the *Janjaweed*, have been targeting civilians in the Darfur region of Sudan with the stated purpose of reducing the tensions between tribal communities in the region and the growing resistance to government rule.[29] According to a recent Reuters report, international experts estimate that 200,000 people have died and 2.5 million have been driven from their homes in 5 years of fighting in Darfur.[30] Despite much hand-wringing on the part of world leaders, the violence continues.

Unfortunately, violence on this scale is not new. Other comparatively recent examples include the genocide perpetrated in the former Yugoslavia in an effort to ethnically cleanse parts of Bosnia and Croatia of non-Serb citizens, and the genocide in Rwanda in the middle of 1994.[31] As in the other cases to which I have just referred, the most powerful members of

---

[28]Ibid., 60.

[29]Accounts of the situation in Darfur are provided in Gérard Prunier, Chapter 3, Sections 3.1 and 3.2 (above), Catherine Lu, Chapter 18, Sections 18.1 and 18.2 (below) and Luis Moreno-Ocampo, Chapter 16 (below).

[30]Reuters, "China urges Sudan to be 'cooperative' on Darfur," *Reuters*, February 24, 2008, http://www.alertnet.org/thenews/newsdesk/L24571773.htm (Accessed June 12, 2009).

[31]In terms of the effect of economic sanctions, one factor that distinguishes Sudan from both Iraq and South Africa is the state of Sudan's economy *before* sanctions were imposed. The end of British rule in the 1950s, followed by a series of civil wars between the Northern and Southern regions of Sudan and the prolonged famine of the 1970s, created the political vacuum in which authoritarian regimes foster, and has left the region very much impoverished. With scarce resources available only to the elite, there was an even greater worry that sanctions could damage an already frail economic system.

the UN have not mustered the political will to stop the killings, rapes, and persecution of the people of Darfur.[32]

Attempts by the Western permanent members of the Security Council to take meaningful punitive steps against the government of Sudan have largely failed in the face of opposition from China.[33] In 2005, China's direct investment in Sudan exceeded $300 million. In 1997, the China National Petroleum Company (CNPC) purchased ownership of 40 percent of the consortium that dominates oil production in Sudan, Great Nile Petroleum and Oil Company (GNPC).[34] That consortium succeeded in transforming Sudan from a nation dependent on foreign energy suppliers into an oil exporter. GNPC's assets in Sudan now amount to $7 billion. Eight percent of China's oil needs are supplied by Sudan. This accounts for between 60 and 85 percent of Sudan's 500,000 barrel daily production. Moreover, China purchases 71 percent of Sudan's foreign exports. The Sudanese government is reported to funnel a large percentage of its oil revenues into the purchase of arms, and the main supplier of those arms is China. As with the US government's resistance to sanctions imposed on South Africa, China is also reluctant to disentangle its economic interests due to the human rights concerns of the international community.

In September 2004, the Secretary-General of the UN, acting under a Chapter VII resolution of the Security Council, established an international commission of inquiry on the situation in Darfur.[35] He appointed Antonio Cassese, the first President of the Yugoslavia Tribunal, to chair the Commission of Inquiry. In January 2005, the Commission reported that, in its view, the government of Sudan had not pursued a policy of genocide.[36] It reported that the policy of attacking, killing and forcibly displacing members of some tribes did not evince a specific intent to annihilate, in whole or in part, any group.[37] The intent appeared to be directed at driving the victims from their homes as a means of controlling rebel communities. At

---

[32] International inaction in the Darfur situation is addressed in Gérard Prunier, Chapter 3, Section 3.2 (above).

[33] An argument for the need to take into account national interests in genocide prevention, in particular China's oil interests in Sudan, is presented in Yehuda Bauer, Chapter 7, Sections 7.1 and 7.3 (above).

[34] See Russell McAleavey, "Pressuring Sudan: The Prospect of an Oil-for-Food Program for Darfur," in *Fordham International Law Journal* 31, no.4 (2008): 1058–1088. In the following paragraphs I have drawn on the information contained in the McAleavey article.

[35] United Nations Security Council, Res. 1564, U.N. Doc. S/RES/1564 (January 25, 2005).

[36] To view the full report, see United Nations, *Report of the International Commission of Inquiry on Darfur to the Secretary-General of the United Nations*, (Geneva, January 25, 2005), http://www.un.org/News/dh/sudan/com_inq_darfur.pdf (Accessed June 12, 2009).

[37] The difficulty in meeting Genocide Convention criteria particularly in relation to intent is addressed in Gérard Prunier, Chapter 3, Section 3.1 (above) and Francis M. Deng, Chapter 4, Section 4.2 (above).

the same time, it reported that whether individuals, including government officials, might have committed acts with genocidal intent was a matter for a competent court to determine. The report of the commission added that:

> The conclusion that no genocidal policy has been pursued and implemented in Darfur by the Government authorities, directly or through the militias under their control, should not be taken in any way as detracting from the gravity of the crimes perpetrated in that region. International offences such as the crimes against humanity and war crimes that have been committed in Darfur may be no less serious and heinous than genocide.[38]

The commission recommended that the Security Council should refer the situation for investigation to the International Criminal Court. A list of some of those responsible for the massive crimes was given to the Secretary-General.

On March 31, 2006 the Security Council accepted the recommendation of the Commission and referred the Darfur situation to the International Criminal Court.[39] It did so using its peremptory powers under Chapter VII of the UN *Charter*.[40] It is thus binding on all member States, including Sudan. In applauding that decision, the Secretary-General issued the following statement:

> The Secretary-General welcomes the adoption today of Security Council resolution 1593 (2005), which refers the situation in Darfur since 1 July 2002 to the Prosecutor of the International Criminal Court. He commends the Council for using its authority under the Rome Statute to provide an appropriate mechanism to lift the veil of impunity that has allowed human rights crimes in Darfur to continue unchecked. He congratulates all Members for overcoming their differences to allow the Council to act to ensure that those responsible for atrocities in Darfur are held to account. He also welcomes the Council's encouragement of undertakings that complement the judicial process and promote healing and reconciliation.
>
> The Secretary-General calls on the Government of Sudan, all other parties to the conflict in Darfur, and all other States and concerned regional and other international organizations to cooperate fully with, and provide any necessary assistance to, the Court and the Prosecutor.[41]

Pursuant to the reference by the Security Council, the Prosecutor, Luis Moreno-Ocampo, reviewed the allegations made against the government of Sudan and on June 6th, 2005, announced that he was opening an

---

[38] Ibid.

[39] The United States, until shortly before the vote was taken by the Security Council had threatened to veto the reference to the ICC. The reference was an important boost to the credibility of the Court and was made possible by the United States' abstention

[40] See *Charter of the United Nations*, Article 41, note 2.

[41] United Nations Secretary-General, "Secretary-General Welcomes Adoption of Security Council Resolution Referring Situation in Darfur, Sudan, to International Criminal Court Prosecutor," SG/SM/9797, AFR/1132, April 1, 2005, http://www.un.org/News/Press/docs/2005/sgsm9797.doc.htm (Accessed June 12, 2009).

investigation into the situation in Darfur.[42] On February 27th, 2007, the Prosecutor sought from the pre-trial chamber the issue of a summons or a warrant of arrest against Ahmad Harun[43] and Ali Kushayb.[44] The chamber held that the Prosecutor had made out a *prima facie* case against both and decided to issue summonses for them to appear before the Court. It did so in the hope that the government of Sudan would cooperate and ensure their appearance.

In the meantime, on May 16th, 2006, the Security Council, again acting under Chapter VII, resolved that a UN peacekeeping force should join that of the African Union for deployment in Sudan.[45, 46] In the following months further peremptory resolutions were passed by the Council.

Through 2006 and 2007 the government of Sudan continued to block the entry of the combined African Union/United Nations peacekeeping force, and consistently refused all cooperation with the International Criminal Court. Indeed, President Omar al-Bashir promoted the accused Ahmad Harun in the cabinet and appointed a notorious leader of the *Janjaweed* militia, Musa Hilal, as his political advisor. The UN Security Council imposed travel and financial sanctions on Hilal and three other individuals in April 2006. US president George Bush issued several executive orders enforcing similar sanctions against them.[47, 48]

---

42 The ICC's treatment of the Darfur situation is examined in Catherine Lu, Chapter 18, Sections 18.1 and 18.2 (below) and Luis Moreno-Ocampo, Chapter 16 (below).

43 Ahmad Haran directed the "Darfur Security desk" as the Minister of State for the Interior of the Government of the Sudan. Haran is acused of using his office to greatly increase the strength and numbers of the *Janjaweed*, who targeted civilians with the justification that they were supporters of the rebels.

44 Kushayb is accused of leading the attacks on four villages and towns, commanding thousands of *Janjaweed*, and ordering and participating in crimes against humanity and war crimes. See *The Prosecutor v. Ahmad Muhammad Harun ("Ahmad Harun") and Ali Muhammad Ali Abd-Al-Rahman ("Ali Kushayb")*, International Criminal Court, Warrant of Arrest for Ali Kushayb, International Criminal Court, ICC-02/05-01/07-3 (April 17, 2007), http://www.icc-cpi.int/Menus/ICC/Situations+and+Cases/Situations/Situation+ICC+0205/Related+Cases/ICC+0205+0107/Court+Records/Chambers/Pre+Trial+Chamber+I/WARRANT+OF+ARREST+FOR+ALI+KUSHAYB.htm (Accessed June 12, 2009).

45 United Nations Security Council, Res. 1679, U.N. Doc. S/RES/1679 (May 16, 2006).

46 The difficulties particular to the peacekeeping mission in Sudan are discussed in Gérard Prunier, Chapter 3, Section 3.2 (above).

47 See Executive Order no. 13,067, 62 FR 59989 (November 5, 1997); Executive Order no. 13,400, 71 FR 25483 (May 1, 2006), Executive Order no. 13412, 71 FR 61369 (October 17, 2006).

48 Civil society groups like Human Rights Watch and Amnesty International have been instrumental in calling the world's attention to the Darfur crisis. NGOs have exerted sustained pressure on governments to vote for sanctions against the Sudanese government and for UN intervention in the conflict. The lack of a vibrant human rights NGO community in China may be another explanation of China's failure to agree to sanctions in

It was against this background that in June 2007, I suggested a modified Oil-for-Food program for Sudan.[49] To implement such a program, the Security Council would impose an embargo on oil revenues to the government of Sudan. Oil exports would be illegal except when the revenues were placed in a special trust fund and could be used only for humanitarian purposes. China need not object to such an embargo as it could continue to purchase Sudanese oil as long as payments were made only to the trust fund. If implemented, such a program would benefit from the lessons learned from the Iraqi Oil-for-Food program, such as increasing participation from the national community, more coordination with NGOs working on the ground in the country, and increasing managerial control tied directly to a democratic process in the country. This proposal has been endorsed by Human Rights Watch and other non-governmental organizations, as well as by the former head of the UN mission to Sudan.[50]

Memories of the problems and corruption that are associated with the Iraq Oil-for-Food Program might cause some to dismiss this idea. That would be a mistake. The weaknesses in that program have been carefully analyzed by the Independent Inquiry Committee.[51] It should be recognized that the Iraq Program diverted $75 billion in oil revenues from Saddam Hussein and, as mentioned earlier, reduced the adverse humanitarian effects of the blanket Security Council oil embargo. The UN has learned much from the systemic failures associated with the Iraq Program and is unlikely to allow them to be repeated in another similar program. In addition, the amounts involved with regard to Sudanese oil are of a substantially lower order than in the case of Iraq. Such a program would place considerable pressure on the government of Sudan. As I put it in an article for the *International Herald Tribune*:

> We should not let the perfect be the enemy of the good. Yes, there were weaknesses in the OFFP. But many of them could be addressed by simple reforms and better management within the UN. Such an embargo would be far better than the bloody status quo, since it would be the best tool that is realistically available to force Khartoum to end the slaughter in Darfur.[52]

Of course, an Oil-for-Food program is but one approach to alleviating a very complex problem. The slaughter and ethnic cleansing has been

---

Sudan. For an example of actions taken by Human Rights Watch towards Darfur see "US slams Sudan's appointee linked to Darfur atrocities," *Agence France-Presse*, January 22, 2009, http://afp.google.com/article/ALeqM5gvhevbfJOD4I9EAeZ5OxHyHtkPUw, (Accessed June 15, 2009).

[49] Richard J. Goldstone, "An Oil-for-food Program for Darfur," *New York Times*, June 12, 2007.

[50] Anne Penketh, "Judge and Activists Demand UN Oil Sanctions on Sudan," *The Independent*, June 16, 2007.

[51] Ibid.

[52] Goldstone, "Oil-for-Food," 2007.

allowed to continue for far too long. Even if the violence were to stop now, there would be many years of suffering in the future as victims seek to rebuild their shattered lives. Attempts to assist in what would require a massive effort to bring justice to Sudan would necessitate not only humanitarian assistance but also forms of transitional justice.

Recently, the situation in Darfur has shown signs of improvement. The combined African Union/United Nations peacekeeping force has replaced the existing African Union force in Darfur.[53] And on July 14th, 2008, ICC Prosecutor Luis Moreno-Ocampo requested the issue of a warrant of arrest against President Bashir to face ten charges, including war crimes, crimes against humanity, and genocide.[54] Since that time, President Bashir has shown some willingness to cooperate with the international community, going so far as to issue a cease-fire on November 12th, 2008.[55] It remains to be seen whether the threat of international justice will at last bring peace to Darfur.[56]

11.5 Conclusion

Economic sanctions might in some cases be a useful tool in deterring serious human rights violations. In order to achieve success, they must be carefully designed and efficiently executed. As the experiences of South Africa, Sudan and Iraq show, sanctions must be used in combination with other measures. Ideally, such measures should be supported by a broad and diverse coalition of governments and civil society organizations that can apply sustained pressure to encourage change. Moreover, this pressure should be directed in part at those countries whose economic interests are adverse to imposing sanctions. For example, China's continued resistance to sanctions in Sudan has been a major obstacle in successful international intervention in the area. Sanctions must take account of these interests and, like the Oil-for-Food program, create structures that will counter these interests.

Sanctions should be compatible with international human rights standards and humanitarian law and not interfere with access to food, shelter and medical care. This is perhaps one of the most difficult tasks for sanctions, especially for countries already ravaged by war and poverty.

---

[53] The Economist, "Sudan: Peacekeepers Into the Fray," *The Economist*, March 15, 2008.

[54] Marlise Simons, Lydia Polgreen and Jeffrey Gettelman, "Arrest is Sought of Sudan Leader in Genocide Case," *New York Times*, July 15, 2008.

[55] Xan Rice, "Sudan's President Announces Unilateral Ceasefire in Darfur," *The Guardian*, November 13, 2008.

[56] See David Blair, "If Peace Comes to Darfur, Thank the International Criminal Court," *The Telegraph*, November 14, 2008.

Sanctions must be designed with a built-in sensitivity to the experiences of those who will be most affected by the deprivation of economic resources. This may be accomplished through greater communication with organizations working in the country at issue, and by working with local elites who demonstrate a willingness to work toward the stability of the country. The purpose of the sanctions should thus be carefully crafted from the outset, and the sanctions themselves must be applied so as to meet their stated aims; if the purpose is to end government-inflicted violence, sanctions must address the areas where state power is accrued and manifested in oppressive force.

Finally, sanctions should be tied to benchmarks and should be accompanied by regular monitoring. As was seen with the corruption that followed the Iraqi Oil-for-Food program, the international community may be hard-pressed to manage the economic and market affairs of a country. If sanctions and programs like Oil-for-Food are to be successful, they must rely upon local as well as international bodies that are accountable for their performance. This, of course, requires financial and personnel support.

These brief comments are not intended to address the myriad issues and problems that the application of sanctions implies. My comments are, however, intended to lend general support to the use of sanctions as a tool for change, while at the same time reflecting the difficulties inherent in the use of sanctions. It is my hope that with the increasing use of sanctions, the world community will develop a more systematic and humanitarian-minded approach to sanctions, so that humanitarian outcomes can more consistently be assured.

Chapter 12
Expectation of Prosecuting the Crimes of Genocide in China

Wenqi Zhu and Binxin Zhang

12.1 Introduction

Genocide is one of the most heinous crimes in human history and under international law. The 1948 Convention on the Prevention and Punishment of the Crime of Genocide (hereafter the "Genocide Convention") for the first time gave a clear definition of the crime.[1] The Genocide Convention imposes obligations on every State party to enact domestic legislation to "give effect to the provisions" of the Convention.[2] The International Court of Justice (ICJ) has constantly observed in its case law that punishing genocide is an obligation *erga omnes*[3]; State practice has further confirmed the existence of universal jurisdiction over the crime.

Until only a few years ago China appeared to be far from prosecuting serious crimes under international law, but has since decided to discuss the possibility of preventing and punishing international crimes, including the crime of genocide. Though China is a party to the Genocide Convention, no domestic legislation on the crime of genocide exists. There is no provision incorporating genocide into Chinese criminal law. While there is

W. Zhu (✉)
Renmin University of China Law School, 100872 Beijing, China
e-mail: wenqizhu@hotmail.com

[1] A survey of the critical articles in the Genocide Convention is undertaken in Francis M. Deng, Chapter 4, Section 4.2 (above).

[2] *Convention on the Prevention and Punishment of the Crime of Genocide*, art.6, Office of the High Commissioner for Human Rights, January 12, 1951.

[3] *Reservation to the Convention on the Prevention and Punishment of the Crime of Genocide, Advisory Opinion*, International Criminal Court, 1951 I.C.J. 15 (May 28, 1951), 23; *Barcelona Traction, Light and Power Company, Limited (Belgian* v. *Spain);* Second Phase, International Court of Justice (ICJ) (February 5, 1970), paras. 33–34, http://www.unhcr.org/refworld/docid/4040aec74.htm (Accessed June 13, 2009); *Case Concerning Application of the Convention on the Prevention and Punishment of the Crime of Genocide, (Bosnia-Herzegovina v. Yugoslavia) (Preliminary Objection)*, International Court of Justice Report (July 11, 1996), para. 31, http://www.un.org/law/icjsum/9625.htm (Accessed June 13, 2009).

R. Provost, P. Akhavan (eds.), *Confronting Genocide*, Ius Gentium: Comparative Perspectives on Law and Justice 7, DOI 10.1007/978-90-481-9840-5_12,

no question that a State's domestic legislation is within its sovereign power, the current situation of the world today means that individual States are more closely related to each other than ever. As a result, the development of international criminal law has an effect on every State in the world, including China.

States are increasingly being faced by practical challenges as a result of the development of international criminal law: the introduction of universal jurisdiction over international crimes like genocide; the establishment of the International Criminal Court (ICC); as well as the ICC's special mechanisms and jurisdiction over State parties and non-State parties.[4] As increasingly more States sign on to the ICC and establish domestic legislation for prosecuting the most serious international crimes, the trend for preventing and punishing international crimes becomes ever more prevalent. China is faced with a practical need to catch up with this trend and contribute to the international effort of combating international crimes, including genocide. After examining the crime of genocide under current international law and introducing the legal framework in China, this article argues that it is both necessary and possible for China to legislate on the issue.

12.2 Genocide Under International Criminal Law

Examples of the brutal act of genocide are not rare in human history.[5] Yet only after World War II did it become a separate crime under international law. The Nuremberg International Military Tribunal was the first to charge and try the act of genocide as a crime against humanity. The Genocide Convention of 1948 distinguished genocide as a crime in its own right and provided the first clear definition of the crime.[6,7] Later, genocide was included in the Statutes of the two Security Council ad hoc tribunals, the International Criminal Tribunal for the Former Yugoslavia (ICTY) and the International Criminal Tribunal for Rwanda (ICTR), as well as in the Rome Statute of the ICC.[8] *Akayesu* became the first case in which an

---

[4]The establishment and role of the ICC are discussed in Luis Moreno-Ocampo, Chapter 16 (below).

[5]See Joshua M. Kagan, "The Obligation to Use Force to Stop Acts of Genocide: An Overview of Legal Precedents, Customary Norms, and State Responsibility." *San Diego International Law Journal* 7, No. 461, 462.

[6]Antonio Cassese, *International Law*, 2nd ed. (New York: Oxford University Press, 2005), 443.

[7]A survey of the critical articles in the Genocide Convention is undertaken in Francis M. Deng, Chapter 4, Section 4.2 (above).

[8]*Statute of the International Tribunal for the former Yugoslavia*, art. 4., adopted by United Nations Security Council Res. 827, (May 25, 1993), http://www.un.org/icty/legaldoc-e/index.htm (Accessed June 14, 2009); *Statute of the International Criminal Tribunal for Rwanda*, art. 2, 2007, http://www.ictr.org/ENGLISH/basicdocs/statute.

international tribunal was called upon to interpret the meaning of genocide as defined in the Genocide Convention.[9,10]

Genocide has been viewed as one of the most heinous crimes in human history and described as the "crime of crimes" by the Rwanda Tribunal.[11] The ICJ has declared that genocide is a crime that "shocks the conscience of mankind and results in great losses to humanity, and which is contrary to moral law and to the spirit and aims of the United Nations."[12] The extremely severe nature of the crime warrants its status as a crime under customary international law. What is more, the punishment of genocide has even been recognized as an *erga omnes* obligation of every State, thus giving rise to universal jurisdiction over the crime.

12.2.1 Genocide as a Crime Under Customary Law

The customary nature of the prevention and punishment of the crime of genocide is uncontroversial.[13] In its 1951 Advisory Opinion concerning the Reservation of the Genocide Convention (hereafter the "1951 Opinion"), the ICJ observed that "the principles underlying the Convention are principles which are recognized by civilized nations as binding on States, even without any conventional obligation."[14] This was a clear confirmation of the customary nature of the underlying principles of the Genocide Convention which obliges States to give effect to the Convention through legislation in order to prevent and punish genocide and related acts, such as conspiracy to commit genocide.[15] State practice has been affirmed, not only by the 104 States that have incorporated the crime into domestic

---

html?sess=24cff403f7d1ae05a8c4a3bef2c7b8d (Accessed June 13, 2009); *Rome Statute of the International Criminal Court*, arts. 5–6 (July 1, 2002), http://www.un.org/children/conflict/keydocuments/english/romestatuteofthe7.html (Accessed June 14, 2009).

[9] *The Prosecutor v. Jean-Paul Akayesu*, Case No. ICTR-96-4-T (September 2, 1998), http://69.94.11.53/ENGLISH/cases/Akayesu/judgement/akay001.htm (Accessed June 15, 2009).

[10] The contribution of the *Akayesu* case is higlighted in Francis M. Deng, Chapter 4, Section 4.2 (above) and Irwin Cotler, Chapter 9, Section 9.2 (above).

[11] *Prosecutor v. Niyitegaka, Case No. ICTR-96-14-A*, (Jul. 9, 2004), 53; see also *Prosecutor v. Stakic*, Case No. IT-97-24-T, Judgment (Jul. 31, 2003), 502.

[12] *Reservation to the Genocide Convention*, 1951, 23.

[13] See *Attorney General of Israel v. Eichmann* (1961), 36 I.L.R. 18, 39 (Dist. Ct.); *Attorney General of Israel v. Eichmann* (1962), 36 I.L.R. 277, 36 ILR 18 (Supreme Ct.), and William A. Schabas, "Genocide, Crimes Against Humanity, and Darfur: the Commission of Inquiry's Findings on Genocide," in *Cardozo Law Review* 27, No. 4 (February 2006): 1703.

[14] *Reservation to the Convention on the Prevention and Punishment of the Crime of Genocide, Advisory Opinion*, International Criminal Court, 1951 I.C.J. 15 (May 28, 1951), 23.

[15] *Genocide Convention*, Article 1, 3, 5, 1951.

legislation,[16] but also by a resolution adopted by the General Assembly in 2005. The *Outcome Document* of the United Nations summit declares that "each individual state has the responsibility to protect its populations from genocide, war crimes, ethnic cleansing and crimes against humanity."[17] It is without doubt therefore that the crime of genocide has a solid basis in customary international law.

12.2.2 *Punishing Genocide as a* Jus Cogens *Rule*

A *jus cogens* rule is binding upon all States: they can neither derogate from such a rule nor contract out of their obligations under it.[18] *Jus cogens* is situated at the top of the normative hierarchy of international legal principles. Article 53 of the 1969 Vienna Convention on the Law of Treaties, for the first time in history, equivalently confirmed the legal effect of a *jus cogens* rule.[19] In the 1951 Opinion, before the creation of the Vienna Convention, the ICJ explicitly recognized the condemnation of genocide as a *jus cogens* rule. The Court opined that both the "condemnation of genocide" and "the co-operation required" for its punishment are of "universal character."[20] About 20 years later, in the *Barcelona Traction* case, the ICJ made it clear that "the outlawing of acts ... of genocide" was an obligation *erga omnes*.[21] The Court asserted this once again in its 1996 judgment of the Genocide Convention case by observing that "the rights and obligations enshrined in the Convention are rights and obligations *erga omnes*."[22] While there is no consensus as to which rules are subject to *jus cogens*, outlawing and punishing genocide has been held as one of "the least controversial examples of a" *jus cogens* rule.[23]

12.2.3 *Universal Jurisdiction*

The *jus cogens* nature of outlawing genocide makes it the responsibility of every State to prevent and punish the crime of genocide, and gives basis

[16] Prevent Genocide International, "Implementing the Genocide Convention in Domestic Law," http://preventgenocide.org/law/domestic/ (Accessed July 14, 2009).

[17] United Nations General Assembly, *2005 World Summit Outcome*, UN Doc. A/60/L.1 (September 15, 2005), 31, para. 138.

[18] Ian Brownlie, *Principles of Public International Law*, 6th ed. (New York: Oxford University Press, 2003), 489.

[19] Dinah Shelton, "Normative Hierarchy in International Law," in *American Journal of International Law* 100 (2006): 291, 300.

[20] *Reservation to the Genocide Convention*, 1951, 23.

[21] *Barcelona Traction, 1970*, paras. 33–34.

[22] *Case Concerning Application of the Genocide Convention*, 1996, 616, para. 31.

[23] Brownlie, *Principles*, 2003, 488–490.

to the argument that States have universal jurisdiction over the crime. The Genocide Convention itself does not contain an *aut dedere aut judicare* provision like many other conventions on international crimes. Article 6 of the Convention provides two fora in which to try persons charged with the crimes contained therein. Firstly, it details that a "competent tribunal of the State in the territory of which the act was committed" can take jurisdiction or, secondly, that an "international penal tribunal" may have jurisdiction where the Contracting Parties have accepted its jurisdiction. Therefore, to examine the issue of universal jurisdiction over genocide, two questions should be answered: first, is Article 6 an exhaustive enumeration of jurisdiction? Second, can a State prosecute genocide based on universal jurisdiction under customary law?

Article 31 of the Vienna Convention on the Law of Treaties details the general rules for the interpretation of a treaty that has been recognized as part of customary international law.[24] It establishes that, "[a] treaty shall be interpreted in good faith in accordance with the ordinary meaning to be given to the terms of the treaty in their context and in the light of its object and purpose." As seen above, Article 6 of the Genocide Convention only provides two means by which to prosecute perpetrators of genocide. However, it cannot be inferred that this is the only meaning to be taken exclusively from the ordinary meaning of the text. Considering that the purpose and object of the Convention is to "liberate mankind from such an odious scourge" as genocide,[25] it is therefore obvious that the General Assembly and the drafters of the Convention intended for genocide to be punished as effectively as possible. Bearing this in mind, it is hard to conceive that the Convention meant to limit the jurisdiction to only the two fora indicated.

Furthermore, Article 31 of the Vienna Convention has set out other elements that should be "taken into account" when interpreting a treaty, including "any application of the treaty." The International Court of Justice, in its 1951 Advisory Opinion, as well as in its judgment on the Genocide Convention case, has consistently asserted the view that genocide is a crime under customary international law, and that every State is obliged to outlaw and punish genocide, even without a conventional basis.[26] State practice also supports this. For example, Spain's National Court, when examining the extradition application for Pinochet, observed that Article 6

[24] *Territorial Dispute (Libyan Arab Jamahiririya/Chad)*, *International Court of Justice Reports 1994*, 6, para. 41; *Oil Platforms (Islamic Republic of Iran v. United States of America)*, Preliminary Objections, Judgement, International Court of Justice Reports 1996, 803, para. 23; *Kasikili/Sedudu Island (Botswana/Namibia)*, *International Court of Justice Reports 1999*, 1045, para. 18.

[25] *Genocide Convention*, preamble, 1951.

[26] *Reservation to the Convention on the Prevention and Punishment of the Crime of Genocide, Advisory Opinion*, International Criminal Court, 1951 I.C.J. 15 (May 28, 1951), 23.

of the Convention does not place a limitation upon the jurisdiction of State parties; instead, it only sets out an obligation for the State in whose territory the crime took place to take action to punish the crime.[27] The legal effect of Article 6 is that it gives priority to the two fora enumerated therein in terms of exercising jurisdiction. However, where these two fora do not or cannot take action, other States are not precluded from asserting universal jurisdiction.[28]

Since the Genocide Convention itself does not place a limitation on the jurisdiction, it is also possible that universal jurisdiction over the crime of genocide may be exercised based on customary law as a State is free to exercise its sovereign rights unless there is a prohibitive rule forbidding it.[29] In 2001, Belgium took the lead in becoming the first country to domestically prosecute genocide as four Rwandans were prosecuted for their crimes committed during the 1994 Rwandan genocide.[30] In the aforementioned *Pinochet* case, the Spanish National Court ruled that Spain could exercise universal jurisdiction over Pinochet for possible acts of genocide.[31] Furthermore, during the Rome Conference, the delegation of Germany expressed the view that States had a legitimate basis under international law to assert universal jurisdiction over the crimes listed in Article 5 of the Rome Statute, which included genocide.[32] It was declared that the crime of genocide was so serious that it is deemed to be committed not only against victims but against the whole of mankind. Therefore, the gravity of the crime warranted that no perpetrators of genocide should be allowed to escape from punishment. As a result, there should be no jurisdictional vacuum for the perpetrators of such a crime to escape to and hide.

---

[27]*In Re Pinochet, Spanish National Court*, Criminal Division (Plenary Session) Case 19/97, November 4, 1998; Case 1/98, November 5, 1998; Genocide Convention, 1951, art. 6.

[28]Maria Del Carmen Marquez Carrassco and Jaquin Alcaide Fernandez, *In re Pinochet: Spanish National Court, Criminal Division (Plenary Session).* Case 19/97, November 4, 1998; Case 1/98, November 5, 1998, (1999) 93 A.J.I.L. 690, at 693.

[29]*SS Lotus Case (France v. Turkey)* (1927), P.C.I.J. Series A, No. 10.

[30]Linda Keller, *Belgian Jury to Decide Case Concerning Rwandan Genocide*, in American Society of International Law (May 2001), http://www.asil.org/insights/insigh72.htm, (Accessed June 16, 2008); Wenqi Zhu, *The Trigger Mechanism of the International Criminal Court and the Reaction of USA*, Henan Social Science 11, No. 5 (September 2003): 66.

[31]Maria Del Carmen Marquez Carrassco and Jaquin Alcaide Fernandez, *supra* note 19, at 693.

[32]Sharon A. Willianms, in Otto Triffterer, eds., *Commentary on the Rome Statute of the International Criminal Court*, article 12, (Germany, Nomos Verlagsgesellschaft, Baden-Baden, 1999): 332–334.

12.3 Legal Framework in China

Chinese criminal law offers a glimmer of hope in the prosecution of genocide. Article 9 of the Chinese Criminal Code reads: "For crimes stipulated in the international conventions which the People's Republic of China concluded or acceded to, if the People's Republic of China exercised criminal jurisdiction within the scope of its obligations under the conventions, the present law applies." According to this provision, it seems possible that China can exercise criminal jurisdiction over international crimes in situations where it has become a party to the relevant international convention. China signed the Genocide Convention in 1949 and ratified it in 1983.[33] Therefore, where an action of genocide has been committed on Chinese territory, China bears the obligation to exercise jurisdiction over persons charged with those crimes.[34]

China has also shown an active attitude towards the application of the Convention and the efforts to punish genocide. Four days before China resumed its exercise of sovereignty over Hong Kong and 3 days before resuming sovereignty over Macau, the Chinese government sent notification of the depositary of the Genocide Convention and notified the UN that the Convention would be applicable in these two areas.[35]

However, according to the principle of *nullum crimen sine lege*, there can be no crime committed, and no punishment imposed, without a violation of the penal law as it exists at the time. Fortunately, Article 3 of Chinese Criminal Code reflects this principle, which reads as follows: "For acts that are explicitly defined as criminal acts in law, the offenders shall be convicted and punished in accordance with law; otherwise, they shall not be convicted or punished." However, there is no "law" in China criminalizing the act of genocide.[36] The fact that "genocide" is not an independent crime under Chinese criminal law, and therefore has not been specifically defined, seems to result in, according to Article 3, the conclusion that the acts of genocide cannot be convicted or punished under the charge of "genocide." Instead, they may constitute other lesser crimes, such as murder or rape, but these acts cannot be prosecuted and punished as genocide.

---

[33] *Status of the Convention on the Prevention and Punishment of the Crime of Genocide* (October 9, 2001), http://www.unhchr.ch/html/menu3/b/treaty1gen.htm (Accessed June 14, 2009).

[34] *Genocide Convention*, 1951, art. 6.

[35] *Status of the Genocide Convention*, 2001.

[36] The Criminal Code of China was enacted in 1979 and amended in 1999. It has 6 amendments. There is no provision in the Criminal Code and its amendments dealing with the crime of genocide.

12.4 The Necessity and Possibility of Chinese Legislation on Genocide

From the above analysis it can be seen that there still exist some doubts and difficulties for prosecuting genocide in China. Without specific provisions in the criminal law, or any specific legislation on the prosecution and punishment of genocide, it is not clear whether Article 9 of the Criminal Code can serve as a basis for prosecution. Even if proceedings are brought under Article 9, the court will encounter practical problems, such as defining the elements of the crime and determining the appropriate sentence. China needs to legislate on the crime of genocide. This is a necessary step in fulfilling China's obligation to punish the crime of genocide under both the Genocide Convention and customary international law, and also in addressing the practical needs posed by developments of international criminal law, as discussed further below.

12.4.1 Obligation Under the Genocide Convention

Every State party to a treaty bears the obligation to perform the treaty in good faith.[37] Article 5 of the Genocide Convention requires every contracting party "to enact, in accordance with their respective Constitutions, the necessary legislation to give effect to the provisions of the present Convention, and, in particular, to provide effective penalties for persons guilty of genocide or any of the other acts enumerated in article III."[38] The Convention imposes obligations on every State party to establish jurisdiction over the crime of genocide in the case where the act was committed on the territory of the State.[39] As a party to the Genocide Convention, China is legally obliged to enact legislation on the crime of genocide, to lay down specific procedures for the prosecution and investigation of the crime, and to "provide effective penalties" for the perpetrators.

12.4.2 The Influence of the International Criminal Court

The establishment of the International Criminal Court is of great significance for the development of international criminal law, and has a substantial impact on every State, whether or not they are parties to the

[37]Vienna Convention on the Law of Treaties, art. 26, United Nations, *Treaty Series*, vol. 1155 (May 23, 1969), 331.

[38]*Genocide Convention*, 1951, art. 5.

[39]Ibid, art. 6.

Rome Statute.[40] The ICC contains particularly unique mechanisms for triggering proceedings and for both exercising jurisdiction over non-State parties as well as ensuring that State sovereignty is preserved. Though not yet a party to the Rome Statute, China is faced with the practical need to perfect its domestic criminal legislation under the influence of the ICC's special mechanisms.

The jurisdiction of the ICC is limited to the most serious international crimes of concern to the international community as a whole: the crime of genocide, crimes against humanity, war crimes and the crime of aggression.[41] Under Article 12, the Court's jurisdiction may be exercised in three ways: if the national of a State party to the Statute has committed a crime; if the crime has occurred on the territory of a State party; or if a non-State party has accepted the Court's jurisdiction. The Court has jurisdiction, however, over all cases referred to it by the Security Council.[42] There are also three trigger mechanisms for the Court's jurisdiction, namely (i) a State party refers a case to the Prosecutor; (ii) the UN Security Council refers a case to the Prosecutor under Chapter VII of the UN *Charter*; or (iii) the Prosecutor himself or herself initiates an investigation on the basis of relevant material.[43]

This therefore means two things. Firstly, the Security Council can play an important role in triggering proceedings before the ICC. Secondly, citizens of a non-State party or who have committed crimes in the territory of a non-State party may be tried by the ICC without the State's consent. Both of these implications will be considered in turn. While it is without doubt that they pose challenges to State sovereignty, a fundamental provision is contained within the Rome Statute which guarantees the priority of domestic jurisdiction and balances State sovereignty against the needs to effectively punish international crimes: the principle of complementarity.

12.4.3 *Influential Role of the Security Council*

When the UN Security Council refers a case to the Court for investigation and prosecution, it specifically involves UN member states. In other words, it entails the obligation to cooperate by both State parties and States not party to the ICC. The authority of the UN Security Council is derived from the UN *Charter*. By virtue of Article 25 of the UN *Charter*, all decisions made by the UN Security Council are binding upon all UN member

---

[40] The impact of the ICC on international criminal law is discussed in Luis Moreno-Ocampo, Chapter 16 (below).

[41] *Rome Statute*, 2002, art. 5.

[42] *Rome Statute*, 2002 art. 12.

[43] *Rome Statute*, articles 13–15.

states. Consequently, when the UN Security Council refers a case to the ICC which it deems to be related to the maintenance of peace and security, it can oblige all UN member states to co-operate in the Court's process of investigating that case. There is already one case that demonstrates the influential role of the UN Security Council on the ICC and of its requests for co-operation with the Court.

In view of the war crimes and crimes against humanity that had occurred in the Darfur region of Sudan, the International Commission of Inquiry submitted a report to the UN Secretary-General on 25th January 2005. In the report, the Commission recommended that the Security Council refer the situation in Darfur to the ICC, because "the Sudanese judicial system is incapable and the Sudanese government is unwilling to try the crimes that occurred in the Darfur region and to require the perpetrators to assume the accountability for their crimes."[44]

After receiving the report, the UN Security Council, acting under Chapter VII of the UN *Charter*, adopted Resolution 1593 on 31 March 2005, in which it decided to "refer the situation in Darfur since 1 July 2002 to the ICC Prosecutor."[45,46] The Security Council further decided and declared that:

> the Government of Sudan and all other parties to the conflict in Darfur shall co-operate fully with and provide any necessary assistance to the Court and the Prosecutor pursuant to this resolution and, while recognizing that States not party to the Rome Statute have no obligation under the Statute, urges all States and concerned regional and other international organizations to co-operate fully.[47]

The adoption of Resolution 1593 concerning the situation in Darfur was the first case in which the Security Council triggered the ICC's investigation mechanism in accordance with Article 13(b) of the Statute. It is also the first case in which a non-State party to the Rome Statute has been subjected to the ICC's jurisdiction. Though it has expressed opposition to the Security Council resolution,[48] Sudan, as a UN member State, has no choice but to abide by the provisions of the UN *Charter* and obey the Security Council resolution by co-operating with the Court. The statement in Resolution 1593 that "the Government of Sudan and all other parties to the conflict in Darfur shall co-operate fully with and provide any necessary assistance to the Court and the Prosecutor pursuant to this resolution"

---

[44]International Commission of Inquiry on Darfur, "Report of the International Commission of Inquiry on Darfur to the United Nations Secretary-General," in pursuance with the United Nations Security Council Res. 1564, (September 18, 2004), January 25, 2005, http://www.un.org/News/dh/sudan/com_inq_darfur.pdf (Accessed June 15, 2008).

[45]United Nations Security Council, Res. 1593, (March 31, 2005), para. 2.

[46]The ICC's treatment of the Darfur situation is examined in Catherine Lu, Chapter 18, Sections 18.1 and 18.2 (below) and Luis Moreno-Ocampo, Chapter 16 (below).

[47]Ibid, para. 2.

[48]Beijing Evening News, 1 April 2005, p. 8.

clearly shows that all non-State parties, including Sudan, must co-operate with and assist the ICC accordingly.

While it is certainly true that a Security Council resolution could not require States like China or the US to cooperate without their own consent, given the fact that they have veto powers as permanent members of the Council, these States can still be persuaded to cooperate though somewhat implicitly. Resolution 1593 was adopted by a vote of 11 in favor, none against, and four abstentions.[49] Surprisingly, China and the US decided to abstain, rather than block the adoption of the resolution. This is despite the fact that neither of them has agreed to the ICC's jurisdiction and that both have somewhat differing opinions from the majority consensus on whether crimes have been committed in Darfur.[50] Such an example serves to demonstrate that China is, to a certain extent, still involved in the triggering of proceedings before the Court, despite its non-party status.

12.4.4 Challenge to the Principle of Pacta Tertiis Nec Nocent Nec Prosunt

The aforementioned trigger mechanism and conditions for exercising jurisdiction, however, pose a challenge to a traditional principle of treaty law. Article 35 of the 1969 Vienna Convention clearly provides that "an obligation arises for a third State from a provision of a treaty if the parties to the treaty intend the provision to be the means of establishing the obligation and the third State expressly accepts that obligation in writing." Also, Article 34 clearly details that a treaty does not create either obligations or rights for a third state without its consent. This is one of the general principles of treaty law.

However, the current jurisdictional powers of the ICC potentially contravene this principle. It is possible that a non-State party that has not accepted the ICC's jurisdiction may be involved in proceedings before the ICC. This is because it is sufficient to trigger the jurisdiction of the ICC if either the territorial State or the national State of the accused is a State party to the Rome Statute or has accepted the ICC's jurisdiction by special declaration. As a result, if the territorial State has accepted the jurisdiction of the ICC, then a citizen of a non-State party may be prosecuted for crimes he committed in that State. Or, if the national State of the accused has accepted the ICC's jurisdiction, he may then be tried for crimes that have taken place in the territory of a non-party State. Thus, the Rome

---

[49] United Nations Security Council, Res. 1593, 2005, para. 2.

[50] The impact of economic interests on China's position *vis-à-vis* Darfur is addressed in Yehuda Bauer, Chapter 7, Sections 7.1 and 7.3 (above) and Richard J. Goldstone, Chapter 11, Section 11.4 (above).

Statute has practically influenced the rights and obligations of non-State parties without their consent. Furthermore, for cases referred to the ICC by the Security Council, there are no conditions attached to the exercise of jurisdiction. Again however, this may not have much impact on States like China or the US who could veto any proposition that concerned them.

This potential legal contravention raised much concern both in the process of negotiating the Rome Statute and after its adoption. The US delegation to the Rome Conference, for example, argued that Article 12 of the Rome Statute is a deviation from Article 34 of the 1969 Vienna Convention and contrary to recognized principles of international law. The US was among the group of States that took the view that except for the situations referred to the Court by the Security Council, the Court cannot assert jurisdiction over non-State parties without their consent.[51]

Setting aside the question of whether Article 12 violates a general principle of treaty law, it is enough to point out that the Rome Statute has come into force and the ICC has been functioning somewhat successfully. Therefore, no matter what opinion a State holds, it is of no doubt that every State in the world is influenced by the Rome Statute and is faced with the possibility of becoming involved in the proceedings before the ICC even if it is not a State party. China can choose not to accede to the Rome Statute but it cannot avoid the possibility that its citizens or those responsible for crimes committed within its own territory could be tried at the ICC at some point.

12.4.5 The Principle of Complementarity

The ICC determines that a case is inadmissible where the case is being investigated or prosecuted by a State which has jurisdiction over it, or where the person concerned has already been tried for conduct which is the subject of the complaint.[52] If either of these conditions are met, then a trial by the ICC is not permitted under Article 17 of the Statute. The ICC can only assert jurisdiction over a crime when it has been established that the State who has jurisdiction is unwilling or unable to investigate and prosecute the alleged crime.[53] This is known as the principle of complementarity. This principle was the result of a difficult compromise reached after intense multinational negotiations. It relieved the majority of States

---

[51]Sharon A. Williams, *Commentary on the Rome Statute of the International Criminal Court*, article 12, in ed. Otto Triffterer (Germany: Nomos Verlagsgesellschaft, Baden-Baden, 1999), 336–338.

[52]*Rome Statute*, 2002, articles 1 and 17.

[53]Ibid, art. 17(1)(a).

from the concern that the Court might infringe State sovereignty and thus serves as a cornerstone of the Rome Statute.[54]

In accordance with the principle of complementary any State concerned may challenge the jurisdiction of the ICC. In the aforementioned Sudan situation, Sudan could oppose the investigation and prosecution of the ICC so long as it can prove that it is actually willing and able to exercise jurisdiction in accordance with Article 17. This is unlikely however as the UN Security Council adopted Resolution 1593 on the premise of having determined that the Sudanese legal system was unable to genuinely investigate or prosecute and the Sudanese government was unwilling to try the crimes committed. Therefore, for States who prefer to try the accused in their own courts, it is important to prove their willingness and ability to do so, and to conduct the investigation and prosecution in accordance with their own domestic criminal law.

Paragraph 2 of Article 17 of the Rome Statute, which deals with the issues of admissibility, lists three situations under which unwillingness can be determined, and paragraph 3 deals with inability. The requirement, in brief, is that the State with jurisdiction must investigate or prosecute the accused "genuinely," or in other words, in good faith. It is not explicitly detailed that the accused should be investigated and/or prosecuted for the core crimes listed in Article 5 of the Statute. It seems enough for the case to be rendered inadmissible before the ICC if domestic criminal proceedings have started in good faith and the perpetrator is tried under any kind of criminal charge in accordance with domestic criminal law. In the case of China, the fact that there is no criminal legislation dealing with genocide may not per se affect the proof of willingness and ability.

However, possible loopholes still exist because of the special nature of the crime of genocide, considering its extreme gravity and the "special intent" requirement. Due to the fact that genocide is such a grave crime, some acts like incitement may amount to a charge of genocide while not constituting other crimes generally.[55,56] The special intent required for genocide – destroying a group in whole or in part – transforms acts that may otherwise constitute murder, intentional injury, rape, etc. into the crime of genocide.[57] Without specific provisions dealing with genocide in domestic criminal law, it may be difficult to effectively investigate and prosecute the

---

[54]Williams, *Commentary*, 1999, 385–392.

[55]*Rome Statute*, 2002, art. 25(e); *Genocide Convention*, 1951, art. 3; *Statute of the ICTY*, 1997, art. 4(3); *Statute of the ICTR*, 2007, art. 2(3).

[56]A discussion of what constitutes incitement is provided in Irwin Cotler, Chapter 9, Section 9.2 (above).

[57]The difficulty in meeting Genocide Convention criteria particularly in relation to intent is addressed in Gérard Prunier, Chapter 3, Section 3.1 (above) and Francis M. Deng, Chapter 4, Section 4.2 (above).

offender and prove to the ICC that these acts are underway. Even if investigations and prosecutions can indeed be conducted, the crimes that can be charged and the possible sentence of the accused may not correspond to the gravity of the crime of genocide. To better guarantee that genocidal offenders will not escape national jurisdiction, legislation is vital. Furthermore, for a permanent member of the Security Council and for a State that wants to play an important and responsible role in the international community, it is necessary to show more determination and effectiveness in combating such grave international crimes like genocide.

12.4.6 *Exercise of Universal Jurisdiction*

As analyzed above, the outlawing and punishment of genocide is an obligation *erga omnes*. Existing State practice for exercising extraterritorial jurisdiction over the crime of genocide based on the principle of universality is abundant. Some Chinese scholars believe that the aforementioned Article 9 of the Chinese Criminal Code provides the basis for Chinese courts to assert universal jurisdiction.[58] Arguably national courts may assert universal jurisdiction without specific provisions of domestic law as long as there is a conventional or customary basis.[59] However, from a practical perspective, national courts often refrain from invoking universal jurisdiction without specific domestic legislation.[60] This is fairly understandable. While international conventions and customary law may provide a legal basis for asserting universal jurisdiction, they are usually not as detailed and specific as domestic legislation. Asserting universal jurisdiction based solely on international law would cause the national court many practical difficulties, such as determining the procedure for requesting judicial cooperation in extraterritorial investigations, determining the sentence, dealing with the obligation to punish international crimes and determining how to respect foreign State immunity. Furthermore, the exercise of universal jurisdiction often involves political implications which may add to a national court's reluctance to act without specific legislation requiring it to do so.

---

[58]Gao Mingxuan and Wang Xiumei, "Reflections on the Characteristics and Localization of Universal Jurisdiction," in *Law and Social Development* (June, 2001), 23.

[59]Princeton University Program in Law and Public Affairs, *The Princeton Principles on Universal Jurisdiction*, 28 (2001). For background information of the Princeton Principles, see http://www.derechos.org/nizkor/icc/princeton.html (Accessed June 19, 2008).

[60]Tanaz Moghadam, "Revitalizing Universal Jurisdiction: Lessons from Hybrid Tribunals Applied to the Case of Hissene Habre," in *Columbia Human Rights Law Review* 39, No. 1 (2008): 471, 489.

The *Hissène Habré* case serves as an example to illustrate the importance of domestic legislation in the exercise of universal jurisdiction. In 2000, the former president of Chad, Hissène Habré was accused in Senegal of being an accomplice to torture, committing barbarous acts, and crimes against humanity. The torture charge was based on the Convention Against Torture and Other Cruel, Inhuman, or Degrading Treatment or Punishment (CAT), which Senegal ratified in 1986.[61] Article 7 of the Convention requires parties to either extradite or prosecute an alleged offender of the crime of torture.[62] The Senegalese Chambre d'Accusation however dismissed the complaint citing a lack of jurisdiction. The Senegalese court placed emphasis on Article 5 of the CAT, which provides that "each State Party shall take such measures as may be necessary to establish its jurisdiction" for offences listed in the CAT. The court relied upon Article 5 stating that the lack of domestic legislation establishing its jurisdiction over extraterritorial torture meant that Senegal was under no obligation to prosecute Hissène Habré if it did not extradite him.[63]

Many believe that this case was a result of political interference by Senegalese President Abdoulaye Wade.[64] Whether this is true or not, the case demonstrates the importance of domestic legislation in exercising universal jurisdiction. Despite an *aut dedere aut judicare* provision in the CAT, which clearly vests the obligation in every State party to prosecute the offenders and deny them the safety of a jurisdictional vacuum, the Senegalese court nevertheless found a way to dismiss the case. The Genocide Convention has no such provision explicitly requiring States to extradite and prosecute. The exercise of universal jurisdiction over genocide can only be based on customary law. It is therefore even more important and necessary to provide specific stipulations in domestic law if a State is ready to prosecute and punish the crime of genocide on the basis of universal jurisdiction. Belgium, Spain and Germany have already domestically incorporated genocide into their legislation.[65]

The Rome Statute only requires State parties to "ensure that there are procedures available under their national law for all of the forms of cooperation."[66] States that are not party to the ICC have no legal obligation

---

[61] Inbal Sansani, "The Pinochet Precedent in Africa: Prosecution of Hissene Habre," in *Human Rights Brief* 8, No. 2 (2001): 32, 33.

[62] *Convention Against Torture and Other Cruel, Inhuman, or Degrading Treatment or Punishment*, art. 7(1) UN Doc. CAT/C/4/Rev.3 (July 18, 2005).

[63] Inbal Sansani, *The Pinochet Precedent*, 2001, 35.

[64] Dustin N. Sharp, "Prosecutions, Development, and Justice: The Trial of Hissene Habre," *Harard. Human Rights Journal* 16 (2003): 147, 169.

[65] See generally M. Cherif Bassiouni, "Universal Jurisdiction for International Crimes: Historical Perspectives and Contemporary Practice," in *Virginia Journal of International Law* 42 (Fall 2001): 1, 81.

[66] *Rome Statute*, 2002, art. 88.

to enact relevant domestic legislation. However, given the fact that non-parties, such as China, can also be involved in proceedings before the ICC, it may be wiser for States to have their own legislation to assert universal jurisdiction, especially when they want to prove that they have the ability and willingness to try the persons charged. Moreover, there is an evident need for the possible exercise of universal jurisdiction bearing in mind that the purpose of the Genocide Convention is "to liberate mankind from such an odious scourge."

China is under the obligation to enact domestic legislation to give effect to the provisions in the Genocide Convention. Despite China's seeming unwillingness to legislate on these issues so far, China has in fact a sufficient legal and psychological foundation to enact legislation that prevents and punishes serious criminal acts perpetrated against specific national, ethnic, religious and racial groups. The Constitution of China enshrines the underlying general principles to equality, unity and mutual assistance among the 56 nationalities in the country.[67] In the Constitution and other legislation and regulations, there are many provisions protecting the rights of minorities in China. For example, while a Chinese couple can generally have only one child,[68] minorities are granted privileges to have more than one child.[69] For certain areas in Tibet and certain nationalities in Inner Mongolia, no restriction on the number of children is imposed.[70] The age limitation of marriage for minorities is also lower than for those of Han nationality.[71] What is more, where Chinese criminal law criminalizes the

---

[67] *Constitution of the People's Republic of China*, Preamble, para.11, art. 4 (December 4, 1982). There are 56 nationalities in China, the majority nationality is called the Han nationality, and other 55 are all clarified as minorities. According to Fifth National Population Census Data, Han are of more than 90% of the country's population. Data available at http://www.chinapop.gov.cn/zwgk/gbgg/t20040326_2819.htm (Accessed June 2008). About how it was confirmed that there were 55 minority nationalities in the country, see Zhao Wei, *About the Identification Process of the 55 Minority Nationalities*, Ethnic Unity (March 1999), 52.

[68] *Law of Population and Family Planning of the People's Republic of China*, art. 18, adopted at the 25th Meeting of the Standing Committee of the Ninth National People's Congress (December 29, 2001).

[69] Ordinance of Population and Family Planning of Xinjing Uygur Autonomous Region, art. 15; Ordinance of Family Planning of Ningxia Hui Autonomous Region; Ordinance of Family Planning of Inner Mongolia Autonomous Region, arts. 9–15; Interim Measures for Family Planning Management in Tibet Autonomous Region, arts. 7–10.

[70] Interim Measures for Family Planning Management in Tibet Autonomous Region, arts. 9–10. Ordinance of Family Planning of Inner Mongolia Autonomous Region, art. 11.

[71] *Marriage Law of the People's Republic of China*, art. 6, amended according to the Decision on Amending the Marriage Law of the People's Republic of China made at the 21st meeting of the Standing Committee of the Ninth National People's Congress (April 28, 2001); Supplementary Provisions concerning the Implementation of the Marriage Law of the People's Republic of China in Xinjing Uygur Autonomous Region, art. 2; Adaptive Provisions concerning the Implementation of the Marriage Law of the People's

act of incitement for certain grave crimes, it includes the crime of incitement to ethnic hatred and discrimination.[72] As a principle enshrined in the Constitution, the idea of unity among nationalities and the protection of specific groups and minorities is a well-rooted concept both in the legal system and in the minds of ordinary Chinese people.

Furthermore, the Chinese legal profession has been calling for legislation on genocide and other international crimes in recent years. Researchers and scholars are conducting research on relevant legislation in other states and have provided specific suggestions for future Chinese legislation.[73] Although this does not mean real legislation is under way, it can provide some guidance for future legislation. Furthermore, it shows that the issue is now being discussed and considered in China. It is therefore reasonable to believe that Chinese legislation on the prosecution and punishment of genocide as well as other international crimes will not be a remote dream.

12.5 Conclusion

Genocide is a crime of extreme gravity, and thus the prevention and punishment of the crime of genocide is an obligation *erga omnes* under international law. In other words, every State in the world is required to prosecute and punish the crime of genocide. Although the Genocide Convention does not establish universal jurisdiction, its application to territorial jurisdiction and jurisdiction of competent international tribunals does not limit universal jurisdiction under customary law, according to the general rules of treaty interpretation. Rulings of the ICJ along with State practices have shown the universal character of States' rights and obligations to prosecute the crime of genocide.

China ratified the Genocide Convention more than 20 years ago, and it has always supported international efforts in combating international crimes, including genocide. However, Chinese criminal law has no specific provisions concerning the crime of genocide. It is unclear whether

---

Republic of China in Tibet Autonomous Region, art. 1; Supplementary Provisions concerning the Implementation of the Marriage Law of the People's Republic of China in Inner Mongolia Autonomous Region, art. 3.

[72]Criminal Law of the People's Republic of China, art. 249, adopted by the Second Session of the Fifth National People's Congress (July 1, 1979), amended by the Fifth Session of the Eighth National People's Congress (March 14, 1997). There are 5 crimes of incitement in Chinese Criminal Law, the other 4 are found in crimes endangering national security, crimes of impairing the interest of national defense and crimes disturbing public order, see arts. 103, 105, 278 and 373.

[73]Shen Hong, *On the Crime of Genocide*, doctoral diss., Renmin University of China (June 2008), 166–174; Leng Xinyu, *On the Universal Jurisdiction*, doctoral diss. Renmin University of China (April 2007), 140–150, 196–198.

or not the investigation and prosecution of a genocidal offender can be conducted in China in accordance with the relevant international conventions to which China is a party. As a result, there are increasing calls for legislation on genocide in China.

China is under an obligation to enact the provisions of the Genocide Convention through domestic legislation. The establishment and functioning of the ICC has further presented practical needs for China to perfect its domestic legislation on international crimes, including genocide. Although not a party to the Rome Statute, China has already been involved in triggering proceedings before the ICC. When the Security Council acted to refer the situation in Sudan to the ICC, China, as a permanent member of the Council, played a role in the procedure. The fact that China did not block the resolution, regardless of its current negative stance towards the ICC, underscored a powerful trend: punishing serious international crimes has increasingly become an international concern and every State should feel obliged to contribute to the international effort in combating international crimes.

Furthermore, under the Rome Statute, it is possible that a non-State party may be directly involved in the proceedings before the ICC without its consent. Due to this, the Rome Statute at the same time emphasizes the principle of complementarity so that the need to deny a jurisdictional vacuum to the offenders is balanced with the need to respect the sovereignty of States. Generally speaking, States with jurisdiction would prefer to try the offenders in their own domestic courts rather than at the ICC. To satisfy the requirement of willingness and ability, and also to effectively deal with the crimes, it is vital for China to have specific domestic legislation.

Domestic legislation is also necessary for the exercise of universal jurisdiction. Understandably, national courts are reluctant to assert universal jurisdiction, and practical difficulties exist for national courts who wish to prosecute extraterritorial crimes. For the crime of genocide, it is perhaps even more difficult because, unlike torture and war crimes, there is no conventional basis for States to exercise universal jurisdiction over genocide. The claim of universal jurisdiction is based solely on customary international law. Specific domestic legislation not only provides national courts with a clear legal basis by which to define and prosecute the crime, but also provides practical guidance.

China is a State with 56 nationalities, and, for the most part, the people of these different nationalities are living peacefully together. The idea of harmonization and unity among nationalities is a cultural tradition as well as a fundamental constitutional principle in China. Though protected groups under the law of genocide are not conceptually the same as nationalities, the well-rooted idea of equality and unity among different ethnic groups may still serve as a good psychological foundation for legislation on genocide. In recent years, this problem has been increasingly discussed by the legal profession, and practical suggestions concerning the possible amendments to current legislation have been proposed. It could be safely concluded therefore that it is both necessary and possible for China to legislate on the prosecution and punishment of the crime of genocide, and that the time has now come to do so.

Part III
Prevention Beyond the State

Chapter 13
Not "Lambs to the Slaughter": A Program for Resistance to Genocidal Law

Frédéric Mégret

The court did not understand him: he had never been a Jew-hater, and he had never willed the murder of human beings. His guilt came from his obedience, and obedience is praised as a virtue[1]

13.1 Introduction

It is hard to think of a goal over which there would be more agreement than preventing genocide. Prevention seems vastly superior to intervention, so that the shift to prevention is also part of a welcome shift away from some of the militarism associated with more "muscular" humanitarian discourses.[2]

One of the difficulties of the field, however, is finding a proper domain for prevention, one that would involve something less than fixing most of the world's problems. This is particularly the case in international law, a discipline that seems to have had remarkably little to say about prevention over the years, except to insist that it should happen. Why is international law relatively mute when it comes to prevention? Morton and Singh note that "While prevention shares an equal status with punishment in the Convention's title, there are no direct prevention provisions in the treaty's articles," arguably because "absent of a compelling theory that reveals the necessary and sufficient causes of genocide, the treaty could not provide

F. Mégret (✉)
Faculty of Law, Centre for Human Rights & Legal Pluralism, McGill University, Montreal, QC H3A 1W9, Canada
e-mail: frederic.megret@mcgill.ca

[1]Hannah Arendt, *Eichmann in Jerusalem; a Report on the Banality of Evil* (New York,: Viking Press, 1963), 225–226.

[2]Anne Orford, "Muscular Humanitarianism: Reading the Narratives of the New Interventionism," *European Journal of International Law* 10, no. 4 (1999).

R. Provost, P. Akhavan (eds.), *Confronting Genocide*, Ius Gentium: Comparative Perspectives on Law and Justice 7, DOI 10.1007/978-90-481-9840-5_13,

explicit prevention measures."[3] I am not sure the problem for international law is the absence of a compelling theory of what causes genocide, but perhaps the theories suggest so many possible causes that international law has failed to see what it could do to specifically prevent genocide, apart from everything it is already doing all the time to make the world a better place.

Or perhaps the problem is that international law operates with, at least in part, the wrong theory, one that is less suited to the particular needs of genocide prevention, than it is an emanation of the international legal project. In this article I will suggest that international law has concentrated excessively on grand, structural ways to prevent genocide and typically pays insufficient attention to how genocides have actually been averted. As a result, it has conceived of ways of preventing genocide that have been only marginally successful and perhaps missed some significant ways in which international law might truly have a role to play in prevention.

Although the article is about prevention broadly understood, it will focus on a particular form of attempt to prevent genocides that is connected to the broad theme of resistance. I will therefore be interested (but not only) in efforts that have a more immediate quality to them than what is sometimes understood by prevention. However, I do so in the belief that prevention is a continuum that goes all the way from remote efforts to protect minorities and create domestic conditions that protect rights to last-ditch attempts to stop atrocities from happening as they are unfolding. What stops and limits genocides, in other words, is also what prevents them. Resistance is the particular form of prevention that arises as soon as there is a breakdown in institutions that requires prevention to take a more distinctly political and oppositional form. Moreover, the important point about resistance is not its chronology but the way it puts human agency rather than structures (domestic or international) at the heart of what prevention should be about.

Instead of a grand theory deploring the persistence of sovereignty and the difficulties of international prevention, I want to propose a more realistic, militant theory of genocide that is rooted in actual resistance put up by those threatened by genocide to protect themselves before and during a genocidal onslaught. But instead of seeing such resistance as something that merely "happens" and that is not particularly connected to the goals of international law, I want to study the role that international law might have in legitimizing, supporting and validating resistance efforts. The exercise is not meant to imply that the international community should not have a role, but should be construed as an appeal to focus less rigidly and exclusively on the international system, and for "internationalists" to

---

[3] Jeffrey S. Morton and Neil Vijay Singh, "The International Legal Regime on Genocide," *Journal of Genocide Research* 5, no. 1 (2003).

listen more actively to what historians, political scientists, philosophers and social psychologists have had to say about how genocides are actually prevented.

I will look at how international law is part and parcel of a broad vision of prevention as the responsibility of the international community and states (I), and therefore implicitly disempowering of victims and their agency (II). I will then briefly sketch the role that scholars of actual genocides ascribe to resistance efforts in averting genocides (III). On the basis of a particular understanding of genocidal conduct as being at least partly determined by blind obedience to orders and the law ("genocidal law") (IV), I suggest that a useful way of looking at resistance is one that sees it as a fundamentally normative activity (V). I then contend that the fundamental challenge is for the international community to better assess ways in which international law might stimulate resistance to such "genocidal law" (IV).

13.2 International Law and Genocide Prevention

In international law and policy circles, thinking about genocide has been dominated by two ideas, that of international criminal justice and that of humanitarian intervention. Rather than examine these mechanisms as such, I simply want to emphasize a number of characteristics that they share as a result of their international formulation, which ultimately make them unlikely prevention tools and limit their ability to deliver.

13.2.1 Reactive Bias

International law is much better at dealing with the consequences of genocide than with preventing its causes. As Michael Reisman was once prompted to remark, when it comes to genocide "we focus on actions after the facts."[4] Both international criminal justice and intervention, in that respect, sit oddly in the prevention category.

To the extent that they operate simultaneously to the commission of a genocide, tribunals, especially the international kind may have a minimally preventive effect. But criminal legal systems are for most purposes quintessentially reactive in that they sanction crimes that were committed in the past. In fact, in the case of international criminal justice, tribunals are doubly reactive in that they were often created, as institutions, after particular atrocities were committed. At times, international lawyers will

[4] W. Michael Reisman, "Legal Responses to Genocide and Other Massive Violations of Human Rights," *Law and Contemporary Problems* 59, no. 4 (1996), 76.

equate punishment and prevention, via the idea of deterrence.[5] But surely criminal deterrence is a poor approximation of genocide prevention, not only because of the well known doubts about its efficacy, but also because of the crucial fact that it will only have an effect long after a genocide has taken place, where prevention's goal is to ensure that genocides do not occur, ideally long before they might.[6]

Humanitarian intervention is not quite after the facts, but it is essentially about disrupting ongoing atrocities rather than prevention *stricto sensu*.[7] However important thinking about the possibility of military intervention to prevent genocides may be, it is already premised on the grim prospect of genocide occurring. Although of late the debate on international intervention has been increasingly geared towards emphasizing prevention, most notably through work on the "responsibility to protect" (R2P),[8,9] the credibility of that system still arguably relies on the credible threat of force at some junction.[10]

In some ways, this reactive bias can be seen as a manifestation of international law's deeper infatuation with the "crisis"[11] or the "event"[12] or the "emergency."[13] Concentration on the event is arguably maximized when it comes to such a considerable event as genocide. International law is much less good at shaping the future than it is at drawing lessons from the past; it addresses consequences rather than causes.

---

[5]The impact of the ICC in the area of prevention is discussed in Catherine Lu, Chapter 18, Section 18.2 (below) and Luis Moreno-Ocampo, Chapter 16 (below).

[6]Thus even sophisticated proponents of deterrence acknowledge that it there for the very long haul, which surely sheds a very particular light on the sort of prevention involved. Payam Akhavan, "Beyond Impunity: Can International Criminal Justice Prevent Future Atrocities?," *American Journal of International Law* 95, no. 1 (2001).

[7]The function of peacekeeping missions is addressed in Wiebe Arts, Chapter 8, Section 8.2 (above).

[8]Alexander J. Bellamy, "Conflict Prevention and the Responsibility to Protect," *Global Governance: A Review of Multilateralism and International Organizations* 14, no. 2 (2008).

[9]The concept of "responsibility to protect" is discussed in Francis M. Deng, Chapter 4 (above).

[10]Ethan Cramer-Flood, "The "Reponsibility to Protect" and Unilateral Humanitarian Interventions: An Emerging Legal Doctrine?" *Minerva* 33 (2008).

[11]Hilary Charlesworth, "International Law: A Discipline of Crisis," *The Modern Law Review* 65 (2002).

[12]Sundhya Pahuja Fleur Johns, Richard Joyce, ed. *Events: The Force of International Law* (London: Routledge, Forthcoming).

[13]Craig Calhoun, "A World of Emergencies: Fear, Intervention, and the Limits of Cosmopolitan Order," *The Canadian Review of Sociology and Anthropology* 41, no. 4 (2004).

13.2.2 International Bias

Also implicit to many contemporary narratives about genocide prevention, especially those coming out of policy and legal circles, is a tendency to see the problem as largely one to be dealt with from outside by the "international community." Since presumably the occurrence of a genocide will in most cases be the result of a state policy, the state principally concerned is understandably written off as a helpful actor, at least by the time genocide has achieved a certain level of imminence. Prevention is therefore first and foremost seen as a matter for the international community, understood broadly as including states, international organizations, and possibly a number of transnational NGOs.[14] To be more precise, this is never quite said, but nor, which amounts to the same, are local actors often mentioned as possibly having a truly positive contribution to make.

The emphasis on the international community's preventive role belongs to the same family of ideas that has traditionally focused on the issue of international (humanitarian) intervention. It is rooted in the legacy of the Holocaust and, to a lesser extent, the Armenian genocide, and the idea that the abandonment of populations under threat by the international community is one of the prime causes of genocides. It is indissociable from a tendency to see these past failures as guilty – a feeling reinforced by the failures of Rwanda and Bosnia – and a mystique of redemption for the "international community," which has increasingly defined its moral tenor in terms of its ability to intervene to prevent atrocities.[15] The resulting understanding is that ultimately populations threatened with annihilation's best hope of rescue is some sort of international effort. This has lead international intervention to be cast even more as a panacea in the case of Darfur.[16] In fact, it is fair to say that the international intervention discourse has largely dominated the debate about what to do to avoid a genocide.

This idea of the international as the prime and natural locus of prevention is both born from and confirmed by international law. The Genocide Convention is of course a treaty between states, agreeing between each other to prevent genocide, and stressing the need for "international cooperation." It is necessarily based on the primacy of states, at least for the purposes of the treaty itself. Genocide is presented as being "contrary to the spirit and aims of the United Nations and condemned by the civilized

---

[14]The mobilization of citizen political will to stop atrocities is discussed in Rebecca J. Hamilton, Chapter 15, Section 15.2 (below).

[15]Chris Brown, "Delinquent States, Guilty Consciences and Humanitarian Politics in the 1990s," *Journal of International Political Theory* 4, no. 1 (2008).

[16]The inability of international intervention to stop atrocities in Darfur is highlighted in Gérard Prunier, Chapter 3, Section 3.2 (above).

world," and if anything "Any Contracting Party may call upon the competent organs of the United Nations to take such action under the *Charter of the United Nations* as they consider appropriate for the prevention and suppression of acts of genocide."[17] The International Court of Justice judgment in the *Bosnia v. Serbia* case merely confirmed that bend. It insisted for example that "the Contracting Parties have a direct obligation to prevent genocide."[18] Indeed, a number of the obligations to prevent genocide are obligations to organize the state machinery in a certain way, and thus essentially only obligations that a state could undertake. The obligation to punish, in particular, is one that is only meant to rest on the state's shoulders.[19]

Of course, the emphasis on the role of the state and the international community is natural given international law's epistemology and prevailing concerns. In the *Bosnia v. Herzegovina* case, the ICJ was interested in an *issue of state responsibility* and that was all it was asked to decide. But there is also a risk that the epistemology will become a source of its own distortions and that international law will occasionally confuse some of its own preoccupations with the reality of genocide prevention. For instance, the Genocide Convention is typically thought of as a little more than a document to spell out the obligations of states *vis-à-vis* genocide, and stands rather as the international community's best attempt at formulating a policy of genocide elimination.

13.2.3 Formal and Humanitarian Bias

Moreover, prevention is typically seen as a long term activity, one that is political but not confrontational, and that focuses on institution building, "early warning mechanisms" and education.[20] There is at times a technocratic feel to the field. Much is invested in liberal protections, the rule of law and human rights. The emphasis of international legal efforts on genocide prevention is geared towards what is more neatly apprehended by the law. One might argue that international law spends more time defining the phenomenon than it arguably does finding innovative solutions to fight it

---

[17] *Convention on the Prevention and Punishment of the Crime of Genocide*, 1948, art. 8.

[18] *Case concerning the application of the Convention on the Prevention and Punishment of the Crime of Genocide (Bosnia and Herzegovina v. Serbia and Montenegro)*, Judgment, International Court of Justice Reports, 2007 I.C.J (February 27, 2007), para. 165; see also paras. 428–438.

[19] State responsibilities emerging from the Genocide Convention are outlined in Francis M. Deng, Chapter 4, Section 4.2 (above), the nature of obligations under the Genocide Convention and the necessity for implementation of domestic legislation are discussed in Wenqi Zhu and Binxin Zhang, Chapter 12, Sections 12.2 and 12.4 (above).

[20] Examples of prevention mechanisms are outlined in Francis M. Deng, Chapter 4, Section 4.5 (above).

and of course that, in its insistence on definitions, it creates more reasons for inertia.[21,22] Genocide is seen essentially as a crime, secondarily as an international delict that might lead to state responsibility, but less as a phenomenon that might be averted regardless of who it is attributable to. Domestically, the emphasis is on incorporation of international provisions, particularly the Genocide Convention. The prevention provisions in the Genocide Convention are typically not susceptible to any easy incorporation, and are not what is targeted. Furthermore, prevention tends to be focused on the long term but seems to have less to say about the more immediate response to a threat of genocide or even an ongoing campaign of atrocities. It is almost as if this form of prevention was destined to make intervention of some sort at one point necessary.

In some cases, there will be a tendency to often conflate the categories of war and genocide, and to see genocide as a humanitarian and relief problem, rather than as a fundamentally political and normative, involving fundamental patterns of discrimination and oppression rather than, for example, a problem of regulation of force. The classic case of this was the ICRC's visit to Therensendstad, and the more general inability to understand the Holocaust for what it was. Clearly Auschwitz was never a humanitarian problem involving a failure by the Nazis to abide by certain humanitarian obligations, any more than the systematic slaughtering of the Tutsis was a humanitarian disaster. Both were a deliberate and absolute rejection of there being such obligations in the first place. Even though the international community has progressed significantly on that front, the debate still rages and has both an over and under-inclusive dimension: the risk of treating as genocide that which is not, and the risk of not treating as genocide that which should be.[23]

13.3 The Problem with the International Prevention Paradigm

13.3.1 The Failures of International Prevention

The emphasis on the reactive, international and legal is not only interesting as a study of the particular ideological biases of a project and discipline. It is also relevant in light of what must surely be assessed as the catastrophic

---

[21]David Scheffer, "Genocide and Atrocity Crimes," *Genocide Studies and Prevention* 1, no. 3 (2006).

[22]Problematic consequences of applying Genocide Convention definitions leading to the exclusion of certain groups are discussed in Gérard Prunier, Chapter 3, Section 3.1 (above) and Francis M. Deng, Chapter 4, Section 4.2 (above).

[23]Jerry Fowler, "Beyond Humanitarian Bandages-Confronting Genocide in Sudan," (2004).

record of the international community in actually preventing atrocities. It is as if the discourse were immune to its cyclical failure, only prompting more soul searching and hand wringing.

Rather than simply blaming the failures of international prevention on the powers that be, their egotism and ill will, it may be more interesting to understand what might be problematic and even a little pernicious about the discourse itself. The discourse of international prevention is typically part of a broader narrative of global socialization and governance that sees genocide as a test case of its resolve and its ability to enforce its norms. It is a discourse that is heavily top-down, often technocratic and that easily falls prey to the aporia and indecisiveness of the international.

What is important to note at this stage is that this emphasis on the state and the international community comes with a number of costs in the form of mental habits and standard expectations. Insistence on making the international community the agent of all prevention leads to significant problems of collective action, sovereignty, and politics. On the one hand, the Genocide Convention is part of an attempt to see beyond sovereignty by "piercing the sovereign veil" and as such part of the great post-Holocaust drive to promote human rights on an international basis.[24] On the other hand, as soon as one raises the specter of strong meddling in "internal" affairs, one reactivates strong defenses of sovereignty. This is a problem that the international community regularly announces solved but which constitutes one of the most durable obstacles to international efforts at genocide prevention or mitigation.[25] Moreover, issues of international intervention (even for the purposes of preventing) then raise issues of international legitimacy for intervening with a vengeance, whilst potential targets invoke counter-discourses of colonialism, imperialism and third world resistance.[26] The goal then becomes one of "convincing" the "international community" that it has a duty to rescue[27] and the quasi-impossible task of transforming bystander states into states that care,[28] even as others, ever suspicious of the international community's motives, caution against

[24]Amitai Etzioni, "Genocide Prevention in the New Global Architecture," *The British Journal of Politics & International Relations* 7, no. 4 (2005).

[25]Vaughn Shannon, "Judge and Executioner: The Politics of Responding to Ethnic Cleansing in the Balkans," *Journal of Genocide Research* 7, no. 1 (2005). KJ Campbell, "The Role of Individual States in Addressing Cases of Genocide," *Human Rights Review* 5, no. 4 (2004).

[26]Examples of such counter-discourses include the objections raised by the Sudanese government and discussed in Catherine Lu, Chapter 18, Sections 18.1 and 18.2 (below).

[27]Randall Robinson, "The Obligation to Rescue I," *Social Research* 62, no. 1 (1995).

[28]Michael Stohl, "Outside of a Small Circle of Friends: States, Genocide, Mass Killing and the Role of Bystanders," *Journal of Peace Research* 24, no. 2 (1987).

it. It is almost as if international law in trying to address the problem tended to thereby endlessly perpetuate it.[29]

If sovereignty is involved and a crisis has been allowed to ripen to genocidal stage, then the militarized discourse of humanitarian intervention will come relatively easily to the international community, creating its own set of problems. With the discourse of international intervention comes a natural inclination to formulate the problem in "macro" terms; having made the problem into a "big" one, the temptation is to conceive of its solution in "big," institutional terms.[30] It is difficult, then, not to see in the international genocide prevention paradigm a discourse that is slightly surreal (even the current marginally more integrated conditions of international life) in the way it focuses on what should be rather than what is.

13.3.2 Disempowerment of the "Victim"

More important perhaps, is the way in which seeking to strengthen the resolve of the "international community" ends up effectively minimizing alternative accounts of how atrocities might be prevented, particularly those involving civil society.[31] In effect, I would argue that there is a powerful discourse at work which disempowers local non-state actors as participants in the genocide prevention efforts, through the all-encompassing figure of the "victim." International lawyers may not *deny* that civil society has a role in preventing genocide, but nor do they see much of a connection between what international law does and what civil society on the ground is involved in doing to stop it. This disempowerment is effected through a series of rhetorical moves that recur again and again.

Victim-oriented discourse, particularly in the context of the international repression of genocide, has assumed a very considerable prominence since the 1990s. To an extent, it can be seen as having filled the vacuum left by the weakness of other justifications for international criminal justice in the international realm. One of the problems with the concept of the "genocide victim," however, is that it has tended to be very univocal. Central to the conceit is that the victim be only that, in other words that the victim be meek, weak, and subdued ("lambs to the slaughter").[32] The ICTR speaks of the "mainly defenseless Tutsi population at the Mugonero

[29] Siswo Pramono, "An Account of the Theory of Genocide" (2002).

[30] See for example Samuel Totten, "The Intervention and Prevention of Genocide: Sisyphean or Doable?," *Journal of Genocide Research* 6, no. 2 (2004).

[31] The role of civil society and its potential impact on preventing atrocities are discussed in Rebecca J. Hamilton, Chapter 15 (below).

[32] Note that this goes both ways. Here I am interested in the extent to which the victim's role as a resister is often denied, but one could say the same thing about the extent to which the role of the victim as a collaborationist is never discussed.

Complex and in Bisesero,"[33] and attacks against "defenceless civilians,"[34] or "the defenceless civilian Tutsi"[35] as aggravating circumstances.

Victims are by and large deprived of agency. If victim agency is mentioned at all, it is merely in the context of demanding reparations, generally under international lawyerly guidance. This in turn leads to a tendency to portray the victim as always and principally in demand of outside assistance. It is important that the victim be meek and subdued for outside intervention to be validated as all the more necessary and heroic.[36] The victim is objectified as simply that, in a way that dispels anxieties about how its agency, potentially its opposition or reservations about an intervention, might affect the interventionist agenda.

As a result, the dominant international legal discourse on genocide seems to have developed little in terms of the victim as resister.[37] A rigid dichotomy is set out between perpetrator and victim, which highlights the former as the systematic wielder of violence and the latter as its systematic recipient, thus ignoring complex processes of counter-violence and resistance. The "resisting victim" is the figure that is excluded from this confrontation.[38] International criminal law has of course reasons of its own for this sort of portrayal. It is famously every *génocidaire*'s favorite excuse to claim that the victim group was somehow a threat.[39] Thus it may seem crucial to prosecutorial depictions of the Rwandan genocide that Tutsi victims not be presented as having fought back, lest some elements of a *génocidaire* and revisionist account be indirectly vindicated. The idea that the *génocidaires* might occasionally be acting in self-defense individually is clearly unfathomable and has never been considered in the jurisprudence of any international criminal tribunals.[40]

---

[33] *The Prosecutor v. Elizaphan and Gérard Ntakirutimana*, Case Nos. ICTR-96-10 & ICRT-96-17-T, Judgment (February 21, 2003), para. 912.

[34] *The Prosecutor v. Eliézer Niyitegeka, 2003)*, Case No. ICTR-96-14-T, Judgment and Sentence (May 16, 2003), para. 499.

[35] *The Prosecutor v. Juvénal Kajelijeli*, Case No. ICTR-98-44A-T, Judgment and Sentence (December 1, 2003), para. 956.

[36] See David Kennedy, "Spring Break," *Texas L. Review* (1985), 1402–1405. Kennedy, a US human rights lawyer was part of a US delegation visiting Nicaraguan prisons. When faced with passive inmates and their privations, Kennedy felt a sense of indignation and motivation to act. By contrast, in the face of individuals who were not passive but political activists engaged in a struggle, Kennedy's sense of mission waned.

[37] See Martin Cohen, "Culture and Remembrance: Jewish Ambivalence and Antipathy to the History of Resistance," in *Resisting the Holocaust*, ed. Ruby Rohrlich (Oxford: Berg Publishers, 1998), 22.

[38] Mahmood Mamdani, *When Victims Become Killers: Colonialism, Nativism and the Genocide in Rwanda* (Oxford: James Currey Publishers, 2001).

[39] The characterization of genocidal events as acts of self-defense is discussed in Irwin Cotler, Chapter 9, Section 9.4.5 (above).

[40] See Frédéric Mégret, "Why 'War Crimes Tribunals' are not War Crime Tribunals" (forthcoming).

Surely however this is a false problem, and it is not possible "to assume that a lack of effective resistance is a genocidal criterion."[41] In a sense the whole idea of international criminal justice is based on both a rejection of the factual veracity of such assertions (the Tutsis were indeed not a fifth column working for the FPR), and a rejection of their normative relevance on classical deontological grounds (even if it were true that some Tutsis were working for the FPR, that in no way justifies committing any crime against the Tutsi group or its members). Victims of genocide could resist as much as possible and genocide would still be occurring. The resistance of Tutsi civilians on the Bisesero hills in no measure confirms the point that the Tutsis were indeed the allies of the FPR; it simply evidences a basic desire to survive in the face of desperate odds. Victims of the brutal crushing of the Warsaw ghetto insurrection were as much victims of the Holocaust, and could certainly not be considered parties to a larger war effort that would have made them legitimate targets under humanitarian law for example.

13.3.3 Neglect of Resistance

Against an international view that is at least ambivalent about if not indifferent to victim resistance, I want to suggest a much more positive vision of the role that civil society, particularly that civil society that is on the frontlines of resistance can play. International policy prescription on genocide is often singularly at odds with what historians have taught us in at least the last half-century about how genocides are effectively prevented or minimized. I have in mind, in particular, a considerable amount of Holocaust literature that has rediscovered the ways in which many victims, far from the image of "lambs to the slaughter," were in fact often very active in resisting the advance of genocidal plans and genocide.

It is of course very difficult to know how many potential victims of atrocities were saved by these actions. In absolute terms, the numbers are certainly not negligible but they will often pale in comparison to the total of victims, and sometimes verge on the symbolic. The point is a more subtle one, however. Of all those who were saved, the vast majority owed their rescue not to anything like the international community, but to themselves,[42] the courage of strangers[43] or resistance movements. In all the examples

[41]Graham Charles Kinloch and Raj P. Mohan, *Genocide: Approaches, Case Studies, and Responses* (New York: Algora Publishing, 2005), 46.

[42]Michael R. Marrus, *Jewish Resistance to the Holocaust*, vol. 7, *The Nazi Holocaust Historical Articles on the Destruction of European Jews* (Westport, CT: Meckler, 1989). Particularly the sources found in his study provide extensive numbers of individuals who survived the Holocaust due to their efforts.

[43]Mordechai Paldiel, *The Path of the Righteous: Gentile Rescuers of Jews During the Holocaust* (Jersey City, NJ: KTAV Publishing House, Inc., 1993). Paldiel gives an idea of

referred to above, therefore, resistance by the victims of atrocities and by civil society more broadly has proven to be possibly the most significant factor in limiting, pushing back or even stopping atrocities. Conversely, the absence of resistance to atrocities is notoriously one of the ways in which those are allowed to be committed. And of course the point of resistance was that it was often haphazard, uncoordinated and spontaneous; it is very difficult to know what its impact might have been had it been more actively supported by outside actors.

Much of the literature on resistance to genocide has focused on its actors, given that different actors seem to raise different psychological, political and moral dilemmas. Resistance to genocide can be conceived of as operating on a series of concentric circles. The first circle is the victims (or potential) victims themselves, and anything they may do to oppose the logic of genocide and escape victimization. The second circle is relatives, friends, acquaintances who do not belong as such to the targeted group and thus are in a position to help.[44] The third circle is that of "ordinary" bystanders, individuals who are not in any particular way tied to the targeted community but may help nonetheless.[45] The fourth circle is what one might describe as "regime" insiders who, for either personal or ideological reasons, can use their position to oppose, slow down the genocide, or protect certain individuals from it (e.g.: Oscar Schindler).[46] The fifth circle is transnational solidarity and might include foreigners on the territory where the genocide is committed (e.g.: Raul Wallenberg).[47]

---

the number of Jews that were saved by others. For example, in the case of France, it is argued that as many as 200,000 Jews (2/3s of French Jewry) were saved by gentiles. Similarly, Nathan Tec (1986) estimates that 80% of the Jewish survivors studied had benefited from the help of strangers.

[44]Kalyanee Mam, "The Endurance of the Cambodian Family Under the Khmer Rouge Regime: An Oral History," in *Genocide in Cambodia and Rwanda: New Perspectives*, ed. Susan E. Cook (New Brunswick, NJ: Transaction Publishers, 2006).

[45]Ervin Staub, "The Psychology of Bystanders, Perpetrators, and Heroic Helpers," in *Understanding Genocide: The Social Psychology of the Holocaust* (Oxford: Oxford University Press, 2002); Richard G. Hovannisian, "Intervention and Shades of Altruism During the Armenian Genocide," in *The Armenian Genocide: History, Politics, Ethics* (New York: St. Martin's Press, 1992).

[46]Paldiel, *The Path of the Righteous*.

[47]Other examples might include Spanish Blue Division soldiers (Wayne Bowen, "'A Great Moral Victory': Spanish Protection of Jews on the Eastern Front, 1941–1944" in *Resisting the Holocaust*, Ruby Rohrlich, ed. (New York: Berg, 1998). Johannes Lepsius in the case of the Armenian genocide sought to document ongoing atrocities relaying information from the interior to often disbelieving public opinions abroad. J Lepsius, *Rapport secret sur les massacres d'Arménie* (Beiruth: Édition Hamaskaïne, 1968). Some foreign priests in Rwanda are also known to have had a significant role. J.M. Janzen, "Historical Consciousness and 'a prise de conscience' in Genocidal Rwanda," *Journal of African Cultural Studies* 13, no. 1 (2000). Some have a role in relaying information from the scene of crime to the outside world.

This view of resistance to genocide according to its actors is very helpful, except its determinants seem hard to gauge, and not the sort of thing that one could go about creating in the abstract or as a result of policy. An alternative is to look not so much at the types of actors as to the types of resistance they put in place. This leads us to question what sort of resistance may be the most helpful and perhaps more importantly, what the shared elements are of known examples of resistance. Before I do so, I want to briefly outline a particular vision of causes of genocide that will then make it clear why I think a vision of prevention as, fundamentally, boiling down to resistance is opportune.

13.4 Genocide, Law and Habitual Obedience

There are many competing explanations of how and why genocides occur, ranging from the political to the psychological. Among those are surely a range of legal factors in the preparation of genocide. Against a vision of genocide as pure unconstrained violence, a vision has emerged of atrocities being at least permitted by the Law. Genocide often relies deeply on morally enabling circumstances and, beyond, Law's complicity and is not simply or in some cases at all a violation of domestic law.[48]

In that respect, I suggest the term "genocidal law" not so much to describe laws that would authorize genocide (there are unlikely to be any that are that direct), but to designate a complex of norms, both legislative and administrative, which collectively, through designation, stigmatization of certain groups and unleashing of violence against them, are an essential building block of genocides.[49] Genocidal law, in other words, includes both what the law mandates and what it tolerates, the law's letter, its spirit and the great many gaps in between. In relying on such a concept, I do not want to engage in the jurisprudential controversy over whether genocidal law is law properly so-called[50] (I believe it clearly is not, but this is not what I am getting at here), or assess whether genocides are committed more against

[48]See for example Richard H. Weisberg and Michael R. Marrus, *Vichy Law and the Holocaust in France* (Oxford: Routledge, 1996).

[49]The role of the modification of laws regulating citizenship, especially the Nuremberg Laws, in paving the way for genocidal acts is examined in Douglas Greenberg, Chapter 5 (above).

[50]H.L.A. Hart, "Positivism and the Separation of Law and Morals." *Harvard Law Review* 71, no. 4 (1958); Lon L. Fuller, "Positivism and Fidelity to Law: A Reply to Professor Hart," *Harvard Law Review* 71 (1958). Stolleis's views on this jurisprudential debate are interesting because they make the connection with the issue of resistance to emphasize, in particular, the extent to which resistance groups like the White Rose "violated valid law" and that "therein lies their courage and dignity." Michael Stolleis, *The Law under the Swastika: Studies on Legal History in Nazi Germany* (Chicago: University of

or thanks to the law (this will depend on the context).[51] Nor do I want to touch on the complex issue of whether historically law has been abused by enthusiastic racists or whether genocide is a product of rigid positivistic adherence to the law when it has been corrupted. Rather, I simply want to make the case that at least the build-up to genocide and sometimes its dangerous vicinity is almost always reliant on a fundamental *appearance* of law, which imbues the acts of executioners with a very superficial veneer of formal legitimacy.[52]

What the law (or what passes for it) manages to command is a very precious resource, namely a measure of habitual obedience, reinforced in genocidal regimes by a high degree of intimidation and physical threat. For example Herbert Kelman and Lee Hamilton have described how genocide can be understood as one of a series of "crimes of obedience," i.e.: "crimes that take place, not in opposition to the authorities, but under explicit instructions from the authorities to engage in these acts, or in an environment in which such acts are implicitly sponsored, expected, or at least tolerated by the authorities." There are arguably no crimes more based on obedience than international crimes committed by or at the instigation of the state, and genocide is a good example because of its reliance on considerable numbers of agents.[53] In fact, the famous Milgram "obedience experiments" were launched in the wake of the Eichmann trial precisely with a view to understanding the Holocaust.[54] Their application to the Holocaust is rightly considered controversial,[55] especially in light of the

---

Chicago Press, 1998), 160. Indeed, it does seem that there is something particularly honourable about violating superficially valid but profoundly immoral laws (a testimony to clarity of vision, for example, as against the appearance of law), where perhaps the suggestion that Nazi law "was not really law" is historically disconnected from the reality and suggests that ordinary Germans were simply under an illusion about its existence.

[51]A.H. Lesser, "The Holocaust: Moral and Political Lessons," *Journal of Applied Philosophy* 12, no. 2 (1995), 145–147.

[52]At times, obviously the veneer would have gone from thin to absolutely transparent, but the extent to which even discipline within the camps and the reasons for gasing prisoners (e.g.: they were "saboteurs") was justified by pseudo-law remains remarkable. RE Wittmann, "Indicting Auschwitz? The Paradox of the Frankfurt Auschwitz Trial," *German History* 21, no. 4 (2003).

[53]Herbert C. Kelman, "The Policy Context of International Crimes," in *Conference on System Criminality in International Law* (Amsterdam Center for International Law), 2. The example used herein is primarily that of torture, which is presented as a crime that is characteristic of the state and legitimized by some of its founding doctrines, including the need to protect law and order from enemy groups. The analysis, however, is also shown to be applicable to massacres and genocide.

[54]Stanley Milgram, "The Perils of Obedience," *Psychology in Today's World. Boston: Little, Brown* (1975), T Bloss, "The Roots of Stanley Milgranas Obedience Experiments and Their Relevance to the Holocaust."

[55]Ann L. Saltzman, "The Role of the Obedience Experiments in Holocaust Studies: The Case for Renewed Visibility," *Obedience to authority: Current perspectives on the Milgram paradigm* (2000).

existence of a number of "willing executioners" whose sadism cannot be explained by following orders (alone).[56] However, it is not implausible that a number of ordinary Germans would not have been enlisted in an effort that was cumulatively genocidal, had it not been for the presence of a thin layer of law signaling the need to conform.[57]

Notably, the law is an integral part of maintaining discipline in the military. In the context of the Second World War, punishment for various forms of "desertion" relied heavily on the German military justice system, which emphasized the extent to which obedience was a moral duty to the Reich and disobedience not only a military offence but a betrayal of the national community.[58] The number of executions sky-rocketed in a way that one can imagine had a substantial chilling effect on any desire to disobey. More specifically, the law is often an inherent part of the processes of "authorization, routinization, and dehumanization" that make these crimes possible.[59] Alexander Alvarez has applied the "techniques of neutralization" argument[60] to the study of the Holocaust.[61] Neutralization refers to "the specific mechanisms that the participants (in genocide) applied to neutralize internal opposition"[62] and involves, for example, the systematic denial of responsibility in conditions where one sees oneself as following orders. Rather than simply making the fundamentally wrong legal, in some cases the law lends its legitimacy to processes that disaggregate the tasks of genocide, making each step appear independently legitimate even as the taking of all the steps carries out a genocidal intent. As Alvarez puts it, "The participants in genocide are ... conforming to rather than opposing established authority structures and legal codes."[63] In such a context, the highly

[56] Allan Fenigstein, "Were Obedience Pressures a Factor in the Holocaust?," *Analyse & Kritik* 20 (1998). (Pointing out that "the vast majority of those who did the killing believed it was just and necessary and would have been willing to kill Jews, even in the absence of an order to do so.")

[57] Arthur G. Miller, "What Can the Milgram Obedience Experiments Tell Us About the Holocaust," *The social psychology of good and evil* (2004): 234. ("The experiments certainly generalize to those persons in Nazi Germany who obeyed orders, despite having personal reservations about what was happening to the Jews, and who did not harbour what Goldhagen terms eliminationist, anti-Semitic beliefs.") Moreover, one can speculate that those who would have had genocidal behaviour anyhow are even more likely to engage in such behaviour in a context where the law acts as a facilitator.

[58] Steven R. Welch, "Harsh but Just'? German Military Justice in the Second World War: A Comparative Study of the Court-Martialling of German and Us Deserters," *German History* 17, no. 3 (1999).

[59] Herbert C. Kelman, "Violence without Moral Restraint: Reflections on the Dehumanization of Victims and Victimizers," *Journal of Social Issues* 29, no. 4 (1973).

[60] Gresham M. Sykes and David Matza, "Techniques of Neutralization: A Theory of Delinquency," *American sociological review* (1957).

[61] Alexander Alvarez, "Adjusting to Genocide: The Techniques of Neutralization and the Holocaust," *Social Science History* (1997).

[62] Ibid.: 170.

[63] Ibid.: 141.

exceptional punishment of an SS officer for the unauthorized murder of thousands of Jews, for example, can be seen as a way of giving the illusion of normalcy in a situation where the Law has long ceased to be anything but the tool of the exceptional.[64]

Of course, the fact that defendants in genocide trials almost always invoke a superior order defense does not actually mean that they themselves believe in it or, quite aside from whether such defenses should be accepted or not, that orders did indeed have a causal role. But the law is part of a culture of obedience – indeed one of its incarnations – on which genocidal enterprises thrive, an "air of legality" in an atmosphere of permission. Specifically, the law would seem crucial in the early stages of the construction of genocide[65] when the appearance of normalcy needs to be sustained, i.e.: when prevention could be at its most useful before it is too late. The law is also particularly useful in that genocides are in essence massive collective endeavors, requiring the coordination of a great many perpetrators over time and space. The law provides the frameworks of common understanding, hierarchy and regularity that is part of the logistics of genocide.

Admittedly those elements will be stronger in systems previously characterized by the rule of law and where genocidal tendencies manifest themselves slowly through the dismantling of guarantees and perversion of the legal system. The build up and carrying out of the Holocaust may therefore be a better paradigmatic case for this argument because of its unique reliance on legal features than the Armenian, Rwandan or Cambodian genocides which occurred in ways that perhaps more significantly bypassed the need for law altogether.[66] However, even in those cases an element of strong state legitimization of obedience to orders was involved. Indeed, "Law" can be seen as a larger metaphor for habitual obedience to the dictates of the state, so that controlling the levers of formal power and legitimate violence

---

[64]Yehoshua Robert Buchler, ""Unworthy Behavior": The Case of SS Officer Max Täubner," *Holocaust and Genocide Studies* 17, no. 3 (2003). Max Täubner was not convicted so much for the fact of having killed Jews (in fact he was praised for doing so), than because his unit had not been assigned that task, and because his men photographed the deeds, something which might have compromised the security of the Reich. In doing so, the court found that he had highlighted his "disregard for the law."

[65]See Omar McDoom et al., *Rwanda's Ordinary Killers: Interpreting Popular Participation in the Rwandan Genocide* (Crisis States Research Centre, LSE, 2005). The article finds that itegeko, or obedience to authority and the law was one of the crucial factors in explaining why participants in the Rwandan genocide participated in roadblocks. According to McDoom (at p. 6), "it was only once a commitment to genocide had been made by state authority figures who were still authoritative in the eyes of the population that mass mobilisation in an anti-Tutsi programme of action was triggered." Interestingly, obedience also accounts for the Tutsis' "initial faith ... in their sector conseiller after Habyarimana's death."

[66]An analysis of the impact of citizenship laws in the context of the Holocaust, Armenian Genocide, Cambodian Genocide and Rwandan Genocide is provided in Douglas Greenberg, Chapter 5 (above).

was always key to the ability to implement a genocidal plan.[67] For example, Alison Des Forges has said of the Rwandan genocide that:

> Many Rwandans say that they killed because authorities told them to kill. Such statements reflect less a national predisposition to obey orders, as is sometimes said, than a recognition that the "moral authority" of the state swayed them to commit crimes that would otherwise have been unthinkable. Itself the chief actor in a masquerade of legitimacy, the interim government gave its officials and citizens the cover of "legitimate" orders to hide from themselves and others the evil they were doing.[68]

In fact, in the case of Rwanda for example, the legal system lent its support to the colonial practice of registering individuals according to their ethnicity, to the point for example of entertaining court cases in which individuals challenged the ethnic affiliation of others, and of punishing mayors for having abusively changed the affiliation of some under their authority.[69] Moreover, appeals to genocide masqueraded as communal labor obligations in which killing was referred to as "doing the work" and weapons as "the tools," in a context where the state had long fine-tuned an apparatus of control of the population.[70]

If not active persecution by the Law along the lines of the Nuremberg Laws, genocide is manifested by a retreat (rather than dissolution) of the law from those areas where it might be most needed, the organization of power's impunity, and the systematic denial of remedies to victims. "Less law," however, is still very much a recognizably legal phenomenon. Even when sheer force is involved, when duress replaces voluntary obedience, it can be argued that duress takes its cue from obedience and frequently follows existing formal power structures (for example German, Cambodian and Serb executioners who were "forced" to commit genocidal crimes were often forced by de jure or de facto superiors).

13.5 Resistance to Genocide as a Normative Activity

An understanding of genocide as at least in part constituted by abidance with the law can help us refocus the study of resistance to genocide as fundamentally a form of resistance against law's habitual obedience

67 Michele D. Wagner, "All the Bourgmestre's Men: Making Sense of Genocide in Rwanda," *Africa Today* (1998).

68 Alison Des Forges, Human Rights Watch, and Fédération internationale des droits de l'homme, "*Leave None to Tell the Story*": *Genocide in Rwanda* (Human Rights Watch, 1999), 14–15.

69 Jean Mukimbiri, "The Seven Stages of the Rwandan Genocide," *Journal of International Criminal Justice* 3, no. 4 (2005): 827.

70 Helen M. Hintjens, "Explaining the 1994 Genocide in Rwanda," *The Journal of Modern African Studies* 37, no. 02 (1999).

claims. Whilst there are many studies of the role of resistance in genocidal environments, few take into account that specifically legal dimension.

One way of looking at resistance is that, borne of emergency and instinct, it is something that simply "happens," in an often improvised, haphazard and ad hoc way. In some ways, resistance is a-legal. Moreover, to the extent that resistance develops against the law, it is perhaps more specifically anti-legal. However, resistance is hardly a non-normative activity. It takes its inspiration in more than just the survival instinct and a knee-jerk biological reaction to the threat of destruction. It is, crucially, an attempt to visualize the danger that lies ahead and to organize, sometimes collectively, in an effort to fend it off. It is often inspired by an alternative vision of what the law is or should be. Moreover, regardless of how actors subjectively conceive of their resistance (and of course they will be principally motivated by saving their existences rather than just making a point about the law's unjustness), if genocides happen because of the descent of law into lawlessness and scrupulous abiding by false law, then conversely genocides may objectively be prevented by acts of resistance to the law that breeds genocide.

Thus there is a sense in which genocide resistance and prevention is a norm inspired activity, either because it targets laws directly or, more generally, because it posits itself as a challenge and alternative to that law. Seeing resistance as directed at the state's legal order and the sort of blind allegiance it is at times capable of mustering in its genocidal enterprises can be a way of transcending some of the psychologism and romanticization involved in portrayal of "heroic altruism" in times of extreme violence (which has been described as both "apolitical and individualistic")[71] by locating resistance to genocide within the study of resistance to the law and the state more generally.[72] Maybe resistance is a special case thereof, but as I will endeavor to show the ways in which law is resisted are arguably only quantitatively, not qualitatively different from modes of resistance that have been deployed in other circumstances. In doing so, I hope to propose a model of resistance that focuses on "civic virtues" of the highest order, including a strong emphasis on autonomy *vis-à-vis* the state, rather than the sometimes prevalent focus on altruism and empathy to explain

---

[71]David H. Jones, "On the Prevention of Genocide: The Gap between Research and Education," *War Crimes, Genocide and Crimes Against Humanity* 1, no. 1 (2005): 8.

[72]This would be a vast research agenda in itself, and in this article I will only suggest how certain ideal typical forms of resistance to genocide in that they position themselves in defiance to the dominant legal order, raise a number of issues common to all resistance and even activism. For an exploration that seeks to link both literatures, see for example Rachel L. Einwohner, "Identity Work and Collective Action in a Repressive Context: Jewish Resistance on The "Aryan Side" of the Warsaw Ghetto," *Social Problems* 53, no. 1 (2006).

resistance behavior.[73] In what follows, I suggest a five-prong model of resistance to the law, from the least to the most dramatic gestures of defiance within which I believe most acts of resistance can be located.

13.5.1 *Adapting to the Law*

A first attitude to genocide made law or genocide leaning law might be to seek some sort of accommodation within it. Long before genocides occurred, individuals at times sought to adapt to the new legal regime. For example the Reichsvertretung der Juden in Deutschland issued a formal declaration after the adoption of the Nuremberg Laws – in a climate of intimidation in which Hitler threatened the community with "further examination of the Jewish question" if no "tolerable relationship" were to be found – in which they essentially asked for greater autonomy in cultural and educational matters as a newly recognized "national minority." In other words, the formal ghettoization of the Jews was met by demands for control over that ghettoization by community institutions. Some historians have argued that the Nuremberg Laws may even have led to a renewal of Jewish community life in Germany.[74]

Another way of adapting to the law is by failing to challenge it but seeking to have it applied in a way that satisfies some personal or short term interest. Arguing that one is not rightly classified as a member of such or such group, or that as a veteran or someone married to an Aryan one should not fall under the Jewish laws, or that certain Jewish lawyers should be released from prison[75] can all be seen as ways of avoiding the worst effects of discrimination. Similarly in Rwanda, in the years preceding the genocide "many Tutsi had sought to become officially Hutu by using official connections, bribes, or other means to receive new identity cards that marked them as Hutu."[76] Individually useful, such strategies could of course all have the effect of unwittingly reinforcing the discrimination inflicted on the rest of the community.

A more extreme form of adaptation to the order of the oppressor is constituted by some isolated cases of collaboration with the genocidal authorities, in the apparent belief that such collaboration could stave off extermination. Perhaps most notoriously, Chaim Rumkowsky, the leader

---

[73]Jones, "On the Prevention of Genocide: The Gap between Research and Education," 26–27.

[74]David Bankier, "Jewish Society through Nazi Eyes 1933–1936," *Holocaust and Genocide Studies* 6, no. 2 (1991): 118–119, but also 24.

[75]Weisberg, *Vichy Law and the Holocaust in France*, 92.

[76]Timothy Longman, "Identity Cards, Ethnic Self-Perception, and Genocide in Rwanda," *Documenting Individual Identity: The Development of State Practices in the Modern World* (2001): 355.

of the Zionist movement in Lodz, ruled over the ghetto Litzmannstadt supposedly to protect it from deportation. Although cooperation with the authorities and the productivity of the factories set up by Rumkowsky account for the fact that the ghetto was not destroyed until the end of the War, it failed to prevent the eventual deportation of all its members, most notably children.[77]

Another extreme instance of adapting to the law consists in bribing those supposed to enforce it with a view to protecting potential victims of genocide. This is a mode of resistance that involves an attempt to undermine legal rules or at least the administration of rules (in a universe where some rules may have become quite negotiable). There are a few notorious cases of bribery being used during the Holocaust in an attempt to save Jews.[78] For example, a group of semi-underground Slovak Jews successfully bribed Dieter Wisliceny, an SS officer who served as Jewish affairs adviser to the Slovak government, with a sum thought to be equivalent to $50,000 in exchange for an intervention to stop deportations. The "Kastner train" allowed 1,700 Jews to escape to Switzerland after Kastner, a leader of the Hungarian Aid and Rescue Committee, negotiated the escape with Eichmann, in exchange for money. In Rwanda, some of those threatened with extermination managed to escape by bribing some of their tormentors (although, grimly, bribes often served to merely obtain a quick death). Bribing the authors of abominable crimes, however, remains an inherently risky mode of acknowledging genocidal authorities, and one that is often fraught with moral ambiguity.[79]

13.5.2 Challenging the Law

A second degree of resistance to the law involves challenging it. The assumption is already that it is the law itself that is the source of oppression and no remedy can be easily obtained from within it. Challenges to the law

[77]Shmuel Huppert, "King of the Ghetto Mor Decai Haim Rumkowski, the Elder of Lodz Ghetto," *Yad Vashem Studies* 15 (1983).

[78]Milton Goldin, "Financing the SS," *History Today* 48, no. 6 (1998), Michael Burleigh, "Jews for Sale? Nazi-Jewish Negotiations, 1933–1945," *The Journal of Modern History* 69, no. 4 (1997), Szabolcs Szita, *Trading in Lives?: Operations of the Jewish Relief and Rescue Committee in Budapest, 1944–1945* (Central European University Press, 2005).

[79]Kastner, who subsequently became the spokesperson for the Ministry of Trade and Industry in Israel, was eventually assassinated by a Holocaust survivor who accused him of having "sold his soul to the devil" when he failed to alert the rest of the community to its fate. See Leora Bilski, "Judging Evil in the Trial of Kastner," *Law and History Review* 19, no. 1 (2001), David Luban, "A Man Lost in the Gray Zone," *Law and History Review* 19 (2001).

still operate within legality, but they express forcefully disagreement with the law's content and typically seek redress of a political sort.

The Nazis T4 program of euthanasia of the disabled was met by such strong protests from the Bishop of Münster and the population that it had to be gradually abandoned. When the Nuremberg Laws were adopted, Leo Baeck composed a Yom Kippur prayer which read in part "... we express our abhorrence of the lie directed against us and the slander of our faith and its expressions."[80] The Union of Jewish War Veterans similarly published pamphlets challenging the law. The Central Union of German Citizens of the Jewish Faith financed historical work aimed at demonstrating the antiquity of Jewish life in Germany "to prove that German Jewry was so integral a component of the German landscape that no anti-Semitic legislation could affect it."[81]

Some in Germany protested the Nuremberg Laws and pogroms, such as Bernhard Lichtenberg, a Berlin priest who wrote to Göring about the concentration camps and led prayers for its victims and was arrested by the Gestapo for "endangering the public peace from the pulpit." Challenges to the law might come from within the legal community itself. For example, upon the occupation of Belgium and the adoption of the first German Law on the status of Jews, three leading Belgian lawyers wrote a letter of protest to the Military Field Commander for Belgium in which they expressed opposition to the law (which, among other things, excluded Jews from the bar and from being judges), and challenged its compatibility with Belgian constitutional law.[82]

However, challenges to the law might take an altogether more direct and practical form. It is said that during the 1933 Nazi boycott of Jewish businesses, amidst the violence and intimidation, some Jewish World War I veterans "stood in front of their own stores wearing their uniforms and medals." Non-Jewish Germans also occasionally helped: "While SA men stood in front of businesses owned by Jews, threatening and taunting those who dared to enter, some Germans chose precisely that day to visit a Jewish doctor or grocer."[83]

In times of great danger, challenges to the law may come from close relatives of members of the targeted group, who can still use their status to argue against its merits without being put too much at risk.

[80]Dalia Marx, "Liturgy Composed on the Brink of Catastrophe," in *Leo Baeck-Philosophical and Rabbinical Approaches*, ed. W Homolka (Frank & Timme GmbH, 2007), 90, Bankier, "Jewish Society through Nazi Eyes 1933–1936."

[81]Bankier, "Jewish Society through Nazi Eyes 1933–1936," 121.

[82]Although characteristically they did not challenge legitimacy of the principles underlying the Reich and the protest only applied to Jewish lawyers. Maxime Steinberg, *La Persécution des Juifs en Belgique (1940–1945)* (Editions Complexe, 2004), 111.

[83]Marion A. Kaplan, *Between Dignity and Despair: Jewish Life in Nazi Germany* (Oxford University Press, USA, 1998), 21–23.

The demonstration of German women married to Jewish men on the Rosenstrasse to obtain the release of their husbands is a good example of this.[84] It has been said more generally that the "non-compliance of intermarried Germans, by the time the deportation of Jews in Germany began, had influenced Hitler to hesitate" because of an apparent reluctance to be "publicly associated with divisive matters."[85]

Challenges to the law may be effective to an extent but still typically acknowledge the fundamental legitimacy of the law. For example, some manifestations of discontent at the Nuremberg Laws by Jewish officials were coupled with affirmations of loyalty to the "fatherland," seemed to welcome the clarification in legal status and to have partly fallen prey to the Nazi lie that the laws were essentially meant to protect the Jewish minority through "dissociation."[86]

13.5.3 Disobeying the Law

Disobedience, the third stage of reaction to genocidal law, involves a more conscious and deliberate attempt to bypass, albeit not seriously confront, the law. It occurred against Nazi law on a fairly large scale. For example, after the prohibition of kosher butchering in 1933, it is known that "in spite of state directives and potentially severe punishment ... a small group of kosher slaughterers continued to perform their work in secret, slaughtering thousands of chickens every week."[87] A typical act of resistance to the law would eventually consist in refusing to obey orders that one present oneself at a certain time and place, or refuse to register as a certain member of a group. In the killing fields of Cambodia, even stealing rice on a small scale from collectivized property might prolong one's life and the life of others through the ordeal.[88]

Disobedience is a strategy that is particularly relevant for groups that have not been so marginalized that they already operate on the fringes of legality or within clandestinity, and in fact may include individuals who are very much in a position to disobey. Harboring Jews during the Second World War was often not only illegal, but criminal and punishable by death. Every person who did so was therefore very consciously defying the law.

---

[84]Nathan Stoltzfus, "Protest and Silence: Resistance Histories in Post-War Germany: The Missing Case of Intermarried Germans," in *Resisting the Holocaust*, ed. Michael Marrus (Berg, 1998), 151–178.

[85]Ruby Rohrlich, *Resisting the Holocaust* (Berg Publishers, 1998), 163.

[86]Abraham Margaliot, "The Reaction of the Jewish Public in Germany to the Nuremberg Laws," *Yad Vashem Studies* 12 (1977).

[87]Kaplan, *Between Dignity and Despair: Jewish Life in Nazi Germany*, 33.

[88]Haing Ngor and Roger Warner, *A Cambodian Odyssey* (New York: Macmillan, 1987).

Particularly interesting is the case of disobedience by officials, i.e.: individuals who are agents of the state and are meant to be particularly at the forefront of the law's implementation. The mass fabrication of fake passports or visas by the likes of Wallenberg, Feng-Shan Ho, San Briz, Perlasca, Chiune Sugihara, Frank Foley was often in direct contradiction to orders or instructions. Aristides de Sousa Mendes, the Portuguese consul in Bordeaux, had been given explicit orders not to give visas to "foreigners of indefinite or contested nationality; the stateless; or Jews expelled from their country of origin." Notwithstanding, he issued visas to over 30,000 refugees escaping Nazi advance, 12,000 of whom were Jews.[89] Swiss border guards who allowed Jewish refugees into Switzerland despite a clear prohibition are in the same category. In Bosnia, one could argue that, even temporarily, General Morillon's disobedience to the UN in promising assistance to the population of certain safe-zones was, by the standards of UNPROFOR, a remarkable instance.[90] Captain Mbaye Diagne, an unarmed Senegalese UN observer in Rwanda, decided to ignore UN orders and saved many innocent lives, losing his own life in the process.

Among the disobeyers, most notably, have at times featured a small but revealing number of individuals within the genocidal system. Perhaps one of the most striking cases of disobedience is that of Georg Ferdinand Duckwitz, a special envoy and trade attaché to occupied Denmark and a Nazi party member, who secretly paid a visit to neutral Sweden to convince its Prime Minister to allow Danish Jewish refugees to escape there. Duckwitz also notified leaders of the Jewish community of the imminent threat of deportation, allowing over 6,000 Jews to eventually escape to Sweden.[91] Helmuth von Moltke, a lawyer working for the German Intelligence Service, smuggled copies of the White Rose tracts to neutral countries. Karl Plagge, a German officer sent to the Eastern front who opposed the Nazis' racialist theories, gave work certificates to Jewish men, certifying them as essential and skilled labor regardless of their backgrounds and eventually covertly warned them of their imminent deportation.[92] Kurt Gerstein, an SS officer who, during a trip and early witness of gassing of Jews who, upon accidentally meeting a Swedish diplomat in a train, told him of what he had seen and urged him to spread the information internationally.[93] Dimitar Peshev, the Bulgarian Minister of Justice

[89]Mordecai Paldiel, *Diplomat Heroes of the Holocaust* (Ktav Publishing House, 2007).

[90]The difficulties encountered by peacekeepers in Bosnia are analyzed in Wiebe Arts, Chapter 8, Section 8.1 (above).

[91]Emmy E. Werner, *A Conspiracy of Decency: The Rescue of the Danish Jews During World War II* (Westview Press, 2002).

[92]Michael Good, *The Search for Major Plagge: The Nazi Who Saved Jews* (Fordham University Press, 2005).

[93]Valérie Hébert, "Disguised Resistance? The Story of Kurt Gerstein," *Holocaust and Genocide Studies* 20, no. 1 (2006).

during the Second World War obtained the cancellation of the order to deport Jews.[94] Cases of Arab tribesmen and even Iraqi army personnel who protected Kurds from executions during Anfal are known.[95] In Rwanda, we know of the Hutu insider ("Jean Pierre") who warned Dallaire of impending massacres.[96] Finally, in a more anonymous way, thousands of soldiers have also over the decades refused to lend their support to genocidal campaigns in World War II,[97] Bosnia,[98] Cambodia, and Darfur,[99] often at considerable risk to themselves. Although these cases remain very much the exception rather than the rule, they were often each in their own way quite successful at undermining genocidal policies.[100]

13.5.4 Escaping the Law

Once there is nothing to be expected from the law or any hope of changing it, a second stage is what one might describe as "escaping" the law, an attempt to more or less entirely subtract oneself from its reach. Escaping the law might be temporary, as for example in the case of refusing to take particular Nazi oaths or to execute certain missions, even if that meant considerable personal risk, in addition to loss of professional status. It might also mean premature retirement by those who would not lend their credibility to an enterprise they disapproved of. In many cases, it meant exile. In the 1930s in Germany, thousands of Jews emigrated to other European countries, the US or Palestine rather than be subjected to second class

---

[94]Gabriele Nissim, "Dimiter Peshev, the Vicepresident of the Bulgarian Parliament Who Made a Whole Nation Feel Ashamed."

[95]Stephanie Nolen, "Split by War: Kurd to Seek His Past in Baghdad," *Globe and Mail*, 5 April 2003, A8.

[96]Touko Piiparinen, "Reconsidering the Silence over the Ultimate Crime: A Functional Shift in Crisis Management from the Rwandan Genocide to Darfur," *Journal of Genocide Research* 9, no. 1 (2007).

[97]Douglas Peifer, "Commemoration of Mutiny, Rebellion, and Resistance in Postwar Germany: Public Memory, History, and the Formation Of" Memory Beacons,"" *Journal of Military History* (2001).

[98]Katharina Schnoring, "Deserters in the Federal Republic of Yugoslavia," *International Journal of Refugee Law* 13, no. 1_ and_ 2 (2001).

[99]*BBC*, "Confessions of a Sudanese Deserter," March 4, 2009, http://news.bbc.co.uk/2/hi/africa/7921311.stm.

[100]It is worth pointing out however, that not all disobedience is virtuous, and that the very selectivity of disobedience by some can in fact evince a deeper desire to broadly collaborate with the state. See for instance, *The Prosecutor v. Tharcisse Muvunyi*, Case No. ICTR-2000-55A-T, Judgment and Sentence (Sep 12, 2006), para 540: (after noting that the accused had saved some Tutsis, the Appeals Chamber insisted that "does not consider this to be a mitigating factor. On the contrary, the Chamber considers that the selective exercise by the accused of his power to protect civilians based on friendship or family ties, was further evidence of his abuse of office and authority. His duty was to protect all civilians in danger irrespective of ethnicity or personal relationships").

citizen status. More radically, especially once the possibilities of escape diminished, it might mean going into hiding ("submerging" is the word that Jews used in Germany). This involved a particular life outside or beyond the law, that is without law's threat but also without what might have been law's protection.

Of course, it would be hard to "escape" the law without also disobeying it. In many cases, the law was used as an instrument to bind populations to a territory, whist their fate was being decided.[101] Not only is living in clandestinity itself typically illegal in a variety of ways, but it also often involves resort to specific unlawful means, that might be illegal even in a non-genocidal context (e.g.: the forgery of documents, bribery, the illegal crossing of borders). However, unlawful behavior in this case is really a means to a more radical end.

Particularly central to resistance to genocide is shedding the markers that make one a target of the administrative state as a Jew, a Cambodian intellectual, or a Tutsi. The centrality of identification of individuals as belonging to certain groups to genocidal enterprises has long been documented.[102] Resistance to such designation might begin with the tearing off of the yellow star, a first foundational offence in what was to then become a life of clandestinity. In Rwanda, those escaping the genocide and who were ordinarily forced to carry with them an identity card occasionally used "documentation as a tool to mold their identity, contravening the intentions of those who established the systems of documentation."[103] Such efforts are a very real challenge to the law's attempt to lend its help to the construction of a dubious ethnicity.[104]

Life beyond the law might be individual, family-based or involve entire communities. Although often not considered as part of resistance, there is a case that in a situation of impending massacre, merely heeding one's survival instinct to escape capture, often at huge personal risk and cost, is in fact an act of resistance. Individual and collective escapes have, at any rate, had a significant impact on the mitigation of atrocities. In some cases, like the Bielski otriad in the Byelorussian forests, entire communities were recreated in difficult but safe conditions.[105] Similarly, groups of fugitives

---

[101] For example, a proclamation by Ludwig Fischer, the German district governor of Warsaw, announced that "Any Jew who illegally leaves the designated residential district will be punished by death." Quoted in Paldiel, *The Path of the Righteous: Gentile Rescuers of Jews During the Holocaust*, 3.

[102] Jim Fussell, "Group Classification on National Id Cards as a Factor in Genocide and Ethnic Cleansing. Presented on 15 Nov" (2001). HM Hintjens, "When Identity Becomes a Knife: Reflecting on the Genocide in Rwanda," *Ethnicities* 1, no. 1 (2001).

[103] Longman, "Identity Cards, Ethnic Self-Perception, and Genocide in Rwanda," 347.

[104] Problematic aspects of conceptions of ethnic identity, particularly in the context of Rwanda, are discussed in Francis M. Deng, Chapter 4, Section 4.2 (above).

[105] Nechama Tec, "Jewish Resistance in Belorussian Forests: Fighting and the Rescue of Jews by Jews," in *Resisting the Holocaust*, ed. Ruby Rohrlich (1998), 77–94.

during the Rwandan genocide managed to await the end of massacres. In escaping or hiding, many might benefit from various bystanders whether it is the Danish population's help to Jews escaping to Sweden,[106] gentile families hiding Jewish children,[107] Hutus protecting Tutsis,[108] or Arab civilians bringing assistance and even rising against the deportation of the Kurds during Anfal.

13.5.5 Confronting the Law

A fifth stage of resistance, once hiding will not do because one has been caught or because hiding is unbearable or because hiding is not enough, consists in confronting the genocidal order for what it is.

The confrontation need not be violent. Mere presence and the ability to relay information to the outside world may be instrumental in slowing down the onset of a genocidal enterprise. The famous Vrba-Wetzler report, written by two Auschwitz escapees, was the first attempt to estimate the number of people killed at the camp.[109] In many cases, confrontation will be clandestine since there will be no position of safety from which confrontation can occur. In 1942, students from the White Rose group published a leaflet in Germany which stated "We want to inform you of the fact that since the conquest of Poland, 300,000 Jews in that country have been murdered in the most bestial manner."

Resistance might also take some spectacular violent or quasi-military forms, coming close in fact to a fully-fledged insurgency. For victims, a good example is the armed opposition of Armenians at Musa Dagh and Van.[110] Several Jewish armed groups were organized, most famously, the uprising of the Warsaw Ghetto.[111] There were in fact acts of resistance within

---

106 Paldiel, *The Path of the Righteous: Gentile Rescuers of Jews During the Holocaust*.

107 Hillel J. Kieval, "Legality and Resistance in Vichy France: The Rescue of Jewish Children," *Proceedings of the American Philosophical Society* (1980): 482–509.

108 Villia Jefremovas, "Acts of Human Kindness: Tutsi, Hutu and the Genocide," *Issue: A Journal of Opinion* (1995): 28–31.

109 Erich Kulka, "Attempts by Jewish Escapees to Stop Mass Extermination," *Jewish Social Studies* (1985).

110 Franz Werfel, *The Forty Days of Musa Dagh* (New York: The Viking Press, 1934); Rouben Adalian, "Musa Dagh," in *Encyclopedia of the Modern Middle East and North Africa*, 2nd ed., vol. 3, edited by Philip Mattar (New York: Macmillan Reference, 2004), 1612–1613.

111 Eli Tzur, "From Moral Rejection to Armed Resistance: The Youth Movement in the Ghetto," in *Resisting the Holocaust* (Berg publishers, 1998), 39–58; Yisrael Gutman, "The Genesis of the Resistance in the Warsaw Ghetto," *Yad Vashem Studies* 9 (1973): 118–159.

concentration camps, such as Sobibor and Treblinka.[112] In Rwanda, 50,000 Tutsis resisted in the hills of Bisesero.[113] Desperate attacks were launched by members of the Cham ethnic group against the Khmer Rouges;[114] the Peshmergas resisted fiercely during Anfal;[115] the Patriotic League in Sarajevo successfully fended off countless Serb assaults.[116]

Confrontation, as the ultimate form of resistance to genocidal law, has at times been successful,[117] and often ended tragically. The deeper point of confrontation between victims and perpetrators may lie less in the number of those saved than the powerful symbolic point made about the dignity of those who are being targeted.

13.6 Assisting Resistance: How Can the International Community Help?

If I am correct in assuming that the best hope of averting or limiting the consequences of genocide lie with an infinity of small, local acts of resistance rather than a univocal focus on big, structural and international solutions to the problem, then what if anything can be done to bridge the gap between the two? Can international law imagine much more concrete ways of being at the service of those involved in resistance efforts, rather than a pure alternative to them?

It bears emphasizing, to begin with, that states have clearly not always been on the side of genocide resistance, for reasons that have very much to do with sovereignty and the structure of international affairs. Swiss border-guards who let in Jews in violation of the law were often demoted; Varian Fry had his American passport withdrawn from him after the Vichy government complained of his activities in helping Jews escape to the American government (which was neutral at the time); one of the reasons for refusing

[112] Yitzhak Arad, "Jewish Prisoner Uprisings in the Treblinka and Sobibor Extermination Camps," in *The Nazi Holocaust. Historical Articles on the Destruction of European Jews*, ed. Michael Marrus (1989), 240–283.

[113] For an interesting study of the much higher survival rate of those Tutsis who fled and resisted attacks, see Philip Verwimp, "Death and Survival During the 1994 Genocide in Rwanda," *Population Studies* (2004).

[114] Ben Kiernan, "Introduction: Conflict in Cambodia, 1945–2002," *Critical Asian Studies* 34, no. 4 (2002): 483–495.

[115] Robert G. Rabil, "Operation "Termination of Traitors": The Iraqi Regime through Its Documents," *Middle East Review of International Affairs* 6, no. 4 (2002).

[116] Irfan Ljubijankic, "New World Order and Bosnia and Herzegovina," *Journal of Muslim Minority Affairs* 16, no. 1 (1996).

[117] United Nations. Office of the High Commissioner for Human Rights., *The Core International Human Rights Treaties* (New York: United Nations, 2006).

to send ransom money for the Europa Plan was that transfers to Axis countries were not permitted; the British Foreign Office felt that no special effort was required to rescue the Bergen Belsen Jews because the camp was to be visited by the ICRC; the State Department Legal Advisor's Office returned a memo against radio jamming when asked whether it might be used in Rwanda to stop genocide.[118] Belgian UNAMIR soldiers were ordered to and complied with orders to abandon 2,000 refugees in the Don Bosco school, almost all of which were subsequently killed.[119] As Richard Holbrooke put it: "We mocked the defense of many Germans after World War II when they said that they were just following orders or did not know about the death camps. But a similar rationale was used by an overwhelming majority of non-German diplomats in Europe during the 1930s to deny Jews entry into their countries."[120]

Legal obedience therefore also obviously extends to the principal actors of the international legal order. Notwithstanding, there is a need for international law to not only subvert the sources of oppression, but more generally uphold resistance. Rather than the classic post-Auschwitz question of whether the international community should bomb the railway lines to the camps, the question might be something more like what can international law do to help the Anne Franks and Raul Wallenbergs of this world?

In the same way that I have argued adaptation to the law as a normative strategy of resistance to genocide may have perverse effects, so too can rescue efforts that merely adapt rather than tackle genocide. The international community cannot afford except in the most dire cases to engage in some of the compromises with the genocidal regime that some of its victims have at times had to engage in.[121] Consider, for example, the following word of caution by Harff:

> we should recognize that despite good intentions, rescue may in fact have negative effects. If we rescue the select few—the prominent scientists, literary figures, gifted and healthy children—or those who have ethnic ties to us, we may play into

[118]The refusal to resort to radio jamming on grounds of freedom of expression as a means to cover political objectives is discussed in Mark Thompson, Chapter 6 (above).

[119]Paolo Tripodi, "When Peacekeepers Fail Thousands Are Going to Die. The Eto in Rwanda: A Story of Deception," *Small Wars & Insurgencies* 17, no. 2 (2006).

[120]Richard Holbrooke, "Defying Orders, Saving Lives-Heroic Diplomats of the Holocaust," *Foreign Affairs* 86 (2007).

[121]Bribing was used towards the end of the Second World War to extricate some Jewish victims from deportation, most notoriously by Wallenberg in Budapest. Bribing remains controversial, however. At the end of the war a number of Nazi dignitaries sought to protect themselves from future prosecutions by collaborating in the rescue of Jews. Others sought to exchange lives for goods that could have been used to continue the war, or even as part of a larger peace deal. Richard Breitman and Shlomo Aronson, "The End of The" Final Solution"?: Nazi Plans to Ransom Jews in 1944," *Central European History* (1992).

the hands of the perpetrators. Rescue based on talent, intelligence, and usefulness mimics the selection rationale of the perpetrators of massive human rights violations—only the motives are reversed.[122]

On the assumption that accommodation is not a viable strategy of prevention and not something that qualifies as resistance, what does international law have to offer civil society in resistance? If it is the case that civil society is the crucial actor in preventing genocide, then what kind of legal ideas might reinforce that role? If traditional international law came up with a paradigm of external intervention, then conversely what vision of international law does the paradigm of resistance presuppose?

13.6.1 Helping Victims Help Themselves

13.6.1.1 The Importance of Legitimizing

The reluctance of international law to engage matters of resistance to oppression when it comes to genocide is a manifestation of a more general reluctance to internationally legitimize resistance to the Law. Notwithstanding, there is clearly a normative basis for a right to resist genocide, even in flagrant violation of domestic norms. I have argued elsewhere that there is a case for a general right to resist oppression in international law, and that international law could even one day reframe itself as an "international law of resistance."[123] If a right of resistance is defendable for anything, it should be to resist genocide. There would be something profoundly awkward if international law legalized national liberation struggles against decolonization on the one hand, and failed to recognize a right to resist genocide. The Genocide Convention does recognize that "at all periods of history genocide has inflicted great losses on humanity" and that "mankind" needs to be liberated "from such an odious scourge." Obviously the Convention is not exhaustive of all means that are susceptible of being deployed to mitigate genocide.

There are easily understandable reasons why not more was said about the rights of populations threatened by genocide. The Convention was drafted at a time where to suggest that states and the international community might not be able to prevent the next genocide, in the wake of the Holocaust, would have been almost inconceivable. It is the same paradox that led the drafters of the Universal Declaration of Human Rights to not proclaim a right to resist oppression, or that made the UN gladly relinquish

[122] Barbara Harff, "Rescuing Endangered Peoples: Missed Opportunities," *Social Research* 62, no. 1 (1995).

[123] Frédéric Mégret, "Le Droit International Peut-Il Être Un Droit De Résistance? Dix Conditions Pour Un Renouveau De L'ambition Normative Internationale," *Etudes internationales* XXXIX (2008).

the effort to codify international humanitarian law to a third party external to the system (the ICRC). The UN could not on the one hand embark on the grand task of promoting human rights worldwide and already anticipate its demise by suggesting that if it failed then people should have the right to resist oppression (although the UDHR came close in its Preamble); nor could the UN outlaw war in grand fashion and enter the detailed exercise of regulating its pursuit.[124]

Be that as it may, the passing of time and a better understanding of the strength and limitations of the international community, as well as what it is that has actually prevented, hindered, limited genocides makes it necessary to expand our legal concept of what can be done legitimately to resist genocide. A clear signal by the international community delegitimizing a genocidal domestic order, and encouraging resistance could at least deprive the genocidal state of the luxury of habitual obedience, and possibly energize resistance effort. More importantly, it could form the basis of a whole series of legal policies to stop genocide in its tracks.

13.6.1.2 The Importance of Warnings

A powerful role for international prevention might consist in finding ways to help victims and potential victims better protest against or extricate themselves from genocidal situations. One first contribution that can be made from outside to resistance is informing populations of some of the specific risks that await them. This may be particularly necessary when the enormity of deeds threatened is such as to raise incredulity from potential victims, and delay important decisions. How different might the Holocaust have been if more victims had been informed and convinced of the fate that awaited them?[125]

During the Second World War, some efforts were conducted in that respect: the allies dropped thousands of leaflets reproduced from the ones originally written by the White Rose. Various rescue efforts sought to document what had happened in some countries in an effort "to arouse an increased awareness of what was liable to occur in a certain community, on the basis of past experience elsewhere." Dalia Ofer cites the example of letters sent to Hungary before Nazi takeover, instructing "the leaders of the Rescue Committee in Hungary ... not to cooperate with the Germans – even in a passive manner – by carrying out activities which

[124]The idea of a right to resist genocide has been pursued more exhaustively in David B. Kopel et al., "Is Resisting Genocide a Human Right?," *Notre Dame Law Review* 81, no. 4 (2006).

[125]This was, among other things, the object of a significant controversy surrounding the Vrba-Wetzler report.

were 'preparation for destruction,' such as census, concentration, yellow star etc."[126]

13.6.1.3 The Importance of Protection

Creating the conditions in which victims can then act to fight or escape genocidal plans should be a second priority. International human rights law retains a strong residual role here in helping reinforce civil society against the repression of the state, particularly various challenges to genocidal law. It should stand by to resist the state's attempt to qualify certain resistance behavior as in violation of domestic law, by instead insisting (when such is the case, of course) that it is in fact an exercise of perfectly protected political rights. For example, if an individual involved in a campaign to protect the rights of a minority and fight back certain genocidal tendencies is imprisoned for defamation or treason, international human rights law (through its usual channels) has a very characteristic role to play in restraining the state's repressive thrust.

If the threat is more pressing, the international refugee regime can provide avenues of escape for threatened populations. The idea that what is at stake is avoiding genocide against an entire group rather than simply preventing persecution of certain individuals is one that should ultimately inform the creation of the sort of policies that the Allies, tragically, never implemented during the Second World War. In the 1990s, however, the Humanitarian Evacuation Programme to airlift threatened Kosovars provided an instance of what has become known as "temporary protection of refugees."[127] In opening borders widely, and even assisting threatened groups in their escape rather than fixating them in places where they will continue to be vulnerable, the international community might provide various forms of collective and temporary asylum, whose modalities still need to be invented. International law still has a long way to go to transcend its overwhelmingly humanitarian approach to the issue of refugee protection.

13.6.1.4 The Importance of Assisting

Once escaping is no longer a solution and that the genocidal state is being confronted by groups within it, it should be a duty of the highest order of the international community to operationally stand besides groups spearheading the effort. At times, the presence of international troops, whilst

---

[126] Dalia Ofer, "The Activities of the Jewish Agency Delegation in Istanbul, 1943," in *Rescue Attempts During the Holocaust: Proceedings of the Second Yad Vashem International Historical Conference, Jerusalem, April 1974*, ed. Efraim Zuroff Ysrael Gutman, 442.

[127] Joan Fitzpatrick, "Temporary Protection of Refugees: Elements of a Formalized Regime," *American Journal of International Law* (2000).

too limited to stop a genocide, can at least provide immediate shelter and protection for fugitives. During the Rwandan genocide, for example, up to 25,000 Rwandans are estimated to have assembled at positions held by UNAMIR. In fact, it seems that "it did not take many soldiers to dissuade the Hutu from attacking,"[128] and one Senegalese captain is credited with having saved hundreds of lives.

During the Second World War the Polish Council for Matters Relating to the Rescue of the Jewish Population had as one of its instructions:

> (. . .) to provide food for the Jewish population in the homeland, to provide arms to that portion of the Jewish population that is suited to do battle with the Germans, to hide the Jewish population in the cities and villages, to provide the Jewish population with documents that might shield it from deportation and murder, to transmit funds to the homeland for the purpose of covering expenditures connected with on-site action, to organize the passage of a certain portion of the Jewish population to neighboring countries, to insure the maintenance of those Polish Jews who make it across the border, to organize assistance for Jewish Polish citizens located upon the occupied territory or threatened by the enemy beyond the borders of the homeland, to undertake any other steps aimed at improving the situation of the Jewish population in Poland, and to carry out these plans by using any means attainable through government activity.[129]

Other agencies followed suit, with the International Rescue Committee facilitating visa granting to socialist militants from occupied Europe, or the Jewish Agency Delegation in Istanbul channeling resources to struggling Jewish communities. It is ironic that whilst governments have so often channeled resources and even weapons to groups ill worthy of them, thinking about operational assistance to groups confronting genocidal regimes is almost non-existent.

13.6.1.5 The Importance of Giving a Voice

Genocide prevention tends to be monopolized by international bodies. However, there is a case that potential genocide victims will be the best placed to trigger an early warning because of their early sensitivity particularly to laws to which they are exposed. Local knowledge and sensitivity are irreplaceable.

A classic example of what might have been a long term genocide prevention is provided by the today slightly forgotten Bernheim petition presented to the League of Nations in 1933. Franz Bernheim, a 33 year old store clerk complained that he had been dismissed on the basis of his Jewishness in

---

[128] Samantha Power, "Bystanders to Genocide," *Atlantic Monthly* 288, no. 2 (2001).

[129] Quoted in David Engel, *Facing a Holocaust: The Polish Government-in-Exile and the Jews, 1943–1945* (University of North Carolina Press, 1993), 138–139. The creation of the Council was very tardy and followed several refusals to engage in rescue plans, but I am interested here in the fact of its existence and the diversity of the means it anticipated.

application of Nuremberg Laws in Upper Silesia, in violation of the German Polish treaty on Upper Silesa of 15 May 1922. The case is particularly interesting because of the connection it makes between an individual act of challenge to the law and the responsibilities of the international community.[130] Although the petition obviously in no way averted the Holocaust nor was it of course formulated as an effort of genocide prevention as such,[131] it did stave off the implementation of the Nuremberg Laws in Upper Silesia until 1937 (when the treaty expired), no small feat. As one contemporary commentator put it the League's decision that Germany was in contravention of its treaty obligations "was a great demonstration of Germany's loneliness among the nations on the basic issue of human rights, and served to focus public opinion on the Jewish situation in Germany."[132] Indeed, "the Czech and Polish representatives on the Council made it clear that they would bring the question up again, using it as a lever for extending the principle of minority rights to the whole of Germany." Obviously that was not to be, but perhaps had more resolute action been taken by the League of Nations on the matter, the Allies might have been more sensitized or at least more formally put on notice of the particular dangers ahead. Tragically, the League's failure to intervene more forcefully was one of the ingredients that transformed discrimination into genocide.

More generally, the idea of the Bernheim petition as a sort of paradigm of early genocide prevention suggests the need for a richer communicational interaction between potential victims of genocide and the international community. "The study of genocide," in the words of Siswo Pramono, "must establish linkage between the 'international' and the 'individual' within national borders,"[133] especially in a context where humanitarian intervention can have severe unintended consequences.[134] Victims and some

---

[130] Gerg Burgess, "The Human Rights Dilemma in Anti-Nazi Protest: The Bernheim Petition, Minorities Protection, and the 1933 Sessions of the League of Nations," in *CERC Working Paper Series* (Contemporary Europe Research Centre, 2002).

[131] Although clearly some parts of it were premonitory. See Bernheim Petition to the League of Nations, AJYB, vol. 35 (1934/1935), 74–101 ("The reason for this request is that, as the above-quoted laws and decrees demonstrate, the application of the principle of inequality to German nationals of non-Aryan and Jewish descent is being systematically pursued in all spheres of private and public life so that already an enormous number of Jewish lives have been ruined, and if the tendencies at present prevailing in Germany continue to hold sway in a very short time, every Jew in Germany *will have suffered permanent injury so that any restoration or reparation will become impossible, and thousands and tens of thousands will have completely lost their livelihood*"). My emphasis.

[132] Harry Schneiderman, "Review of the Year 5693," *American Jewish Year Book* 35 (1932–1933): 53.

[133] Pramono, "An Account of the Theory of Genocide," 6.

[134] Jide Nzelibe, "Courting Genocide: The Unintended Effects of Humanitarian Interventions," *Jide O Nzelibe* (2008). Allan J. Kuperman, *The Limits of Humanitarian Intervention: Genocide in Rwanda* (Brookings Institution Press, 2001). Sarah Kenyon

victims' groups have a key role in encouraging rescue efforts and should be given the legal recognition that enables them to do so. The debate on the international duty to intervene, in its legal or "just war" form, has been dominated by criteria that have very little to do with victim agency.[135] However, victims or potential victims would seem ideally placed to prescribe whether they want to be rescued (e.g.: whether the costs of a rescue might not be bigger than its benefits), and if so how. One specific way for humanitarian intervention not to be unilateral is through the bilateralism implicit in an understanding between the international community and the victim population.

13.6.2 Disrupting Genocidal Law

Individuals may become "law-breakers in the interests of maintaining what they considered the norms of their society,"[136] but what the "true" norms of that society are may become difficult to assess in times of radical upheaval. International law, conversely, can provide a normative referent that is relatively constant over time. Contra incitement to genocide, what is needed is – rather than simply jamming the radio waves – a public incitement to resist genocide or disobey orders to commit it. This involves both an element of threat and incentives.

13.6.2.1 The Importance of Threats

In order to open up space for strategies of resistance, international law should use all of the resources at its disposal to delegitimize genocidal laws and genocidal policies, with a view to shaking off the stranglehold of habitual obedience. If nothing else, international law, through such initiatives as the adoption of the Genocide Convention and its effort to name what had happened during the Holocaust and beyond, has powerfully influenced the ability of all actors involved to understand genocide as a specific form of violence. The identification of a threat of genocide can have powerful mobilizing effects, given the political, historical and legal associations that come with it. In that respect, the Genocide Convention is also a tool to de-particularize victims' experience, by framing it in the universal language

---

Lischer, "Collateral Damage: Humanitarian Assistance as a Cause of Conflict," *International Security* 28, no. 1 (2003).

[135] Bryan Hehir, "Expanding Military Intervention: Promise or Peril?," *Social Research* 62, no. 1 (1995). This article is typical of a forward looking exercise which nonetheless relies on a characteristically Westphalian grammar even as it explores the potential to subvert it through the just war tradition. Victims' wishes are not mentioned.

[136] Bob Moore, "The Rescue of Jews in Nazi-Occupied Belgium, France and the Netherlands," *Australian Journal of Politics & History* 50, no. 3 (2004): 389.

of a particularly abhorrent crime, when the temptation might otherwise be strong to describe massacres as not specifically genocidal.[137]

Whilst it is true that international law is better at sanctioning past or at best ongoing instances of genocide, more can probably be done of international law's deterrent potential to fulfill the promise of prevention. As has been mentioned, the limit of international criminal justice is that if often operates for the long run. Although courts would presumably be prevented from doing so, there is nothing that stops a number of authorized international actors from threatening prosecutions in specific situations and against specific individuals. This can usefully bridge the gap between long term deterrence and special deterrence directed at specific individuals, long before and independently of their being found guilty of crimes.

Rather than judging individuals *ex post* on the basis of resort to natural law concepts, as has been done from Nuremberg to the East German border guard cases, the international community could be clear about what laws it intends to use, with a view to dispelling any notion that domestic law will provide a cover. In 1944, Raul Wallenberg threatened SS Commander August Schmidthuber with future prosecutions and execution if he followed Eichmann's order to execute 100,000 remaining Jews in Budapest, to apparently significant effect. At around the same time, it is thought that Prime Minister Horthy stopped deportations after a cable between the Jewish Agency and England was intercepted that asked that all members of the Hungarian government be eventually held accountable for their participation. In the wake of the bombings of Serbia in 1998, British NATO commanders made it known to Serb officers that they would be held liable for any atrocities committed in Kosovo. Somewhere at the intersection of psychological ops and criminal justice lies a potential for intimidation of would-be *génocidaires*.

13.6.2.2 The Importance of Disobedience

In terms of threats, international law is also the locus of some norms that suggest it not a duty at least a clear right to disobey the state. Perhaps the most clear is the Nuremberg judgment. If it is the case that having obeyed superior orders is indeed not a defense under international criminal law, then it follows that a duty to disobey unlawful orders exists – at least if one wants to avoid committing international crimes. International criminal law, over the last decade, has gone quite far in refusing to recognize not only superior orders but also situations of duress as full defenses (although they may be taken into account as mitigating circumstances). This only reinforces the pressure on all echelons of the military to do their utmost to

[137] The Genocide Convention's aspiration for universality is discussed in Gérard Prunier, Chapter 3, Section 3.1 (above).

resist in cases where genocide is involved. It requires a sustained effort of education, particularly of the military,[138] which applies not only to armies potentially involved in genocide, but also to those who one would expect to be able to protect victims.[139,140] In addition, outside military contexts there is even less doubt that one should disobey unlawful instructions.

Thinking about certain standards of "manifest illegality" has been dominated by the idea that identification of such illegality is particularly clear in cases of international crimes.[141] Manifest illegality is constituted by much behavior that does not make it remotely to the level of genocide (e.g.: any war crime). The only ambiguity when it comes to genocide is whether the person executing the order also shared the "special *mens rea*" of the person giving it to "destroy a group as such." However, arguably even if he does not the acts involved might qualify as crimes against humanity and thus be manifestly illegal. The international community might also emphasize in some cases the extent to which threats of punishment by the state is sometimes partly a bluff, and that genocidal regimes will not always have the resources or the willingness to discipline unwilling executioners.[142]

More positively, the international community might provide a degree of protection to disobeyers, deserters or "whistle blowers" in the case of an impending genocide, granting them some sort of protection. For example, Eric Talbot Jensen, a Judge Advocate for the US Army, has made a sophisticated argument in favor of creating ways to "incentivize and protect

[138] Martha Minow, "What the Rule of Law Should Mean in Civics Education: From the 'Following Orders' Defence to the Classroom," *Journal of Moral Education* 35, no. 2 (2006).

[139] On the need to encourage a sense of moral autonomy amongst peacekeepers so that massacres such as that of the ETO school in Rwanda are not repeated, see Paolo Tripodi, "Peacekeepers, Moral Autonomy and the Use of Force," *Journal of Military Ethics* 5, no. 3 (2006).

[140] Guidelines for peacekeeping missions and the possibility of creating a UN school for peacekeeper training are discussed in Wiebe Arts, Chapter 8, Section 8.2.4 (above).

[141] For example, Mark Osiel has discussed the possibility of extending the "manifestly illegal order" rule to "unjust wars and coups." M Osiel, *Obeying Orders: Atrocity, Military Discipline and the Law of War* (Transaction Pub, 2002), 83. If soldiers are expected to be able to distinguish just from unjust wars under threat of liability, in the current stage of very complex jus ad bellum developments, then a fortiori they should see the illegality that is in genocide.

[142] I say this on the basis of the oft mentioned analysis that "There is not a single instance on record of harsh punishment ever being used, or even being possible, for disobeying a killing order." Also CR Browning, *Ordinary Men: Reserve Police Battalion 101 and the Final Solution in Poland* (HarperCollins Publishers, 1992). This is not to minimize the risks taken, which were extremely real, but to point out that nor should invocations of superior orders by those responsible systematically be taken at face value. Another example where even the Nazi machine seemed paralysed is the Rosenstrasse protests. With characteristic chutzpah, Wallenberg also managed to escape Arrow Cross thugs.

informants prior to mass atrocities such as genocide."[143] Rather than complex and institutionalized "early warning systems" that have shown their limits, the idea is to take maximum advantage of the possibility that some "insiders" at least will be willing to consider revealing plans to commit atrocities. That initial willingness must be exploited internationally, through a mixture of offers of protection, immunity and possibly monetary reward. In some cases, the incitation to disobey should probably be coupled with more political concessions, for those involved but also for their country.[144]

13.6.2.3 The Importance of Responsibility

Another area in which the law, particularly international law, could make progress is by developing a better concept of bystander responsibility, essentially making the at least nominal case that individuals who fail to do anything to prevent that which they could have prevented might be found liable of something. "Silent majorities" have generally been treated very leniently as part of transitional justice settlements and as the work of Laurel Fletcher has shown (one of the few to have paid attention to these issues) "liberal law adjudication implies a false moral innocence among bystanders."[145] The difficulty is that the criminal law is rightly reluctant to condemn on the basis of pure omissions. However, this may be because the person condemned would be condemned for the full offence (e.g.: genocide), rather than a specific offence (failure to rescue someone threatened with genocide in a situation where one could have). Moreover, what is needed is to determine with some precision in what circumstances a "duty to rescue" would arise, presumably on the basis of some special responsibility.

A higher recognition that passive bystanders are not entirely innocent, that there is no neutral ground in the face of genocide, could perhaps go some way to delineating the boundaries of moral and legal responsibility. It might contribute to create a culture of intranquility *vis-à-vis* some of the more glaringly unjust outcomes of the law, especially from those who are

143 Eric Talbot Jensen, "Incentivizing and Protecting Informants Prior to Mass Atrocities Such as Genocide: An Alternative to Post Hoc Courts and Tribunals," *Houston Journal of International Law* 29, no. 1 (2006).

144 A contrario, it has been argued that the Allied doctrine of unconditional surrender meant that "those Germans-and particularly those German generals-who might have been ready to throw Hitler over, and were in a position to do so, were discouraged from making the attempt by their inability to extract from the Allies any sort of assurance that such action would improve the treatment meted out to their country." Michael Balfour, "Another Look at Unconditional Surrender'," *International Affairs (Royal Institute of International Affairs 1944-)* (1970).

145 Laurel E. Fletcher, "From Indifference to Engagement: Bystanders and International Criminal Justice," *Mich. J. Int'l L.*: 1079.

in a position to intervene.[146] As Fletcher argues, such a recognition could be obtained by criminal judgments of perpetrators that at least emphasize the facilitative impact of bystanders and caution that they "should not be considered to exonerate those who are not before the court."[147] If not through the criminal law then the problematique of bystanders might become more intrinsic to truth and reconciliation processes. The question of international peacekeepers who, even though they do not strictly have the mandate, stand by idly as populations are massacred is one that is very apt to be analyzed from a bystander perspective.[148]

13.6.2.4 The Importance of Rehabilitation

In terms of positive incentives, the promise of rehabilitation to those condemned by the genocidal regime or in any way disparaged by third states could provide a measure of incentive, especially for those whose moral sense needs to be energized by more concrete incentives. Rehabilitative efforts should be expected and included in all transitional strategies, partly to restore the dignity of the resisters and emphasize their heroism; partly to throw the basis of a new rule of law, expunged of the sins of the past; and partly, sadly, if all is too late for the victims of the previous bout of atrocities, as a contribution to the reinforcement of protections in societies that have been affected by genocide. The international community could act as a sort of guarantor that rehabilitation will take place.

To a degree, rehabilitative strategies have become more prominent in transitional justice efforts, and are a distinct element of thinking about genocides.[149] Many of the main actors of the German resistance to Nazism were eventually recognized. The widows of some Rwandan genocide victims have been known to intervene on behalf of some accused of atrocities to emphasize the extent to which they had saved Tutsis.[150] The international criminal tribunals have, somewhat contentiously in this case, occasionally included rescue efforts by some of the accused as at least a mitigating circumstance at the sentencing stage.[151] However, rehabilitation does remain

---

[146] Arne Johan Vetlesen, "Genocide: A Case for the Responsibility of the Bystander," *Journal of Peace Research* 37, no. 4 (2000).

[147] Fletcher, "From Indifference to Engagement: Bystanders and International Criminal Justice," 1082.

[148] Robert Siekmann, "The Fall of Srebrenica and the Attitude of Dutchbat from an International Legal Perspective," *Yearbook of International Humanitarian Law* 1 (1998).

[149] Digne Rwabuhungu, "Synthèse Du Colloque: « Les Justes face au génocide: réflexion sur une attitude héroïque » Organisé par la communauté rwandaise de Belgique," (2008).

[150] "Les Justes: entre oubli et réconciliation," (*Penal Reform International*, 2004), 29.

[151] Assistance to potential victims has been given "limited weight" in final sentencing outcomes (see, e.g.: *The Prosecutor v. Eliezer Niyitegeka*, Case No. ICTR-96-14-A,

under-theorized and little understood by lawyers. For example it took four decades for Swiss border guards to be fully and almost always posthumously rehabilitated by the Swiss government. The German army long opposed too emphatic a rehabilitation of Wehrmacht deserters during the Second World War. Various "legal pluralist" efforts such as Yad Vashem's award of the "Righteous" title have had a tremendous impact[152] and more could be done in terms of proactively seeking those who have sought to disobey.[153] But they are no substitute for full legal rehabilitation in the countries where the acts were committed.

A serene confidence that that which is wrong will be righted and that some time in the future acts that are at one point presented as treasonous and abhorrent will be considered fully in accordance with both law and morality might have a certain impact in encouraging strategies of resistance. One can only wonder what might have happened had some of the UN battalions stationed in Rwanda in 1994 decided, out of their own initiative and in violation of orders, to actively and militarily seek to protect as many potential victims of the genocide as they did. Too often from the Jean Bosco School to Srebrenica, peacekeeping forces did exactly the contrary, either handing over victims to their tormentors or, if not quite that, turning a blind eye to their imminent plight.

Appeal Chamber Judgment (July 9, 2004), paras. 264–265; *The Prosecutor v. Tihomir Blaskic*, Case No. IT-95-14-T, Judgment (March 3, 2000), para 782; *The Prosecutor v. Kajelijeli*, Case No. ICTR-98-44A-A, Appeals Judgement (May 23, 2005), paras. 310–311. However, it has been considered as a mitigating factor, such as in *The Prosecutor v. Joseph Nzabirinda*, Case No. ICTR-2001-77-T, Sentencing Judgment (Feb 23, 2007), paras. 74–77: "the Chamber is of the view that there is sufficient evidence that Joseph Nzabirinda personally assisted Tutsi refugees by way of moral, financial and material support in Sahera secteur during the 1994 events and that he assisted in organising the departure of certain refugees to Burundi. According to the evidence submitted, Joseph Nzabirinda's acts contributed to saving the lives of some of the Tutsi refugees. Therefore, the Chamber finds that Joseph Nzabirinda's assistance to certain victims constitutes a mitigating factor." See however *The Prosecutor v. Tihomir Blaskic*, Case No. IT-95-14-T, Judgment (March 3, 2000), para 781–782. The Court found that the accused "allegedly maintained, here and there, good relations with the Muslims throughout the conflict (...). Notwithstanding this, the Trial Chamber observes that these good relations were sporadic and above all on an individual basis. These factors are all the less decisive when one notes that criminals frequently show compassion for some of their victims even when perpetrating the most heinous of crimes."

[152]The transposability of the "righteous" model to other genocides is nonetheless a matter of debate, and there is some local wariness that the idea is instrumentalized in post-colonial ways. V Rosoux, "The Figure of the Righteous Individual in Rwanda," *International Social Science Journal* 58, no. 189 (2006).

[153]The emphasis in identifying "righteous" has been on fostering reconciliation, much more than it has been exalting disobedience per se. Claudine Vidal, "Les Commémorations du génocide au Rwanda," *Les temps modernes*, no. 613 (2001).

13.7 Conclusion: Rescue v. Intervention?

I have sought to suggest that maybe the international lens is not allowing us to see the diversity of ways in which genocides are avoided, or their effects limited. The acts of resistance I have highlighted are only the most known and they occur closer to the resistance end of the spectrum than the prevention one, but they are arguably a metaphor for the latter. Disobedience should begin when genocidal plans are conceived, and its impact should be maximized and multiplied by targeted, thoughtful international assistance. At a certain level, a society based on a spirit of resistance is one where genocides are not likely to occur in the first place, whereas the massive marshalling of allegiances is a necessary first step to all enterprises of mass killing.

Although resistance will always happen in some way or other, the radical solitude of resisters must be underlined.[154] When confronted with the massive weight of the state and its law, citizens must refuse to answer calls, soldiers need to break ranks, civil servants must refuse to implement directives. Disobedience is unlikely enough in ordinary circumstances, let alone in a genocidal context in which it can translate into death, that it will need all the normative encouragement it can get. To disobey the law of the state is, inevitably, to shake some of the bounds of a communal life, bounds that may have all the appearances of authority and some of the trappings of normality. It is to enter a world of solitude, clandestinity and danger on account of a belief that genocidal law is either not law or not a law worth respecting. It is, in other words, to radically reassess oneself as a citizen of the world, brought back to that bare and precarious condition because of the enormity of the stakes and because the sovereign has ceased to deserve even minimal adherence to its norms. Although individuals will engage in such actions out of sheer courage and sense of moral values it is crucial that this be seen not simply as an issue of weighing morality against law, but also as one of weighing illegitimate v. legitimate law.

International law, in this sort of environment, can be a powerful ferment in cautioning against, eroding and blunting genocidal law. Its role in that respect is perhaps a more modest one than the grand narrative of stopping genocide through intervention or prosecuting those guilty of genocidal crimes. It may involve taking second stage to the efforts of others. But it is also a more profoundly humanistic project than the paternalism implicit in some efforts at genocide prevention. More importantly, it may be more successful and do away with some of the complexities that inevitably beset the international community when it seeks to intervene as such in the affairs of states.

[154]This point is particularly underlined in Klemens Klemperer, " 'What Is the Law That Lies Behind These Words?,' Antigone's Question and the German Resistance Against Hitler," *Journal of Modern History* 64.

There is room for creativity in encouraging a spirit of resistance to mass crimes in every society long before their commission even appears plausible. Indeed, although this paper has concentrated on the more last ditch efforts to avert genocide, it is clear that these are only archetypical and heroic versions of a number of smaller and more discreet gestures that can be posed long before genocide is even conceivable. Civil society initiatives should be developed whose goal is to "immunize" societies from the temptation of atrocities. The objective should be to create a civil society that is a powerful antidote against and ultimately impediment to genocidal enterprises. That break may on its own impede or it may help save lives whilst a larger international intervention is planned. But we need to rediscover guerilla tactics, agit prop, sabotage, psy-ops, *levée en masse* and *francs tireurs*, underground railroads, camouflage, disobedience, and tyrannicide. In view of the massive machinery of the state, one may think that these tactics are puny. But as Satterwhite argues, "it is too easy to dismiss such efforts out of hand, under the assumption that they are not realistic. The problem with this easy dismissal is that, having dismissed alternatives as unrealistic by definition, it proceeds to state that violence represents the only realistic course of action."[155]

None of this obviates the need to pay more attention to what can be done internationally to foster rescue, is not meant to diminish the need, in some cases, for intervention. Indeed, it may well be that "once a Stalin or a Hitler is in the saddle ... the dictatorship cannot be removed by popular revolt," and that "only outside military intervention can do it."[156] But there is a difference between helping rescue victims of genocide and stopping a genocide, in the same way a distinction is often emphasized, for instance during the Second World War, between ordinary rescuers of Jews and anti-Nazi resisters.[157] Although the two may occasionally have been the same and their goals are certainly not incompatible, the latter strove for the resolution of the overall problem (e.g. the end of occupation and the war), whilst the former attended the more immediate task of saving those who could be saved. The international community needs to see itself as more than a "resister," especially in cases where "resistance" is likely to be slow and protracted (Bosnia and Darfur come to mind).

The tension between these two potential roles played out very clearly in one Second World War incident, which may be replicated in other contexts,

155 James Satterwhite, "Forestalling War in Kosovo: Opportunities Missed," *Peace & Change* 27, no. 4 (2002): 607.

156 Franklin H. Littell, "Essay: Early Warning," *Holocaust and Genocide Studies* 3, no. 4 (1988): 484.

157 Samuel P. Oliner, *The Altruistic Personality: Rescuers of Jews in Nazi Europe* (Touchstone, 1992), 170. Peter Suedfeld and Stefanie de Best, "Value Hierarchies of Holocaust Rescuers and Resistance Fighters," *Genocide Studies and Prevention* 3, no. 1 (2008).

and can be seen as a metaphor for the tension at stake. In 1943, the Bergen-Belsen concentration camp was set up. Bergen Belsen was meant as a camp to detain Jews who had been temporarily exempted from deportation to the East. The British Foreign Office was approached by the Germans who offered to release some of the incarcerated Jews in exchange for German civilians held abroad. The British Office immediately rejected such proposals as little more than blackmail and emphasized that "we can best help the Jews by bringing about the defeat of the Nazi regime."[158] This has led Rainer Schulze to comment that "there is no avoiding the fact that it was not only the German side that prevented larger numbers of Jews from Bergen-Belsen from being rescued before the end of the war."[159] As Ofer put it:

> Many believed that the chances of rescue depended solely on winning the war. To a certain extent, this feeling was justified, even though it was liable to impede the practical activities which later led to the rescue of several small groups .... The end of the war would, obviously, end the destruction, but the question was what to do until then? What about those refugees who succeeded in escaping, the remnants who were still alive even after the large-scale waves of destruction, those communities which the Germans had still not reached?[160]

Such dilemmas suggest that there is a middle way between massive intervention to stop a genocide and the many smaller scale efforts that a responsible international community, knowing the limits of its powers, should be prepared to undertake if genocidal threats are to be fought effectively.

Measured against the criticism by Frank Chalk that much current genocide prevention work is informed by "ahistorical optimism" and an "incongruous" combination of humanism and positivism,[161] one of the strengths of the approach to genocide prevention that I have described in this chapter is that it is bottom-up, spontaneous, and decentralized. It does not rely on any grand scheme or solution to all genocides, and is therefore ideally suited to particularized responses, as well as the challenge of tackling genocidal regimes in all available ways.

In recasting itself as an "international law of resistance to atrocities," international law would also inevitably change its character. International law traditionally emphasizes obedience to domestic law and, as a law of states, is unlikely to want to be seen as legitimizing rebellion, be it in the face of genocide. Yet international law has in a sense put itself in front of

---

[158] Rainer Schulze, "Keeping Very Clear of Any 'Kuh-Handel': The British Foreign Office and the Rescue of Jews from Bergen-Belsen," *Holocaust Genocide Studies* 19, no. 2 (2005), quoted at 238.

[159] Ibid.: 243.

[160] Ofer, "The Activities of the Jewish Agency Delegation in Istanbul, 1943," 443.

[161] Frank Chalk, "Definitions of Genocide and Their Implications for Prediction and Prevention," *Holocaust and Genocide Studies* 4 (1989), p. 150.

that dilemma, one that pits its theory of the legitimate actors of the international system against its increasingly vocal support of certain substantive norms. If the international community is indeed serious about genocide prevention, then it should give itself all the means available to try and avert atrocities, even if that means empowering actors and modes of action that it has traditionally seen as of marginal relevance.

Chapter 14
Privatizing Humanitarian Intervention? Mercenaries, PMCs and the Business of Peace

Krzysztof Kotarski and Samuel Walker

14.1 Introduction

It is 1944. The Allies have received credible reports that a Nazi death machine of unprecedented efficiency is operating in Auschwitz, Poland. They refuse to bomb the railroad tracks leading to the concentration camp, citing a need to concentrate precious military resources on the front lines. The Jewish World Congress, refusing to stand by while the slaughter continues, reaches out to a group of enterprising Polish veterans and hires them to destroy the railroad. The saboteurs enter Poland and plant explosives at several critical junctures along the tracks, shutting down Auschwitz. They save thousands of lives and collect a handsome fee. Was it the right thing to do?

It has been nearly 4 years since the United States House of Representatives unanimously declared in July 2004 that "the atrocities unfolding in Darfur, Sudan, are genocide."[1] That this slow-motion annihilation continues to march steadily onwards, even perhaps recently picking up speed,[2] is a radical indictment of the international community and the echoes of "never again" emanating from Cambodia, Bosnia and Rwanda. It is enough to make anyone question whether the ideal of swift, humanitarian intervention by the community of "civilized nations" is a chimera.[3]

K. Kotarski (✉)
Centre for Military & Strategic Studies, University of Calgary, Calgary, AB T2N 1N4, Canada
e-mail: Kkotarski@gmail.com

[1] *Declaring Genocide in Darfur, Sudan*, H.R. Con. Res. 467 (rfs), 108th Cong., 2nd sess. (June 24, 2004).

[2] Lydia Polgreen, "Scorched-Earth Strategy Returns to Darfur," *The New York Times*, March 2, 2008.

[3] The inability of peacekeeping forces to stop atrocities in Darfur is highlighted in Gérard Prunier, Chapter 3, Section 3.2 (above).

R. Provost, P. Akhavan (eds.), *Confronting Genocide*, Ius Gentium: Comparative Perspectives on Law and Justice 7, DOI 10.1007/978-90-481-9840-5_14,

We remain hopeful that one day our political leaders, or the United Nations they control, will mobilize national militaries to bring a swift end to mass atrocities. Those working toward realizing this ideal are engaged in a noble endeavor and we share their vision. But 4 years is long enough to declare that, even should the international community eventually intervene in Sudan, we have already failed the people of Darfur and are likely to do the same when the next genocide occurs. And the next time, we will probably not have 4 years to contemplate inaction.

Recall that it took only 3 months to kill roughly 800,000 people in the 1994 genocide in Rwanda.[4] The moral imperative to stop genocide and similar atrocities demands urgent action, using the tools that the realities of the present world afford us. Bill Clinton declared that his "greatest regret"[5] as President was not taking swift action to save some of the 800,000 slaughtered, estimating that "I believe if I had moved we might have saved at least a third of those lives."[6] If we are serious about our moral outrage against genocide, are we not then bound to honestly consider *all* reasonable options available for stopping it?

This paper explores one such possible alternative, the use of mercenaries. For some the idea will come as a shock, considering that mercenaries generally do not have a much better reputation in popular culture than *génocidaires* themselves. However, put in the proper context, the use of a modern "Private Military Company" (PMC)[7] to protect vulnerable populations threatened by mass extinction can be morally and legally justified. Even Sir Brian Urquhart, considered one of the founding fathers of UN peacekeeping, has acknowledged their obvious advantages, stating that it would be "very foolish to close the door" to the possible use of PMCs in peacebuilding.[8] They present a beguiling alternative to the international

[4]See Arthur Asiimwe, "Rwanda census puts genocide death toll at 937,000," *Reuters*, April 4, 2004, which also cites the lower figure of 800,000 given by the International Criminal Tribunal for Rwanda.

[5]John F. Harris, "Bill Clinton Takes Spot On Global Stage," *The Washington Post*, June 1, 2005.

[6]Scott Helman, "His big regret: not acting in Rwanda," *The Boston Globe*, December 11, 2007.

[7]Some authors have eschewed use of the term "mercenary" when discussing PMCs, as the former tends to elicit visceral condemnation, clouding legitimate debate. Given that our paper seeks to help overcome this knee-jerk reaction, we do not see the point in employing solely euphemistic labels that obscure the basic question – the legitimacy of private, non-state force. See, for example, Katherine Fallah, "Corporate actors: the legal status of mercenaries in armed conflict," in *International Review of the Red Cross*, No. 863 (2006): 602: "the 'mercenary' label is frequently 'applied to express the speaker's disapproval, rather than to describe an individual satisfying the specific criteria under international law' taking on a political rather than legal meaning. In order to defuse the loaded uses of these terms, I shall instead use the expression 'corporate actor'..."

[8]Sir Brian Urquhart, "Dogs of War," interviewed by Tony Jones, Lateline, *Australian Broadcasting Corporation*, May 18, 2000, transcript at http://www.abc.net.au/lateline/archives/s128621.htm (Accessed June 11, 2009).

political deadlock characterizing current responses to genocide, a professional military force that can quickly and cheaply intervene without the associated political cost of state soldiers coming home in body bags.

Objections to funding a "private peace" generally come in two forms: based on principle and on feasibility. Past debates reveal that advocates generally emphasize the obvious practical benefits of mercenaries, suggesting that they somehow override uncontended theoretical objections.[9] We argue instead that there are both principled and pragmatic justifications for employing a PMC to humanitarian ends.

First, we explore the historical and cultural background, revealing that today's puritanical distaste for PMCs arises primarily from a particular historical anomaly, the use of mercenaries in the brutal decolonization struggles of 1960–1970s Africa. We then examine how current laws and international norms carve out exceptions for the legitimate use of PMCs. Finally, we briefly survey some of the main practical concerns, including accountability, command and control, and tactical feasibility. While overall we remain skeptical, under certain circumstances the use of mercenaries could save lives. It is time that this option is ushered out from under the labels of "far-fetched" or "radical" and into the realm of serious discourse.

14.2 The Mercenary in History

Although there is little in the international press to suggest otherwise, modern mercenaries do not all descend from Bob Denard or "Mad" Mike Hoare.[10] Mercenaries have been referred to as the world's second-oldest profession,[11] and while today's PMCs do share at least one main

[9]See, for example, the discussion in the UN regarding using a PMC in Goma, Zaire, as recounted by Bruce D. Jones, *Peacemaking in Rwanda: the Dynamics of Failure* (Boulder, CO: Lynne Rienner Publishers, 2001), 142.

[10]Mike Hoare was the most famous of the Congo mercenaries raising the 5th Commando for secessionist Moishe Tshombe. An ex-British soldier, he has been convicted of hijacking a plane to escape from an aborted coup attempt in the Seychelles in 1981. His account of his mercenary service can be found in: Mike Hoare, *Congo Mercenary* (London: Robert Hale Ltd, 1991). Robert Denard began his mercenary career in the Congo as well. From Denard's obituary, in the *Economist*: "In the breakaway Katanga Province in the 1960s Bob Denard propped up Moishe Tshombe, and Belgian mining interests in Congo, against a United Nations force. He tried to launch coups in Yemen and Benin and fought for secession in Biafra. His men – usually only a few dozen of them – were generally French, Belgian or South African, well equipped with guns and armoured jeeps, whipping the untrained blacks into shape. Denard himself seemed less racist than his troops, and in the Comoros, having converted to Islam, he wore the robes and cap of a native as he limped to Friday prayers. But he laughed at the thought of democracy in Africa." Obituary of Bob Denard," *The Economist*, October 18, 2007.

[11]Sarah V. Percy, "Mercenaries: Strong Norm, Weak Law," *International Organization* No. 61 (Spring 2007), 367.

characteristic with the infamous decolonization era mercenaries – that they work for money – the wide range of modern security companies serving worldwide is best understood as belonging to an older historical stream, one that winds back all the way to antiquity.

Today, as it has in history, much of the debate surrounding the use of private force inevitably begins with the polarized moralizing that comes with the "mercenary" label.[12] A 1993 report by the UN Special Rapporteur on mercenaries [13] categorically condemned soldiers-for-hire as "cold-blooded, dehumanized individual[s]," "intrinsically intolerant or violent persons" and proclaimed that "there must be no attempt to justify mercenaries in the media nor any misconceptions regarding this type of human behaviour. A mercenary is not a hero nor is he the last romantic guerrilla, but a criminal whose actions are associated with the vilest crimes against life."[14] They have variously been called "whores of war,"[15] "the scourge of the Third World,"[16] "hired assassins,"[17] "black knights,"[18] and, of course, "dogs of war." Kofi Annan himself intimated that there was no such thing as a "respectable" mercenary.[19]

Such vehement criticism is not new. Writing centuries ago, Niccolo Machiavelli condemned mercenaries in his magnum opus, *The Prince*.[20]

> Mercenaries are disunited, thirsty for power, undisciplined, and disloyal; they are brave among their friends and cowards before the enemy; they have no fear of God, they do not keep faith with their fellow men; they avoid defeat just so long as they avoid battle; in peacetime you are despoiled by them, and in wartime by the enemy.

---

[12] David Shearer, *Adelphi Paper 316: Private Armies and Military Intervention* (London: Oxford University Press, 1998), 76: "The moral debate over private military force has centred largely on the moral issues attached to the 'mercenary' label."

[13] The official title is in fact, "UN Special Rapporteur on the question of the use of mercenaries as a means of violating human rights and impeding the exercise of the right of peoples to self-determination."

[14] United Nations General Assembly, 49th Session, UN Doc. A/49/362 (1993).

[15] Wilfred Burchett and Derek Roebuck, *The Whores of War: Mercenaries Today* (Middlesex, UK: Penguin, 1977).

[16] Guy Arnold, *Mercenaries: The Scourge of the Third World* (London: MacMillan Press, 1999).

[17] Shearer, *Adelphi Paper*, 1998, 11.

[18] McGill University Faculty of Law, *Quid Novi*, October 30, 2008.

[19] Secretary-General Kofi Annan, "SECRETARY-GENERAL: First of all, I don't know how one makes a distinction between respectable mercenaries and non-respectable mercenaries,"transcript of Press Conference by at UN Headquarters, SG/SM/6255,June 12, 1997, http://www.un.org/news/Press/docs/1997/19970612.sgsm6255.html (Accessed June 11, 2009).

[20] Niccolo Machiavelli, *The Prince*, trans. George Bull (London: Penguin Classic, 1961), 77–78.

Mercenaries have indeed been associated with "the vilest crimes against life" and there is no doubt that many have proven "undisciplined and disloyal." Hired guns popularly known as *les affreux* ("the dreaded ones") propped up brutal dictators and fueled bloody civil wars in 1960–1970s Africa, from the Congo crisis to the Nigerian civil war in Biafra. In Machiavelli's day "free companies" roamed throughout Europe, and the Grand Catalan Company, the historical precursor to today's PMCs, betrayed its benefactor in 1311, and established a duchy in Athens, where it survived for 63 years.[21]

But these incendiary episodes obscure a much more complex history that demonstrates that while modern anti-mercenary arguments can be traced back to the Middle Ages,[22] the continued employment of mercenaries throughout different eras signifies that there has always been some conception of a "legitimate" mercenary, just as there are "legitimate" mercenaries today.

14.2.1 *The "Mercenary" Label in History*

Historian Janice E. Thomson suggests that the contemporary organization of global violence is "neither timeless nor natural."[23] While states in the twentieth century enjoyed a monopoly on force unparalleled in history, it was "democratized, marketized, and internationalized" non-state violence that dominated the international system before 1900.[24] As such, the present-day rise of PMCs should not be understood as a revolutionary development in military and geopolitical strategy, or even as a continuation or expansion of Cold War-era norms. Rather, it is a permutation of past forms of mercenarism adapted to the demands of the post-Cold War world.[25]

Thomson outlines four primary forms of twentieth century mercenarism:

1. Foreigners may join an army individually and without their home state's complicity, as in the case of the French Foreign Legion.

---

[21] Janice E. Thomson, *Mercenaries, Pirates and Sovereigns: State-Building and Extraterritorial Violence in Early Modern Europe* (Ewing: Princeton University Press, 1994), 27–28.

[22] Sarah Percy, "Morality and Regulation," in *From Mercenaries to Market: The Rise and Regulation of Private Military Companies, eds.* Simon Chesterman & Chia Lehnardt, (New York: Oxford University Publishers, 2007), 11–28.

[23] Thomson, *Mercenaries*, 1994, 3.

[24] Ibid.

[25] Juan Carlos Zarate, "The Emergence of a New Dog of War: Private International Security Companies, International Law, and the New World Disorder," in *Stanford Journal of International Law* 34.75 (1998), 81.

2. Like the Gurkhas, they may be recruited under an interstate treaty or contract.
3. A state may pay a per capita charge for the use of another state's troops, as the United States did during the Vietnam War.
4. Individual foreigners may be hired directly by a state for use in a particular conflict. This ad hoc recruiting of individuals was used, for example, in the Congo, Nigeria, and Angola.[26]

Each form has evolved from a previous historical trend, and although all can be grouped under the controversial "mercenary label," it is the last variant that has met with the most significant legal and cultural opposition in the modern era.

In the first instance, individual soldiers have served under foreign flags since antiquity, without permission from their own sovereign. When Alexander the Great invaded Asia in 334 B.C. his army included 5,000 mercenaries, and the Persian army that faced him at Issos contained 10,000 Greeks. Xenophon's famous account of 10,000 Greek mercenaries in the service of a Persian pretender to the throne[27] offers another such example, and while the French Foreign Legion has a relatively modern date of inception, 1831,[28] the practice of recruiting and hiring foreign troops in one's army can be found throughout European history.[29]

On the second point, the famed Nepalese Gurkha troops have been fighting for the British Crown since 1816[30] and are currently serving as part of the NATO deployment to Afghanistan.[31] They can find their predecessors in the Swiss regiments that served under the King of France after the Perpetual Peace signed in Fribourg in 1515.[32]

---

[26]Thomson, *Mercenaries*, 1994, 89–90.

[27]Although Cyrus perished in 399 B.C. before seizing the throne from his brother, the story of the Ten Thousand was recorded by Xenophon in *Anabasis* and curiously inspired the 1979 film *The Warriors*, where the journey of the Ten Thousand was re-imagined with youth gangs in 1970s New York. The main gang leader, who falls to his death setting "the Warriors" on their journey home, was named Cyrus.

[28]Thomson, *Mercenaries*, 1994, 89.

[29]Historian David Potter vividly describes British efforts to contract German troops when Henry VIII declared war on France in 1543 in: Potter, David "The International Mercenary Market in the Sixteenth Century: Anglo-French Competition in Germany, 1543-50," in *The English Historical Review* 111.440 (1996), 111.

[30]Thomson, *Mercenaries*, 1994, 89.

[31]For example, Alastair Leithead, "Tough task ahead for Nato troops," *BBC News Online*, July 31, 2006, http://news.bbc.co.uk/2/hi/south_asia/5232766.stm (Accessed June 11, 2009).

[32]For a fascinating account of Swiss mercenaries in the European middle ages see, Anthony Mockler, *The Mercenaries* (New York: The Macmillan Company, 1969), 74–104 and John McCormack, *One Million Mercenaries: Swiss Soldiers in the Armies of the World* (London: Leo Cooper, 1993).

On the third point, the United States hired South Korean, Philippine and Thai troops during the Vietnam War, when under separate agreements with the three governments, the US paid an overseas allowance, a *per diem* for each soldier, plus an additional allowance according to rank.[33] The Swiss pioneered this practice as well, when after the Peace of Westphalia some individual cantons received direct payment for the services of cantonal armies.[34]

It is the fourth point, the *ad hoc* hiring of mercenaries outside of normal military structures and outside of state authority that has raised the most objections. However, it has to be noted that although this practice has been condemned, there have been notable exceptions. When volunteers flocked to the Republican cause during the Spanish Civil War for what are generally understood to be ideological reasons, their presence in Spain was tolerated (and, in some circles, even celebrated).[35] However, both popular and legal opinions turned sharply against the practice when independent mercenaries commonly referred to as "soldiers of fortune," "wild geese," or *les affreux*, took up arms in the 1960s on the African continent.[36]

Such independent mercenaries, hired outside the constraints of the twentieth century nation-state system, presented a threat to fledgling African states, and their actions are commonly advanced as the basis for much of the blanket distaste that envelops mercenaries today. When foreign mercenaries rampaged through the newly independent Republic of Congo, the United Nations Security Council took the unprecedented step of mandating blue helmets to engage the foreign troops. The United Nations Operation in the Congo (ONUC), as envisioned by the Security Council in February of 1961, was initially deployed as a peacekeeping force that would: "[t]ake immediately all appropriate measures to prevent the occurrence of civil war in the Congo, including arrangements for ceasefire, the halting of all military operations, the prevention of clashes, and the use of force, if necessary, in the last resort."[37]

Some 9 months later, because of the outbreak of mercenary violence, a second resolution was drafted authorizing ONUC "to take vigorous action, including the use of the requisite measure of force, if necessary, for the immediate apprehension, detention pending legal action and/or deportation

---

[33] Thomson, *Mercenaries*, 1994, 94.

[34] Ibid., 30–31.

[35] There are many accounts of the motivations and actions of volunteers fighting in the Spanish Civil War. For a detailed ideological account, see George Orwell, *Homage to Catalonia* (New York: Harcourt Brace, 1952).

[36] Zarate, "The Emergence of a New Dog of War," 1998, 86.

[37] United Nations Security Council, Res. 161, UN Doc. S/4741, February 21, 1961.

of all foreign military and paramilitary personnel and political advisers not under United Nations Command, and mercenaries."[38]

Although the UN force crushed the mercenary-supported secession in 1963 and departed in 1964, the effectiveness of mercenary troops in combat led to the proliferation of soldiers-for-hire across the African continent. According to Gerry Thomas, mercenaries have played three roles in Africa since 1960:

1. as "operational maneuver groups" acting under the direct control of heads of state;
2. as "coup strike forces" financed to overthrow existing governments; and
3. as "internal paramilitary security" popular in South Africa as defensive ranch-and-range security forces for private farms.[39]

In all three cases, the lethal force employed by mercenaries took place in environments with weak or non-existent national regulation and in the absence of other legal accountability mechanisms. As such, the modern distaste for soldiers of fortune and the modern labels against the use of mercenaries emerged not only from the well-documented cases of excess and abuse, but also from the inherent exploitation of weak states and weak legal systems.

In the 1990s a new form of mercenarism emerged: the Private Military Company.[40] Zarate posits that the retreat of the Soviet Union and the US from the affairs of distant regions after the end of the Cold War created a power vacuum that was filled by sophisticated military professionals who created the modern, private, international security corporation.[41] He notes that PMCs "have sprouted in countries with a large pool of military expertise, due to military downsizing, early retirement incentives, and the sheer profitability of such work compared to regular military pay."[42] These companies provide a wide spectrum of military and security services usually reserved for state armies, ranging from creating military doctrine or training established national militaries to engaging in actual combat in ongoing conflicts. They have a "clear corporate structure" designed to show

---

[38]United Nations Security Council, Res. 169, UN Doc. S/5002, November 24, 1961.

[39]Gerry S. Thomas, *Mercenary Troops in Modern Africa* (Boulder, Colorado: Westview Press, 1986), 6–7.

[40]Percy, "Mercenaries," 2007, 14. Percy makes the distinction between combat PMCs such as Executive Outcomes and Sandline, and non-combat PMCs that engage support or training but avoid combat roles.

[41]Zarate, "The Emergence of a New Dog of War," 1998, 76.

[42]Ibid., 91. In this respect, the post-Cold War era was as conducive to the rise of PMCs as the post-Peloponnesian War environment that allowed Greek veteran Xenophon and his Ten Thousand to march with a Persian pretender to the throne.

accountability and to buck the mercenary label, and both often take additional steps to appear as accountable as possible.[43] Today PMCs comprise a $100 billion per year industry, operating in over 100 countries.[44]

These new "corporate soldiers" represent a significant departure from the loose mercenary units that rampaged through Africa in the middle of the twentieth century. But, not only have PMCs been unable to shirk their horrifying African legacy, they continue to be haunted by an embedded moral norm against the use of private force that is rooted in a deeper historical context.[45]

While at the core of the very nature of the modern PMC is the need to escape the mercenary label, Sarah Percy argues that two moral objections to their existence remain. By presenting a pragmatic, modern and even humanitarian façade, modern combat PMCs try to mitigate much of what Percy outlines as the two persistent moral objections against the private use of force: killing without attachment to a cause, and threatening democratic control over force. Both these norms continue to haunt modern PMCs, despite their best efforts to break with the mercenary label in the post Cold War world.

The first objection stems from the persistent feeling that "killing in warfare is usually justified by some sort of attachment to an appropriate cause."[46] Such causes have differed over time: for example, in the Middle Ages it was morally acceptable to die for one's sovereign or one's honour, while after the French Revolution it became acceptable to die for the freedom of one's countrymen. Mercenaries have differed from soldiers in that they are usually perceived to fight for causes that are not deemed appropriate by the opinion of their day. Fighting for monetary gain has been particularly frowned upon in European tradition, and the Crimean War marked the last time that a major European power recruited a significant number of mercenaries for a European war.[47] Percy argues that even when a PMC was directly ordered by a state government to engage in combat, as was the case for Executive Outcomes in Sierra Leone in 1995, the moral disapproval over financial motivation continued.[48]

[43]For example, Executive Outcomes had a policy of only taking contracts from national governments.

[44]Peter. W. Singer, "Peacekeepers Inc." in *Policy Review*, No. 119 (June/July 2003), http://www.hoover.org/publications/policy%20review/3448831.html (Accessed June 15, 2009).

[45]Percy, "Mercenaries," 2007.

[46]Ibid., 14.

[47]Zarate, "The Emergence of a New Dog of War," 1998, 86. Britain hired 16,500 Germans, Italians, and Swiss mercenaries to fight in the Crimean War, although they were never deployed.

[48]Percy, "Mercenaries," 2007, 17–18.

The second moral objection comes from the persistent idea that "there is something morally important about a citizen's military contribution to the state."[49] Machiavelli's notions of duty to the state were grounded in the idea that a republic could fall victim to tyranny because mercenaries would serve their paymaster and not the public good, and this idea found its continued expression in the Enlightenment. Jean-Jacques Rousseau argued that leaders prefer mercenaries to free men "if only to use the former at a suitable time and place to subjugate the latter more effectively."[50] This line of reasoning leads us to the modern day arguments employed by opponents of PMCs, who contend that their use by weak states furthers oppression and emboldens states to go to war.

The recent rise of the modern PMC is a post-Cold War phenomenon and has been lauded by some as an escape from the worst elements of the mercenary tradition. UK Foreign Secretary Jack Straw wrote in a 2002 Green Paper, "Today's world is a far cry from the 1960s when private military activity usually meant mercenaries of the rather unsavoury kind involved in post-colonial or neo-colonial conflicts."[51] The implication that modern PMCs are somehow different from the unregulated mercenaries of yesteryear has been advanced by scholars, politicians and the PMCs themselves, and in many respects, especially in the realm of professionalism, this can be argued with considerable success. However, while modern PMCs have been able to escape the legal label of "mercenary" they have been unable to entirely escape the moral stigma that accompanies their work.

14.2.2 The "Mercenary" Label Today

From this historical background, some conclusions can be drawn: mercenaries are not a new and terrifying phenomenon, the modern PMC is a significant departure from the lone, rogue mercenary typified in popular culture, and there has always been some conception of a "legitimate" mercenary. Indeed, when we try and put our finger on what exactly a "mercenary" is in the modern context, sweeping moral condemnation becomes most difficult.

The modern legal definition resides in Article 47 of the 1977 First Additional Protocol to the Geneva Conventions, which states:

2. A mercenary is any person who:

[49]Ibid, 18.

[50]Ibid.

[51]United Kingdom, Foreign and Commonwealth Office (UK), "Private Military Companies: Options for Regulation," (February 12, 2002), http://www.fco.gov.uk/Files/kfile/mercenaries,0.pdf (Accessed June 11, 2009).

(a) is specially recruited locally or abroad in order to fight in an armed conflict;
(b) does, in fact, take a direct part in the hostilities;
(c) is motivated to take part in the hostilities essentially by the desire for private gain and, in fact, is promised, by or on behalf of a Party to the conflict, material compensation substantially in excess of that promised or paid to combatants of similar ranks and functions in the armed forces of that Party;
(d) is neither a national of a Party to the conflict nor a resident of territory controlled by a Party to the conflict;
(e) is not a member of the armed forces of a Party to the conflict; and
(f) has not been sent by a State which is not a Party to the conflict on official duty as a member of its armed forces.

Suffice it to say that this definition is "characterized by loopholes, imprecisions, technical deficiencies and obsolete elements."[52] The person in question must actually participate in armed conflict, which excludes training or protection missions. They must be motivated purely by profit, excluding ideological mercenaries, and be paid substantially more than the average soldier, excluding cheap mercenaries. They must also have no patriotic stake in the conflict, excluding for example the US employees of Blackwater in Iraq. The problem is best summed up by Geoffrey Best's quip that "a mercenary who cannot exclude himself from this definition deserves to be shot – and his lawyer with him."[53]

Even the simplest definition is problematic. The UK Green Paper notes:

> The Oxford English Dictionary defines a mercenary as "a professional soldier serving a foreign power." This is a wide definition, which would include many people engaged in legitimate activities, for example Gurkha troops in the British and Indian Armies, troops in the British Army who have been recruited in Commonwealth countries, loan service personnel, the French Foreign Legion and the Swiss Guard in the Vatican.

It would also include Marine Lance Cpl. Jose Gutierrez, a native of Guatemala and the first US service member to die in the Iraq War, and the 20,500 others like him who comprise the US military's non-citizen "green-card warriors."[54]

---

[52] Enrique Bernales Ballesteros, "Use of mercenaries as a means of violating human rights and impeding the exercise of the right of peoples to self-determination," UN Doc. A/58/115 (July 2, 2003).

[53] Geoffrey Best, *Humanity in Warfare: The Modern History of the International Law of Armed Conflict*, (London: Weidenfeld and Nicolson, 1980), 328.

[54] Thelma Guttierez and Wayne Drash, "'Green-card Marine' prepares for third deployment," *CNN*, March 20, 2008, http://www.cnn.com/2008/US/03/19/greencard.marine/index.html (June 11, 2009).

Alternatively, if fighting only for monetary gain is the definitive criteria, we might well question whether all those volunteering for national militaries do so purely out of a sense of patriotic pride rather than as a career choice. UK Foreign Secretary Jack Straw suggested that the United Nations was already in a sense employing mercenaries as some poorer countries notoriously contribute to peacekeeping missions only because the UN pays more.[55]

To help understand just how difficult it is to define "mercenary" consider the following two poems:

Epitaph on an Army of Mercenaries
These, in the day when heaven was falling,
The hour when Earth's foundations fled,
Followed their mercenary calling
And took their wages and are dead.
Their shoulders held the sky suspended;
They stood, and earth's foundations stay;
What God abandoned, these defended,
And saved the sum of things for pay.
– A.E. Housman, 1917
Another Epitaph on an Army of Mercenaries
It is a God-damned lie to say that these
Saved, or knew, anything worth any man's pride.
They were professional murderers and they took
Their blood money and impious risks and died.
In spite of all their kind, some elements of worth
With difficulty persist here and there on earth.
– Hugh MacDiarmid, 1935

Readers may be surprised to learn that both were written about the British Expeditionary Force (BEF) after it was nearly wiped out at the 1914 Battle of Ypres.[56] At the time, the BEF was referred to by some as a "mercenary" army because it was comprised of paid professionals, as opposed to the conscripted armies of France or Germany.

In sum, confusion over the definition of "mercenary" reveals that nothing is gained by indignantly dismissing the entire practice as morally corrupt. It is the *means* individual mercenaries employ, and the *ends* to which they are put, that should be more seriously examined and, where appropriate, condemned.

This point becomes particularly salient when considering the wide diversity of firms in the emerging "private military and security company

---

[55]Matthew Tostevin, "Focus – Could dogs of war become doves of peace?" *Reuters*, May 28, 2002.

[56]David Kovacs, "A Cautionary Tale," in *Transactions of the American Philological Association*, 123 (1993), 405.

industry."[57] Abdel-Fatau Musah has claimed that "private military companies are nothing but the old poison of vagabond mercenaries in new designer bottles,"[58] but the broader consensus[59] seems to be that PMCs vary as widely as their customers do, and they are "ranged across the moral spectrum from 'ruthless dictators, morally depraved rebels and drug cartels' to 'legitimate sovereign states, respected multinational corporations and humanitarian NGOs.'"[60] Painting all mercenaries with the same brush would be like trying to formulate a single comprehensive judgment about state militaries around the globe. Still, the moral and rhetorical weight of the mercenary label cannot be denied.

14.3 The Normative and Legal Context: Whither Sovereignty?

Would a mercenary intervention be legal? In short, almost surely it would be. There does exist an international treaty that explicitly prohibits mercenaries, the 1989 *Convention against the Recruitment, Use, Financing and Training of Mercenaries*. However, to date the Convention has been signed by only thirty states, including none of the major powers.[61] Moreover, the Convention only prohibits the use of mercenaries in "armed conflict." This could be interpreted as excluding strictly internal conflicts such as civil war,[62] and would at the least permit protection missions not amounting to active combat.

More importantly, the Convention depends on the highly technical definition of mercenaries in Article 47 of the 1977 Additional Protocol I to the Geneva Conventions (discussed above). Here, even one of the most virulent opponents of soldiers-for-hire, the former UN Special Rapporteur for mercenaries Enrique Ballesteros, has reluctantly admitted that modern Private Military Companies "cannot be strictly considered as coming within the legal scope of mercenary status."[63] International legal scholar Antonio

---

[57]Benjamin Perrin, "Promoting Compliance of Private Security and Military Companies with International Humanitarian Law," in *International Review of the Red Cross*, No. 863 (2006), 628.

[58]Peter W. Singer, *Corporate Warriors: The Rise of the Privatized Military Industry*, (Ithaca: Cornell University Press, 2003), 44.

[59]See, for example, Perrin, "Promoting Compliance," 2006, 628; Deborah Avant, *The Market for Force: The Consequences of Privatizing Security* (New York: Cambridge University Press, 2005), 226; Percy, "Morality and Regulation," 2007.

[60]Singer, *Corporate Warriors*, 2003, 9.

[61]For an up-to-date list of signatories: http://www.icrc.org/ihl.nsf/WebSign?ReadForm&id=530&ps=P (Accessed June 11, 2009).

[62]Shearer, *Adelphi Paper*, 1998, 19.

[63]United Nations ESCOR, 53rd Sess., UN Doc. E/CN.4/1997/24, February 20, 1997.

Cassese forcefully contends that Article 47, drafted in the aftermath of *les affreux* in Africa, was propelled by a desire to eradicate the unsavoury, rogue mercenaries impeding post-colonial stability. However, it was deliberately constructed to allow states to retain the option of using them to support legitimate governments.[64]

"Legal" opposition to the use of mercenaries *qua* private military firms is therefore not usually framed in terms of *formal* illegality. Opponents, rather, are typically concerned with the erosion of a fundamental norm of international law: state sovereignty.

By now it is trite to observe that since the 1648 Peace of Westphalia, the paradigm of the sovereign state has been the governing principle of our international system. As Max Weber observed in 1918, *the* defining characteristic of a state is its exclusive control of violence: "a state is a human community that (successfully) claims the monopoly of the legitimate use of physical force within a given territory."[65]

In a recent article advocating the use of mercenaries in Darfur, political philosopher Michael Walzer wrote: "It is a very dangerous business to loosen the state's grip on the use of violence, to allow war to become anything other than a public responsibility." But, as he went on, "There are, of course, exceptions to every rule."[66]

For some, the use of mercenaries – non-state violence – poses a fundamental challenge to the sovereign monopoly on force, threatening to undermine our quaint "billiard-ball" view of international relations.[67] Yet, in recent years it has been increasingly recognized that the once "ironclad" principle of sovereignty is no *carte blanche*. In 2001, the *ad hoc* International Commission on Intervention and State Sovereignty issued its report on the "Responsibility to Protect" (R2P), enshrining what has become a "broadly accepted international norm."[68] R2P carved out an exception to sovereignty founded on two basic principles:

A. State sovereignty implies responsibility, and the primary responsibility for the protection of its people lies with the state itself.

B. Where a population is suffering serious harm, as a result of internal war, insurgency, repression or state failure, and the state in question is

---

[64]Antonio Cassese, "Mercenaries: Lawful Combatants or War Criminals," in *Zeitschrift fur auslandisches offentliches Recht und Volkerrecht* 40, (1980): 1-30.

[65]Max Weber, "Politics as a Vocation," in *From Max Weber: Essays in Sociology*, eds. H.H. Gerth and C. Wright Mills (New York: Oxford University Press, 1946), 77–128.

[66]Michael Walzer, "Mercenary Impulse: Is there an ethics that justifies Blackwater?" *The New Republic*, March 12, 2008.

[67]We refer here to the classic analogy typically taught in International Relations 101 classes in universities everywhere, where the world is viewed as a giant pool table upon which lie states – the billiard balls – knocking each other about.

[68]Gareth Evans, "Crimes against humanity: overcoming indifference," in *Journal of Genocide Research* 8, No. 3 (September 2006): 335.

unwilling or unable to halt or avert it, the principle of non-intervention yields to the international responsibility to protect.[69]

This R2P, then, falls first and foremost upon the individual state and, second, upon the "international community" when that state has failed to prevent a local population from suffering "serious harm."[70]

At the core of R2P is the principle that concerns for sovereignty can be no excuse for failing to protect vulnerable populations from mass atrocity. As Secretary-General Kofi Annan observed in a speech encouraging the development of the as-yet named R2P, the protection of human rights must "take precedence over concerns of state sovereignty...As long as I am Secretary General, the United Nations will always place human beings at the center of everything we do."[71]

It is true that R2P principally envisions humanitarian intervention by an ill-defined collective of enlightened states acting under Security Council authorization.[72] As Frédéric Mégret observes, "R2P, as a 'guiding principle for the *international community of states*,' seems irretrievably wedded to an interstate paradigm, which it contributes to reinforce even as it claims to depart from it."[73]

Nevertheless, it could be argued that R2P emerges from the common sense observation that a principle which demands us to stand idly by as genocide unfolds is not one worth respecting in all circumstances. This is reinforced by the prohibition of genocide as a *jus cogens* norm of international law, meaning "a norm from which no derogation is permitted," which, if only rhetorically, supports the supposition that the imperative to stop genocide comes before all else.[74] Put as such, the use of PMCs in order to halt or prevent mass atrocities is a justified contravention of sovereignty, whether it be the sovereignty of the individual aggressor state or the general preservation of the state monopoly on force in the "international community." The R2P report itself seems to acknowledge as much when it states that, if Security Council authorization is not forthcoming, "it is difficult to

---

[69]International Commission on Intervention and State Sovereignty (ICISS), *The Responsibility to Protect*. Report of the International Commission on Intervention and State Sovereignty. (Ottawa: International Development Research Centre, 2001), 13.

[70]An analysis of the "responsibility to protect" concept and of the respective roles of individual states and international community is provided in Francis M. Deng, Chapter 4, Section 4.1 (above).

[71]Judith Miller, "The World: Checkered Flags; Sovereignty Isn't So Sacred Anymore," *The New York Times*, April 18, 1999.

[72]Parameters for military intervention in keeping with the "responsibility to protect" requirements are outlined in Wiebe Arts, Chapter 8, Section 8.2 (above).

[73]Frédéric Mégret, "Responsibility to Protect (Others) v. the Power of Protecting Oneself: Beyond the 'Salvation' Paradigm." (unpublished paper).

[74]The *jus cogens* nature of the prohibition of genocide is examined in Wenqi Zhu and Binxin Zhang, Chapter 12, Section 12.2.2 (above).

argue that alternative means of discharging the responsibility to protect can be entirely discounted."[75]

A similar justification for usurping sovereignty can be found if, in a particular case, the use of mercenaries can be cast as falling within victims' inherent right of resistance. That Jewish militants had the moral right to violently resist their Nazi oppressors in the Warsaw ghetto uprising of 1943 seems obviously justifiable according to all but the most pacifist of ethical standards. It also finds expression in international law. For example, the Universal Declaration of Human Rights acknowledges that should a state fail to protect human rights, a people may "be compelled, as a last resort, to rebellion against tyranny and oppression."[76] If the hiring out of a private military firm can somehow be construed as emanating from the victims themselves, perhaps in a situation where a victims' group is the source of the firm's financing or mandate, its use is eminently justified as a form of legitimate internal resistance against an illegitimate sovereign power.[77]

As a final thought, it is also worth noting that the emergence of the private military firm may have *already* undermined the international commitment to sovereignty whether we like it or not. Both Peter Singer and Deborah Avant, the leading political scientists on "the market for force," observe that the remarkable rise of mercenaries, particularly in the last two decades, seems to be irretrievably charting us towards a "neomedieval"[78] paradigm of global security where "power is more fungible than ever."[79] Whether or not this development should be heralded is not within the scope of our argument, but the relevant fact remains that the private use of force cannot be ignored. Mercenaries are back, and they seem to be here to stay. PMCs are currently employed on every continent, in every major war zone, have been involved at some level in every UN peacekeeping operation since 1990, and by some estimates comprise a $100 billion per year industry.[80] As Singer writes:

---

[75] ICISS. *The Responsibility to Protect*. 2001, 53.

[76] Of course, this preambular statement is ambiguous as to whether it legalizes resistance *per se*, but as Frédéric Mégret observes in a chapter in this volume, there are multiple references to the right to resistance in international law. See Mégret, Chapter 13.

[77] The argument that international law should legitimize victims' resistance to genocide is put forward in Frédéric Mégret, Chapter 13, Section 13.6 (above).

[78] Avant, *The Market for Force*, 2005, 261.

[79] Singer, *Corporate Warriors*, 2003, 171. Avant, *The Market for Force*, 2005, 264: "The market for force has undermined states' collective ability to monopolize violence in the international system... Rather than arguing about its overall costs or benefits, both policy makers and their constituents would be well served by thinking about the trade-offs involved in the different strategies for participating in and managing this market."

[80] Singer, *Corporate Warriors*, 9; Avant, *The Market for Force*, 2005, 7; Willis Witter, "Private firms eye Darfur," *The Washington Times*, October 2, 2006.

> In sum, the privatized military services phenomenon appears likely not only to endure, but also thrive in the coming years. Indeed, some groups have described the further proliferation of PMFs [Private Military Firms] as almost "inevitable." Thus, as shocking as private firms supplying military services might have been a few years back, it is no exaggeration to say that [they] are "the wave of the future in terms of defense and security."[81]

Our argument is not that sovereignty is or should be irrelevant, but rather that in order to do the most good we must think pragmatically about harnessing the realities of the world we live in, and not the ideals of the imagined world we seek to build. Humanitarians seeking to end genocide should not be the last to resort to private military force and thereby ironically become sovereignty's lone, stubborn standard bearers.

14.4 Practical Concerns: Accountability, Applicability and the Chain of Command

Although it is not our goal to comprehensively address all the practical aspects of a privatized genocide intervention (such questions necessarily vary case by case), principled justifications ring hollow without some review of universally applicable pragmatic concerns. While the debate on principles is hotly contested in polarized terms, the pragmatic case for a privatized genocide intervention is plainer to see.

Deploying a PMC can in certain cases be faster, cheaper, and avoid the political complications of spilling national blood to stop a far-off crisis. Doug Brooks, head of the International Peace Operations Association (effectively an industry lobby group), notes that in many cases, "if the UN plans to wait for proper Chapter Six conditions, it will be a long wait."[82] He quotes an e-mail sent by former President Frederick Chiluba of Zambia, who mediated the Lusaka Agreement in 1999. There, the former statesman complains that when contemplating forces to support the Agreement, the UN was waiting for "a perfect score on some performance chart."[83]

---

[81] Singer, *Corporate Warriors*, 2003, 233.

[82] Doug Brooks, *Creating the Renaissance Peace: The Utilization of Private Companies for Peacekeeping and Peace Enforcement Activities in Africa* (Pretoria, SA: Africa Institute of South Africa, 2000), 2.

[83] Frederick Chiluba, "Call for Support for Lusaka Agreement, Speedy Establishment of UN Peacekeeping Mission," quoted in an e-mail distributed by the African Policy Information Center (APIC), January 26, 2000 cited in Brooks, *Creating the Renaissance Peace*, 2000, 3.

Fitzsimmons[84] notes that PMCs do not share such constraints. Politically, unlike the United States and other developed countries, PMCs have no constituency that would demand immediate disengagement in the event of casualties. Operationally, PMCs are unfettered by arcane military structures or UN bureaucracy, and remain free to utilize training, military skill, speed and coordination to act as a force multiplier within the scope of their contract.[85] They can also provide cheaper services. For example, in Sierra Leone, a 21-month presence by Executive Outcomes (EO) cost the government $35 million, a very low sum considering that EO managed to turn the tide of a war in favour of their employer and to force a ceasefire. A UN observer force, which was never deployed, was to cost $47 million for an 8-month mission.[86] Also, according to Singer, EO offered to deploy 1,500 soldiers, along with air and fire support in Rwanda, in 1994. The cost for a 6-month operation to provide safe havens from the genocide was estimated at $150 million (around $600,000 a day). The eventual UN relief operation, which deployed only after the killings ended, cost $3 million a day.[87]

Of course, cost and might are not everything, and some significant practical obstacles remain, in particular with respect to accountability, the chain of command and the inherent limitation that mercenaries are best suited to narrowly-tailored, functional missions.

14.4.1 Accountability Problems

Lack of accountability for potential human rights violations by PMCs is often mentioned as a major stumbling block, particularly in the humanitarian community.[88] Whereas state militaries are accountable through the political process, and individual soldiers are, at least in theory, prosecutable for crimes by their national authorities, employees of PMCs can be said in some instances to operate in a "legal vacuum."

Before briefly outlining possible ways to hold mercenaries accountable, two preliminary points should be made. The first is that while accountability is a pressing concern, it may strike some as lacking in moral perspective to be excessively worried about the potential human rights abuses of a force sent to stop the much greater evil of genocide. Second, it need hardly be pointed out that national militaries have also often acted with callous

[84]Scott Fitzsimmons, "Dogs of Peace: A Potential Role for Private Military Companies in Peace Implementation," in *Journal of Military and Strategic Studies* 8, No. 1 (Fall 2005): 1–27.

[85]Ibid., 4–5.

[86]Shearer, *Adelphi Paper*, 1998, 49–51.

[87]Singer, *Corporate Warriors*, 2003, 171.

[88]See, for example, Willis Witter, "Private firms eye Darfur," *The Washington Times*, October 2, 2006.

disregard for the civilians they are sent to protect.[89] Indeed, it is not clear that, empirically, PMCs on the whole behave worse than state armies. Doug Brooks seems right to say that "[o]ddly, what worries the international community enough to shy away from utilizing PMCs is the *potential* harm that they could do, not any particular past incident."[90] In fact, some have made the point that PMCs, on average, operate with a higher degree of military professionalism than the local forces of the troubled countries where they typically operate. Their presence can thereby enhance the "social control" of violence by importing international values.

For example, Deborah Avant argues that Executive Outcomes, a decidedly questionable firm started by ex-apartheid South African special forces troops, brought a "short-run increase in integration with international military professional values" amongst the Sierra Leonean army. "Compared with the RSLMF, the RUF, and the militias, [Executive Outcomes'] record looks stellar," she writes, "[a]nd, under EO's protection, Sierra Leone did hold elections."[91]

Of course, those now looking for "particular incidents" need look no further than, for example, the involvement of employees of DynCorp International in setting up an underage sex trade ring for UN peacekeepers in Bosnia,[92] or the recent murder of 14 Iraqi civilians by Blackwater Worldwide in Iraq.[93] In both cases, the alleged perpetrators were never prosecuted because of deficiencies in the law. Indeed, there is a disturbing lack of regulation in the private military industry, and ensuring that mercenaries are accountable to someone should be an important consideration in hiring them.

14.4.2 Legal Accountability

The *civil* liability of a PMC itself is, according to the International Committee of the Red Cross (ICRC), "generally accepted" in most countries.[94] Thus companies could always be sued for monetary damages

---

[89]See, for example: David J. Bercuson, *Significant Incident: Canada's Army, the Airborne, and the Murder in Somalia* (Toronto: McClelland and Stewart, 1996).

[90]Doug Brooks, "Messiahs or Mercenaries? The Future of International Private Military Services," in *International Peacekeeping* 7, No. 4 (2000): 129.

[91]Avant, *The Market for Force*, 2005, 91.

[92]Stewart Payne, "Teenagers 'used for sex by UN in Bosnia'," *The Daily Telegraph*, April 25, 2004.

[93]David Johnston and John M. Broder, "F.B.I. Says Guards Killed 14 Iraqis Without Cause," *The New York Times*, November 14, 2007.

[94]International Committee of the Red Cross (ICRC), "The ICRC to expand contacts with private military and security companies," April 8, 2004, http://www.icrc.org/Web/Eng/siteeng0.nsf/iwpList571/21414DE8FCAF2645C1256EE50038A631 (Accessed June 15, 2009).

resulting from abuses. On the other hand, the *criminal* responsibility of the firm itself is rare and limited in most states.[95] The more likely scenario is that the employees be held individually culpable for their crimes. Under international law, staff members of PMCs, like any other individual, are bound to obey international humanitarian law (in armed conflict) and human rights law. Depending on the context, such crimes are prosecutable before courts of the state where the crime occurred, the state of the victim, the state of the perpetrator, or any state if the crime falls under universal jurisdiction (e.g. genocide, crimes against humanity, torture, etc.). Where there are grave breaches of either humanitarian or human rights law, it is always possible for the International Criminal Court to intervene.

Under national criminal law, the problem is more complex. The country where the crime was committed can always prosecute, but this is not always feasible, particularly since mercenaries typically operate in weak states seized with armed conflict or internal turmoil. The state of nationality of the perpetrator can also usually prosecute, providing it can secure the alleged perpetrator's extradition, although not all countries permit the extra-territorial application of their criminal law.

At the risk of vastly oversimplifying the matter, it can be said that most of the problems regarding lack of accountability for mercenaries are political rather than strictly legal in nature. Where the law clearly applies, there are a host of political reasons for countries not to intervene. Where there is a lack of regulation in national law, there is typically nothing in theory barring a more proactive government stance. As Singer notes, "all but a few states' domestic statutes currently ignore PMFs' very existence."[96]

A solution to filling the "legal vacuum" surrounding mercenaries, then, rests in large part with state legislators, particularly those in the United States and the United Kingdom where the majority of established PMCs are headquartered. The US approach to the use of private force in Iraq is perhaps instructive in how *not* to hold mercenaries accountable. Not only has the US imprudently employed what Avant terms "cowboy" firms,[97] but they also forced the passage of an Iraqi law immunizing all contractors from domestic prosecution. Coupled with the fact that until recently private contractors did not fall within the scope of the US *Military Extraterritorial Jurisdiction Act*, this helps explain why Blackwater employees accused of murdering Iraqi civilians were inexcusably let off scot free.

This loophole was recently closed in the wake of the Blackwater shooting controversy, when the US Congress passed a bill making all private

[95] Ibid.

[96] Peter W. Singer, "War, Profits, and the Vacuum of Law: Privatized Military Firms and International Law," in *Columbia Journal of Transnational Law* 12 (2004), 524.

[97] Avant, *The Market for Force*, 2005, 226.

contractors working in combat zones subject to prosecution in US courts.[98] While this provides some reassurance, the mere existence of a law does not mean that a US prosecutor will have the political incentive to investigate and bring to trial an American mercenary operating independently outside US borders.

Thankfully, there is reason to believe that accountability for PMCs will only increase in the future. The recent reforms to American law indicate that other countries may follow suit. A UK "Green Paper" urged the adoption of common regulatory standards,[99] and the International Committee of the Red Cross has also recently embarked on a project to systematically engage PMCs in a dialogue "to ensure that they know and respect fundamental humanitarian principles and the relevant provisions of the law."[100] Peter Singer has proposed the creation of an international regulatory body that would license, monitor and sanction recognized private military firms.[101] Skeptics still seeing the present lack of accountability as a dealbreaker should therefore be open to re-evaluating their position in the future.

Still, it must be admitted that the most powerful risks and incentives with regard to legal compliance by private military and security companies are grounded in behaviour and norms which fall *outside* formal law.[102]

14.4.3 Market Accountability

While some may not be convinced that the law can ever provide adequate accountability, there are powerful arguments for how mercenaries can also be held accountable through a supplementary layer of responsibility: the market.

First, an entity hiring a mercenary firm to halt mass violence can set strict contractual terms. These should include outside vetting of personnel, on the ground monitoring by an independent party, pre-calculated monetary sanctions for human rights violations (or the possibility of withholding payment), and a forum selection clause submitting the company or its

---

[98]U.S. Congress. House. 2007. *MEJA Expansion and Enforcement Act 2007*, HR 2740,110th Congress, 2007.

[99]United Kingdom, Foreign and Commonwealth Office, *Private Military Companies*, 2002.

[100]ICRC. The ICRC has also recently devoted an entire issue of the *International Review of the Red Cross* to legal accountability for PMCs. Available at: http://www.icrc.org/Web/Eng/siteeng0.nsf/htmlall/section_review_2006_863?OpenDocument

[101]Singer, "War, Profits, and the Vacuum of Law," 2004, 545.

[102]Benjamin Perrin, "Promoting compliance of private security and military companies with international humanitarian law," in *International Review of the Red Cross*, No. 863 (2006), 634.

employees to the jurisdiction of a particular tribunal. The International Peace Operations Association (IPOA), a US-based association of private military and security firms, has even called for such an approach, arguing that "contractual obligations can be much more specific and invasive than general guidelines and regulations. They could include military observers, increased transparency and detailed financial and legal penalties for non-compliance."[103] Like any other company, private military firms are driven by profit. If a client ties payment to good behaviour, firms can be expected to act in their self-interest.

Second, the existence of a market for well-behaved mercenaries is, in a sense, somewhat self-regulating. The private military industry itself is perhaps the only transnational industry actively seeking international regulation.[104] Put simply, it badly wants to be perceived as legitimate. As Tim Spicer, the colourful head of Sandline International, wrote in his autobiography:

> Given that a PMC is a business, it is acknowledged that a fundamental law of successful business is that the supplier is only as good as his last contract. Ethical businesses first build a reputation and then work hard to protect it. If a particular PMC performed badly or unethically, exploited the trust placed in it by a client, changed sides, violated human rights or sought to mount a coup, then the company and its principals would find that their forward order book was decidedly thin. Discarding ethical and moral principles can therefore only be a one time opportunity. The chance will not recur and the company's prospects would disappear.[105]

That these firms see respect for human rights as sound business strategy is reflected in the creation of the IPOA and its adoption of a Code of Conduct, written largely by NGOs, in which its members agree to respect the major international humanitarian and human rights law treaties.[106] Blackwater and other PMCs have also made aggressive pitches to deploy to Darfur and peacekeeping missions elsewhere.[107] While the sincerity of their commitment to human rights remains open to question, we can at least conclude that such companies see human rights as good business.[108]

---

[103] Ibid., 625.

[104] See, for example, Toni Pfanner, "Interview with Andrew Bearpark," in *International Review of the Red Cross*, No. 863 (2006), 449, in which the Head of the British Association of Private Security Companies describes how they are "keen on regulation." See also Singer, "War, Profits, and the Vacuum of Law," 2004, 545.

[105] Tim Spicer, *An Unorthodox Soldier: Peace and War and the Sandline Affair* (Edinburgh: Mainstream Publishing, 1999), 25–6, quoted in Andrew Clapham, "Human rights obligations of non-state actors in conflict situations," *International Review of the Red Cross*, No. 863, (2006), 517.

[106] Perrin, "Promoting compliance," 2006, 627.

[107] Willis Witter, "Private firms eye Darfur," *The Washington Times*, October 2, 2006.

[108] This, we hasten to add, should also dispose of the more sensationalist arguments offered against mercenaries, such as the fact that they might be paid more by a rival

Some may be uncomfortable with paying for feigned altruism, but perhaps we should be thankful that, for once, enforcing human rights rather than avoiding them is seen as a sure path to profit.

At the end of the day, it must be acknowledged that there are always inherent risks with privatizing humanitarian intervention. The profit motive can be wielded for good, but it also has the potential to backfire. What if, for example, a PMC decided that continuing its protection mission was no longer in its financial interest and suddenly withdrew? What if, like the United States when it left Somalia after the death of 18 soldiers, a PMC took heavy casualties and simply changed its mind? While this would likely destroy any future humanitarian business for that PMC, the possibility remains. The world is messy and humanitarian intervention is never without its costs. But we will never stop genocide without, as Holocaust historian Yehuda Bauer has put it, a certain degree of "cold-blooded, cold-headed thinking."[109] If we want to save lives, we must be prepared to take calculated risks.

14.5 Military Feasibility and the Chain of Command

It would be pointless to talk about mercenaries without discussing who would hire them. A private military firm should not be let loose without clear lines of command and control and a shared understanding of specific goals. The most obvious scenarios are that a state would hire them as a kind of proxy force, or that the United Nations would employ them as peacekeepers in lieu of contributions from individual nations. In both cases, the concerns of command and control do not seem to be insurmountable or unique. States have highly developed chains of command and already effectively make ample use of mercenaries. We surmise that the UN, without too much difficulty, could also feasibly command a mercenary force, a task that would perhaps be even simpler than the usual path of combining different national peacekeeping contingents with wildly varying levels of commitment and ability.[110]

---

faction and abruptly switch sides. See for example the worry of Behrooz Sadry, deputy head of the UN mission in Sierra Leone: "Then there is the question of loyalty. Suppose a faction can pay more than the U.N?" in Matthew Tostevin, "Focus-Could dogs of war become doves of peace?," *Reuters*, May 28, 2002.

[109] Yehuda Bauer, "Genocide in History: The Onward Progress of Civilisation?" (Speech given during a panel discussion at the Global Conference on the Prevention of Genocide, McGill University, Montreal, Canada, October 11–13, 2007).

[110] The difficulties of past peacekeeping missions especially in relation to the establishment of coordination between different national contingents and the lack of resources are examined in Wiebe Arts, Chapter 8, Section 8.1 (above).

A ready-made example of a state-sanctioned mercenary intervention in a humanitarian disaster area already exists. In May 1995 Executive Outcomes arrived in Sierra Leone to bolster the National Provisional Ruling Council (NPRC) government of Valentine Strasser in its struggle against the Revolutionary United Front (RUF). EO was hired by the government of Sierra Leone, silencing, for a time, questions of sovereignty, but the company was not hired to pursue primarily humanitarian aims. Rather, Shearer quotes an EO executive saying that "on arrival, EO and the government set our four military objectives:

- to secure Freetown;
- to regain control of crucial resources, in particular the Sierra Rutile mine and the diamond fields (generating revenue for the government and helping to guarantee EO's payment);
- to destroy RUF's headquarters; and
- to clear remaining areas of RUF occupation."[111]

The first three objectives were achieved in the course of five military operations between May 1995 and October 1996. It was a Clausewitzian clinic in limited warfare, and this swift campaign bolstered the national government and allowed Sierra Leone to hold national elections in February-March 1996. EO's 21-month presence, which included both combat and training, cost the government $35 million. Comparatively, a UN observer force, which was never deployed due to RUF opposition, was to cost $47 million for an 8-month deployment.[112]

Subsequent criticism of the EO force has centered on its economic motivations, and the fact that the peace collapsed shortly after EO left. Critics have argued that even where EO was successful in its immediate objectives, "security in Sierra Leone was geographically specific; it was not supplied as a public good."[113] Jeremy Harding posits that even though civilians stopped dying whenever Executive Outcomes arrived, "they [EO] only went where the payoff was high,"[114] such as the diamond rich area of Kono. Yet, perhaps the most important lesson from Sierra Leone lies not in what Executive Outcomes did not do, but in what they managed to accomplish. Percy notes that "moral objections can prevent clear-headed analysis of the situation,"[115] and such arguments miss the broader fact that when given a specific set of clearly defined military objectives, a PMC proved to be a

[111]Shearer, *Adelphi Paper*, 1998, 49.

[112]Ibid., 49–51.

[113]Percy, "Morality and Regulation," 2007, 17.

[114]Jeremy Harding, "The Mercenary Business: Executive Outcomes," in *Review of African Political Economy*, 24, No. 71 (1997), 93.

[115]Percy, "Morality and Regulation," 2007, 17.

very effective tool, if only in the short term. As Singer notes, "A number of people in [...] Sierra Leone are alive today due to the rise of the PMF industry."[116]

The United Nations has never hired a PMC for anything resembling a combat mission; however, in late 1994 the UN Department of Peacekeeping Operations (DPKO) considered employing a PMC to help deliver humanitarian aid to the over 1.2 million Rwandan refugees who had fled across the border to Zaire. The dilemma was that the *génocidaires* had deliberately engineered the refugee crisis in order to create a "human shield" between them and the advancing Rwandan Patriotic Front (RPF). Any aid sent to the refugees, therefore, risked falling into the wrong hands unless accompanied by an aggressive security mission to help separate the killers from the innocent civilians. Bruce Jones, relying on confidential interviews, describes discussion of the mercenary option at the UN:

> DPKO also floated Option C, a truly innovative alternative: use a private-sector security company to provide protection. DPKO received an informal proposal from an experienced British company to which the firm offered to provide training and logistical support to Zairian troops. The perceived attraction was that Option C would avoid the political difficulty that had scuppered the UNAMIR option: countries unwilling to face the political repercussions of body bags returning from an operation in Zaire that their populations little understood. The proposal did receive some support in the Security Council, including one member of the Permanent Five, as a practical solution to a difficult situation. *Other states, however, rejected it because of high costs and on the basis of principle.* Some states argued that using a private security company to fulfill an international public responsibility was tantamount to shirking that responsibility. Those who supported Option C responded that principle was all well and good if one were willing to act upon it; given that opponents were unwilling to provide troops to a UN force, it did seem reasonable to pursue such practical solutions. Nevertheless, the nay-sayers won the day.[117]

Jones then recounts how political deadlock resulted in the eventual expenditure of $2.5 billion in humanitarian aid, something all states agreed needed to be done, but could not unless accompanied by a security force. However, the delay helped "the genocide forces to recuperate and resuscitate, inside Zaire, and thereby to pose a continuing threat to Rwanda."[118] It is astonishing that states were willing to spend *billions* on humanitarian aid, but not the little extra needed to make sure that the aid did not have precisely the opposite of its desired effect. If they were unwilling to sacrifice their own troops, then surely employing a PMC would be a preferable moral response, whatever "principle" was at stake, than to do nothing and actually contribute to prolonging the conflict.

---

[116] Singer, *Corporate Warriors*, 2003, 228.
[117] Jones, *Peacemaking in Rwanda*, 2001, 142. [emphasis added]
[118] Ibid., 140.

Finally, the availability of private military firms on the open market raises an intriguing third possible customer: a humanitarian NGO or wealthy philanthropist. Could George Soros hire Blackwater to protect refugee camps in Darfur for a measly few hundred million? Or what if an organization solicited small donations on the Internet from millions of people worldwide to pay for a private protection force, giving new meaning to the term "people power"?

It may sound far-fetched, but humanitarian NGOs around the world are already employing private military firms in more limited capacities. One study, described as "by no means a comprehensive survey," found more than forty contracts between PMCs and humanitarian actors.[119] In Kenya, the UNHCR currently pays ArmorGroup to guard refugee camps.[120] ArmorGroup has also worked for UNICEF, the International Rescue Committee and CARE, among others.[121] In the Democratic Republic of the Congo, the World Wildlife Federation financed park guards to protect endangered white rhinos from poachers.[122] Worldvision and Caritas hired the firms Lifeguard and Southern Cross to provide security in Sierra Leone,[123] and Defense Systems Limited protected Red Cross workers around the world.[124] Considering that more ICRC workers were killed in the 1990s than US military personnel, the use of private guards is only logical.[125]

In 2005, the Genocide Intervention Fund (GIF), an American NGO, approached over 100 private military firms about the possibility of deploying them to protect refugee camps in Darfur. A Blackwater representative assured Andrew Sniderman, co-founder of GIF, that they could deploy in 2–3 weeks, had no qualms about entering without Sudanese government approval, and would even "bloody the noses of the Janjaweed" if it were necessary. Ultimately, GIF rejected the idea, in part because they only had $250,000 to spend, but primarily for a host of other practical and moral reasons. What if the *Janjaweed* decided to retaliate against unprotected towns or camps? Would GIF embarrass and delegitimize the African Union, undermining security in the long run? Could GIF really keep Blackwater employees in line should anything go awry? And who would address the

---

[119] Singer, *Corporate Warriors*, 2003, 255.

[120] http://www.armorgroup.com/globalreach/africa/africacasestudies/kenya/

[121] Peter W. Singer, "Humanitarian principles, private military agents: some implications of the privatized military industry for the humanitarian community," in *Resetting the Rules of Engagement: Trends and Issues in Military-Humanitarian Relations*, eds. Victoria Wheeler and Adele Harmer, Humanitarian Policy Group Report 21 (London: Overseas Development Institute, 2006), 5.

[122] Avant, *The Market for Force*, 2005, 206.

[123] Singer, "War, Profits, and the Vacuum of Law," 2004, 5.

[124] Avant, *The Market for Force*, 2005, 25.

[125] Singer, *Corporate Warriors, 2003*, 119.

underlying political and social issues that prompted the conflict, problems that would persist after GIF's money dried up?[126]

Faced with these daunting uncertainties, and the stark reality that an NGO led primarily by college students could hardly be expected to spearhead a humanitarian intervention, GIF contemplated a more narrow use of private force. They approached Evergreen International about hiring an Unmanned Aerial Vehicle (UAV) that would scour the plains of Darfur from above, looking for signs of *Janjaweed* movement and relaying their locations to the African Union Peacekeeping force. Evergreen offered a high-grade UAV for $22 million or a less reliable version for $5 million. Neither were within GIF's projected budget, and experts advised them that the utility of their investment would evaporate the minute a sandstorm knocked out the drone or it was shot down by the Sudanese government.[127]

In the end, GIF ended their brief courtship with private military firms and decided to give their money to an African NGO that provides female escorts to accompany Darfuri women when they leave refugee camps to search for firewood. *The New Republic* describes the lessons learned:

> [T]rying to do as private citizens what should, after all, be the job of governments has proved tougher than the group ever expected. "Some of us thought we'd do the fund-raising, hand it over, and they'd do the rest," [GIF cofounder Mark] Hanis says. He adds, somewhat wearily, "With giving money, there are a lot more details."[128]

The devil, as always, is in the details. It seems fanciful to think GIF could have tackled perhaps the world's most intractable crisis alone. It is never as simple as "Write a Cheque, End a War," as one industry representative has put it.[129] Yet GIF's short-lived UAV proposal demonstrates that there are more limited, feasible ends toward which NGOs can potentially put mercenaries, helping to fill the gaps that sovereign states are unable or unwilling to address. GIF's failure is also in part a testament to the exceeding complexity of the crisis in Darfur, a remote region the size of France with multiple factions competing for control. It is at least conceivable that future problems may be more discrete and solvable.

A potentially more manageable context for a humanitarian role for PMCs may lie in the smaller scale experiences of individual NGOs. In the violence that erupted after the December 27th, 2007, presidential election in Kenya, Nan and Gerry Hardison, a retired couple from San Diego, found themselves at the epicenter of escalating tribal violence. They had been

---

[126] Andrew Sniderman, " 'If lives matter, then you use the private industry:' Blackwater USA and the Genocide Intervention Fund," November 12, 2005, unpublished paper.

[127] Jason Zengerle, "Student Aid: Raising Money to Save Darfur," *The New Republic*, March 20, 2006.

[128] Ibid.

[129] Doug Brooks, "Write a Cheque, End a War," *Conflict Trends*, No. 6 (July 2000).

working as missionaries for the US-based Episcopal Church in Maseno, a town in Western Kenya. After criminal gangs took to the streets and an ambulance containing nine young American nurses was stoned and the windshield smashed, the Church decided to get the Hardisons and ten of their colleagues out of harm's way. They reached out to ArmorGroup Kenya, a division of ArmorGroup International,[130] who quickly dispatched a "Close Protection Team." By January 10th, the missionaries were safely ensconced in Nairobi.[131]

If ArmorGroup could evacuate the Hardisons and ten friends, could they also have saved more? At what point does the number of victims become large enough that we are no longer talking about "personal bodyguards" *per se* and about a "protection force"? What if you knew that a village was about to be liquidated by genocidal death squads, and the only way to save them in time was to hire a PMC to either guard or evacuate the populace? If you had the money and the means, would it be moral to do *nothing*? What if it were not a small town, but a country? These are tough questions. It is time we started asking them more often.

14.6 Conclusion

During the 1994 genocide in Rwanda Executive Outcomes offered to deploy 1,500 soldiers to create havens and stop the mayhem at a cost of $150 million over 6 months. The plan was considered by the Clinton administration but rejected.[132] Yet, considering the events in 1994, it seems rather clear that there lies a grave error in failing to even consider using mercenaries to humanitarian ends on the righteous belief that to do so would signal a compact with the devil. Modern mercenaries are neither all good nor all bad. As David Shearer has put it: "Private military forces cannot be defined in absolute terms. They occupy a grey area that challenges the liberal conscience. Moral judgments on the use of mercenaries are usually passed at a distance from the situations in which these forces are involved. Those facing conflict and defeat have fewer moral compunctions."[133]

[130]ArmourGroup International. "ArmorGroup International plc Leads evacuation of US missionaries and nurses from Kenya," *ArmourGroup International*, 28 January 2008. http://www.armorgroup.com/files/news/19880/Kenya_rescue.doc (Accessed June 12, 2009).

[131]Matthew Davies and Janet Kawamoto, "Kenya missionaries return to work despite continuing unrest," *Episcopal Life* Online, January 30, 2008, http://www.episcopal-life.org/79901_94360_ENG_HTM.htm (Accessed June 12, 2009).

[132]See Singer, "Peacekeepers Inc.," 2003. Also, Eric Pape and Michael Meyer, "Dogs of Peace," *Newsweek International Edition*, August 25, 2003.

[133]Shearer, *Adelphi Paper*, 1998, 13.

Percy's normative analysis of the historical prejudices against the private use of force offers a window into the almost visceral distaste for mercenaries that has also touched modern PMCs. However, when taking a detached perspective, it is difficult to see why PMCs should be judged *a priori* on what they may or may not be, in contrast to what they actually do. If PMCs can be successfully employed in the context of genocide prevention or for broader humanitarian ends, then it serves to reason that the historical disdain for modern forms of private force need not apply in the present context.

The norm which, for some, invalidates use of mercenaries is that of the state monopoly on force. But, as we have suggested, R2P effectively creates a hierarchy of norms whereby the imperative to stop genocide comes before sovereignty concerns. More important, perhaps, is the simple fact that the use of PMCs to stop genocide would be an exceptional remedy, whereas it is the routine use of mercenaries in other contexts, such as their abundant employment by the US in Iraq that should concern advocates of sovereignty.

The feasibility of privatized humanitarian intervention depends largely on the anatomy of the particular crisis. We suggest that using mercenaries be seriously considered if two criteria are met: (a) there is clearly a genocide or similar mass atrocity taking place; (b) there is an obvious need for the "functional" application of force. Deborah Avant's "dimensions of control" theory posits that managing violence requires three types of control: functional, political and social.[134] Political and social control refer essentially to the underlying causes of a conflict, demanding diplomacy, reconstruction, humanitarian assistance and other measures in order to address violence in the long-term. There is clearly very little room for PMCs or other private actors in this context. However, the functional dimension, essentially the tactical side of military intervention, does leave ample room for PMCs.

Mercenaries are extremely good at deploying cheaply, rapidly and at accomplishing discrete military goals. In other words, they are ideally suited to exercising "functional control." What they cannot do, however, is solve the more complex roots of violence. Any privatized humanitarian intervention, therefore, would ideally be accompanied by a wider political and humanitarian effort. This would imply that mercenaries are best used as a component of a larger initiative engineered by a state or the UN.

One should not, however, be seduced by the complexities of intervention into taking an "all or nothing" approach. The emerging literature on genocide *prevention*, a concept to which this volume is devoted, asks that we intervene in a crisis as early as possible when the measures taken are likely

[134] Of course, Avant's theory is a bit more complex, in that applications of functional control can have ramifications on the political and social dimensions, and vice versa – i.e. applications of military force can also in some respects be considered political or social.

to be more manageable. Thus, even if PMCs cannot put to rest the long-term causes of conflict, a task at which national governments often fail as well, lives can be saved by quick, decisive and purely functional action. The story of Executive Outcomes in Sierra Leone illustrates that although mercenaries failed to bring about a lasting peace, they did accomplish their concrete military objectives and allowed for a short-term increase in stability. They carved out the breathing room needed to hold elections, and saved lives in the process. If given a humanitarian mandate, there is reason to believe PMCs could be just as effective protecting civilians.

In the end, perhaps we should listen to the voices of victims. It is they who will ultimately bear the costs of inaction and the risks of intervention. Salih Mahmoud Osman, a Darfuri human rights activist and lawyer, pointed out that "the United Nations Charter begins with 'We the Peoples of the United Nations' not 'We the States.' My people are being killed. If there are ways of stopping genocide and defending victims that fall outside of the state, they must be pursued."[135]

---

[135] Salih Mahmoud Osman, remarks made at the International Young Leaders Forum, Global Conference on the Prevention of Genocide, McGill University, Montreal, Canada, October 11–13, 2007. ArmourGroup International. "ArmorGroup International plc Leads evacuation of US missionaries and nurses from Kenya," *ArmourGroup International*, 28 January 2008. http://www.armorgroup.com/files/news/19880/Kenya_rescue.doc (Accessed June 12, 2009).

Chapter 15
Creating the Outcry: Citizen-Driven Political Will for Genocide Prevention in the US Context

Rebecca J. Hamilton

Those of us who had our first experience of working out how to respond to genocide in the context of the Darfur crisis took as received wisdom that a lack of political will was the key obstacle to overcome if we wanted to see the rhetoric of "never again" translated into effective action. Samantha Power's Pulitzer Prize winning history of the US government's failure to stop genocide had made a compelling argument for the necessity of political will.[1] And the words with which Lt-General Roméo Dallaire signed off his ill-fated cable to the United Nations, as he struggled to stave off those with genocidal intent in Rwanda, were seared into our minds: "Peux ce que veux. Allons-y" [Where there's a will, there's a way. Let's go.][2]

That political will had been lacking in response to every genocide of the 20th century was not a point upon which anyone needed further convincing. However there is a vast gap between identifying a problem and actually fixing it.

The following article is adapted from a speech I gave at the 2007 Global Conference on Genocide Prevention. Firstly, I explore why citizen-generated political will for genocide prevention matters, and why it has historically been lacking in the US context. Secondly, I describe some of the work now being done by the Genocide Intervention Network, a US-based NGO, borne out of the new generation of activists who responded

R.J. Hamilton (✉)
Princeton, NJ 08540, USA
e-mail: bec.hamilton@gmail.com

The term "prevention" is used throughout this article to mean both the prevention of genocide and other mass atrocity crimes before they begin, and the halting of further killing once violence is already underway.

[1] Samantha Power, *A Problem from Hell: America and the Age of Genocide*, Basic Books (2002).

[2] Dallaire, quoted in Phillip Gourevitch, *We Wish to Inform You That Tomorrow We Will Be Killed With Our Families*, (Farrar, Straus and Giroux, 1998).

R. Provost, P. Akhavan (eds.), *Confronting Genocide*, Ius Gentium: Comparative Perspectives on Law and Justice 7, DOI 10.1007/978-90-481-9840-5_15,

to the Darfur crisis.[3] In particular, I focus on the steps they have taken to start to "create the outcry" needed to build political will for genocide prevention.

15.1 Getting Our Hands Dirty: Advocacy Through Politics

There are two basic channels through which the political will needed to prevent genocide can be generated amongst decision-makers in a democratic system: internal and external. On the rare occasion that genocide prevention coincides with the set of foreign policy items defined to be in the "national interest," the political will to prevent genocide may arise from within government.[4] However, genocide prevention was only included in the US National Security Strategy for the first time in 2006[5] and continues to generally be thought of as a humanitarian issue, rather than as a strategic issue attended to by those working within a traditional "national interests" framework.[6] The internal generation of political will can be bolstered by those within government who, for idiosyncratic reasons like a personal tie to the region in crisis, or a strong identification with the horror of genocide, will attempt to elevate genocide prevention above competing policy objectives. However, the net result is that unless violence is erupting in a country of strategic value to the US, the goal of protecting civilians from genocide tends not to be a priority. To rely solely on the generation of political will from inside government creates a risk, borne out by history, that genocide prevention is lost in the hierarchy of national interest issues

[3]Accounts of the situation in Darfur are provided in Gérard Prunier, Chapter 3, Sections 3.1 and 3.2 (above), Catherine Lu, Chapter 18, Sections 18.1 and 18.2 (below) and Luis Moreno-Ocampo, Chapter 16 (below).

[4]The need to take into account national interests in genocide prevention is addressed in Yehuda Bauer, Chapter 7, Sections 7.1 and 7.3 (above).

[5]As recently as 2002, genocide prevention was not addressed in the US National Security Strategy (NSS). The 2002 NSS made a passing reference to genocide, saying that it was a goal of the US Government to use its influence to make clear that terrorism is illegitimate and should be viewed in the same light as genocide. See National Security Council, *The National Security Strategy of the United States of America 2002*, Washington D.C., September 2002, Part III. Not until 2006 did genocide prevention merit its own section of the NSS. See National Security Council, *The National Security Strategy of the United States of America 2002*, Washington D.C., September 2006, Part IV(C)(4).

[6]The recently completed report of the Taskforce on Genocide Prevention, co-chaired by Madeleine Albright and William Cohen, offers a promising pathway through which the traditional thinking about the role of genocide prevention in the foreign policy context can and should be updated. However it is too early to tell whether the report's recommendations will be meaningfully implemented. See Taskforce on Genocide Prevention, *Preventing Genocide: Blueprint for U.S. Policymakers*, (2008). Available at: http://www.usip.org/genocide_taskforce/report.html.

that traditionally consume the US government's foreign policy expertise and resources.[7]

The alternative, then, is for political will to be generated by pressure from outside the government. At first glance, this seems like an obvious approach; the moral imperative behind genocide prevention may not earn it top billing in the hierarchy of national interests, but it certainly seems to captivate regular citizens. A 2002 study by the Chicago Council on Foreign Relations found that 77% of Americans would be in favor of the government sending US troops to stop genocide.[8] In 2005, a poll by Zogby International found that 86% of Americans view it as unacceptable for any government to engage in wholesale attacks against its own civilians.[9] Yet throughout the 20th century, this citizen-based concern about genocide was never channeled effectively to create the political will to act among those making US foreign policy. The question is, why?

One possibility is that, despite their survey replies to the contrary, people just do not care – or do not care enough – about the lives of strangers to take time out of their daily routines in order to put political pressure on their representatives to respond to genocide. Undoubtedly this is part of the answer, and it echoes David Rieff's widely read critique that the average American has not yet been convinced of the value of human rights ideals.[10]

Yet even if we assume that a lack of concern is what prevented a significant portion – or even a majority – of the population from taking political action in response to information about an ongoing genocide throughout the 20th century, it is insufficient to argue that indifference alone provides a full accounting of the historical failure by those outside government to generate sufficient political will to spur effective government action. Certainly the phenomenon of the Darfur activism movement in the US has uncovered a reservoir of citizen-based concern about genocide prevention that mirrors the polling data, and presumably education could play a role in expanding that number further.

15.2 Citizen-Driven Political Will

In the aftermath of the genocides of the late 20th century, government officials bemoaned the fact that no sizeable number of voters ever expressed

[7] Of course there is no good reason why the status quo in this regard should not be subject to challenge, but that is not the topic of this article.

[8] Chicago Council on Foreign Relations, "American Public Opinion and Foreign Policy," p. 23, 2002.

[9] Zogby International poll, May 2005, available at: http://www.africaaction.org/resources/docs/DarfurPolls05.pdf.

[10] David Rieff, "The Precarious Triumph of Human Rights," *New York Times Magazine*, August 8, 1999.

concern to their political representatives while the killing was underway. Don Steinberg, Special Assistant for African Affairs to President Clinton during the 1994 Rwandan genocide, described the options for halting the atrocities as constrained by others in government who asked, "where's the public outcry? the 'hallelujah chorus' of support?"[11] Such questions were often accompanied by a tendency to blame regular citizens for failing to take up this channel of opportunity, and an assumption that citizens just did not care. For the most part, that was where the questions stopped.

But for those of us residing on college campuses as the Darfur crisis unfolded, there was a different perspective for the taking. We had seen our sleep-deprived classmates turn up at late-night campus meetings to organize fundraising events for civilian protection in Darfur; we had witnessed the way we could, with relatively little effort, turn our family discussions over Thanksgiving to the plight of Darfuris. We noticed signs coming from the broader community – the piano teacher in Salt Lake City who started donating a percentage of her earnings to protect civilians in Darfur, or the religious leaders who chose to make Darfur the topic of their sermons.[12] The conventional wisdom that regular citizens in the US do not care about the plight of those on the other side of the world overlooked what we were observing. When one starts from the assumption that at least a segment of the population does care about stopping genocide (and that this number could be expanded with effort), then the space is created for a new question: what obstacles have historically prevented that segment of the population from conveying their concern in a politically effective manner?

Firstly, there is a prevalent belief that on an issue as overwhelming to most people as genocide, there is very little that can be done. People assume that if smart, effective policies to prevent genocide did exist, they would have been implemented already. Additionally, there is a not-unreasonable assumption on the part of most people that, with a problem as significant as genocide, someone else – someone with more power, wealth, or expertise – is dealing with it. In order to transform the concept of citizen-driven political will from a scapegoat into a solution, people have to be convinced that as voters, or potential voters, they have an inbuilt source of leverage over politicians operating on the calculation of getting into or staying in elected office. This leverage, if exercised effectively, can at a minimum get an issue onto the political agenda, and in the best case scenario it can build the political will necessary for action. Convincing citizens of their power in this

[11]Warren Hoge, "Intervention Hailed as a Concept is Shunned in Practice," *New York Times*, January 20, 2008. See also, Paul Ritcher, "Rwanda Violence Stumps World Leaders" *Los Angeles Times* April 30, 1994, p. A13 (Representative Schroeder of New York explaining that she received more calls from her constituents about the threat to Rwandan gorillas during the 1994 genocide than about the destruction of people).

[12]See generally, Hamilton & Hazlett, "Not on Our Watch" in *War in Darfur and the Search for Peace*, (Alex deWaal, ed.) (Harvard University Press: 2007).

regard forms a pathway to breaking down the notion, prevalent in the North American context, that human rights activism is not the business of every person, but rather is something that lawyers and political elites deal with. Secondly, even if people can be convinced that their individual actions can have an impact, there remains the very practical question of exactly what actions they should take to build political will.

The Genocide Intervention Network (GI-Net), a Washington-based non-profit, borne of the newfound commitment among students to protect civilians from genocide, has led the charge in answering just that question. Founding executive director 26-year old Mark Hanis says "Everyone had been talking about the need for political will. But talking about it was not going to save lives. Political will doesn't just show up on the doorstep – it takes people to actively create. We knew that's what we needed to work out how to do."[13]

15.2.1 Communication Between Voters and Their Representatives

In the US context, one of the most obvious means of building political will is for people to communicate their concerns to their political representatives. GI-Net staff member, Allyson Neville, observes that:

> while it sounds simple enough, in reality there is an obstacle that stops many U.S. voters speaking to their representatives: they have never done it before. Many people just don't know who their representatives are, and even if they find out that information, there are additional hurdles posed by finding the telephone number for their representatives' office and then working out what exactly to say.[14]

GI-Net decided to see whether these obstacles could be overcome by launching a toll-free number, 1-800-GENOCIDE. The number was easy to remember, and citizens could call it from anywhere in the country. Callers would be prompted to put in their zipcode, based upon which GI-Net could put them through to the representative for their area. To address the difficulty of people not knowing what to say, GI-Net also gave callers a list of talking points about any upcoming legislation that needed support before putting them through to their representative.

In the 2 years following its launch in January 2007, the toll-free number has generated over 18,000 individual calls by constituents to their representatives on the Darfur crisis.[15] This is a distinct contrast to the

[13] Interview with Mark Hanis, 29 March 2008.
[14] Interview with Allyson Neville, 24 April 2008.
[15] Interview with Allyson Neville, 1 February 2009.

resounding silence that political representatives reported hearing from their constituents during the Rwandan genocide.[16]

15.2.2 *Creating Accountability: Rewarding Those Who Act and Shaming Those Who Do Not*

Another component to building political will in any democratic system is to have a means of creating accountability – the ability to generate costs for representatives who fail to act and rewards for those who do act. In the US context, organizations that are successful in getting their issue seen as a political priority often build a system of accountability by releasing scorecards grading members of Congress on how they vote on legislation that advances their issue.[17]

Following this approach, GI-Net set up a scoring system to grade every member of Congress from A+ to F on how they had responded to Darfur.[18] Once this information was published, citizens represented by low-scoring politicians could use the scorecards to pressure their representatives into action. In some cases citizens used the scorecards in their face-to-face meetings with representatives, while others published articles in their local paper to publicly shame low-scoring representatives from the area. Meanwhile, those representatives with high scores found themselves receiving calls of support from their constituents, calls that for the first time created a positive political incentive to respond to ongoing atrocities. These representatives strengthened the accountability system further by publicizing their high scores on their websites and press releases, thus distinguishing themselves from those without such scores to promote.

As citizens made greater use of the accountability mechanism, the GI-Net office found itself the recipient of phone calls from members of Congress themselves – not only their staff – asking what actions they would need to take to get a score upgrade. 166 out of the 167 representatives who scored an "F" in 2006 had taken action to improve their scores by 2008. Since the launch of *DarfurScores* in 2006, 255 representatives took action that moved them from a score of "D" or lower, to a score of "C"

[16] See *supra* at note 6.

[17] Of all the unlikely role models, GI-Net looked to the National Rifle Association, who had been using a scorecard system to successfully protect the rights of US gun owners for years. See, www.nra.org. If you can hold politicians accountable for protecting the rights of rifle owners, you should be able to hold them accountable for protecting civilians from genocide.

[18] See http://www.DarfurScores.org [Note: from February 2009, this website will be transitioned to www.GenocideScores.org]

or higher.[19] One Congressional staffer reported that her boss "complains at least once a week about the fact that he was given a C+ and yells about finding a way to raise his grade because every time he goes back to his district he gets harassed by high-schoolers who've checked out the *DarfurScores* website."[20]

It is no surprise that elected officials are uncomfortable with scores that show them to be "soft on genocide." What is surprising is that in a long history of US representatives failing to take any effective action in the face of mass atrocity, this was the first time they had been systematically held to public account.

15.2.3 Citizens Leading the Government

Another way to build political will is to lead the government by example. The campaigns to divest funds from companies doing business with the Sudanese government have been an example of this approach in the Darfur context.[21] Citizen-driven divestment campaigns began to appear in the US shortly after then-Secretary of State, Colin Powell, publicly declared that genocide was taking place in Darfur. The first campaign was launched by students at Harvard University, which by April 2005 had agreed to divest its endowment of funds held in the oil company, Petro-China.[22] This decision in turn spurred a wave of other universities and colleges to divest (61 at time of writing, with a further 55 having initiated divestment campaigns).[23] From there the campaign branched out to non-academic settings, with divestments from state pension funds being the next target.

The benefit of this sequencing was that by the time divestment decisions made it to the various State legislatures, there was already a wealth of examples of divestment policies being implemented by the fund managers of the university endowments, which served to minimize any claims that such a policy was impracticable. At the time of writing, 27 states have divested from companies doing business with the GOS, most of them using

[19]"DarfurScores.org Donor report," *Genocide Intervention Network* (on file with author).

[20]Interview with Allyson Neville, February 1, 2009.

[21]The impact of divestment on the South African government and an argument for the use of economic sanctions to effect changes in the Darfur situation are examined in Richard J. Goldstone, Chapter 11, Sections 11.2 and 11.4 (above).

[22]See "Statement by Harvard Corporation Committee on Shareholder Responsibility (CCSR) Regarding Stock in PetroChina Company Limited" *Harvard Gazette*, April 4, 2005.

[23]See http://www.sudandivestment.org/statistics.asp.

a targeted divestment model created by the Sudan Divestment Taskforce,[24] now housed within GI-Net. On the last day of 2007, President Bush signed the *Sudan Accountability and Divestment Act* into law, ensuring that the divestment decisions made by States would not be subject to constitutional challenge and requiring companies seeking US government contracts to certify that they are not conducting certain business operations in Sudan.[25] The divestment campaign has now gone international, with seventeen other countries having initiated divestment campaigns.[26]

15.3 Results

If it is true that political will is a central ingredient in genocide prevention, and if more political will has been built to push members of the US Congress to act on the situation in Darfur than was built in relation to any genocide of the 20th century, then one would expect to see the US Congress acting more effectively to stop atrocities in Darfur than it has in response to previous atrocities. In essence, this hypothesis plays out. Relative to other atrocities in Africa, Darfur has received a disproportionate amount of Congressional attention as indicated through the amount of funds appropriated ($996 M over fiscal years 2004–2006) and the number of resolutions proposed and passed.[27] So it seems that regular citizens can, in real terms, bump the issue of genocide prevention up on the list of policy priorities. It was just that, until recently, no one was systematically giving people the tools to translate the care they felt into a politically effective

[24]The Sudan Divestment Task Force's targeted divestment policy affects only companies that meet very stringent criteria: companies that (1) have a business relationship with the government of Sudan, (2) impart minimal benefit to the country's underprivileged, and (3) have demonstrated no substantial corporate governance policy regarding the Darfur situation. See www.sudandivestment.org.

[25]Sudan Accountability and Divestment Act: S.2271 (passed December 13, 2007).

[26]See http://www.sudandivestment.org/statistics.asp The countries are: Australia, Belgium, Brazil, Canada, Denmark, Germany, India, Ireland, Italy, Japan, the Netherlands, New Zealand, Norway, South Africa, Sweden, Switzerland, and the United Kingdom.

[27]In the US House of Representatives, 8 Congressional resolutions were passed in the period June 2006 – December 2007. *Darfur Peace and Accountability Act*: H.R. 3127 (passed June 26, 2006); NATO Bridging Force: H.R. 723 (passed September 26, 2006); House Amendment 709 to H.R. 4939 (passed June 16, 2006); Presidential Special Envoy: House Resolution 992 (passed September 26, 2006); China Resolution: House Resolution 422 (passed June 5, 2007); *Darfur Accountability and Divestment Act*: H.R.180 (passed July 31, 2007); *Genocide Accountability Act*: H.R.2489 (passed December 5, 2007); *Sudan Accountability and Divestment Act*: S.2271 (passed December 13, 2007). See also, Hamilton & Hazlett, "Not on Our Watch" in *War in Darfur and the Search for Peace*, (Alex de Waal, ed.) (Harvard University Press: 2007).

voice. But what sounds like a hopeful conclusion may, for the memoirs of our current political representatives, be a thorn in their sides.

Until Darfur, the persistent failure of the US government to protect civilians from genocidal violence could be readily attributed, at least in part, to the absence of a politically relevant outcry from citizens. The simplicity of that alibi is now under threat. Undoubtedly citizen activism for genocide prevention is not nearly as strong or deep as it could and should be. For certain, the Darfur activism movement has made, and continues to make, significant strategic mistakes. Activists have attempted to internationalize their efforts only belatedly, and have still not yet worked out how to most effectively pressure the executive branch, which has a more significant role to play than Congress on this issue. But as the crisis in Darfur remains unresolved, no one who has been in government during this genocide can say that the public did not care.

Chapter 16
The Role of the International Community in Assisting the International Criminal Court to Secure Justice and Accountability

Luis Moreno-Ocampo

16.1 Overview of the International Criminal Court

Sixty years ago at the Nuremberg Trials, perpetrators of massive crimes were held accountable before the international community. For the first time, the victors of a conflict chose to turn to the law to define responsibilities regarding the conduct in armed conflicts. In the words of the Nuremberg Prosecutor Justice Robert H. Jackson: "That four great nations, flushed with victory and stung with injury, stay the hand of vengeance and voluntarily submit their captive enemies to the judgment of law is one of the most significant tributes that power has ever paid to reason."[1]

Nuremberg was a landmark. However, the world was not ready to transform such a landmark into a lasting institution. Subsequently, the Cold War produced massive crimes in Europe, Latin America, and Asia, while Africa was still under the rule of colonialism and Apartheid.

In the end, the world would wait for almost half a century after Nuremberg and would again witness two genocides – first in the Former Yugoslavia, and then in Rwanda –before the United Nations Security Council decided to create the *ad hoc* Tribunals for the former Yugoslavia ("ICTY") and Rwanda ("ICTR"), thus connecting peace and international justice once again.

The contribution of these *ad hoc* Tribunals is yet to be fully recognized and measured. The ICTY and ICTR developed the law and prosecuted the

L. Moreno-Ocampo (✉)
International Criminal Court, Office of the Prosecutor, The Hague, Netherlands
e-mail: luis.moreno-ocampo@icc-cpi.int

[1] J. Robert H. Jackson, "*The United States of America, the French Republic, the United Kingdom of Great Britain and Northern Ireland, and the Union of Soviet Socialist Republics v. Hermann Wilhelm Göring, et al.*" (opening statement to the International Military Tribunal, Case No. 1, Palace of Justice, Nuremberg, Germany, November 21, 1945).

R. Provost, P. Akhavan (eds.), *Confronting Genocide*, Ius Gentium: Comparative Perspectives on Law and Justice 7, DOI 10.1007/978-90-481-9840-5_16,

worst perpetrators, including generals and members of governments.[2] They also contributed to restoring lasting peace in conflict-torn regions. Most significantly, the ICTY and ICTR paved the way for the decision to establish a permanent criminal court.

For centuries, conflicts were resolved through negotiations without legal constraints. In Rome in 1998, a new and entirely different approach was adopted. Lasting peace requires justice: this was the decision taken in Rome by 120 States.[3] They committed to putting an end to impunity for the most serious crimes of concern to the international community and to contributing to the prevention of such crimes. To this end, the Rome Statute created an International Criminal Court ("ICC"), a permanent court with jurisdiction over genocide, crimes against humanity and war crimes. International justice was not a moment in time any longer, nor an *ad hoc* post conflict solution: it became an institution.

The Rome Statute created a comprehensive and global criminal justice system that included the following key elements:

- Substantial law was codified in one detailed text; the content of different international conventions such as the Genocide Convention and the Geneva Conventions were incorporated; elements of crimes were meticulously defined; based on the jurisprudence by the ad hoc Tribunals the definition of sexual violence was further elaborated upon; special emphasis was put on crimes against children.
- Different legal and procedural traditions were integrated into a new international model; victims were given the right to participate in proceedings, with their voices and interests formally included at different stages of the process; a trust fund was created for reparations or compensation in the victims' favour.
- The scope of ICC jurisdiction reaches beyond any national or regional boundary; whereas its predecessors were each limited in scope to a particular territory, the ICC is a worldwide criminal justice system; its jurisdiction extends over crimes committed on the territory or by the nationals of more than a 100 State parties; its jurisdiction could extend to the entire world, since the United Nations Security Council can refer any situation to the Court.[4]
- Even more important, and the object of strong debate in Rome, was the decision of States to give the Prosecutor the ability to trigger the jurisdiction of the Court. By establishing the *proprio motu* powers

---

[2]The contribution of ICTR case law, particularly the *Akayesu*, *Ruggiu*, *Kambanda* and *Bikindi* decisions, is examined in Irwin Cotler, Chapter 9, Section 9.2 (above).

[3]*Rome Statute of the International Criminal Court,* U.N. Doc. A/CONF.183/9, entered into force July 1, 2002.

[4]The scope and impact of ICC jurisdiction is discussed in Wenqi Zhu and Binxin Zhang, Chapter 12, Section 12.4.2, (above).

of the Prosecutor to open an investigation, the treaty created a new autonomous actor on the international scene. Such a provision, which allows the Court to act without an additional trigger from States or the UN Security Council, ensures that the requirements of justice will prevail over any political decision. This is a key defining provision for the new legal framework.

It should be emphasized that the Rome Statute was not drafted overnight. It is a strong and consistent body of law. The drafters were well aware that rendering justice in the context of conflict or peace negotiations would present particular difficulties, and they prepared the ICC well to meet those challenges. Careful decisions were made: a high threshold of gravity for the jurisdiction of the Court was established; a system of complementarity was designed whereby the Court intervenes as a last resort, when States are unable or unwilling to act; and the UN Security Council was given a role in cases of threats to peace and security.

States demonstrated their understanding of, and firm support for, this new design by the tremendous speed of the ratification process. Less than 4 years after its adoption in Rome, the Statute entered into force. The issue is no longer about whether we agree or disagree with the pursuit of justice in moral or practical terms; we must follow the law.

The next challenge was to make this body of law operational, to transform ideas and concepts into a working system. This has been my objective as the Prosecutor of the ICC during the first 5 years of the Court's existence. This process involved many issues, such as, how to select the gravest situations to investigate? How to trigger the jurisdiction of the Court? How to protect witnesses and investigate in ongoing conflict situations?

16.2 The Current Situation

Over these 5 years, the Office of the Prosecutor of the ICC has opened investigations in 4 situations – the Democratic Republic of Congo, Northern Uganda, Darfur in Sudan, and Central African Republic, all countries still engulfed to various degrees in conflict. We also analyzed the situation in Venezuela and the activities of nationals of 25 State parties involved in Iraq.[5] We are currently monitoring other situations in three different continents. In each case, we collected evidence. The Court protected the witnesses. Victims started participating in the proceedings. As of today, the Judges of the ICC have issued 12 arrest warrants.

[5]Update on Communications received by the Office of the Prosecutor of the ICC, February 17, 2006; Annexes: Iraq response and Venezuela response, http://www.iccnow.org/documents/Update_on_the_Court_CommunicationsReceivedOTP_10Feb06.pdf.

16.2.1 The Democratic Republic of Congo ("DRC")

In the DRC situation, we currently have three suspects in custody and one arrest warrant has yet to be executed.

In the case of the Prosecutor versus Thomas Lubanga Dyilo, in which the accused is charged with the war crimes of conscripting and enlisting children under the age of 15 and using them to participate actively in hostilities in Ituri, we are preparing to go to trial in mid-2008. Mr. Lubanga is the alleged founder of the *Union des Patriotes Congolais* ("UPC") and the *Forces patriotiques pour la libération du Congo* ("FPLC"), the alleged former Commander-in-Chief of the FPLC and the alleged President of the UPC. The trial will be a defining moment for the Court. Regardless of the outcome of this case, it will send – it has in fact already sent – a signal to the DRC and around the world that using children as soldiers is a serious crime that will be prosecuted.

The arrest warrant against Mr. Bosco Ntaganda remains outstanding. Mr. Ntaganda is the former Deputy Chief of the General Staff of the FPLC, Mr. Lubanga's former armed group; in addition, Mr. Ntaganda is also a leading member of Laurent Nkunda's *Congrès National pour la Défense du Peuple* ("CNDP"), which is currently active in the Kivus.

With regard to the second suspect in custody, Mr. Germain Katanga, alleged commander of the *Force de résistance patriotique en Ituri* ("FRPI") in the DRC, the Office presented its evidence to the ICC Judges in the summer of 2007 and a sealed arrest warrant was issued on July 6th, 2007. On October 17th, 2007, the Congolese authorities surrendered and transferred Mr. Katanga to the International Criminal Court. Mr. Katanga is alleged to have committed war crimes and crimes against humanity.

Based on an arrest warrant issued under seal on July 6th, 2007, Mr. Mathieu Ngudjolo, a former senior commander of the *Front des Nationalistes et Intégrationistes* ("FNI") and the *Force de Résistance Patriotique en Ituri* ("FRPI") in the DRC, was arrested in Kinshasa on February 6th, 2008. He was surrendered to the Court by the Congolese authorities and transferred the next morning to the ICC detention center in The Hague.

Both Mr. Ngudjolo and Mr. Katanga are being prosecuted for ordering their FNI-FRPI forces to attack and "wipe out" the village of Bogoro on February 24th, 2003 in the early hours. Approximately 200 civilians were murdered, and countless others were attacked. The village was pillaged by the FNI-FRPI forces.

With the arrest and transfer of Mathieu Ngudjolo to the Court, the Prosecution has completed a first phase of its DRC investigation, focusing on the horrific crimes committed by leaders of armed groups active in Ituri since July 2002. My Office is now moving on to a third investigation in the

DRC, with other applications for arrest warrants to follow in the coming months and years.

Different options are being analyzed regarding alleged crimes committed by individuals and armed groups in different provinces and at different periods. Among others, there are reports of massive sexual violence of shocking brutality, of forced displacements, and of killings in the Eastern parts of the DRC, in particular the Kivus, where we have documented allegations of crimes committed by the regular soldiers of the DRC, by the FDLR and by Laurent Nkunda's forces. Other options include the case of officials having financed and organized militias. It will not be the last investigation in the DRC.

16.2.2 Central African Republic ("CAR")

On May 22nd, 2007, my Office announced the opening of an investigation in the Central African Republic.

The Office's investigation is focusing on the most serious crimes, which were mainly committed during a peak of violence in 2002–2003, including a particularly high number of allegations of rapes and other acts of sexual violence, perpetrated against hundreds of reported victims and involving a number of armed groups from CAR or from the DRC, such as the MLC.

I visited Bangui on February 7th, 2008. The investigation into CAR is the end of impunity for those responsible for sexual crimes. It is a promise to the victims. It is a message to the criminals. It is a commitment by the Court. It must also be the commitment of each State party to the Rome Statute, particularly the DRC, CAR and Uganda, but also those State parties involved in humanitarian, development or conflict management initiatives in the region. All State parties have to show a consistent approach. Individuals who commit crimes falling under the Court's jurisdiction cannot receive promises of impunity.

On May 24th, 2008, Mr. Jean-Pierre Bemba, chairman of the *Mouvement de Libération du Congo* ("MLC"), an armed group which intervened in the 2002–2003 armed conflict in CAR, was arrested in the suburbs of Brussels. Mr. Bemba has been charged by the ICC for crimes against humanity and war crimes committed in CAR. The MLC pursued a plan of terrorizing and brutalizing innocent civilians, in particular during a campaign of massive rapes and looting. Mr. Bemba had already used the same tactics in the past in the DRC, always leaving a trail of death and destruction behind him.

The Prosecution presented the document containing the charges in the case of Mr. Jean-Pierre Bemba on October 1st, 2008. The Judges have decided that the confirmation hearing will take place between December 8th and 12th, 2008.

16.2.3 Darfur, the Sudan

In March 2005, the UN Security Council referred the situation in Darfur to my Office. On June 1st, 2005, after evaluation of the relevant information under the Rome Statute, I decided to open an investigation.[6]

For 20 months we investigated the worst crimes committed in Darfur in 2003 and 2004. We reviewed thousands of documents, but mostly we interviewed victims – victims who took terrible risks to speak to us. Victims who wanted to tell us their stories. One woman described how they killed her baby and then raped her. A man told us: "They raped my 8-year-old daughter. They forced me to watch. I was asking, 'why?'"

Those stories became evidence, evidence unveiling a well-organized system of persecution against the civilian population in Darfur. The situation in Darfur is neither the result of "climate change" nor the consequence of some ancestral tribal strife: it is a planned operation.

On April 27th, 2007, the ICC Judges issued arrest warrants against Ahmad Harun, former Minister of State for the Interior and current Minister of State for Humanitarian Affairs of the Sudan and Ali Kushayb – a *Janjaweed*/militia leader – for war crimes and crimes against humanity. The Prosecution demonstrated that they joined together to persecute and attack civilians in Darfur who were not participants in the conflict; that Ahmad Harun coordinated a system through which he recruited, funded and armed Militia/*Janjaweed* to supplement the Sudanese Armed Forces, and incited them to attack and commit massive crimes against the civilian population, based on the rationale that they could be rebel supporters. Ali Kushayb was a key part of that system, personally delivering arms and leading attacks. These two arrest warrants remain outstanding.

On December 5th, 2007, I officially informed the UN Security Council that the Sudan was not cooperating with the Court.[7] I also reported on present crimes, finding that ongoing acts of violence are not chaotic occurrences but represent a pattern of attacks against 2.5 million displaced persons. In Darfur, the first phase of Ahmad Harun's plan was to force the people out of their villages and into camps. In the second phase – happening right now – he is controlling them inside the camps, controlling their access to food, humanitarian aid, and security. There are consistent reports that the land and villages which the displaced left behind are being occupied by new settlers. There is a strategy to attack the displaced who try to organize themselves in the camps such as Kalma: some are arrested, others are

---

[6]The ICC's treatment of the Darfur situation is examined in Catherine Lu, Chapter 18, Sections 18.1 and 18.2 (below).

[7]Sixth Report of the Prosecutor of the International Criminal Court, to the Security Council pursuant to UNSC 1593 (2005), http://www.icc-cpi.int/NR/rdonlyres/C197560D-EE9C-42C0-B9AE-9E7054D15A83/277773/OTPRP20071205UNSCENG.pdf, (Accessed December 5, 2007).

forcibly expelled from the camps with no means of survival and relocated in hostile areas.

Following the June 5th, 2008 report to the Council, on June 16th, 2008, the UN Security Council unanimously adopted Presidential Statement 21, which states that the Security Council takes note of the OTP's efforts to bring to justice the perpetrators of war crimes and crimes against humanity in Darfur, in particular the arrest warrants for Ahmad Harun and Ali Kushayb and urges the government of the Sudan and all other parties to the conflict in Darfur to cooperate fully with the Court, consistent with Resolution 1593 (2005), in order to put an end to impunity for the crimes committed in Darfur.

On July 14th, 2008, I presented to the Judges my second case in the Darfur situation covering crimes committed from March 2003 to the present. I requested an arrest warrant against Mr. Al Bashir for 3 counts of genocide, 5 counts of crimes against humanity and 2 counts of war crimes.

Today, Judges of the International Criminal Court are considering my Application. Should they rule in favour of the request, they will issue an arrest warrant and transmit it to the government of the Sudan for enforcement.

Arrest is the responsibility of the territorial state. The Court is not asking for international forces to intervene. But there will be need for innovative, strong and consistent diplomatic and political action by all actors to ensure compliance with the Court's decision. Solutions that favour impunity, such as deferrals and immunities, are not an option.

We have also proceeded with the investigation into allegations of rebel crimes, focusing on the Haskanita attack against AU peacekeepers on September 29–30th, 2007. We are now ready to proceed to the Judges with an application in the third investigation before the end of 2008.

16.2.4 Uganda

Warrants of arrest for Joseph Kony and senior leaders of the LRA were issued on July 8th, 2005. They have committed unspeakable atrocities. They are charged with crimes against humanity and war crimes, such as rape, murder, enslavement, sexual enslavement, enlisting of children, attacking civilian populations, cruel treatment, pillaging and inhumane acts.[8]

My Office had to formally, confidentially and then publicly approach States to request that they should audit in depth the assistance they were giving to the Juba peace talks to ensure that no assistance of any form should go to the indictees. There is a strong need to criminalize any activity

[8]The impact of the ICC on the situation in Uganda is addressed in Catherine Lu, Chapter 18, Section 18.1 (below).

that serves, directly or indirectly, to harbor suspects. This could be done by States through monitoring who receives the humanitarian assistance that they give, as well as by freezing the assets of the indictees, and by States cooperating to carry out searches.

The ICC does not have the authority to execute warrants directly on the territory of States; rather, arrests are the responsibility of the relevant States. Securing arrests is a process that may require the commitment of significant police, military, political and/or legal resources. Where suspects are mobile and able to move across borders, as in the Uganda case, there is a need for specific forms of coordination among relevant States and organizations. Suspects may also retain support networks (perhaps with a global reach) which are in turn able to provide safe havens or logistical and financial support. Eradicating these forms of support is crucial to enhancing the prospects for arrests.

Kony and the other two LRA commanders charged with crimes against humanity and war crimes committed in Northern Uganda remain at large. They continue to commit crimes and to threaten the entire region. Arrest is long overdue.

Kony used the Juba peace talks to gain time and support, to re-arm and attack again. We have collected information indicating that at the end of 2007, Joseph Kony issued orders to abduct 1,000 persons to expand the ranks of the LRA. The price paid today by civilians is high. The LRA is attacking civilians in Southern Sudan and in the CAR, and is now also committing atrocities in the DRC.

On September 17th, 2008, the LRA attacked Congolese villages in the DRC (Dungu Territory). These attacks all follow a similar method, with markets surrounded and looted, students abducted from school, properties burned and dozens of civilians killed, including several local chiefs. Tens of thousands have now been displaced.

We urge all actors, including regional and international organizations, to support and work together with the DRC, CAR, Southern Sudan, Uganda and the MONUC in the planning and execution of the arrests.

16.3 Current Challenges: The Enforcement of Decisions and the Interdependency Between Peace and Justice

On a general level, the ICC, and the Office of the Prosecutor in particular, has obtained cooperation from a number of States (including non-State parties) and international organizations, as well as concluding agreements to facilitate additional cooperation. Such cooperation has overall been forthcoming.

Experience demonstrates, nonetheless, that obtaining cooperation in practice may be influenced by issues of feasibility, resources, policy and prioritization, and by the existence of effective domestic procedures enabling practical execution of requests within and across ministries and institutions. The degree to which the goals of the Rome Statute are achieved depends in large part on the actions taken by all those actors in furtherance of the Statute's goals, and in the level of support they offer the ICC.

What are some of the challenges the ICC has faced in its early days of operation? Among these challenges are many with which the international tribunals have been familiar:

- The investigation of the most massive crimes, while focusing on suspects who bear the greatest responsibility, as opposed to the physical perpetrators of crimes;
- Working without our own enforcement powers and in situations where the perpetrators may be protected or the communities divided;
- Conducting investigations in the context of ongoing violence, as our work is often contemporaneous with an ongoing conflict, with the attendant issues this raises for the protection of victims and witnesses and the security of staff; and
- The challenge of delivering results in a manner that is efficient and cost-effective while respecting the highest standards of justice.

However, the issue of arrest and surrender forms the principal area of concern of the International Criminal Court, as it has been for the *ad hoc* Tribunals. As we all recognize only too well, without arrests, trials will simply not take place.

While it is for the relevant actors to decide how best to facilitate arrests, we have in particular called on all State parties to consider the following:

- Diplomatic and political pressure from State parties, with support of other States and organizations, as, for example, that of the UN in the context of the DRC;
- Support to those States on whose territory suspects are located through, for example, sharing information on suspect tracking, logistical support and specialized training for arrest operations;
- Investigating issues of supply and support and tackling these networks through domestic or international action; for example, imposing UN Security Council sanctions and freezing assets;
- Including, where feasible, provisions enabling cooperation with efforts to bring to justice individuals responsible for crimes under the jurisdiction of the ICC within the mandate of relevant peacekeeping missions (and ensuring that the necessary resources are provided to secure arrests);
- Creating operational groups comprised of relevant States and organizations to exchange information and coordination on military and diplomatic efforts to secure arrests.

Allowed to remain at large, the persons sought by the ICC can continue to threaten the victims, the very victims who took tremendous risks to tell their stories.

In particular there are efforts from some quarters to sideline the ICC at the very moment we are trying to encourage others to marginalize persons sought by the ICC. In particular, there are those who wish to pit the ICC's justice mandate against the requirements of peace and security, in efforts to avoid compliance with the ICC's warrants. These calls will be familiar to those from the ICTY in the context of the Dayton Peace Accords in Bosnia, or the Special Court for Sierra Leone after the indictment of Charles Taylor.

What we have said is that international justice, national justice, the search for the truth, and peace negotiations can and must work together; they are not alternative ways to achieve a goal but can be integrated into one comprehensive solution. The tension we see in Uganda or Darfur is not between peace and justice. It is not the decisions of the ICC that undermine peace processes and conflict resolution initiatives.

On the contrary, the beneficial impact of the ICC and the value of the law to prevent recurring violence is clear. Deterrence has started to show its effect as in the case of Cote d'Ivoire, where the prospect of prosecution of those using hate speech is deemed to have kept the main actors under some level of control.[9] In Colombia, legislation and proceedings against paramilitary were influenced by the Rome provisions, and there are examples of military officials incorporating the constraints of the Rome Statute in their operational planning. In Uganda arrest warrants have contributed to bringing the LRA to the negotiating table, focused national debates on accountability and reducing crimes, and exposed the criminals and their horrendous crimes, all of which has contributed to weakening the support they were enjoying, to de-legitimizing them and their practices such as conscription of children. In the long term, the ICC will contribute to the peaceful coexistence between former enemies as a sense of justice and reparation is achieved.

It is the lack of enforcement of the Court's decisions which is the real threat to enduring peace. Allowed to remain at large, the exposed criminals are continuing to threaten the victims; allowed to remain at large, the criminals ask immunity under one form or another as a condition to stopping the violence. They threaten to attack more victims. This is nothing more than extortion and blackmail. The ICC has reminded States of their responsibilities in this regard to uphold the law.

16.4 Conclusion

The ICC is a new instrument of peace in a world where conflicts transcend borders.[10] It has been built on the lessons learned of decades of violence

---

[9]The impact of the ICC in the area of prevention is discussed in Catherine Lu, Chapter 18, Section 18.2 (below).

[10]Different conceptions of the role of the ICC are discussed in Noah Weisbord, Chapter 17 (below).

and atrocities. As citizens of the global community, States, the UN, and the AU, we cannot separate our efforts. It must be our shared commitment to deal with massive crimes. There are no safe borders for each and every one of us if we choose to turn a blind eye to the plight of the people of Darfur or elsewhere.

What is happening in Darfur is not a distant reality. Resolving the problem, giving victims their dignity back and holding those responsible for crimes accountable, must not be just a dream: together we can make it an obtainable reality. We must stigmatize, isolate, marginalize and disrupt criminal activities, and we must exclude from the negotiating table those responsible for the most serious crimes of concern to the international community. Violence shall not be rewarded any longer. Impunity will not prevail.

The mandate of the Office is justice: justice for the people of Darfur, people who are dying in full sight of the international community, people dying from the indifference of governments. Ignoring such violence today in Darfur is accepting it tomorrow anywhere in the world. In today's world, no citizen is protected if we do not protect all of them; in Darfur, in Montréal, around the world.

I am the Prosecutor of a permanent Court. I can wait. The destiny of individuals accused of massive crimes is the courtroom. But victims cannot wait.

Chapter 17
International Justice: From the Twilight to the Dawn? International Criminal Court Prosecutor Luis Moreno-Ocampo at McGill University

Noah Weisbord

In his 1948 essay, *The Twilight of International Morality*, Hans Morgenthau describes a "deterioration of moral limitations of international politics," which he attributes to two historical forces: "the substitution of democratic for aristocratic responsibility in foreign affairs and the substitution of nationalistic standards of action for universal ones."[1] According to Morgenthau, the French Revolution introduced a new era of nationalism that "corroded" the aristocratic cosmopolitan morality that had previously exerted a humanizing influence on the conduct of international affairs. The result was the total wars of the 20th century: war waged without moral restraint because the violence is justified by ideology.[2] *The Twilight of International Morality* closes ominously and decisively: "[l]ittle do they [the nationalistic masses] know that they meet under an empty sky from which the gods have departed."[3]

Sixty years have passed since Morgenthau wrote *The Twilight of International Morality*. Where does the story go from here? The answer matters because, as one of the canonical political science essays of the 20th century, *The Twilight of International Morality* helped frame the Cold War for a generation of international law and international relations scholars and their students, who became the leaders of states and militaries. The way the story continues is significant because this disciplinary narrative has the potential to affect the next generation's understanding of the trajectory of international morality, Prosecutor Moreno-Ocampo's speech at McGill University, and the events related to the arrest – or failure to arrest – Ahmad Harun.

N. Weisbord (✉)
Duke University Law School, Durham, NC 27708, USA
e-mail: weisbord@law.duke.edu

[1] Hans Morgenthau, "The Twilight of International Morality," *Ethics* 58, no. 2 (1948): 88.
[2] Ibid., 93.
[3] Ibid., 99.

R. Provost, P. Akhavan (eds.), *Confronting Genocide*, Ius Gentium: Comparative Perspectives on Law and Justice 7, DOI 10.1007/978-90-481-9840-5_17,

Since *The Twilight of International Morality*, the Cold War materialized and concluded in an "unabashed victory of economic and political liberalism" over communism.[4] In the wake of the Cold War, there have been a number of historical developments of specific relevance to Morgenthau's tale that he could not have anticipated as he wrote after World War II. These include the proliferation of international criminal laws and *ad hoc* tribunals to enforce them (but failure to act to prevent international crimes), the arrest and trial of a number of military leaders and heads of state breaking those laws (in the midst of widespread impunity), the extensive ratification of the statute establishing a permanent international criminal court (amid resistance from the most militarily powerful states),[5] the incorporation of the criminal prohibitions contained in the Rome Statute into legal systems worldwide (with analogous rules in the national legislation of the most militarily powerful states), the creation of a functioning international criminal court in The Hague (with no independent enforcement capacity),[6] and the arrest of the first two suspects (and the inability or unwillingness of States Parties to the ICC to arrest others). Taken together, these developments reveal key information about the current trajectory of international morality and hint at possible avenues for Morgenthau's story.

Here are three alternatives. Either the emergence of the ICC is: (1) a false dawn, a superstructure of morality that serves as an apology for the exercise of raw power by the liberal democracies;[7] (2) a reverie, a utopia dreamed up by idealists;[8] or (3) the dawn of international justice. There are certainly additional scenarios and, after considering these, the reader may want to imagine alternatives.

The false dawn. International relations scholars from Machiavelli[9] to Hobbs[10] to Marx[11] have told the story of international morality as a superstructure on a substratum of great power interests. The evolution of international justice after the Cold War and Prosecutor Moreno-Ocampo's inability to impel states to arrest Ahmad Harun, due, as many commentators have suggested, to the vested interests of great powers in oil reserves

---

[4]Francis Fukuyama, "The End of History?" *The National Interest* 16 (1989).

[5]Rome Statute of the International Criminal Court, 2187 U.N.T.S. 90, July 17, 1998.

[6]The establishment and role of the ICC are discussed in Luis Moreno-Ocampo, Chapter 16 (above).

[7]Arguments raised by states such as Sudan characterizing the ICC as a tool of the great powers are addressed in Catherine Lu, Chapter 18, Sections 18.1 and 18.2 (below).

[8]Martti Koskenniemi, *From Apology to Utopia: The Structure of International Legal Argument* (Cambridge: Cambridge University Press, 1989).

[9]Niccolo Machiavelli, *The Prince* (New York: The Modern Library, 1950).

[10]Thomas Hobbes, *Leviathan* (Oxford: Oxford University Press, 1881).

[11]Karl Marx and Friedrich Engels, *The Communist Manifesto* (New York: Penguin Classics, 1848).

controlled by the government of Sudan, may be described this way.[12] Yet, the false dawn scenario is less credible in light of the fact that the Rome Statute has been ratified by 105 states worldwide, many of them not liberal democracies.[13] Furthermore, some of the leading liberal democracies, great powers that fought and won the Cold War, most notably the United States, have made significant efforts to oppose the Court or undermine its effectiveness.[14] This is a tale that does not easily accommodate its contradictions.

The reverie. In the second scenario, international morality is a reverie, a utopia dreamed up by idealistic scholars and diplomats, with little realistic capacity to humanize the cold reality of international relations or improve human security. Ideals are simply not as significant as interests in motivating the behavior of political and military leaders. Certainly, international morality seems like a hopeful dream in light of the continuing violence in Darfur,[15] States' inability or unwillingness to enforce the outstanding ICC arrest warrants, and Prosecutor Moreno-Ocampo's bleak report at McGill, "[t]he same man we allege as Minister of State for the Interior, attacked civilians and forced people out of their homes and into the camps is today in charge of the camps and controlling the fate of his victims." However, this scenario does not explain the fact that the Darfur referral was successfully pushed through the UN Security Council, despite the resistance of some of the world's most militarily powerful states. Nor does it account for the effect of the ICC intervention in Northern Uganda, which galvanized a concerted international effort to marginalize the Lord's Resistance Army, push them to the bargaining table, and drastically reduced attacks on the civilian population.[16]

The dawn of international justice. Under the third scenario, the ICC represents the dawn of international justice and demonstrates that a cosmopolitan international morality can exist absent an aristocratic elite

---

[12] The implications of China's interests in the Sudan on the situation in Darfur are discussed in Yehuda Bauer, Chapter 7, Sections 7.1 and 7.3 (above) and Richard J. Goldstone, Chapter 11, Section 11.4 (above).

[13] See The Assembly of States Parties to the International Criminal Court, "The States Parties to the Rome Statute," http://www.icc-cpi.int/iccdocs/asp_docs/ICC-ASP-7-SWGCA-INF.1%20English.pdf (Accessed November 29, 2007).

[14] US Department of State, "Article 98 Agreements and the International Criminal Court," http://www.state.gov/t/pm/art98/ (last Accessed: November 29, 2007); Human Rights Watch, "Letter to State Parties and Signatories to ICC on Article 98 Agreements," New York, August 9, 2002, http://hrw.org/press/2002/08/article98letter.htm (last accessed November 29, 2007).

[15] An account of the deteriorating situation in Darfur is provided in Gérard Prunier, Chapter 3, Sections 3.1 and 3.2 (above).

[16] The impact of the ICC on the situation in Uganda is addressed in Catherine Lu, Chapter 18, Section 18.1 (below) and Luis Moreno-Ocampo, Chapter 16 (above).

with intra-group loyalties and a shared culture. The post-Cold War international criminal justice movement, an emerging network of scholars, statesmen, students, parliamentarians, diplomats, law enforcement agencies, philanthropists, religious and humanitarian groups, has replaced the cosmopolitan aristocratic elite Morgenthau identifies as the template for the international morality of the day. The contemporary international justice network, the audience for Prosecutor Moreno-Ocampo's mobilizing speech at McGill, has, by creating or commandeering international rules, national legislation, supranational institutions and transnational networks of all types, eroded the norms of sovereign immunity, act of state, and *droit de guerre* associated with the nationalistic and democratic ethos Morgenthau imagines under an empty and godless sky. Yet, the dawn of international morality, or, more accurately, international justice, is overcast and there are islands of outlawry. Sudan has placed Ahmad Harun in charge of the camps where his victims have amassed for safety. Militarily powerful states are blocking decisive Security Council action to stop government-endorsed violence in Darfur. When asking for international cooperation to marginalize and arrest individuals suspected of committing mass atrocities, Prosecutor Moreno-Ocampo is meeting with resistance that is regularly defended on the basis of the nationalistic and democratic ethos Morgenthau forecasts in *The Twilight of International Morality*.

According to Max Weber: "We are *cultural beings*, endowed with the capacity and the will to take a deliberate attitude towards the world and lend it *significance*."[17] The "we" in the story of international morality is no longer Morgenthau's cosmopolitan aristocratic elite, but instead the interested hodgepodge represented in Prosecutor Moreno-Ocampo's audience at McGill. Prosecutor Moreno-Ocampo's call to arrest Ahmad Harun signifies an important moment in the story of international justice insofar as the way it is interpreted by this gathering shapes their hopes, expectations, and efforts. It remains to be seen which story will prevail, how it will effect their involvement, and ultimately, how their involvement will influence the fate of Ahmad Harun's charges in Darfur. Whatever story prevails, the manifestation of a network around the international justice project indicates that, even without an aristocratic elite, even if the gods have departed, the sky is no longer empty: a new cosmopolitan ideal has emerged.

[17]Max Weber, *Sociological Writings* (New York: The German Library, 1949), 81.

Chapter 18
The Politics of Legal Accountability and Genocide Prevention

Catherine Lu

Does holding perpetrators of genocide accountable through legal criminal prosecutions contribute to the prevention of genocide? In cases of ongoing or recently concluded violent political conflict, does the indictment of key perpetrators help to prevent or mitigate atrocities, or contribute to the peaceful resolution of conflict? For example, does the International Criminal Court's (ICC) indictment of top commanders in the Lord's Resistance Army in Uganda help to lessen the severity of human rights violations or conclude the peace in the region? Or does the ICC's March 2009 arrest warrant for Sudanese president Omar al-Bashir on charges of war crimes and crimes against humanity – including targeting civilians and pillage in war, as well as murder, extermination, forcible transfer, torture, and rape – help to end civilian suffering in Darfur or bring about a peace settlement between warring parties? What is the relationship between the politics of accountability and the politics of prevention? Do international criminal tribunals help us to progress towards a world in which genocide and other mass atrocities will "never again" haunt humanity?

18.1 The Politics of Accountability

In a 2007 address in Nuremberg, called, "Building a Future on Peace and Justice," the Chief Prosecutor of the ICC, Luis Moreno-Ocampo, argued that his office constituted "a new autonomous actor on the international scene" whose primary, if not sole duty, was "to apply the law without political considerations." Adopting a strict legalistic view of the

C. Lu (✉)
Department of Political Science, McGill University, Montréal, QC H3A 2T7, Canada
e-mail: catherine.lu@mcgill.ca

R. Provost, P. Akhavan (eds.), *Confronting Genocide*, Ius Gentium: Comparative Perspectives on Law and Justice 7, DOI 10.1007/978-90-481-9840-5_18,

ICC's responsibilities, the Prosecutor stated, "there can be no political compromise on legality and accountability."[1]

Moreno-Ocampo's statement implies that law is above politics or separate from politics, rather than another form of politics. I have asserted in previous work that law cannot be viewed in isolation from its normative and political contexts. The International Criminal Court is not only a legal institution with legalistic objectives; its purposes and operation should also be understood and assessed in moral and political terms.[2] I draw from the work of the late American political theorist, Judith Shklar, who has argued, "law is a form of political action, among others, which occasionally is applicable and effective and often is not. It is not an answer to politics, neither is it isolated from political purposes and struggles.... The question is not, 'Is law politics?' but 'What sort of politics can law maintain and reflect?'"[3] This acknowledgement of the inseparability of law from politics and morality should not be read as an endorsement of a cynical interpretation that law is (or ought to be) a mere servant to power, or right a slave to might. Rather, it should lead us to interrogate the politics of accountability, and the political and normative conditions that give shape to legal rules, practices and outcomes.

The key question to ask, then, is not whether or not the ICC is political – it inescapably is – but, rather, what kinds of politics is it able to support, maintain and reflect? In particular, an international criminal tribunal raises the issue of what influence or impact an international institution of accountability can have on the shape of various sites of domestic politics. The current situations before the Court illuminate the dynamic and conflicted relationships between the ICC, and international and domestic political actors.

The Office of the Prosecutor of the ICC is actively pursuing four situations currently: the Democratic Republic of Congo, Northern Uganda, the Darfur region of Sudan, and the Central African Republic.[4] All are ongoing or tenuously stabilized conflicts. An early worry about the ICC has been that rather than dispensing impartial justice and accountability for all, it would operate more as an instrument of globally dominant states to teach manners to the weak. The situation in the Darfur region of Sudan

---

[1] Luis Moreno-Ocampo, "Building a Future on Peace and Justice" (address, Nuremberg, June 24/25, 2007), http://wwwold.icc-cpi.int/library/organs/otp/speeches/LMO_nuremberg_20070625_English.pdf.

[2] See Catherine Lu, "The International Criminal Court as an Institution of Moral Regeneration: Problems and Prospects," in *Bringing Power to Justice: The Prospects of the International Criminal Court*, eds. Joanna Harrington, Michael Milde and Richard Vernon (Montreal: McGill-Queen's University Press, 2006), 191–209.

[3] Judith N. Shklar, *Legalism: Law, Morals, and Political Trials* (Cambridge, MA: Harvard University Press, 1964), 143–144.

[4] An account of current cases before the ICC is provided in Luis Moreno-Ocampo, Chapter 16 (above).

was referred to the ICC by the United Nations Security Council (UNSC) in 2005, and led to several indictments in 2007 against Ahmad Harun, former Minister of State for Interior of the Sudan, and Ali Kushayb, a *Janjaweed* militia leader, for crimes against humanity and war crimes. On March 4, 2009, the ICC issued an arrest warrant for the President of Sudan, Omar al-Bashir, on two counts of war crimes and five counts of crimes against humanity. The prosecution of these cases, however, has been blocked due to lack of cooperation from the Sudanese government – indeed, Ahmad Harun remains part of the government as the minister in charge of humanitarian affairs. Sudanese government representatives have accused the UN Security Council of basing justice on "exploitation of crises in developing countries and bargaining among major Powers," and argued that the UNSC resolution "exposed the fact that the ICC was intended for developing and weak countries and was a tool to exercise cultural superiority."[5] Although clearly a self-serving response by the Sudanese government, it does highlight the reality that in current global political conditions, the ICC is incapable of disciplining the world's most powerful states, and potentially most egregious human rights offenders – China, Russia and the United States. Being able to achieve *some* justice, such as in Sudan, by vindicating the worth of *some* victims and ending the impunity of *some* violators would herald a step in the right direction. But the real test for the ICC, in terms of its promotion of an impartial and universal system of international criminal justice, will be whether it can hold the world's most powerful to account.[6]

Despite Sudan's protests about victimization by "major powers," the other situations before the Court indicate that weak states may also attempt to exploit the ICC for their own advantage in local power disputes. Somewhat unexpectedly, three of the current cases were self-referrals, where the ruling government in question referred its own conflict to the ICC. For example, the Ugandan government's self-referral has led to indictments against key leaders of the rebel Lord's Resistance Army (LRA) – the first warrants to be issued by the ICC in October 2005. Mark Drumbl has noted, however, that the Ugandan government is an "illiberal regime" involved in committing atrocities. Bringing in the ICC thus becomes one strategy that ruling governments can employ to "consolidate power and avoid enfranchising the policy preferences of afflicted local populations."[7] As Paola Gaeta has put it, "By requesting ICC intervention, that state could be using the Court as a political weapon in the hope that its intervention

---

[5]United Nations Security Council, "United Nations Security Council Resolution 1593 (2005), adopted by Vote of 11 in Favour To None Against, with 4 Abstentions (Algeria, Brazil, China, United States)," SC/8351, March 31, 2005, http://www.un.org/News/Press/docs/2005/sc8351.doc.htm.

[6]Different conceptions of the role of the ICC are discussed in Noah Weisbord, Chapter 17 (above).

[7]Mark A. Drumbl, *Atrocity, Punishment, and International Law* (Cambridge: Cambridge University Press, 2007), 144–146.

could assist it in achieving its domestic political and military aims."[8] This use of the Court becomes apparent in situations where the cooperation of governments with the investigations of the ICC is limited to the pursuit of cases against rebel or anti-government factions. Given that self-referring governments such as Uganda are themselves parties to the violent conflict, self-referral can undermine the perceived impartiality of the ICC. As Drumbl observes, "In local eyes, the fact that the ICC was invited by the Ugandan government spoils its putative impartiality."[9]

Clearly, the ICC cannot determine alone the course of the politics of accountability or its results, but given the vagaries of both international and domestic politics, the ICC Chief Prosecutor was perhaps more right than wrong in asserting the independence of his office and the Court. At the same time, participants in the politics of accountability must recognize how dependent the labours of the Court will be on the quality and character of international and domestic political conditions. As Shklar asserted, "Formal justice depends for its social impact upon the total political environment in which juridical actions occur, and its functions cannot be understood in isolation."[10] The ICC must operate currently in at least two nonideal contexts: a global context of gross political and economic disparities in which powerful states consider themselves peerless and are largely indifferent to politically induced humanitarian disasters, and domestic contexts of violent political conflict and instability in which the agents who are responsible for atrocities are also among the most powerful local parties who can derail any peace negotiations. In such nonideal contexts, the work of the ICC risks becoming instrumentalized by international and/or domestic political actors seeking their own political advantage through legalistic means. In the short and medium terms, proponents of the ICC must therefore confront and assess the challenge of unexpected harms produced by the intervention of the Court on local and domestic politics. At the same time, the attempt by various actors to instrumentalize the Court can produce other unintended consequences; politicizing accountability may in the long term strengthen the notion of legal accountability as a legitimate and far-reaching political demand in both international and domestic politics.

18.2 The Politics of Prevention

How do the politics of accountability relate to the politics of prevention? I have observed elsewhere that in the aftermath of atrocities, survivors face

[8] Paola Gaeta, "Is the Practice of 'Self-Referrals' a Sound Start for the ICC?" *Journal of International Criminal Justice* 2, no. 4 (2004): 952.

[9] Drumbl, *Atrocity, Punishment, and International Law*, 145.

[10] Shklar, *Legalism*, 146.

three pressing questions: "Who is to blame? How could such evil happen? And how can it be prevented in the future?"[11] The tasks of moral or legal judgement, causal explanation, and prevention or deterrence are interrelated, but also distinct. For example, while legal accountability may be important for vindicating the view of individual human beings as moral agents at all, the task of prevention or deterrence, given the structural nature of socially and politically organized violence, will likely require much more than holding individual agents accountable for their actions or omissions. If the goal is prevention, then the individual "liability model" of responsibility is inadequate, and needs to be buttressed by a notion of "political responsibility" for the structural dysfunctions that produce politically organized crimes such as genocide.[12]

Proponents of the ICC see no conflict between two of its main declared aims: achieving justice for victims and ending the impunity of violators, and helping to deter future violators and end conflicts.[13] The ICC faces criticism from two directions about its role in deterring violators and promoting peace. The first criticism emanates from a worry that in the nonideal conditions of societies experiencing violent conflict, the quest for legal accountability conflicts with the task of reaching a peace agreement between warring parties; peace and justice may not go together, and sometimes one must shake hands with devils in order to secure the peace.[14] The second avenue of criticism comes from those who argue that justice, understood as legal criminal accountability, is insufficient and perhaps even counterproductive in terms of the long-term goal of building a sustainable future without genocide. Proponents of restorative justice approaches to peacebuilding argue that amnesties may not only be politically expedient, but they may also serve better the broader goals of collective accounting and political inclusion in the aftermath of divisive political conflict that has culminated in mass atrocity.[15] In addition, some critics worry that the significant economic costs of running criminal prosecutions divert limited international funds away from the more important task of economic reconstruction in severely impoverished countries.[16]

---

[11]See Catherine Lu, "Agents, Structures and Evil in World Politics," *International Relations* 18, no. 4 (2004): 499.

[12]See Iris Marion Young, "Responsibility and Global Labor Justice," *The Journal of Political Philosophy* 12, no.4 (2004): 365–388, on responsibility for structural injustice, and the distinction between the blame model and political model of responsibility.

[13]See United Nations, "Rome Statute of the International Criminal Court: Overview," United Nations Treaty Database, http://untreaty.un.org/cod/icc/general/overview.htm.

[14]The argument that there is no conflict between justice and peace is presented in Luis Moreno-Ocampo, Chapter 16 (above).

[15]Helena Cobban, *Amnesty After Atrocity? Healing Nations after Genocide and War Crimes* (Boulder, Colorado: Paradigm Publishers, 2007).

[16]Ibid., 208–211.

Interestingly, the Sudanese government has explicitly raised the potential problem of a trade-off between peace and justice, warning that the involvement of the ICC would "only serve to weaken prospects for settlement and further complicate the already complex situation."[17] While this is a crude self-serving argument, it is also, unfortunately, an argument with traction, in the nonideal circumstances in which the Sudanese government is an essential partner to any durable agreement to end the violence in the Darfur region. While it is far from obvious that the Sudanese government would quickly terminate the conflict in Darfur if the ICC charges were dropped, it is also plausible that, as in the case of Mozambique or South Africa, a negotiated settlement might require the granting of amnesties rather than the pursuit of criminal prosecution. Against those who have criticized the involvement of the ICC in ongoing conflicts as a threat to fragile peace negotiations, ICC Prosecutor Moreno-Ocampo has maintained that ICC decisions cannot be blamed for undermining peace processes. Rather, he has highlighted the Court's "beneficial impact," including bringing belligerents to the negotiating table.[18, 19] By justifying the ICC in these terms, however, the ICC Prosecutor gives credibility to the view that accountability mechanisms should be an instrument of the consequentialist goal of achieving peace or deterring violators. If justice claims are subordinate to consequentialist political aims, then it may turn out that while arrest warrants are instrumental in bringing violators to the negotiating table, their withdrawal would also be instrumental once peace negotiations are taking place.

Given the potentially serious political implications of the work of the ICC, some may argue that the ICC Prosecutor should show more deference to governments or state agents because (1) those in the judicial profession are not trained political actors, and (2) state agents are better at balancing consequentialist political aims with the quest for accountability. Historically, however, state agents have not been obviously better able to balance the interests of justice and peace. When criminal tribunals have been dominated by state agents, their operation exhibited defective commitments to justice, sometimes unnecessarily so or for ill-conceived political reasons. The case of Japan after World War II provides an illuminating example. After the war, the United States was the main power that assumed the task of holding Japanese leaders to account in the Tokyo trial. Historian John Dower has argued that the trial, rather than representing a

[17]United Nations Security Council Resolution 1593, U.N. Doc. S/Res/1593 (March 31, 2005).

[18]Luis Moreno-Ocampo, "Building a Future on Peace and Justice"(address, Nuremberg, June 24/25, 2007), http://wwwold.icc-cpi.int/library/organs/otp/speeches/LMO_nuremberg_20070625_English.pdf.

[19]The positive impact of the ICC is illustrated in Luis Moreno-Ocampo, Chapter 16 (above).

vindication of justice as legal accountability, actually failed to hold significant perpetrators accountable for major crimes: "No heads of the dreaded Kempeitai (the military police) were indicted; no leaders of ultranationalistic secret societies ...The forced mobilization of Korean and Formosan colonial subjects was not pursued as a crime against humanity, nor was the rounding up of many tens of thousands of young non-Japanese who were forced to serve as 'comfort women' providing sexual services to the imperial forces." In addition, in return for access to the research results, American officials granted "blanket secret immunity" to "the officers and scientific researchers in Unit 731 in Manchuria who had conducted lethal experiments on thousands of prisoners." These omissions did not reflect concerns that pursuing such cases might lead to social chaos, or undermine the reconstruction of post-war Japan; rather, Dower suggests that the Tokyo trial, run by the Western liberal victors, "mirrored a world still skewed by the harsh realities of race, power, and powerlessness."[20]

The ethical challenge of achieving a morally appropriate balance between the pursuit of legal accountability and consequentialist political considerations is thus not solved by subordinating prosecutors or the criminal justice process to nonideal political state agents. Although prosecutors and judges are not trained or self-styled politicians, they are political actors, whose mandate is to promote a certain practice of legalism and justice as legal accountability for the exercise of political power. The introduction of the ICC as an institution of legal accountability thus creates a presumption in favour of prosecution in the cases of genocide, war crimes and crimes against humanity. My understanding of "presumption" is similar to that of the philosopher Charles Taylor; it "is a starting hypothesis"[21] with which we should approach the task of accounting for genocide, war crimes and crimes against humanity. But a presumption in favour of prosecution does not amount to an unconditional duty or right to prosecute; the presumption can be defeated by more compelling moral/political considerations. The consequence of introducing this presumption in world politics is that exemption from prosecution for these serious offences must be publicly justified at local, domestic *and* international levels. While political actors at every level may seek to instrumentalize the ICC, the politics of accountability between these diverse, contesting publics may help to establish the legitimacy of the international institution. Even though the ICC is currently a severely constrained institution, its efforts to establish a transparent, fair and politically independent process of judging individual accountability for

---

[20] John W. Dower, *Embracing Defeat: Japan in the Wake of World War II* (New York: W.W. Norton, 1999): 464–465. For a more nuanced view of the achievements and failures of the Tokyo trial, see Yuma Totani, *The Tokyo War Crimes Trial: The Pursuit of Justice in the Wake of World War II* (Cambridge: Harvard University Press, 2008).

[21] Charles Taylor, "The Politics of Recognition," in *Multiculturalism* (Princeton: Princeton University Press, 1994), 66–67.

genocide, war crimes, and crimes against humanity may have salutary long term consequences for both domestic and international politics.

18.3 The Long View

"Never again" has been a powerful appeal since the Nazi holocaust, but the appeal has also been labeled "the world's most unfulfilled promise."[22] There are two versions of the appeal, which I will call "utopian" and "practical." In the utopian version, "never again" refers to an ideal world in which the various political dysfunctions that precipitate atrocities cease to exist, a world in which genocides and other atrocities would literally "never again" appear. In such a world, genocides would be eradicated, in the same way that the polio virus could be eradicated as a human health concern. Of course, such a world would also be one in which the ICC would cease to have a function. Given the corruptibility of human politics, I favour the more "practical" version of the "never again" appeal, that imagines a world in which political dysfunctions still exist, but their destructive manifestations in the form of genocide and other mass atrocities are "never again" met with global indifference or resignation.[23] In such a world, various forms of political dysfunction may still spiral into genocide, war crimes, and crimes against humanity, but the incidence and scale of atrocities would be mitigated by timely, effective interventions – diplomatic, military and otherwise – and there would still be a need for an ICC to prosecute the most culpable individual political leaders. In such circumstances, the politics of prevention at the international level would work hand in hand with the politics of accountability, leaving little bargaining room for domestic political actors who engage in serious human rights violations to further their political objectives.

In our current world of defective domestic and international political agents and structures, however, the price of peace may indeed sometimes be justice, or even worse, vulnerable populations will have to endure years of organized killing, raping, and burning of villages with neither peace nor justice in sight. In the case of Darfur, given the absence of a serious international diplomatic effort or an effective peace-making force that can alter the political reality on the ground, it is difficult to see how either peace or justice can be obtained. Indeed, in response to contemporary ongoing violent political conflicts that have resulted in genocide, crimes against

[22]Samantha Power, "Never Again: The World's Most Unfulfilled Promise," *Frontline* http://www.pbs.org/wgbh/pages/frontline/shows/karadzic/genocide/neveragain.html (accessed July 15, 2009).

[23]Pragmatic ways short of intervention to stop mass atrocities are examined in Frédéric Mégret, Chapter 13, Section 13.5 (above).

humanity or war crimes, the UN Security Council has been thick on resolutions and thin on tangible political commitment to ending serious human rights violations. Thus even with a Security Council mandate, the hybrid United Nations/African Union force in the Darfur region suffers from a lack of troops, equipment and resources, even to defend themselves from attack, much less to protect vulnerable populations. Disturbingly, the international community may be employing the politics of accountability to displace its political responsibility to engage in the politics of protection or prevention. In frustration, Moreno-Ocampo has repeatedly called on the international community and the UN Security Council to stop the crimes and arrest the leaders. He has stated that, "Darfur is a test for the international community,"[24] but so far, only the civilians and refugees of Darfur are paying the price of the international community's political failures. As Gary Bass commented at the Prevention of Genocide conference, this current scenario is tantamount to "holding the Nuremberg Trials without fighting World War II."

When power is indifferent to both the aims of prevention and accountability for genocide, ICC practitioners will find their work and its consequences constantly thwarted or subverted, in intentional and unintentional ways. In the end, there is no institutional substitute for good moral and political leadership and judgement. When these are lacking, the quality of institutional practices and their outcomes suffer accordingly. The potential of the International Criminal Court to contribute positively to our practical ideals thus depends on great transformations in world politics.

[24]Luis Moreno-Ocampo, "ICC Prosecutor on Darfur: "Stop the Crimes, Stop the Criminals," International Criminal Court, http://www.icc-cpi.int/menus/icc/situations%20and%20cases/situations/situation%20icc%200205/press%20releases/icc%20prosecutor%20on%20darfur_%20%E2%80%9Cstop%20the%20crimes_%20stop%20the%20criminals%E2%80%9D.

Chapter 19
A Psychological Investigation of Individual and Social Transformations in Post-Genocide Rwanda

Jobb Arnold

The aims of life are the best defense against death
– Primo Levi[1]

The purpose of this paper is to explore the relationship between the micro level psychological reactions of individuals exposed to genocidal violence and the impact this has on current attitudes toward programs of social reconciliation. Recent social science research has clarified the complex interaction of individual and collective trauma in the aftermath of extreme mass violence, its relation to cycles of violence, and its capacity to undermine reconciliation efforts.[2] Less research attention has focused on the reasons why some individuals and communities exposed to violence are able to break cycles of violence and effectively work toward rebuilding their own lives and aid in the reconstruction of the lives of other survivors. The paucity of research investigating these more optimistic patterns can be attributed in part to the nature of the questions asked by social science and the assumptions held regarding the life trajectories of those who have lived through mass violence.[3]

Research that explores cycles of violence and the role of trauma in perpetuating them finds a natural complement in efforts that facilitate peaceful and sustainable change at the individual and societal levels. Trauma healing is important in terms of violence prevention as well as a means of promoting sustainable reconciliation and is an important element of moving from

J. Arnold (✉)
PhD Candidate, Cultural Studies Program, Queen's University, Belfast, UK
e-mail: jobbera@gmail.com

[1]Primo Levi, *The Drowned and the Saved, trans.* Raymond Rosenthal (New York: Random House, 1987) 140.

[2]Ervin Staub, "Reconciliation After Genocide, Mass killing, or Intractable Conflict: Understanding the Roots of Violence, Psychological Recovery, and Steps Toward a General Theory," *Political Psychology* 27, no.6 (2006).

[3]Derek Summerfield, "A Critique of Seven Assumptions Behind Psychological Trauma Programmes in War-Affected Areas," *Social Science & Medicine* 48, no. 10 (1999).

R. Provost, P. Akhavan (eds.), *Confronting Genocide*, Ius Gentium: Comparative Perspectives on Law and Justice 7, DOI 10.1007/978-90-481-9840-5_19,

negative peace, denoting the absence of violence, to *positive peace*, where quality of life can begin to increase.[4] The following sections provide an overview of the psychological concept of *post-traumatic growth* (PTG) and explore its relation to reconciliation.[5] Subsequent sections present the first known empirical research to explore PTG in a sample of Rwandan genocide survivors and provides support for the theoretical connection between PTG and openness to reconciliation.

19.1 Variation in Responses to Trauma

There is a substantial psychological literature concerned with the pathogenic nature of traumatic events, individual and social *traumatization* and factors affecting the onset of *post-traumatic stress disorder* (PTSD). While the identification of biomedical symptoms is an invaluable tool in the assessment and treatment of individuals following traumatic experiences, an over-reliance on diagnostic criteria may also be problematic for reasons both typological and cultural. Although the term *traumatization* carries a distinctly biomedical connotation, its widespread usage has emerged more from the journalistic tradition than the psychiatric one.[6] This colloquial rendering of traumatization has led to the false assumption that people exposed to horrible events will *all* experience traumatization in a similar way resulting in PTSD. There are reasons to question assumptions about the inevitability of PTSD based on the growing psychological literature on variant prototypical responses to trauma. This more nuanced psychological perspective is corroborated by ethnographic research that draws on the narrative experiences of individuals who have been exposed to objectively stressful life events (e.g. ethnic violence, internment in concentration camps, physical injury) whose experiences reflect a broad spectrum of responses.[7]

Although PTSD as a psychological construct has contributed a great deal to the understanding of trauma, a secondary result of its dominant

---

[4]Johan Galtung, *Peace by Peaceful Means: Peace and Conflict, Development and Civilization* (Thousand Oaks California: Sage, 1996).

[5]Richard G. Tedeschi, Crystal L. Park and Lawrence G. Calhoun, "Posttraumatic Growth: Conceptual Issues" in *Posttraumatic Growth: Positive Changes in the Aftermath of Crisis*, ed. Richard G. Tedeschi, Crystal L. Park and Lawrence G. Calhoun (New Jersey: Erlbaum, 1998).

[6]Although traumatization is frequently used to refer to less severe cases as well.

[7]Lindi Cassels and Peter Suedfeld, "Salutogenesis and Autobiographical Disclosure Among Holocaust Survivors," *Journal of Positive Psychology* 4, no. 4 (2006); George A. Bonanno, "Loss, Trauma, and Human Resilience: Have We Underestimated the Human Capacity to Thrive After Extremely Aversive Events?" *American Psychologist* 59, no. 1 (2004).

usage has been less engagement with alternative models for conceptualizing trauma. While measures of PTSD provide a quantitative basis for assessing the prevalence and frequency of psycho-somatic symptoms they do not take into account the existential and societal disruption which follows destructive events such as genocide.[8] Complementary models of trauma are useful in filling these gaps and providing a broader understanding of the disorienting nature of trauma at the individual, interpersonal and socio-cultural levels and the liminal spaces between each of these levels of analysis. A recurrent theme across disciplinary discussion of trauma (especially psychology, anthropology, sociology and psychoanalysis) is the subjective experience of ungrounded chaos. Rwandan psychologist Deogratias Bagilishya characterizes trauma in the Rwandan context as the loss of all internal and external points of reference, leaving the individual separated from both community and a meaningful sense of self.[9] Psychoanalyst Yolanda Gampel notes that Freud's early notion of *unheimlich*, or *the uncanny*, describes an internal state of disorganization and a breakdown of the integrating elements of the ego, a feature common among survivors of large-scale social violence.[10] Sociologist Aaron Antonovsky conceptualizes trauma as incoherence which impedes the individual's ability to comprehend, manage, and derive meaning from life.[11] A similar view is held by Ronnie Janoff-Bulman: trauma is the shattering of an individual's *assumptive worldview* which contains expectations of predictability and controllability.[12]

Each of the theories mentioned above resonates deeply with scholarship that has explored the ongoing consequences of genocide. Genocide shatters the normalcy of a society, dislocating worldviews and supplanting dominant conventions with radical rules which mandate extreme violence and in-group compliance, shredding the social and cultural fabric of communities and belief systems.[13] Culturally bound knowledge provides the basis for

---

[8]Antonious C. G. M Robben and Marcelo M. Suarez-Orozco, "Interdisciplinary Perspectives on Violence and Trauma" in *Cultures Under Siege: Collective Violence and Trauma* ed. Antonious C. G. M. Robben and Marcelo M. Suarez-Orozco (Cambridge: Cambridge University Press, 2000); Summerfield, "Critique of Seven Assumptions."

[9]Deogratias Bagilishya, "Mourning and Recovery from Trauma: In Rwanda, Tears Flow Within," *Transcultural Psychiatry* 37, no. 3 (2000).

[10]Yolanda Gampel, "Reflections on the Prevalence of the Uncanny in Social Violence," in *Cultures Under Siege: Collective Violence and Trauma*, ed. Antonious C. G. M Robben and Marcelo M. Suarez-Orozco (Cambridge England: Cambridge University Press, 2000).

[11]Aaron Antonovsky, "The Salutogenic Perspective: Toward a New View of Health and Illness," *Advances* 4, no. 1 (1987).

[12]Ronnie Janoff-Bulman, "Assumptive Worlds and the Stress of Traumatic Events: Applications of the Schema Construct," *Social Cognition* 7, no. 2 (1989).

[13]Scott Straus, *The Order of Genocide* (Ithica: Cornell University Press, 2006).

a collective understanding of dominant messages which, in genocide, rigidify identity boundaries, polarize and demonize out-groups,[14] and provide categorical social behaviour scripts for carrying out violence.[15] In Rwanda the local dynamics of genocide unfolded through stages of cumulative radicalization. The locus of power became indeterminate after Habyarimana's assassination, and hardline elements quickly gained control, imposing rigid laws of killing and mobilizing broad sections of the population which, up to that point, had not been genocidal.[16]

Following genocide, societies are left depleted and ravaged by lingering malice, urges for revenge and pervasive suspicion between and within groups. Although social scripts which facilitated killing are not prevalent in post-genocide periods, the category changes in identity leading up to and during the violence cannot simply be undone, nor can the pre-genocide social conditions which gave life a predictable flow be re-instituted. The result of this is a period of liminality both at the individual and social level. Individuals and communities are forced to cope with the past while trying to create a new future; feeling unable to move out of the terrible suspension of the in-between is the experience of trauma. Presently Rwanda has a very powerful and directive government which has instituted a great deal of social order at a superficial level, through top-down programs and a strong military backing. While the need for such *negative peace* is evident, it is doubtful that this top-down approach alone is capable of providing the individual level structure needed to re-establish an internal sense of coherence and move toward positive peace. Finding a way to assess the effectiveness of these programs is a great challenge. The nature of community change makes it difficult to map out in broad macro level assessments. Community and individual level research attempt to understand the extent to which governmental programs are effecting actual change in line with the aims of social justice and reconciliation.[17]

The capacity for individual change after trauma – inoculating small sections of society against mass mobilization trauma – is a paradigm which has yet to be developed fully. The exploration of such a possibility requires closer examination of the dynamic interaction of individual and social

[14]The impact of pejorative characterization of "out-groups" is analyzed in Yehuda Bauer, Chapter 7, Section 7.2 (above) and Irwin Cotler, Chapter 9, Section 9.4 (above).

[15]Andreas Wimmer, "The Making and Unmaking of Ethnic Boundaries: A Multilevel Process Theory" *American Journal of Sociology* 113, no. 4 (2008); Ervin Staub, *The Roots of Evil: The Origins of Genocide and Other Group Violence* (Cambridge: Cambridge University Press, 1989); Christopher Taylor, *Sacrifice as Terror: The Rwandan Genocide of 1994* (Birmingham: Berg Publishers, 1999).

[16]Straus, *Order of Genocide*.

[17]Filip Reyntjens, "Rwanda Ten Years On: From Genocide to Dictatorship," *African Affairs* 103 (2004); Alana E. Tiemessen, "After Arusha: Gacaca Justice in Post-Genocide Rwanda," *African Studies Quarterly* 8, no. 1 (2004).

transformation. Although "clinical" symptoms of trauma can be anticipated based on diagnostic predictor variables including the nature of the traumatic event, this predictability can exaggerate the homogeneity of experiences. Exposure to mass violence is clearly a highly stressful experience and will predictably lead to drastic psychological responses such as dissociation, numbing and hyper-arousal; however, to see such responses as *abnormal* often misrepresents a very typical human response in the face of horrible events.[18] Although a percentage of individuals exposed to such events will certainly experience persistent disruptive psychological symptoms at a level which becomes incapacitating, there are also those who will demonstrate greater resilience, speedy recoveries and, in some cases, a level of personal growth from these experiences.[19]

An individualistic focus, however, can overshadow the importance of cultural belief systems (the rites and rituals which provide cosmological and ontological order for both individuals and communities) and are thus highly relevant to the understanding of trauma responses.[20] In Rwanda, symbolic practices such as burial ceremonies have been widely disrupted since many families are unable to find those members killed in the genocide. The inability of communities to fulfill these rites can prevent individuals from re-establishing a sense of coherence, perpetuating the manifestation of individual trauma symptoms.

Enmeshed in this dynamic of individual and collective trauma, interpersonal and interethnic conflict persists in Rwanda, even though the government is loath to acknowledge it.[21] A 2007 report by Human Rights Watch entitled *Killings in Eastern Rwanda* presents two cases where Tutsi genocide survivors who were witnesses at a local community *Gacaca* Court were killed. Following both initial incidents there were extrajudicial reprisal killings of three Hutu men in one case, and 8 men, women, and children in the other. These events are demonstrative of ethnic tensions within traumatized communities; dozens of other reported deaths further indicate the very real potential for renewed large-scale violence in Rwanda.[22] Unresolved traumas can sharpen identity boundaries and fuel low level cultural violence. This in turn provides an insidious legitimation

[18] Bonanno, "Loss, Trauma and Human Resilience."

[19] Peter Suedfeld, "Reactions to Societal Trauma: Distress and/or Eustress," *Political Psychology* 18, no. 4 (1997); Richard G. Tedeschi and Lawrence G. Calhoun, "Special Issue: Editorial Note," *Traumatology*, 11, no. 4 (2005).

[20] Bagilishya, "Mourning and Recovery."

[21] Examples of the persistence of conflict in Rwanda as evidenced by reports of human rights abuses in prisons are discussed in Francis M. Deng, Chapter 4, Section 4.2 (above).

[22] Human Rights Watch, *Killings in Eastern Rwanda* (New York: Human Rights Watch, 2007).

of "othering," which threatens to destabilize fundamental aspects of the reconciliation process.[23]

19.2 Collective Trauma and Renewed Violence

Large-scale violence impacts the individual while simultaneously affecting social unity by changing the saliency and source of cultural meaning. This leaves individuals bereft of a meaningful worldview, and provides a collective basis for establishing historic evils perpetrated by out-groups as cultural touchstones for legitimating violence in the years or even generations to come.[24] In many Rwandan communities, suspicion, distrust and fear continue to hinder reconciliation programs, raising important questions concerning how far social change can proceed while high levels of fear, in-group isolationism, and threats of violence continue.

Although the Rwandan government publicly espouses egalitarian ideals, there are concerns regarding the extent to which this image of popular and peaceful change is belied by unresolved ethno-political tensions which are kept in check by political censorship and strict internal policing. The official discourse of unity and reconciliation strongly asserts a shared Rwandan identity eschewing ethnic identifications and seeking to convert the population to a new Rwandan identity free from past categories.[25] Despite the obviously desirable and pragmatic appeal of such widespread change, the authenticity and stability of such a broad-based conversion within the current centralized power structure is doubtful.[26] The creation of superordinate goals such as economic development and national unity is a valuable initiative, championed by the RPF, which shows signs of weakening sectarianism and making the boundaries of ethnic in-groups more permeable. Such gradual modes of change allow for more flexibility across circumstances; ironically, this flexibility may be hampered by rigid top-down mandates for identity change that override local realities.[27]

The situation in post-genocide Rwanda is complex and the intra-personal, inter-personal and socio-cultural realms cannot be understood in isolation. What is clear is that healing individual psychological wounds

---

[23]Johan Galtung, "Cultural Violence," *Journal of Peace Research* 27, no. 3 (1990).

[24]Robben and Suarez-Orozco, "Interdisciplinary Perspectives."; Vamik D. Volkan, *Bloodlines: From Ethnic Pride to Ethnic Terrorism* (Colorado: Westview Books, 1998); Mahmoud Mamdani, *When Victims Become Killers: Colonialism, Nativism, and the Genocide in Rwanda* (New Jersey: Princeton University Press, 2001).

[25]The notion that maintaining ethnic identities can only turn victims into killers is addressed in Douglas Greenberg, Chapter 5 (above).

[26]Wimmer, "Making and Unmaking."

[27]Musharraf Sherif, "Superordinate Goals in the Reduction of Intergroup Conflict," *The American Journal of Sociology* 63, no. 4 (1958).

is essential for generating the collective will at the local level to drive community participation in local acts of reconciliation, moving away from patterns that facilitate renewed violence.[28] Exactly how, and at what stage of post-trauma healing, individuals begin to conscientiously contribute to the broader aims of reconciliation between ethnic groups is a question that has received little attention. In an attempt to contribute to the body of research from which this question may be answered, I sought to empirically investigate the relationship between individual psychological healing and attitudes toward societal transformations.

19.3 Individual Healing and Societal Reconciliation in Kibungo Province

In collaboration with Professor Sigfried Musangwa at the *Université d'Agriculture, de Technologie et d'Education de Kibungo* (UNATEK), I collected data in Rwanda's Eastern province to explore how individual exposure to trauma impacted attitudes toward societal reconciliation. The sample was comprised of forty-two students in their first year of a teachers' college program. The sample consisted of 21 Tutsi, nine Hutus and nine individuals who did not indicate their ethnicity or identified as "other." The main demographic difference was that Tutsis experienced more traumatic events on average ($M = 4.25$) than Hutu participants ($M = 2.86$). Although there were other slight variations across the sample (e.g. religiosity, number of years in exile), since the present study sought to investigate social change, the sample was assessed as a whole.

My hypotheses were that (1) individuals who were exposed to high levels of objective trauma and also indicated high levels of a *sense of coherence* (SOC) in their lives would be more likely to report having experienced subjective *post-traumatic growth* (PTG) than those who reported lower levels of coherence or had less exposure to violence; (2) individuals who reported more PTG would be more likely to indicate a greater openness to societal level reconciliation and report greater resistance to the use of state violence. In order to explore these hypotheses I used an empirical measure of trauma so as to minimize the variations in what was perceived as traumatic by participants. This included a checklist of 7 forms of violence which typified direct forms of genocide-related trauma in Rwanda.[29] I also gathered questionnaire data which indicated self-reported levels of coherence

[28] Staub, "Reconciliation After Genocide."

[29] Phuong N. Pham, Harvey M. Weinstein and Timothy Longman, "Trauma and PTSD Symptoms in Rwanda: Implications for Attitudes Toward Justice and Reconciliation," *Journal of the American Medical Association* 292, no. 5 (2004).

and PTG.[30] I employed a Rwanda-specific measure of openness to societal reconciliation which concerned individual willingness to put aside ethnic differences in order to promote reconciliation (e.g. people must learn to depend upon each other, no matter what their ethnic group; our community would be a better place if there were only people of my own ethnic group (reverse coded)). I also employed a questionnaire which asked individuals to indicate situations in which state violence would be acceptable.

19.4 Predictors of Post-Traumatic Growth

The sample showed a remarkably high level of post-traumatic growth, even when compared to other samples of war-affected populations.[31] Hypothesis one was confirmed: individuals who reported a stronger sense of coherence (SOC) and had also been exposed to more objectively traumatic events demonstrated significantly more PTG. To assess the impact of SOC and trauma on post-traumatic growth, a comparison of mean scores was carried out. The sample was divided into a 2 × 2 table using a high/low median split on both scores of trauma and SOC to create four cells containing PTG scores. These cells consist of individuals with: (1) low SOC, high trauma; (2) high SOC, high trauma; (3) low SOC, low trauma; and (4) high SOC, low trauma (See Table 19.1). Examination of the means demonstrates the anticipated result with substantially higher levels of PTG in the high SOC, high trauma group ($M = 97.58$, SD = 14.34). The other three cells have much lower levels of PTG and their mean scores do not vary greatly. A comparison of the high-high group with the three other groups indicates that this result is statistically significant, $t = 3.16$, $p < 0.01$, one-tailed test.

Table 19.1
Post-traumatic growth

	Low coherence	High coherence
High Trauma	$M = 84.00$ $\sigma = 14.34$ $n = 11$	$M = 97.58$ $\sigma = 15.56$ $n = 12$
Low Trauma	$M = 83.00$ $\sigma = 17.15$ $n = 4$	$M = 84.20$ $\sigma = 16.56$ $n = 15$

[30] Antonovsky, "Salutogenic Perspective."; Richard G. Tedeschi and Lawrence G. Calhoun, "The Posttraumatic Growth Inventory: Measuring the Positive Legacy of Trauma," *Journal of Traumatic Stress* 9, no. 3 (1996).

[31] Steve Powell and others, "Posttraumatic Growth After War: A Study with Former Refugees and Displaced People in Sarajevo," *Journal of Clinical Psychology* 59, no. 1 (2003).

19.5 Discussion

These results provide the first known empirical evidence of post-traumatic growth in Rwanda. The predicted interaction between SOC and high levels of trauma exposure supports theories of trauma which emphasize the centrality of a strong sense of coherence in developing a new sense of purpose following mass violence.[32] While recent research has focused on four prototypical responses to severe stress (chronic reactions, delayed responses, recovery following initially high stress, and a general resilience characterized by moderate to low stress after a potentially traumatic event), the present findings suggest that PTG may be considered a fifth prototypical response.[33]

The importance of SOC to the Rwandan sample provides cross-cultural corroboration of past research which has demonstrated the centrality of SOC in trauma healing primarily in Western samples. These findings suggest that although Rwandans and Americans do not have the same experience of SOC in terms of content, there appears to be a common structural basis of coherence independent of culture which provides the basis for post-traumatic growth.[34] Rwanda is a much more collectivistic society than North America and it is likely that the sources of coherence are more rooted in community-based cultural practices than they are in Western societies, which tend to be more individualistic. This has important implications for post-violence interventions in locations where a coherent worldview is comprised of elements of cultural and community referents, and is central for both individual and collective healing. The imposition of foreign forms of trauma intervention may prove ineffective or worse, as they may disrupt the community's ability to restore a culturally grounded SOC.[35]

Recognizing individual PTG following genocide does not imply that individuals do not experience severe pain and loss. A forward-looking orientation can be an important part of individual, spiritual, and cultural renewal.[36] As time passes following genocide and a degree of stability returns, the course of individual recovery will inevitably change. During

---

[32] Antonovksy, "Salutogenic Perspective."

[33] Bonanno, "Loss, Trauma and Human Resilience."; Suedfeld, "Reactions to Societal Trauma."; Tedeschi and Calhoun, "Special Issue."

[34] Peter Suedfeld, "Cognitive Managers and Their Critics," *Political Psychology* 13, no. 3 (1992).

[35] Nancy Peddle and others, "Trauma, Loss, and Resilience in Africa: A Psychosocial Community Based Approach to Culturally Sensitive Healing," in *Honoring Differences: Cultural Issues in the Treatment of Trauma and Loss*, ed. Katherine Nader, Nancy Dubrow and B. H. Stamm (New Jersey: Brunner/Mazel, 1999).

[36] Sousan Abadian, "Cultural Healing: When Cultural Renewal is Reparative and When it is Toxic," *Pimatisiwin, A Journal of Aboriginal and Indigenous Community Health* 1, no. 2 (2006).

these post-genocide times it is important not only that individual healing take place, but that sectarian tendencies that promote future mass violence be subverted by movements toward collective healing and peace building.[37] As Rwanda's large scale unity and reconciliation program continues, the healing of psychological wounds is an important aspect of moving society toward reconciliation and deserves continued attention.[38] The following section investigates how PTG influences individual attitudes towards social transformation and reconciliation, and how it impacts the potential for future state violence.

19.6 Individual Growth and Societal Reconciliation

Having established the presence of PTG in a sample of genocide survivors, I turn to my second hypothesis, which predicts that this will lead to more positive attitudes towards reconciliation. Religiosity, marital status and years married were identified as possible confounding variables and were controlled for.[39] As predicted, PTG was positively related to greater openness to reconciliation ($r = 0.34$, $p = 0.03$), as were higher levels of SOC ($r = 0.34$, $p = 0.04$). High levels of SOC also positively correlated with more positive perceptions of society ($r = 0.42, p = 0.04$). Linear regression was used to predict openness to reconciliation using willingness to endorse state-sponsored violence as a means of conflict resolution and PTG as predictor variables. The regression model was significant (F (2, 37) = 3.28, $p < 0.05$ ($R^2 = 0.15$)) with standardized effect sizes which approached significance for both PTG ($\beta = 0.27$, $p = 0.07$) and willingness to resort to violence ($\beta = -0.23$, $p = 0.10$), indicating that PTG relates to attitudes more supportive of reconciliation.

19.7 Discussion

A renewed sense of coherent meaning in individual lives is an important aspect of reconciliation and non-violence which is resistant to renewed violence. Openness to reconciliation that is based on, or present alongside, individual transformation appears to provide a more solid basis for deep reconciliation. The tendency for ethnic violence to move in cycles is

---

[37] Galtung, *Peace by Peaceful Means*.

[38] Staub, "Reconciliation After Genocide."

[39] Kenneth I. Pargament, Kaushik M. Desai and Kelly M. McConnell, "Spirituality: A Pathway to Posttraumatic Growth or Decline," in *Handbook of Posttraumatic Growth: Research & Practice*, ed. Lawrence. G. Calhoun and Richard. G. Tedeschi (New Jersey: Erlbaum, 2006); Sherry A. Falsetti, Patricia A. Resick and Joanne L. Davis, "Changes in Religious Beliefs Following Trauma," *Journal of Traumatic Stress* 16, no. 5 (2003).

a tragic reality often masked by a discourse of reconciliation which does little more than obscure lingering hatred and a desire for revenge.[40] This is particularly worrisome since the tendency for collective trauma to give rise to renewed violence does not dissipate over time; post-violence societies sometimes experience a form of time collapse that creates the sense of temporal proximity to atrocities which happened in generations past. These culturally grounded *chosen traumas* can lead to renewed mass movements of dehumanization, fear and violence.[41] While patterns do not change easily, the individual's capacity to transcend historic hatreds may be a means for bottom-up action able to redirect large scale social trends.

A common response to the shattering of assumptive worldviews as a result of violent trauma is to seek a rigidly defined, safe in-group which can help ameliorate the anxiety of incoherence and massive internal and external upheaval.[42] This may lead to a form of *toxic* cultural renewal in which traumatized individuals become embroiled in hate-mongering and vengeance, effectively sowing the seeds for new violence.[43] The impulse for individuals to turn to socially rigid forms of coping following trauma highlights the important role of social and political institutions. These are looked to for a new sense of normalcy following chaos – for better or worse.[44] If the social and political discourse that emerges is one of restraint and tolerance, it can be instrumental in establishing the groundwork for peace; if the discourse is one of hatred and sectarianism, it is the best predictor of renewed ethnic violence.[45] In the present research there is a trend for individuals exposed to a great deal of trauma to support government led programs of reconciliation, presumably, at least in part, as a means of ameliorating their disrupted SOC. This is potentially dangerous, since the individual who surrenders agency in return for social authority becomes vulnerable to imbibing the rhetoric of ethnic nationalism which can fan the flames of great loss and injustice, and turn them into a willingness to retaliate against the perceived enemy.

While many positive attitudes reflected in this research are compatible with the governmental discourse of reconciliation, these two levels should not be seen in an aggregate form. While governmental involvement is an important aspect of social change, the complexity of individual change cannot be seen in terms of individuals who did or did not embrace

[40] Mamdani, *When Victims Become Killers*.

[41] Volkan, *Bloodlines*.

[42] Jeff Greenberg and others, "Evidence for Terror Management Theory: The Effects of Mortality Salience on Reactions to Those Who Threaten or Bolster the Cultural Worldview," *Journal of Personality and Social Psychology* 8, no. 2 (1990).

[43] Abadian, "Cultural Healing."

[44] Gampel, "Reflections."

[45] Straus, *Order of Genocide*.

the government discourse as the easiest way to restore a ruptured SOC. The research findings indicate that only individuals with high exposure to trauma and a high SOC experienced a deep existential re-evaluation, referred to here as post–traumatic growth. This suggests that it is an important mechanism, making individuals less likely to endorse violence and more likely to show awareness of the need to end cycles of violence. Although state-led programs of reconciliation may facilitate inter-ethnic integration, there are limits to such top-down models which do not attend to the internal state of individuals. Intra-personal insight is a necessary element of deep and sustainable social transformation since it operates at the level of individual identification and therefore of social-behavioural scripts. The centrality of individuals' sense of coherence to PTG, and the fact that SOC independently predicts openness to reconciliation, illustrates the importance of grounded individual agency and awareness in transforming post-genocide societies from the bottom up.

It would be over-simplistic to suggest a mono-causal flow of reconciliation from the individual level of transformation, especially considering the fact that community and collective practice heavily influence individual identities. Nevertheless, the present research gives cause for optimism regarding the capacity of individuals exposed to extraordinarily adverse life conditions to establish a new sense of meaning which includes a willingness for reconciliation. The tension between the individual and society is ongoing; group-think, propaganda, and bureaucratic social structures are just a few examples of how social influences can lead otherwise "normal people" to commit inhuman acts.[46] Increasing attention is being paid to individual agency in genocide, and with this has come a renewed focus on individual responsibility during atrocities and the individual capacity for moral action in preventing such events.[47] The presence of individual PTG and existential re-evaluation following mass violence suggests a psychological correlation between the renewal of self and the re-determination of individual level actions toward others.

19.8 Conclusion

Despite the historic focus on the pathogenic nature of trauma, exposure to extremely negative life events is not always debilitating, and in some cases can result in an increased sense of meaning in post-conflict contexts. The present study of Rwandan student-teachers exposed to genocidal violence

[46] Hannah Arendt, *Eichmann in Jerusalem: A Report on the Banality of Evil*, (New York: Penguin, 1963); Staub, *Roots of Evil*.

[47] The concept of a potential bystander responsibility is discussed in Frédéric Mégret, Chapter 13, Section 13.3.3 (above).

provides the first known evidence of post-traumatic growth in Rwanda. It must be noted that the present sample is not representative of the general population and the findings should not be generalized. Nevertheless, the interaction between exposure to objectively traumatic events and high levels of coherence leading to more positive outcomes supports theories which emphasize the importance of culturally bound sources of coherence in understanding the nature of trauma and the process of trauma healing. Finally, individuals who demonstrated high levels of PTG and SOC were also more likely to indicate attitudes which are favourable to societal reconciliation and more opposed to violence as a means of conflict resolution, establishing the link between individual and social transformations. These findings provide empirical corroboration of theories of deep reconciliation and suggest that individual level healing is an important place to begin the process of sustainable societal reconciliation.[48] The process of individual transformation is a necessary step toward meaningful social transformation and the prevention of unhealed traumas manifesting themselves as future violence.

Acknowledgement I would like to thank Gordon and Penny Echenberg for their support and dedication to preventing genocide, as well as the coordinators and facilitators of the Young Leaders Forum at the Global Conference on the Prevention of Genocide. I would also like to thank Dr. Peter Suedfeld for his support and guidance with this research as well as Lama Mugabo, Lindi Cassels and Sigfried Musangwa for their assistance at the research stage. I am also grateful for the support of the Social Sciences and Humanities Research Council of Canada for supporting this project.

[48]Jean Paul Lederach, *Preparing for Peace: Conflict Transformation Across Cultures* (Syracuse: Syracuse University Press, 1995).

Chapter 20
Creating the Essential Middle Ground: Using Media to Enhance Tolerance and Co-Habitation in Africa

Mary Kimani

20.1 Introduction

The process of media liberalization in Africa essentially mirrors the continent's difficult and painful transition from autocratic governance to democracy. In the early stages of that history, media organs, often owned by the state or its clients, proffered to the public the sanitized views and activities of state officials rather than factual and unbiased reporting of events. At the point of liberalization, rather than turning into a purveyor of factual reporting, media often became a tool that elites competing for power could use to advance their political agendas. A proliferation of media owned by political operatives often followed such liberalization. It is Rwanda that we most associate with this tendency. Media and political liberalization in Rwanda happened simultaneously. The newly liberalized media became the venue of an ideological war between Hutu political elites that preferred peaceful coexistence with ethnic Tutsi elites, and those that considered them a threat to their political power. The now infamous *Kangura* newspaper, and hate radio *Radio Television Libre Des Mille Collines* (RTLM) took this logic to the extreme, inciting ethnic hatred and genocide.[1] But this scenario is not unique to Rwanda. Similar media abuses occurred in Côte d'Ivoire and preceded the January 2008 ethnic killings in Kenya's rift valley. However, the lessons from these experiences can transform traumatized societies. A number of innovative media projects are working to bring communities together and create a middle ground in societies once polarized by war, fear, ethnic hatred or propaganda.

For 6 years, beginning in 1999, I worked with Internews, an international non-profit media organisation operating primarily in transitional and

M. Kimani (✉)
United Nations, Office of the Special Advisor on Africa, New York, NY 10017, USA
e-mail: kimanim@un.org

[1]The role played by RTLM in the Rwandan Genocide and the concept of an ethics of communication are examined in Mark Thompson, Chapter 6 (above).

R. Provost, P. Akhavan (eds.), *Confronting Genocide*, Ius Gentium: Comparative Perspectives on Law and Justice 7, DOI 10.1007/978-90-481-9840-5_20,

post conflict countries. I was assigned to report on the genocide trials at the International Criminal Tribunal for Rwanda (ICTR), based in Arusha, Tanzania from 1999 until 2002. One of the trials I covered was the "Media Trial," a case against three media managers accused of persecution and direct and public incitement to genocide, among other charges. I took the opportunity of working at the court to study the media's role in the killings.[2]

In January 2003, I moved to Rwanda, where Internews was working closely with the Ministry of Justice and civil society organisations to generate dialogue about justice and reconciliation in the aftermath of the genocide. Based in a small studio in Kigali, about a dozen members of our staff developed film news reels in the local Kinyarwanda language. The newsreels typically covered key trials in the international, national and local courts. They included the views and questions posed by victims and perpetrators and the responses given by judicial and other officials. We screened these in remote villages and prisons in the country using a portable projector and a diesel engine generator and held lively debates about the issues. It is these experiences that have, to a large extent, informed the views expressed in this paper.[3]

20.2 Media and Extremism

One of the most apt explanations that I have come across of why the genocide in Rwanda occurred is the one advanced by Dr. Alison Des Forges in the publication, *Leave None to Tell the Story*. Dr. Des Forges, a Rwandan historian and the Human Rights Watch Advisor for the Great Lakes, wrote that "Hutus who killed Tutsis did so for many reasons, but beneath the individual motivation lay a common fear rooted in firmly held but mistaken ideas of the Rwandan past."[4]

In that one paragraph, Dr. Des Forges encapsulated the fundamental and recurrent reason behind not just the massacres in Rwanda, but also the ongoing ethnic killings in Eastern Democratic Republic of Congo (DRC) and the recent ethnic massacres in the Rift Valley province of Kenya. I am referring here to the "common fear rooted in firmly held but mistaken ideas." These mistaken ideas relate to power and resources and perceptions of how these have been or are being distributed between the aggressors and the victims.

[2]See Mary Kimani, "RTLM: The Medium that Became a Tool for Mass Murder," in *The Media and the Rwanda Genocide*, ed. Allan Thompson (London: Pluto Press, 2007), 110.

[3]For more on the cine-mobile program visit http://www.internews.fr/spip.php?article126.

[4]Alison Des Forges, *Leave None to Tell the Story: Genocide in Rwanda* (New York: Human Rights Watch, 1999).

Such ideas have at their basis the belief that the targeted group, ethnic Tutsis in the Rwandan case, are beneficiaries of unequal allocation of resources and power, or the reason why a country is undergoing war, famine or economic downturn. In Rwanda, these ideas were advanced by political elite over many decades. Their purpose was to manipulate and distort historical grievances (of the Hutu against the Tutsi) for political ends.[5] The aggressor community, in this case the Hutus, thus came to perceive itself as having been "cheated" or "victimised" by the target community, the Tutsis.[6]

This state of affairs is hardly unique to Rwanda. The Ivorians, Congolese and, most recently, Kenyans have all, to some extent, experienced the political manipulation of reality by their leaders, usually as a means of galvanising the support of ethnic groups in power struggles. However, for these ideas to morph into the extreme expressions of fear, anger and attempts at perceived self-preservation that led Hutus to kill Tutsis, Ivorians to target "Burkinabe foreigners" or Kenya's ethnic Kalenjin to burn Kikuyu families sheltering in a church, the ideas must first become ingrained in the aggressing society, find acceptability and appear justifiable. Media – in particular radio, and, to a smaller extent, papers published in local languages – has become the tool for this propagation.

> In Rwanda, the *Kangura* newspaper and FM station RTLM were the key propagators of these beliefs. In Côte d'Ivoire, it was *Notre Voie, Les Echos du Matin, Le Courrier d'Abidjan* and *Le Temps* newspapers. These Ivorian papers promoted government-sponsored violence by relaying disinformation and rumours that encouraged looting, forced expulsions of "foreigners" and fomented street violence by pro-government rioters. In Kenya, Strategic Communications, an organisation hired by the UN Development agency (UNDP) to study media coverage of the 2007 general elections, found that vernacular stations broadcast many inflammatory messages that contributed to violence before and after the elections. One such station was *Kass FM*, a Kalenjin language radio station that carried messages denouncing "outsider" ethnic groups such as Kikuyus and Kisii living in the Rift Valley area. Such messages are seen as having partly contributed to the subsequent ethnic massacres in the province.[7]

So why, instead of being independent and impartial, do certain media outlets end up playing such a polarising and often deadly role?

---

[5] For a more detailed argument on this aspect of Rwandan history please refer to Fujii Lee Ann, "Origins of Power and Identity in Rwanda," paper presented at the Annual Conference of the International Studies Association, Chicago, IL, February 20–24, 2001.

[6] An account of the principal events of the Rwandan Genocide is provided in Douglas Greenberg, Chapter 5 (above).

[7] Reporters Without Borders, "Côte d'Ivoire – Annual Report 2005," Reporters Without Borders, May 3, 2005, http://www.rsf.org/article.php3?id_article=13569 (Accessed June 9, 2009).

20.3 Beholden

The answer to this question lies in the history of the media in Africa. Most of sub-Saharan Africa had little or no privately-owned media prior to 1990. Existing media was mostly state-owned. In some instances, powerful politicians and/or the Catholic Church owned newspapers and even radio stations. What the media at the time had in common was that journalists typically had to adhere to a very strict political or religious line laid down by media owners. Poorly paid and often trained by the very institutions that hired them, most of the journalists and editors were financially beholden to the owners and their interests. From its very inception, therefore, African media was understood (at least by the journalists and editors) as serving the interest of its owners. News was not a series of "objective reports" to be communicated to the people. Instead, news was "whatever information the owners wished to have communicated" to the population. Although the media in Africa has become a lot more liberal and open following multi-party democratization in the late 1990s, the notion that news is whatever a publication or radio owner wishes to communicate is still very prevalent among journalists and editors.[8]

In Rwanda, this approach to the "news" ended up producing devastating results. Prior to 1990, media in Rwanda was predominantly state owned. Then in 1990, the Rwanda Patriotic Front, a largely Tutsi army, invaded Rwanda from Uganda. It was made up predominantly of the children of Tutsis forced into exile by prior Hutu-dominated governments. The invasion, combined with growing internal opposition against the regime of then President Juvenal Habyarimana, forced many changes in Rwanda's democratic space. These included the declaration of multi-party democracy and media liberalisation.

The impact of media liberalisation was immediate. By 1993, there were over 40 publications in the capital alone, although some quickly became defunct. But what seemed like a brave step ahead into freedom of thought and expression hid the seeds of the impending tragic role that the media would play in fomenting genocide. From the very onset, the new media that developed was owned and controlled by political elites. The editorial goal of most of these newspapers was hardly an impartial, accurate or balanced reporting of the ongoing conflict. On the contrary, the purpose of these publications was to advance, often by any means, the respective viewpoints of their owners, who also happened to be parties to the conflict. Consequently, as the internal and external contest for power grew, the respective editorial lines of these party-owned and party-affiliated media grew increasingly polarised along political and ethnic lines.

---

[8]The argument that rights of broadcasters are privileged over rights of the receiving public is put forward in Mark Thompson, Chapter 6 (above).

In established democracies such as those in Europe and the United States, politically polarised media would not be a problem. Clear rules on defamation and incitement and codes of journalistic ethics, backed by rule of law, functional courts and peer review mechanisms, would have ensured that egregious violations were penalised and falsehoods unmasked. Additionally, the relative exposure and sophistication of the audiences in established democracies would work to push extreme views to the fringe. However, in Rwanda, as elsewhere in Africa, the media liberalisation came at a critical time. Institutions of democratic governance, including laws on how mass media organisations could operate, were just in the process of being discussed or had just been put in place. Negotiations on whether democratic institutions, including free media, should exist often followed violent conflict or long internal power struggles. Moreover, the legitimacy of these new democratic institutions was often contested even after agreements had been reached. As a result, factions in government and opposition groups had deeply vested interests in these processes, including which version of "facts" was propagated and which versions quashed.

What happened then, in countries like Rwanda and Côte d'Ivoire, is that substantially less sophisticated and less exposed audiences were left to figure out which political elites were telling them the truth. Backed by powerful politicians and their media, extreme views, rather than existing on the fringes of society, came to hold centre stage. Worse, egregious violations such as direct incitement to genocide went largely unpunished as politicians condoned the impunity of journalists supporting their ethnic and political causes.

In Rwanda, politically-sponsored media unabashedly merged military, political and ethnic identities. The invading Rwanda Patriotic Front (RPF), Parti Liberal (PL), and a section of the Mouvement Démocratie République (MDR) became identified as Tutsi or pro-Tutsi and therefore against the interests of Hutus. *Kangura*, a magazine commonly described as a Hutu response to RPF publications, disseminated particularly pernicious propaganda. The paper constantly alleged that the Tutsis and their supporters were working to reverse the gains made by the Hutus since independence. *Kangura* alleged a regional conspiracy by Tutsis and their supporters to dominate all economic and political levels, to subjugate the Hutus, and kill all Hutus that resisted the new power order. Through such allegations, *Kangura* and other extreme media created a sense of victimhood among the Hutus and galvanised them to "defend their rights." *Kangura*, like radio *RTLM*, warned Hutu listeners of the need to "deal" with the enemy in their midst, if they were to survive the war. That enemy in the midst of the Hutu population was understood to mean all Tutsis.[9]

---

[9]See, for example, Kangura, *Kangura Magazine*, (UN ICTR evidence database) February 1992. One excerpt reads: "*If there is no corresponding Hutu union in a quick response*

Kass FM in Kenya and pro-government media in Côte d'Ivoire mirrored this approach to varying degrees. *Kass FM* referred to "outsiders" as "weeds" that needed to be uprooted, language very similar to that employed by radio *RTLM*. Outsiders (in this case, Tutsis in Rwanda and the Kikuyus in Kenya) were typified in broadcasts as greedy, land hungry, domineering and unscrupulous.[10] Pro-government media in Côte d'Ivoire and *Kangura* in Rwanda warned repeatedly of the growing "anger" of the people against such "outsiders" or "oppressors" and "foreigners." The Ivorian media and *Kangura* also decried the alleged omnipresence of the targeted community in positions of wealth and power and argued that such a situation was intolerable. *RTLM* and *Kangura* journalists often explained their role as "awakening the masses" to wrongs being perpetrated against them.

The point of these examples is to show that the message of hate media is often the same regardless of the unique circumstances in which the event is taking place. The purpose of such propaganda is to convince members of an aggressor community that the targeted community's conduct is intolerable, that their motives are suspect, that their way of life is unacceptable, beyond the bounds of what society considers human and proper, and that it is therefore legitimate to target, expel and even exterminate them to protect the aggressor group.

A common argument made in support of such polarising media is that freedom to engage in odious speech is part of the democratic space that should exist in society. The prescription on how to deal with media extremism is to have more newspapers and radio, with the idea that extreme viewpoints will be drowned out by other publications or stations with more centrist views. Ironically, as Andy Sennitt states in his analysis *Replacing Hate with Hope in Kenya*, vernacular stations such as *Kass FM* were allowed to set up in Kenya precisely because it was believed "that the country was politically mature enough to use them responsibly."[11] In Rwanda

---

to the Tutsi union, it will soon be too late for any remedy. In their plans to seize power, Tutsis not only made provisions for armed conflict, they also thought of another form of fighting, which could be used in the event of the failure of armed conflict. It is on this strategy that the war today rests, since it has helped to prepare the war and will help to continue waging the war for as long as the Hutus have not been subjugated. Kangura will reveal this form, so that methods to free Hutus will be sought. For, they are now in the grip of the Tutsis, who are using this strategy. If nothing is done, they would die, as they should."

[10]The impact of pejorative characterization of "out-groups" is analyzed in Yehuda Bauer, Chapter 7, Section 7.2 (above) and Irwin Cotler, Chapter 9, Section 9.4 (above).

[11]Andy Sennitt, "Replacing Hate with Hope in Kenya: Hate Radio Fans the Flames of Violence," Radio Nederland Wereldomroep, January 31, 2008, http://www.radionetherlands.nl/features/080131-kenya-hate-radio (Accessed June 9, 2009).

too, radio *RTLM* was initially seen as a step forward for media freedom in a country which had, up to that time, only known state-owned radio.[12]

In their judgement convicting the three defendants in the Rwandan media trial, ICTR judges found that the managers had used their respective media to exploit

> the history of Tutsi privilege and Hutu disadvantage and the fear of armed insurrection to mobilize the population, whipping them into a frenzy of hatred and violence that was directed largely against the Tutsi group . . . heightened the sense of fear, the danger, and the sense of urgency giving rise to the need for action by listeners.[13]

Inevitably, the array of evidence presented to the population convinced them of the need to undertake violence as a form of "self defence."[14] False or exaggerated allegations of past Tutsi treachery spurred people into action. *RTLM*, backed by the power and support of the political leadership, presented the ordinary person with an impossible choice: get rid of the Tutsi or the Tutsi will get rid of you; kill or be killed.

Sennitt has a particularly articulate quote from Caesar Handa, Executive Director of Strategic Public Relations and Research, explaining why it worked. "The power of radio to mobilise people in Africa is almost beyond comprehension to a Western mind. What many people hear on the radio they take as gospel truth."[15] The late Andre Sibomana, a former journalist and priest, in an interview with journalists Herve Deguine and Laure Guilbert, also describes the power of the media in Africa: "Through a game of repetition, drop by drop, the media build up moral and cultural constructs which eventually become permanent features. . ..fuelling a climate of intolerance and turn[ing] them into agents of destruction."[16]

The argument to be made here is that while odious and polarising speech may be completely protected and defensible under freedom of expression laws, it does little to help the already ethnically fragmented countries in Africa find common ground. More often than not, such broadcasts or publications unwittingly provoke violence or, worse, cross the line into deliberately inciting massacres. This is not to say that we should ban such media wholesale but it suggests that journalists, donors, and aid agencies

---

[12] The formulation of media rights in terms of freedom of expression is examined in Mark Thompson, Chapter 6 (above).

[13] *Prosecutor v. Ferdinand Nahimana, Jean-Bosco Barayagwiza and Hassan Ngeze*, ICTR-99-52-T (ICTR December 3, 2003), http://69.94.11.53/default.htm (Accessed June 10, 2009).

[14] The characterization of genocidal events as acts of self-defense is discussed in Irwin Cotler, Chapter 9, Section 9.4.5 (above).

[15] Andy Sennitt, "Replacing Hate with Hope," 2008.

[16] Andre Sibomana, *Hope for Rwanda: Conversations with Laure Guilbert and Hervé Deguine* (London: Pluto Press, 1999).

working in countries with ethnic tensions need to look at how better to prevent media abuse, and how, where possible, to reverse the effects of such abuse.

20.4 The Alternative

The one good thing that has come out of the Rwanda crisis is a keen awareness of the role that media can play in instigating massacres and even genocide. That awareness has led to a boost for "peace media." Peace media is a type of media mostly run by NGOs like Internews, usually in post-conflict countries. This alternative form of media sees itself as an agent for cohabitation, reconciliation and a rebuilding of societies. A lot of controversy exists about such media, especially in the West. Reporters in countries such as France, Canada and the United States do not see it as their role to actively advocate for tolerance and cohabitation. Their role, as many a Western journalist will often assert, is to simply report the issues and leave people to make up their minds.

Unfortunately that does not always work in Africa. Rwanda, Côte d'Ivoire and Kenya have had no shortage of news reports from international media such as BBC, RFI and VOA that provide news and let people make up their own minds about whom they believe. But when extremist political voices penetrate local media, their ideas can quickly overwhelm these "neutral" sources of information. The essential middle ground disappears quite quickly, partly because of the ethnically splintered nature of African states, which makes it relatively easy to polarise communities by tapping into ethnic loyalties and grievances.

Frances Fortune is Africa Director of Search for Common Ground (SFCG), one of the NGOs bucking this trend. SFCG produces and airs pro-peace programmes in eight countries, including Angola, Burundi, Sierra Leone and Liberia. All these are countries that have witnessed gross human rights violations, massacres and forms of ethnic cleansing. In an interview with a UN publication, Ms. Fortune told me that "many people would argue that just providing information, strictly news, is adequate. That is not so. Media has to be utilized to support peace. Even prevention of conflict is possible if you provide people with alternative ideas early enough."[17]

One of SFCG's most successful projects was in Burundi, where their station, *Studio Ijambo*, brought journalists from across the tribal divide, Tutsi and Hutu, to work jointly on pro-peace broadcasts. The programmes by the studio came to be known for their depth of coverage of the civil conflict in Burundi. *Studio Ijambo* earned respect and legitimacy as the

[17]Mary Kimani, "Broadcasting Peace: Radio a Tool for Recovery," in *Africa Renewal*, October, 2007, 3.

producer of programmes in which the issues underlying the conflict were truly being discussed, without fear of taboo, and not from a position of ethnic bias. *Studio Ijambo* urged an approach of working together, of trying to understand the interests of the political class and how those interests may differ from those of the ordinary person. Its programming helped change the internal dialogue in Burundi from an adversarial one, Hutus against Tutsis, to a communal one, Burundians tackling the issues facing everyone together.

Today, *Studio Ijambo* is emulated by radio stations countrywide. Thus, by encouraging dialogue on problematic issues throughout the Burundi peace process and influencing how new stations behaved, *Studio Ijambo* contributed to the creation of a truly vibrant, open and impartial media in Burundi, and one of the most progressive in Africa. This positive impact on media throughout an entire country is not limited to *Studio Ijambo* in Burundi. In Liberia alone, SFCG works with 22 partner radio stations – 10 in the capital Monrovia and 12 in rural communities. The same is the case in Sierra Leone. Many local radio stations now broadcast SFCG programmes because of their legitimacy and the interest they generate. SFCG also helps train journalists and raise the standard of their work in the countries where they are based.

But there is resistance to this proactive approach to media work. At the heart of criticism is the argument that such journalism turns journalists into peace advocates rather than unbiased reporters of events. Peace building, critics argue, requires skills beyond the scope of mere journalists, and such proactive work, in effect, puts the media in the position of taking sides, a very dangerous place to be. But Gordon Adam of the Scotland-based NGO Media Support and Lina Holguin of Oxfam in Quebec, Canada, argue that such work can be successful if there are effective partnerships "between members of the media and conflict resolution specialists, NGOs, funding organizations and communities."[18] Such partnerships, they argue, provide journalists with the knowledge they may lack and facilitate their ability "to meet the needs of the audience."[19] *Mega FM* in Northern Uganda, for instance, is jointly run by the UK's Department for International Development (DFID) and the Ugandan government. Its primary audience is composed of members of the Lord's Resistance Army (LRA), a rebel movement responsible for the abduction, enslavement, rape and use of hundreds of children as child soldiers. The station also targets the communities that the LRA has terrorised. One former child soldier, profiled by the station, explains the impact of the station:

---

[18]Linda Holguin and Adam Gordon, "The Media's Role in Peace-building: Asset or Liability?," The Media Research hub: Social Science Research Council, http://mediaresearchhub.ssrc.org/the-media-s-role-in-peace-building-asset-or-liability/resource_view (Accessed June 10, 2009).

[19]Ibid.

> I did not feel anything bad about killing. Not until when I started listening to Radio *Mega*. They were having programmes, music, and people sending greetings . . . about peace: come back home . . . I actually heard over the radio, how we used to move: we burnt homes . . . And I started to think: are we really fighting a normal war? That is when I started realizing that maybe there is something better than being here in the bush.[20]

Indeed *Mega FM* was so successful at making child soldiers rethink what they were doing that the LRA banned any soldier below the rank of captain from listening to radio.

Interactive Radio for Justice (IRFJ) based in Ituri, in Eastern DRC, is another example of peace media. It was set up by Wanda Hall, a former Internews manager, with funding from the US-based MacArthur Foundation. IRFJ broadcasts have made a huge impact in an area previously only known for the violent massacres between the Hema and the Lendu militia. IRFJ concentrates on human rights, bringing in interviewees to explain measures put in place to punish violators of international crimes locally and internationally. It deals with the question of child soldiers and how they can re-integrate into society, and it allows call-ins aimed at helping communities experiencing conflict to hear each other and peacefully discuss their differences. Most importantly it broadcasts in Swahili, Lingala, French, Kikongo and Kiluba, the main languages in the region, and it can be heard over Bunia, Southern Sudan and Western Uganda. The project has been so successful that its creator, Wanda Hall, has been invited to start a similar project in the Central Africa Republic. Richard Pituwa, a Congolese national and owner of Radio *Canal Revelation*, which co- produces IRFJ's programmes, told me in an interview for a UN publication, that "people will believe propaganda if they do not have the proper information. But if you bring them the actual information, it changes everything. It helps people go beyond what they were told."[21]

Radio Okapi in the Eastern part of the DRC is another example of a successful peace radio project. *Okapi* is jointly run by the UN peace keeping mission in the Congo and a Swiss Foundation, Hirondelle. It is credited by regional analysts with easing tensions; counteracting propaganda and helping people in Eastern DRC rebuild their lives after the war.

The ways in which these organisations convey the message of cohabitation varies. In Liberia and Sierra Leone, the most effective peace programmes by SFCG are soap operas. These allow the society to view the issues through the medium of humorous storylines and characters they can easily identify with. The soap operas that SFCG produces are supplementary to news programmes but are often much more effective than news in promoting co-existence. In Côte d'Ivoire for example, SFCG produced

[20] See full story at http://www.dfid.gov.uk/Media-Room/Case-Studies/2007/Can-radio-help-end-conflict-peacefully-in-Uganda/ (Accessed June 15, 2009).

[21] Mary Kimani, "Broadcasting Peace," 2007, 3.

a football soap opera called "L'Équipe." The simple story is built around characters who reflect the Ivorian adoration of local footballers. Through the characters, the show addresses the issues of ethnicity, unequal distribution of wealth and politics. It is being used to rebuild a sense of national identity which has been marred by years of ethnic and class divisions. L'Équipe currently airs on 14 local radio stations, including the UN peace keeping radio *ONUCI FM*, and is paid for by the EU commission and the US-based Skoll Foundation. Ten other community stations have received funding from other donors to produce similar programming.

In Kenya, *Ghetto FM* station is targeting youths living in various informal settlements in Nairobi. The Nairobi slums were some of the areas hardest hit by the post-electoral ethnic violence of January and February 2008. Thousands of slum residents were forcibly expelled and scores killed because of their ethnicity. *Ghetto FM* concentrates on the message of cohabitation and peace. It strives to shift the focus from ethnicity to the other pressing needs facing the slum population as a whole, regardless of their ethnic background. It is one of the first attempts to promote peace media in Kenya.

Increasingly, churches, UN bodies, and even donor agencies are setting up broadcasting stations with the specific intention of bringing communities closer. Programming on these stations emphasizes similarities rather than differences between communities. It raises issues that separate communities and gets people to talk in constructive ways rather than let bitterness, mutual silence and suspicion grow. So significant have these kinds of media been in creating peace and de-escalating violence that the UN Security Council voted to continue supporting *Radio UNAMSIL*, a radio station set up in Sierra Leone by the peace-keeping mission.

20.5 Conclusion: Potential Obstacles

However, peace media can experience substantial backlash from extremist groups and leaders. For example, when *Mega FM* convinced an LRA commander from Pagak town in Northern Uganda to announce on air that he had left the rebel group, many younger combatants followed suit. In reprisal, the LRA attacked his home area, killing 53 people. IRFJ and, *Okapi* have had security threats and concerns for their staff because of their proactive work. But closing operations and moving away is not seen as an option. It would only allow extreme ideas to take centre-stage once again, so all these organisations have continued their work. *Okapi*, for instance, started a partnership with Benevolencia, an NGO that works on conflict resolution. The joint broadcasts teach the community the nature of conflict and how wars begin, grow and get out of hand. Former programme director Yves Laplume says it is not an easy message to get across:

Table 20.1 Political alignment of the media

Church owned and neutral papers	*Papers owned by MRND and CDR party members or supporters.*	*Government papers and MRND papers*	*Papers owned by MDR party, its members or supporters*	*RPF papers*	*Papers owned by RPF or supporters*
Kinyamateka and Dialogue, Amakuru Ki I Butare	Kangura, Intera, L'echo des Mille Collines, Interahamwe, La Médaille Nyiramacibiri, Kamarampaka, Zirikana Ikinani, Power-pawa, Kangurwa-Nyabarongo, Umuranga	Imvaho, La Relève, Umurwana-Shyaka, Ijisho Rya Rubanda	Isibo, Urumuli Rwa Demokarasi, Le Démocrate, L'opinion, Le Tribun, Le Flambeau,	Rwanda Rwe'ejo Rwanda Review	Kanguka, Impuruza Le Soleil, Imbaga, Murangi, Kiberinka

> It was very intellectual at the beginning and it was difficult to show examples, because if you mention ethnicities you can reverse the whole trend of peace right now. You had to speak in general about how conflict occurs between people, neighbours, and becomes a problem of societies. People like it now. It is able to make people understand how they can be manipulated by politicians and people with an interest in conflict.[22]

Probably the most important thing that these stations do is to create dissonance. They introduce viewpoints that the politically partial media may ignore when compiling news content, and they challenge individuals who are willing to think differently to begin doing so. Obviously, long held beliefs, especially negative ones, do not change rapidly and this process will take time. However, if not confronted, polarizing beliefs and ideas tend to become even more potent and virulent, supplying fodder for unscrupulous leaders who see benefits in tapping into them.

The one major drawback that all these stations struggle with is that what they do, while valuable, is not commercially profitable. Unlike commercial media, they cannot depend on advertisers. Moreover, given Africa's poor purchasing power, subscriptions are not likely to work. As a result, none of these organizations is self-sustaining. They all depend, almost entirely, on donor funding. While funding media to undo years of hate propaganda is finally becoming acceptable, nobody is yet willing to support these media in their preventative work. There is a need for greater recognition of the potential of this type of media to prevent genocide and other gross violations of human rights. The Director of IRFJ, Wanda Hall, puts it best: "Media is the most important tool for social change; it has been used for many things from teaching about the use of mosquito nets and condoms to inciting genocide. I believe activists should use it for peace. We are not changing the nature of news; we are just giving an alternative."[23]

See Table 20.1 below for the political alignment of the media.

---

[22]Yves Laplume, interviewed by author via telephone, July 27, 2007.

[23]Mary Kimani, "Broadcasting Peace," 2007, 3.

References

Cruelty in the Congo Free State: Concluding Extracts from the Journals of the Late E.J. Glave *The Century Illustrated Monthly Magazine* 32 (May–October 1897): 699–715.

Ireland – Past Measures and Their Results *The Economist*, January 16, 1847.

Penal Reform International. *Les Justes: entre oubli et réconciliation*. 2004. Available online at http://www.penalreform.org/download/Gacaca/Rapport%20Kibuye%20III_FR.pdf

Political: The Actual Condition of Ireland *The Economist*, October 14, 1843.

Security Council Refers Situation in Darfur, Sudan, to Prosecutor of International Criminal Court. Resolution 1593 (2005), adopted by Vote of 11 in Favour to None Against, with 4 Abstentions (Algeria, Brazil, China, United States). SC/8351, March 31, 2005. http://www.un.org/News/Press/docs/2005/sc8351.doc.htm

Sudan: Peacekeepers Into the Fray *The Economist*, March 15, 2008.

The New Measures of the Government *The Economist*, January 30, 1847, 115.

The Political Economist: Ireland *The Economist*, January 30, 1847, 113.

The Political Economist: Three Measures for the First Day of the Session *The Economist*, January 16, 1847, 1.18, no. 4 (2004): 498–509.

Tutsis and Hutus: More Blood to Come *The Economist*, July 22, 1995.

Abadian, Sousan. Cultural Healing: When Cultural Renewal is Reparative and When It Is Toxic, *Pimatisiwin, A Journal of Aboriginal and Indigenous Community Health* 1, no. 2 (2006): 5–28.

Africa Watch. *The Forgotten War in Darfur Flares up Again*. London: Africa Watch, April 6, 1990.

Akçam, Taner. *A Shameful Act: The Armenian Genocide and the Question of Turkish Responsibility*. New York, NY: Metropolitan Books, 2006.

Akhavan, Payam Beyond Impunity: Can International Criminal Justice Prevent Future Atrocities?, *American Journal of International Law* 95, no. 1 (2001): 7–31.

Albright, Madeleine, and William Cohen. *Preventing Genocide: A Blueprint for U.S. Policymakers*. United States Institute for Peace: Taskforce on Genocide Prevention. United States: United States Holocaust Museum, The American Academy of Diplomacy, and the Endowment of the United States Institute of Peace, 2008, http://www.usip.org/genocide_taskforce/report.html (Accessed June 9, 2009).

Allen, John. *Rabble Rousers for Peace: The Authorized Biography of Desmond Tutu*. Glencoe, IL: Free Press, 2006.

Almedom, Astier M. Resilience, Hardiness, Sense of Coherence, and Posttraumatic Growth: All Paths Leading to 'Light at the End of the Tunnel'?, *Journal of Loss & Trauma* 10, no. 3 (2005): 253–265.

Alvarez, Alexander. Adjusting to Genocide: The Techniques of Neutralization and the Holocaust, *Social Science History* 21, (1997): 139–178.

R. Provost, P. Akhavan (eds.), *Confronting Genocide*, Ius Gentium: Comparative Perspectives on Law and Justice 7, DOI 10.1007/978-90-481-9840-5,

Andreopoulos, George J. Introduction In *Genocide: Conceptual and Historical Dimensions*, edited by George J., Andreopoulos, Philadelphia, PA: University of Pennsylvania Press, 1997.

Annan, Kofi. In Larger Freedoms: Toward Development, Security and Human Rights for All, *Report of the Secretary-General of the United Nations* UN Doc. A/59/2005, March 21, 2005, 1–62, http://daccess-dds-ny.un.org/doc/UNDOC/GEN/N05/270/78/PDF/N0527078.pdf?OpenElement

Antonovsky, Aaron. The Salutogenic Perspective: Toward a New View of Health and Illness, *Advances* 4, no. 1 (1987): 47–55.

Appadurai, Arjun. *Fear of Small Numbers: An Essay on the Geography of Anger*. Durham, NC: Duke University Press, 2006.

Arad, Yitzhak. Jewish Prisoner Uprisings in the Treblinka and Sobibor Extermination Camps In *The Nazi Holocaust. Historical Articles on the Destruction of European Jews*, edited by Michael Marrus, Westport, CT: Meckler, 1989: 240–283.

Arendt, Hannah. *Eichmann in Jerusalem: A Report on the Banality of Evil*. New York, NY: Penguin, 1963.

Arnold, Guy. *Mercenaries: The Scourge of the Third World*. London: MacMillan Press, 1999.

Ascherson, Neal. *The King Incorporated: Leopold the Second and the Congo*. London: Granta, 1999.

Asiimwe, Arthur. Rwanda Census Puts Genocide Death Toll at 937,000, *Reuters*. April 4, 2004. Available at: http://www.alertnet.org/thefacts/reliefresources/108117321274.htm

Attorney General of Israel v. Eichmann (1961), 36 I.L.R. 18, 39 (Dist. Ct.)

Attorney General of Israel v. Eichmann (1962), 36 I.L.R. 277, 36 ILR 18 (Supreme Ct.)

Avant, Deborah. *The Market for Force: The Consequences of Privatizing Security*. New York, NY: Cambridge University Press, 2005.

Bagilishya, Deogratias. Mourning and Recovery from Trauma: In Rwanda, Tears Flow Within, *Transcultural Psychiatry* 37, no. 3 (2000): 337–353.

Balfour, Michael. Another Look at Unconditional Surrender, *International Affairs* (Royal Institute of International Affairs 1944) 46 (1970): 719–736.

Bankier, David. Jewish Society through Nazi Eyes 1933–1936, *Holocaust and Genocide Studies* 6, no. 2 (1991): 111–127.

Barcelona Traction, Light and Power Company, Limited (Belgian v. *Spain);* Second Phase. International Court of Justice (ICJ) (February 5, 1970). http://www.unhcr.org/refworld/docid/4040aec74.htm (Accessed June 13, 2009).

Bassiouni, M. Chérif. Crimes Against Humanity, *Crimes of War Project* www.crimesofwar.org/thebook/crimes-against-humanity.html (Accessed May 13, 2008).

Bassiouni, M. Chérif. Universal Jurisdiction for International Crimes: Historical Perspectives and Contemporary Practice, *Virginia Journal of International Law* 42 (Fall 2001): 1–100.

Bauer, Yehuda. Genocide in History: The Onward Progress of Civilisation? Speech given during a panel discussion at the Global Conference on the Prevention of Genocide, McGill University, Montreal, Canada, October 11–13, 2007.

Bellamy, Alexander J. Conflict Prevention and the Responsibility to Protect, *Global Governance: A Review of Multilateralism and International Organizations* 14, no. 2 (2008): 135–156.

Bender, Thomas, ed, *The Antislavery Debate: Capitalism and Abolitionism as a Problem in Historical Interpretation*. Berkeley, CA: University of California Press, 1992.

Bercuson, David J. *Significant Incident: Canada's Army, the Airborne, and the Murder in Somalia*. Toronto, ON: McClelland and Stewart, 1996.

Bernales Ballesteros, Enrique Use of Mercenaries as a Means of Violating Human Rights and Impeding the Exercise of the Right of Peoples to Self-Determination UN Doc. A/58/115 (July 2, 2003).

Best, Geoffrey *Humanity in Warfare: The Modern History of the International Law of Armed Conflict*. London: Weidenfeld and Nicolson, 1980.

Bilski, Leora Judging Evil in the Trial of Kastner, *Law and History Review* 19, no. 1 (2001): 117–160.

Blackburn, Robin. *The Overthrow of Colonial Slavery, 1776–1848*. New York, NY: Verso, 1988.

Blass, Thomas. The Roots of Stanley Milgram's Obedience Experiments and Their Relevance to the Holocaust, *Analyse und Kritik* 20 (1998): S46–S53.

Bonanno, George A. Loss, Trauma, and Human Resilience: Have We Underestimated the Human Capacity to Thrive After Extremely Aversive Events?, *American Psychologist*, 59, no. 1 (2004): 20–28.

Bose, Sugata. Starvation Amidst Plenty: The Making of Famine in Bengal, Honan, and Tonkin, 1942–1945, *Modern Asian Studies* 24, no. 4 (1990): 699–727.

Breitman, Richard, and Shlomo Aronson. The End of the Final Solution?: Nazi Plans to Ransom Jews in 1944, *Central European History* 25 (1992): 177–203.

Breitman, Richard Plans for the Final Solution in Early 1941, *German Studies Review* 17, no. 3 (1994): 483–493.

Enforcement Activities in Africa Pretoria, SA: Africa Institute of South Africa, 2000.

Brooks, Doug *Creating the Renaissance Peace: The Utilization of Private Companies for Peacekeeping and Peace*. A paper for the Africa Institute of South Africa's 40th Anniversary Conference, 30 May–2 June 2000, Pretoria, South Africa.

Brooks, Doug. *Creating the Renaissance Peace: The Utilization of Private Companies for Peacekeeping and Peace Enforcement Activities in Africa*. Pretoria, SA: Africa Institute of South Africa, 2000. Available from http://www.sandline.com/pdfs/brooks.pdf

Brooks, Doug Messiahs or Mercenaries? The Future of International Private Military Services, *International Peacekeeping* 7, no. 4 (2000): 129–144.

Brown v. Board of Education, 347 U.S. 483 (1954).

Brown, Chris. Delinquent States, Guilty Consciences and Humanitarian Politics in the 1990s, *Journal of International Political Theory* 4, no. 1 (2008): 55–71.

Browning, Christopher R., and Jürgen Matthäus *The Origins of the Final Solution: The Evolution of Nazi Jewish Policy, September 1939–March 1942*. Lincoln, NE: University of Nebraska Press, 2007.

Browning, Christopher R. *Ordinary Men: Reserve Police Battalion 101 and the Final Solution in Poland*. New York, NY: HarperCollins Publishers, 1992.

Brownlie, Ian. *Principles of Public International Law*, 6th ed. New York, NY: Oxford University Press, 2003.

Buchler, Yehoshua Robert 'Unworthy Behavior': The Case of SS Officer Max Täubner, *Holocaust and Genocide Studies* 17, no. 3 (2003): 409–429.

Burchett, Wilfred, and Derek Roebuck. *The Whores of War: Mercenaries Today*. Middlesex.: Penguin, 1977.

Burgess, Gerg. The Human Rights Dilemma in Anti-Nazi Protest: The Bernheim Petition, Minorities Protection, and the 1933 Sessions of the League of Nations. In CERC Working Paper Series: Contemporary Europe Research Centre, 2002.

Burleigh, Michael. Jews for Sale? Nazi-Jewish Negotiations, 1933–1945, *The Journal of Modern History* 69, no. 4 (1997): 893–895.

Calhoun, Craig. A World of Emergencies: Fear, Intervention, and the Limits of Cosmopolitan Order, *The Canadian Review of Sociology and Anthropology* 41, no. 4 (2004): 373–396.

Cambodian Genocide Program. "The CGP, 1994–2008." Genocide Studies Program, Yale University, http://www.yale.edu/cgp/ (Accessed June 4, 2009).

Campbell, Kenneth J. The Role of Individual States in Addressing Cases of Genocide, *Human Rights Review* 5, no. 4 (2004): 32–45.

Carey, Peter. *The Power of Prophecy: Prince Dipanagara and the End of an Old Order in Java, 1785–1855*. Leiden: KITLV, 2007.

Case Concerning Application of the Convention on the Prevention and Punishment of the Crime of Genocide, (Bosnia-Herzegovina v. Yugoslavia) (Preliminary Objection). International Court of Justice Report (July 11, 1996). http://www.un.org/law/icjsum/9625.htm (Accessed June 13, 2009).

Cassels, Lindi, and Peter. Suedfeld Salutogenesis and Autobiographical Disclosure Among Holocaust Survivors, *Journal of Positive Psychology* 1, no. 4 (2006): 212–225.

Cassese, Antonio. Mercenaries: Lawful Combatants or War Criminals, *Zeitschrift fur auslandisches offentliches Recht und Volkerrecht* 40, (1980): 1–30.

Cassese, Antonio. *International Law*, 2nd edn. New York, NY: Oxford University Press, 2005.

Cesarani, David. *Eichmann: His Life and Crimes*. London: William Heineman, 2004.

Chalk, Frank. Re-defining Genocide In *Genocide: Conceptual and Historical Dimensions*, edited by George J Andreopoulos. Philadelphia, PA: University of Pennsylvania Press, 1997, 47–63.

Charlesworth, Hilary. International Law: A Discipline of Crisis, *The Modern Law Review* 65 (2002): 377–392.

Chicago Council on Foreign Relations. American Public Opinion and Foreign Policy. ICPSR03673-v1. Rochester, NY: Harris Interactive [producer], 2002.

Cobban, Helena. *Amnesty after Atrocity?: Healing Nations after Genocide and War Crimes*. Boulder, CO: Paradigm Publishers, 2007.

Cocker, Mark. *Rivers of Blood, Rivers of Gold: Europe's Conflict with Tribal Peoples*. London: J. Cape, 1998.

Cohen, Martin. Culture and Remembrance: Jewish Ambivalence and Antipathy to the History of Resistance In *Resisting the Holocaust*, edited by Ruby Rohrlich, 119–162. Oxford: Berg Publishers, (1998).

Cohen, Roberta, and Francis M. Deng. *Masses in Flight: The Global Crisis of Internal Displacement*. Washington DC, The Brookings Institution, 1996.

Coloroso, Barbara. *Extraordinary Evil: A Brief History of Genocide...and Why It Matters*. Toronto, ON: Viking, 2007.

Cramer-Flood, Ethan The 'Responsibility to Protect' and Unilateral Humanitarian Interventions: An Emerging Legal Doctrine?, *Minerva* 33 (2008): 35–50.

Dallaire, Roméo *Shake Hands with the Devil*. Toronto, ON: Vintage Canada Edition, 2003.

Davies, John L., and Ted Robert Gurr, eds *Preventive Measures: Building Risk Assessment and Crisis Early Warning Systems*. Lanham, MD: Rowman and Littefield, 1998.

Davies, Matthew, and Janet Kawamoto. Kenya Missionaries Return to Work Despite Continuing Unrest. *Episcopal Life* Online, January 30, 2008. http://www.episcopal-life.org/79901_94360_ENG_HTM.htm (Accessed June 12, 2009).

Davis, Mike. *Late Victorian Holocausts: El Niño Famines and the Making of the Third World*. London: Verso, 2001.

de Tocqueville, Alexis. *Writings on Empire and Slavery*. Baltimore, MD: Johns Hopkins University Press, 2001.

den Hond, Bas. *Pers kan blauwhelmen helpen bij hun taak* (The media can help blue berets in their work). *Trouw*, October 20, 2007.

Deng, Francis M. Frontiers of Sovereignty: A Framework of Protection, Assistance and Development for the Internally Displaced., *Leiden Journal of International Law* 8, no.2 (1995): 249–286.

Deng, Francis M. Reconciling Sovereignty with Responsibility: A Basis for Humanitarian Action, In *Africa World Politics*, edited by John Harbeson and Donald Rothchild Boulder, CO: Westview Press, 1995.

Deng, Francis M. Sovereignty and Humanitarian Responsibility: A Challenge for NGOs in Africa and the Sudan. In *Vigilance and Vengeance*, edited by Robert I Rotberg. Washington, DC: Brookings Institution Press and The World Peace Foundation, 1996.

Deng, Francis M., and I. William Zartman, eds. *Conflict Resolution in Africa*. Washington, DC: Brookings Institution Press, 1991.

Deng, Francis M., and I. William Zartman, eds. *A Strategic Vision for Africa: The Kampala Movement*. Washington, DC: Brookings Institution Press, 2002.

Deng, Francis M., and Terrence Lyons, eds *African Reckoning: A Quest for Good*. Washington, DC: Brookings Institution Press, 1998.

Deng, Francis M., Sadikiel Kimaro, Terrence Lyons, Donald Rothchild and I.William Zartman, eds., *Sovereignty as Responsibility: Conflict Management in Africa*. Washington, DC: Brookings Institution Press, 1996.

Des Forges Alison. *Leave None to tell the Story: Genocide in Rwanda*. New York, NY: Human Rights Watch, 1999.

Des Forges, Alison. Silencing the Voices of Hate in Rwanda In *Forging Peace. Intervention, Human Rights and the Management of Media Space*, edited by Monroe Price and Mark Thompson. Edinburgh: Edinburgh University Press, 2002.

Donnelly, Jr., James S. Mass Eviction and the Great Famine In *The Great Irish Famine*, edited by Cathal Póirtéir. Dublin: Mercier, 1995, 155–173.

Dower, John W. *Embracing Defeat: Japan in the Wake of World War II*. New York, NY: W.W. Norton, 1999.

Drumbl, Mark. A. *Atrocity, Punishment, and International Law*. Cambridge: Cambridge University Press, 2007.

Einwohner, Rachel L. Identity Work and Collective Action in a Repressive Context: Jewish Resistance on the 'Aryan Side' of the Warsaw Ghetto, *Social Problems* 53, no. 1 (2006): 38–56.

Engel, David. *Facing a Holocaust: The Polish Government-in-Exile and the Jews, 1943–1945*. London: University of North Carolina Press, 1993.

Etzioni, Amitai. Genocide Prevention in the New Global Architecture, *The British Journal of Politics & International Relations* 7, no. 4 (2005): 469–484.

Evans, Gareth. Crimes Against Humanity: Overcoming Indifference, *Journal of Genocide Research* 8, no. 3 (September 2006): 325–339.

Ewans, Martin. *European Atrocity, African Catastrophe: Leopold II, the Congo Free State, and its Aftermath*. London: Routledge, 2002.

Fallah, Katharine. Corporate Actors: The Legal Status of Mercenaries in Armed Conflict, *International Review of the Red Cross*, 863 (2006): 599–611.

Falsetti, Sherry A., Patricia A. Resick, and Joanne L. Davis. Changes in Religious Beliefs Following Trauma, *Journal of Traumatic Stress* 16, no. 4 (2003): 391–398.

Fein, Helen. *Accounting for Genocide*. New York, NY: Free Press, 1979.

Fein, Helen. Defining Genocide as a Sociological Concept, *Current Sociology* 38, no. 8 (1990): 8–31.

Fein, Helen. Genocide, Terror, Life Integrity, and War Crimes, the Case for Discrimination In *Genocide: Conceptual and Historical Dimensions*, edited by George J Andreopoulos, 95–108. Philadelphia, PA: University of Pennsylvania Press, 1997.

Fein, Helen. Testing Theories Brutally: Armenia (1915), Bosnia (1992) and Rwanda (1994) In *Studies in Comparative Genocide*, edited by Levon Chorbajian and George Shirinian, 157–164 New York, NY: St. Martin's Press, 1999.

Fenigstein, Allan. Were Obedience Pressures a Factor in the Holocaust?, *Analyse & Kritik* 20, (1998): 54–73.

Fitzpatrick, Joan. Temporary Protection of Refugees: Elements of a Formalized Regime, *American Journal of International Law* 94 (2000): 279–306.

Fitzsimmons, Scott. Dogs of Peace: A Potential Role for Private Military Companies in Peace Implementation., *Journal of Military and Strategic Studies* 8, no. 1 (Fall 2005): 1–27.

Fletcher, Laurel E. From Indifference to Engagement: Bystanders and International Criminal Justice, *Mich. J. Int'l L.* 26, (2005): 1013–1096.

Fowler, Jerry. Beyond Humanitarian Bandages-Confronting Genocide in Sudan, *The New England Journal of Medicine*, 351 2004, 2574–2576.

Franklin, John Hope *George Washington Williams*. Durham: Duke University Press, 1998.

Friedlander, Saul. *The Years of Extermination: Nazi Germany and the Jews, 1939–1945*. New York, NY: HarperCollins, 2007.

Fuller, Lon L. Positivism and Fidelity to Law: A Reply to Professor Hart, *Harvard Law Review* 71 no. 4 (1958): 630–672.

Fussell, Jim. *Group Classification on National ID Cards as a Factor in Genocide and Ethnic Cleansing*. Presented on November 15, 2001 to the Seminar Series of the Yale University Genocide Studies Program by Jim Fussell, Prevent Genocide International.

Gaeta, Paola. Is the Practice of "Self-Referrals" a Sound Start for the ICC?, *Journal of International Criminal Justice* 2, no. 4 (2004): 949–952.

Galtung, Johan. "Cultural violence.", *Journal of Peace Research* 27, no. 3 (1990): 291–305.

Galtung, Johan. *Peace by Peaceful Means: Peace and Conflict, Development and Civilization*. Thousand Oaks, CA: Sage, 1996.

Gampel, Yolanda. Reflections on the Prevalence of the Uncanny in Social Violence In *Cultures Under Siege: Collective Violence and Trauma*, edited by Antonious C.G.M Robben and Marcelo M Suarez-Orozco, 43–72 Cambridge: Cambridge University Press, 2000.

Genocide Intervention Network History of Genocide. Genocide Intervention Network, Genocide, http://www.un.org/preventgenocide/rwanda/infokit.shtml (Accessed June 4, 2009).

Genocide Intervention Network Past Genocides. Genocide Intervention Network, http://www.genocideintervention.net/educate/genocide#bosnia1 (Accessed June 4, 2009).

Gerzon, Mark. *Leading Through Conflict: How Successful Leaders Transform Differences Into Opportunities*. Watertown, MA: Harvard Business Press, 2006.

Goldin, Milton. Financing the SS, *History Today* 48, no. 6 (1998) http://www.historytoday.com/milton-goldin/financing-ss.

Goldstein, Abraham. Group Libel and Criminal Law: Walking on the Slippery Slope Paper presentation, International Legal Colloquium on Racial and Religious Hatred and Group Libel, Tel Aviv University, Israel, 1991.

Good, Michael. *The Search for Major Plagge: The Nazi Who Saved Jews*. New York: Fordham University Press, 2005.

Gordon, Gregory. 'A War of Media, Words, Newspapers and Radio Stations': The ICTR Media Trial Verdict and a New Chapter in the International Law of Hate Speech, *Virginia Journal of International Law* 45 (2004): 139–197.

Gordon, Gregory. From Incitement to Indictment?: Prosecuting Iran's President for Advocating Israel's Destruction and Piecing Together Incitement Law's Emerging Analytical Framework, *Journal of Criminal Law & Criminology* 98, no. 3 (March, 2008): 853–920.

Gourevitch, Philip. *We Wish to Inform You That Tomorrow We Will Be Killed with Our Families: Stories from Rwanda*. New York, NY: Picador, 1999.

Greenawalt, Alexander K.A. Rethinking Genocidal Intent: The Case for Knowledge-Based Interpretation., *Columbia Law Review*, 99, no. 8 (1999): 2259–2294.

Greenberg, Jeff, Tom Pyszczynski, Sheldon Solomon, Abram Rosenblatt, Mitchell Veeder, and Shari Kirkland. Evidence for Terror Management Theory: The Effects of Mortality

Salience on Reactions to Those Who Threaten or Bolster the Cultural Worldview, *Journal of Personality and Social Psychology* 8, no. 2 (1990): 308–318.

Guinnane, Timothy. Ireland's Famine Wasn't Genocide. *Washington Post*, September 17, 1997.

Gurr, Ted Robert, and Barbara, Harff. Toward Empirical Theory of Genocides and Politicides: Identification and Measurement of Cases Since 1945, *International Studies Quarterly* 32, no. 3 (1988): 359–371.

Gutman, Yisrael. The Genesis of the Resistance in the Warsaw Ghetto, *Yad Vashem Studies* 9, (1973): 29–70.

Haines, Robin. *Charles Trevelyan and the Great Irish Famine*. Dublin: Four Courts, 2004.

Hamburg, David. *Preventing Genocide: Practical Steps Toward Early Detection and Effective Action*. Boulder, CO and London: Paradigm Publishers, 2008.

Hamilton, Rebecca, and Chad Hazlett. Not on Our Watch In *War in Darfur and the Search for Peace*, edited by Alex deWaal, 337–366. Cambridge: Harvard University Press, 2007.

Harding, Jeremy. The Mercenary Business: Executive Outcomes., *Review of African Political Economy* 24, no. 71 (1997): 87–97.

Harff, Barbara. Rescuing Endangered Peoples: Missed Opportunities, *Social Research* 62, no. 1 (1995): 23–40.

Harff, Barbara. No Lessons Learned from the Holocaust? Assessing Risks of Genocide and Political Mass Murder since 1955, *American Political Science Review* 97, no.1 (2003): 57–73.

Harms, Robert. The End of Red Rubber: A Reassessment, *Journal of African History* 16, no.1 (1975): 73–88.

Harris, John F. Bill Clinton Takes Spot On Global Stage. *The Washington Post*. June 1, 2005.

Hart, H.L.A. Positivism and the Separation of Law and Morals, *Harvard Law Review* 71 (1958): 593–629.

Harvard Corporation Committee. Statement by Harvard Corporation Committee on Shareholder Responsibility (CCSR) Regarding Stock in PetroChina Company Limited. *Harvard University Gazette*, April 4, 2005. http://www.news.harvard.edu/gazette/daily/2005/04/04-sudan_statement.html (Accessed June 9, 2009).

Hawkins, Hunt. Joseph Conrad, Roger Casement, and the Congo Reform Movement, *Journal of Modern Literature* 9, no.1 (1981–1982): 65–80.

Hawkins, Hunt. Mark Twain's Involvement with the Congo Reform Movement, *New England Quarterly* 51, no.2 (1978): 147–175.

Hébert, Valérie. Disguised Resistance? The Story of Kurt Gerstein, *Holocaust and Genocide Studies* 20, no. 1 (2006): 1–33.

Hehir, Bryan. Expanding Military Intervention: Promise or Peril?, *Social Research* 62, no. 1 (1995): 41–51.

Helman, Scott. His Big Regret: Not Acting in Rwanda *The Boston Globe*. December 11, 2007.

Hintjens, Helen M. Explaining the 1994 Genocide in Rwanda, *The Journal of Modern African Studies* 37, no. 2 (1999): 241–86.

Hintjens, Helen M. When Identity Becomes a Knife: Reflecting on the Genocide in Rwanda, *Ethnicities* 1, no. 1 (2001): 25.

Hitler, Adolph. *Mein Kampf*. Translated by James Vincent Murphy. Reedy, WV: Liberty Bell Publications, 2004.

Hoare, Mike. *Congo Mercenary*. London: Robert Hale Ltd, 1991.

Hochschild, Adam. *Bury the Chains: Prophets and Rebels in the Fight to Free an Empire's Slaves*. Boston, MA: Houghton Mifflin, 2005.

Hochschild, Adam. *King Leopold's Ghost: A Story of Greed, Terror and Heroism in Colonial Africa*. Boston, MA: Mariner Books, 1998.

Holbrooke, Richard. Defying Orders, Saving Lives-Heroic Diplomats of the Holocaust, *Foreign Affairs* 86, (2007): 135.

Holguin, Linda, and Adam Gordon. The Media's Role in Peace-Building: Asset or Liability? Media 3 Conference, Barranquilla, Columbia (19–23 May 2003).

Hong, Shen. *On the Crime of Genocide*. Doctoral disserrtation. Renmin University of China (June 2008).

Hovannisian, Richard G. Intervention and Shades of Altruism During the Armenian Genocide In *The Armenian Genocide: History, Politics, Ethics* 173–207. New York, NY: St. Martin's Press, 1992.

Human Rights Watch. *Killings in Eastern Rwanda*. New York, NY: Human Rights Watch, 2007.

Hunt, Nancy Rose. An Acoustic Register, Tenacious Images, and Congolese Scenes of Rape and Repetition, *Cultural Anthropology* 23, no. 2 (2008): 220–253.

Huppert, Shmuel. King of the Ghetto Mor Decai Haim Rumkowski, the Elder of Lodz Ghetto, *Yad Vashem Studies* 15, (1983): 125–158.

Independent Inquiry Committee*The Management of the Oil-for-Food Programme, Volume 2: Report of Investigation, Programme Background*. Independent Inquiry Committee into the United Nations Oil-for-Food Programme, September 7, 2005. http://www.iic-offp.org/documents/Sept05/Mgmt_V2.pdf (Accessed June 12, 2009).

International Commission of Inquiry on Darfur. Report of the International Commission of Inquiry on Darfur to the United Nations Secretary-General," in pursuance with the United Nations Security Council Res. 1564, (September 18, 2004), January 25, 2005. http://www.un.org/News/dh/sudan/com_inq_darfur.pdf. (Accessed June 15, 2008).

International Commission on Intervention and State Sovereignty *The Responsibility to Protect*. Report of the International Commission on Intervention and State Sovereignty. Ottawa: International Development Research Centre, 2001.

International Committee of the Red Cross (ICRC). The ICRC to Expand Contacts with Private Military and Security Companies, April 8, 2004, http://www.icrc.org/Web/Eng/siteeng0.nsf/iwpList571/21414DE8FCAF2645C1256EE50038A631 (Accessed June 15, 2009).

International Convention on the Elimination of All Forms of Racial Discrimination, 660 U.N.T.S. 195 (January 4, 1969), http://academic.udayton.edu/race/06hrights/UnitedNations/CERD/cerd00.htm (Accessed June 12, 2009).

International Criminal Court *Rome Statute of the International Criminal Court*, U.N. Doc. A/CONF.183/9.

International Crisis Group. "Do Americans Care about Darfur: An International Crisis Group/Zogby International Survey." Update Briefing, African Briefing No.26. Washington/Brussels, June 1, 2005. http://www.crisisgroup.org/library/documents/africa/horn_of_africa/b026_do_americans_care_about_darfur.doc (Accessed June 9, 2009).

Jackson, J. Robert H. The United States of America, the French Republic, the United Kingdom of Great Britain and Northern Ireland, and the Union of Soviet Socialist Republics v. Hermann Wilhelm Göring, et al. *Opening Statement to the International Military Tribunal*, Case No. 1, Palace of Justice, Nuremberg, Germany, November 21, 1945.

Jackson, J. Robert H. *The United States of America, the French Republic, the United Kingdom of Great Britain and Northern Ireland, and the Union of Soviet Socialist Republics v. Hermann Wilhelm Göring, et al*. Opening Statement to the International Military Tribunal, Case No. 1, Palace of Justice, Nuremberg, Germany. November 21, 1945.

Janoff-Bulman, Ronnie. Assumptive Worlds and the Stress of Traumatic Events: Applications of the Schema Construct, *Social Cognition* 7, no. 2 (1989): 113–136.

Janzen, John M. Historical Consciousness and a 'prise de conscience' in Genocidal Rwanda, *Journal of African Cultural Studies* 13 no. 1 (2000): 153–168.

Jefremovas, Villia. Acts of Human Kindness: Tutsi, Hutu and the Genocide, *A Journal of Opinion* 23 (1995): 28–31.

Jensen, Eric Talbot. Incentivizing and Protecting Informants Prior to Mass Atrocities Such as Genocide: An Alternative to Post Hoc Courts and Tribunals, *Houston Journal of International Law* 29, no. 1 (2006): 113–154.

Johns, Fleur, Sundhya Pahuja, Richard Joyce, ed. *Events: The Force of International Law*. London: Routledge 2010.

Jones, Bruce D. *Peacemaking in Rwanda: the Dynamics of Failure*. Boulder, CO: Lynne Rienner Publishers, 2001.

Jones, David H. On the Prevention of Genocide: The Gap between Research and Education, *War Crimes, Genocide and Crimes Against Humanity* 1, no. 1 (2005): 5–46.

Judge, Edward H. *Easter in Kishinev: Anatomy of a Pogrom*. New York, NY: New York University Press, 1992.

Judt, Tony The Problem of Evil in Postwar Europe. *The New York Review of Books*, February 14, 2008.

Kagan, Joshua M. The Obligation to Use Force to Stop Acts of Genocide: An Overview of Legal Precedents, Customary Norms, and State Responsibility, *San Diego International Law Journal* 7, no. 2 (2005/2006): 461–490.

Kaplan, Marion A. *Between Dignity and Despair: Jewish Life in Nazi Germany*. Oxford: Oxford University Press, 1998.

Kasikili/Sedudu Island (Botswana/Namibia), Judgement, ICJ Reports 1999.

Keller, Linda. Belgian Jury to Decide Case Concerning Rwandan Genocide, *American Society of International Law*, (May 2001). http://www.asil.org/insights/insigh72.htm, (Accessed June 16, 2008).

Kelman, Herbert C. Violence without Moral Restraint: Reflections on the Dehumanization of Victims and Victimizers, *Journal of Social Issues* 29, no. 4 (1973): 25–61.

Kelman, Herbert C. The Policy Context of International Crimes. Paper prepared for the Conference on System Criminality in International Law, Amsterdam Center for International Law, October 20–21, 2006.

Kennedy, Pagan. *Black Livingstone: A True Tale of Adventure in the Nineteenth-Century Congo*. New York, NY: Viking, 2002.

Kiernan, Ben. *Blood and Soil: A World History of Genocide and Extermination from Sparta to Darfur*. New Haven, CT: Yale University Press, 2007.

Kiernan, Ben. Introduction: Conflict in Cambodia, 1945–2002, *Critical Asian Studies* 34, no. 4 (2002): 483–95.

Kiernan, Ben. Serial Colonialism and Genocide in Nineteenth-Century Cambodia In *Empire, Colony, Genocide*, edited by A. Dirk Moses, 205–228. New York, NY: Berghahn, 2008.

Kieval, Hillel J. Legality and Resistance in Vichy France: The Rescue of Jewish Children, *Proceedings of the American Philosophical Society* 124 (1980): 339–366.

Kimani, Mary. Broadcasting Peace: Radio a Tool for Recovery *Africa Renewal*, 2 no. 3 October, 2007: 3.

Kimani, Mary. RTLM: The Medium that Became a Tool for Mass Murder In *The Media and the Rwanda Genocide*, edited by Allan Thompson, 110–124. London: Pluto Press, 2007.

Kinealy, Christine. *A Death-dealing Famine: The Great Hunger in Ireland*. London: Pluto, 1997.

Kinealy, Christine. Food Exports from Ireland 1846–1847, *History Ireland* 5, no. 1 (1997): 32–36.

Kinealy, Christine. *The Great Irish Famine: Impact, Ideology and Rebellion*. Basingstoke: Palgrave, 2002.

Kinloch, Graham Charles, and Raj P Mohan. *Genocide: Approaches, Case Studies, and Responses*. New York, NY: Algora Publishing, 2005.

Kirkby, Coel. "Rwanda's Gacaca Courts: A Preliminary Critique.", *Journal of African Law* 50, no. 2 (2006): 94–117.

Klemperer, Klemens. 'What Is the Law That Lies Behind These Words?' Antigone's Question and the German Resistance Against Hitler*Journal of Modern History* 64 (1992): S102–S111.

Kopel, David B., Joanne D. Eisen, Paul Gallant, and David Luban. Is Resisting Genocide a Human Right?, *Notre Dame Law Review* 81, no. 4 (2006): 1275–1346.

Kovacs, David. A Cautionary Tale, *Transactions of the American Philological Association*, 123 (1993): 405–410.

Kulka, Erich. Attempts by Jewish Escapees to Stop Mass Extermination, *Jewish Social Studies* 47 (1985): 295–306.

Kuper, Leo. *Genocide: Its Political Use in the Twentieth Century*. New Haven, CT: Yale University Press, 1981.

Kuper, Leo. Theoretical Issues Relating to Genocide: Uses and Abuses In *Genocide: Conceptual and Historical Dimensions*, edited by George J. Andreopoulos. Philadelphia, PA: University of Pennsylvania Press, 1997, 31–46.

Kuperman, Alan J. *The Limits of Humanitarian Intervention: Genocide in Rwanda*. Washington, DC: Brookings Institution Press, 2001.

Lederach, Jean Paul *Preparing for Peace: Conflict Transformation Across Cultures*. Syracuse, NY: Syracuse University Press, 1995.

Lee Ann, Fujii. Origins of Power and Identity in Rwanda. Paper presented at the Annual Conference of the International Studies Association, Chicago, IL, February 20–24, 2001.

Lemkin, Raphael. *Axis Rule in Occupied Europe: Laws of Occupation, Analysis of Government, Proposals for Redress*. New York, NY: Howard Fertig, 1973.

Lepsius, Johannes. *Rapport secret sur les massacres d'Arménie*. Beirut: Édition Hamaskaïne, 1968.

Lesser, AH. The Holocaust: Moral and Political Lessons, *Journal of Applied Philosophy* 12, no. 2 (1995): 143–50.

Levi, Primo. *The Drowned and the Saved*, trans. Raymond Rosenthal. New York, NY: Random House, 1987.

Lieutenant General Mladić and General Halilović. Agreement for the Demilitarization of Srebrenica, article 7, signed agreement, Sarajevo, April 18, 1993.

Lischer, Sarah Kenyon. Collateral Damage: Humanitarian Assistance as a Cause of Conflict, *International Security* 28, no. 1 (2003): 79–109.

Littell, Franklin H. Essay: Early Warning, *Holocaust and Genocide Studies* 3, no. 4 (1988): 483–90.

Litvak, Meir. The Islamic Republic of Iran and the Holocaust: Anti-Semitism and Anti-Zionism, *The Journal of Israeli History* 25, no.1 (March 2006): 267–284.

Ljubijankic, Irfan. New World Order and Bosnia and Herzegovina, *Journal of Muslim Minority Affairs* 16, no. 1 (1996): 65–71.

Longman, Timothy. Identity Cards, Ethnic Self-Perception, and Genocide in Rwanda, *Documenting Individual Identity: The Development of State Practices in the Modern World*. Princeton, NJ: Princeton University Press, 345–357, 2001.

Louis, William Roger Roger Casement and the Congo, *Journal of African History* 5, no. 1 (1964): 99–120.

Louis, William Roger The Stokes Affair and the Origins of the Anti-Congo Campaign, 1895–1896, *Revue belge de philologie et d'histoire* 43, no. 2 (1965): 572–584.

Lu, Catherine. Agents, Structures and Evil in World Politics, *International Relations* 18, 4 (December 2004): 499–510.

Lu, Catherine. The International Criminal Court as an Institution of Moral Regeneration: Problems and Prospects In *Bringing Power to Justice: The Prospects of the International Criminal Court*, edited by Joanna Harrington Michael Milde and Richard Vernon, Chap. 7 Montreal, QC: McGill-Queen's University Press, 2006.

Luban, David. A Man Lost in the Gray Zone, *Law and History Review* 19, (2001): 161–176.

Luwel, Marcel. Roger Casement à Henry Morton Stanley: un rapport sur la situation au Congo en 1890, *Africa-Tervuren* 14, no. 4 (1968): 85–92.

Machiavelli, Niccolo. *The Prince*, translated by George Bull. London: Penguin Classics, 1961.

MacKinnon, Catherine International Decision: Prosecutor v. Nahimana, Barayagwiza, & Ngeze., *American Journal of International Law* 98, no. 2 (April, 2004): 325–330.

Mamdani, Mahmood. *When Victims Become Killers: Colonialism, Nativism, and the Genocide in Rwanda*. Princeton, NJ: Princeton University Press, 2001.

Mann, Michael. *The Dark Side of Democracy: Explaining Ethnic Cleansing*. New York, NY: Cambridge University Press, 2005.

Manvell, Roger, and Heinrich Fraenkel. *Doctor Goebbels. His Life & Death*. London: Greenhill, 2008.

Maréchal, Philippe La controverse sur Léopold II et le Congo dans la littérature et les médias: Réflexions critiques In *La Mémoire du Congo: Le temps colonial*, edited by Jean-Luc Vellut, 43–50. Tervuren: Musée Royal de l'Afrique Centrale/Gand, Snoeck, 2005.

Margaliot, Abraham. The Reaction of the Jewish Public in Germany to the Nuremberg Laws, *Yad Vashem Studies* 12, (1977): 75–107.

Marrus, Michael R. Jewish Resistance to the Holocaust Vol. 7, T*he Nazi Holocaust Historical Articles on the Destruction of European Jews*. Meckler, 1989.

Marx, Dalia. Liturgy Composed on the Brink of Catastrophe In Leo Baeck *Philosophical and Rabbinical Approaches*, edited by W. Homolka. Berlin: Frank and Timme GmbH, 2007.

Mayersen, Deborah. Intermittent Intervention: Europe and the Precipitation of the Armenian Massacres of 1894–1896 In *Terror, War, Tradition: Studies in European History*, edited by Bernard Mees and Samuel P Koehne, 247–270 Unley, SA: Australian Humanities Press, 2007.

McAleavey, Russell. Pressuring Sudan: The Prospect of an Oil-for-Food Program for Darfur, *Fordham International Law Journal* 31, no.4 (2008): 1058–1088.

McCormack, John. *One Million Mercenaries: Swiss Soldiers in the Armies of the World*. London: Leo Cooper, 1993.

McDoom, Omar. London School of Economics, Political Science. Crisis States Programme, Political Science. Development Studies Institute, and Political Science. Crisis States Research Centre. Rwanda's Ordinary Killers: Interpreting Popular Participation in the Rwandan Genocide: Crisis States Research Centre, LSE, 2005.

Mégret, Frédéric. Le droit international peut-il être un droit de résistance? Dix conditions pour un renouveau de l'ambition normative internationale, *Etudes internationales* 39 no. 1 (2008): 39–62.

Mégret, Frédéric. Responsibility to Protect (Others) v. the Power of Protecting Oneself: Beyond the 'Salvation' Paradigm (unpublished paper).

Milgram, Stanley. The Perils of Obedience *Psychology in Today's World*. Boston, MA: Little, Brown (1975).

Mill, John Stuart *Utilitarianism. On Liberty. Essay on Bentham*, edited with an Introduction by Mary Warnock. Glasgow: Collins Fount, 1979.

Miller, Arthur G. What Can the Milgram Obedience Experiments Tell Us About the Holocaust In *The Social Psychology of Good and Evil*, 193–239, New York, NY: Guilford Press, (2004).

Miller, Judith. The World: Checkered Flags; Sovereignty Isn't So Sacred Anymore. *The New York Times*, April 18, 1999.

Mingxuan, Gao and Wang Xiumei. Reflections on the Characteristics and Localization of Universal Jurisdiction. *Law and Social Development* (June 2001).

Minow, Martha. What the Rule of Law Should Mean in Civics Education: From the 'Following Orders' Defence to the Classroom, *Journal of Moral Education* 35, no. 2 (2006): 137–162.

Mockler, Anthony. *The Mercenaries*. New York, NY: The Macmillan Company, 1969.

Moghadam, Tanaz. Revitalizing Universal Jurisdiction: Lessons from Hybrid Tribunals Applied to the Case of Hissène Habré, *Columbia Human Rights Law Review* 39, no. 1 (2008): 471–528.

Moore, Bob. The Rescue of Jews in Nazi-Occupied Belgium, France and the Netherlands, *Australian Journal of Politics & History* 50, no. 3 (2004): 385–395.

Morash, Christopher. *Writing the Irish Famine*. Oxford: Clarendon, 1995.

Morel, Edmund D. *Affairs of West Africa*. London: Heinemann, 1902.

Morel, Edmund D. *King Leopold's Rule in Africa*. London: Heinemann, 1904.

Morel, Edmund D. *Morel's History of the Congo Reform Movement*, edited by William Roger Louis and Jean Stengers. Oxford: Clarendon, 1968.

Morel, Edmund D. *Red Rubber: The Story of the Rubber Slave Trade Flourishing on the Congo in the Year of Grace 1906*. London: Unwin, 1907.

Morel, Edmund D. *The Congo Slave State. A Protest Against the New African Slavery; and an Appeal to the Public of Great Britain, of the United States, and of the Continent of Europe*. Liverpool: Richardson, 1903.

Moreno-Ocampo, Luis. "Building a Future on Peace and Justice." Address, Nuremburg. Conference, Nuremberg, June 24/25, 2007. http://wwwold.icc-cpi.int/library/organs/otp/speeches/LMO_nuremberg_20070625_English.pdf

Moreno-Ocampo, Luis. ICC Prosecutor on Darfur: "Stop the Crimes, Stop the Criminals. International Criminal Court. http://www.icc-cpi.int/menus/icc/situations%20and%20cases/situations/situation%20icc%200205/press%20releases/icc%20prosecutor%20on%20darfur_%20%E2%80%9Cstop%20the%20crimes_%20stop%20the%20criminals%E2%80%9D (Accessed July 15, 2009).

Morton, Jeffrey S., and Neil Vijay Singh The International Legal Regime on Genocide, *Journal of Genocide Research* 5, no. 1 (2003): 47–69.

Mukimbiri, Jean. The Seven Stages of the Rwandan Genocide, *Journal of International Criminal Justice* 3, no. 4 (2005): 823–836.

Murray, Rachel. The Report of the OAU's International Panel of Eminent Personalities to Investigate the 1994 Genocide in Rwanda and Surrounding Events, *Journal of African Law* 45, (2001): 123–133. Quoted in Jeremy Sarkin. The Tension Between Justice and Reconciliation in Rwanda: Politics, Human Rights, Due Process and the Role of the Gacaca Courts in Dealing with Genocide. *Journal of African Law*, 45 (2001): 143–172.

Naimark, Norman M. *Fires of Hatred: Ethnic Cleansing in Twentieth-Century Europe*. Cambridge, MA: Harvard University Press, 2001.

Naji, Kasra. *Ahmadinejad: The Secret History of Iran's Radical Leader*. Los Angeles, CA: University of California Press, 2008.

Netherlands Institute for War Documentation *Srebrenica, een 'veilig' gebied. Reconstructie, achtergronden, gevolgen en analyses van de val van een Safe Area III* (Srebrenica, a 'safe' area. Reconstruction, background information, consequences and analyses of the fall of a Safe Area III). Amsterdam: Boom, 2002.

Ngor, Haing, and Roger Warner. *A Cambodian Odyssey*. New York, NY: Macmillan, 1987.

Nissim, Gabriele. Dimiter Peshev, the Vicepresident of the Bulgarian Parliament Who Made a Whole Nation Feel Ashamed. http://web.ceu.hu/jewishstudies/pdf/02_nissim.pdf.

Noakes, Jeremy and Geoffrey Pridham. *Documents on Nazism 1919–1945*. New York, NY: Viking Press, 1974.

Noone, Val. Famine and Imperialism: Ireland 1845–1852. Paper presented at Colloquium on "Comparative Famine and Political Killings: causation, scale and state responsibility." History Department, Melbourne University, August 13, 1999.

Nzelibe, Jide. Courting Genocide: The Unintended Effects of Humanitarian Interventions. *Jide O Nzelibe* (2008): 1.

Ó Gráda, Cormac *Black '47 and Beyond: The Great Irish Famine*. Princeton, NJ: Princeton University Press, 1999.

Ó Gráda, Cormac The Great Famine and Today's Famines In *The Great Irish Famine*, edited by Cathal Póirtéir, 248–258. Dublin: Mercier, 1995.

Ó Gráda, Cormac *The Great Irish Famine*. London: Macmillan, 1989.

Ó Murchadha, Ciarán *Sable Wings over the Land: Ennis, County Clare, and its Wider Community During the Great Famine*. Ennis: Clasp Press, 1998.

Ó Síocháin, Séamas Roger Casement's Vision of Freedom In *Roger Casement in Irish and World History*, edited by Mary E Daly, 1–10. Dublin: Royal Irish Academy, 2005.

Ó Síocháin, Séamas *Roger Casement: Imperialist, Rebel, Revolutionary*. Dublin: Lilliput, 2007.

O'Callaghan, Margaret 'With the Eyes of Another Race, of a People Once Hunted Themselves': Casement, Colonialism, and a Remembered Past In *Roger Casement in Irish and World History*, edited by Mary E Daly, 52. Dublin: Royal Irish Academy, 2005,.

O'Neill, Onora Practices of toleration In *Democracy and the Mass Media*, edited by Judith Lichtenberg, Cambridge: Cambridge University Press, 1990.

O'Neill, Onora Rethinking Freedom of the Press. Transcript of an address given at the Royal Irish Academy, December 4, 2003, 7. www.ria.ie/reports/pdf/pressfreedom.pdf (Accessed June 10, 2009).

Ofer, Dalia. The Activities of the Jewish Agency Delegation in Istanbul, 1943 In *Rescue Attempts During the Holocaust: Proceedings of the Second Yad Vashem International Historical Conference*, edited by Efraim Zuroff Ysrael Gutman, 435–50, Jerusalem, April 1974.

Oil Platforms (Islamic Republic of Iran v. United States of America), Preliminary Objections, ICJ Reports 1996.

Oliner, Samuel P. *The Altruistic Personality: Rescuers of Jews in Nazi Europe*. New York, NY: Touchstone, 1992.

Orford, Anne. Muscular Humanitarianism: Reading the Narratives of the New Interventionism. European, *Journal of International Law* 10, no. 4 (1999): 679–711.

Orwell, George. *Homage to Catalonia*. New York, NY: Harcourt Brace, 1952.

Osiel, Mark. *Obeying Orders: Atrocity, Military Discipline and the Law of War*. New Brunswick, NJ: Transaction Pub, 2002.

Overview. http://untreaty.un.org/cod/icc/general/overview.htm.

Paldiel, Mordecai. *Diplomat Heroes of the Holocaust*. Jersey City, NJ: Ktav Publishing House, 2007.

Paldiel, Mordecai. *The Path of the Righteous: Gentile Rescuers of Jews During the Holocaust*. Jersey City, NJ: KTAV Publishing House, Inc., 1993.

Pargament, Kenneth I., Kavita M. Desai, and Kelly M. McConnell. Spirituality: A Pathway to Posttraumatic Growth or Decline? In *Handbook of Posttraumatic Growth: Research & Practice*, edited by Lawrence G Calhoun and Richard G Tedeschi, 121–137. Hillsdale, NJ: Erlbaum, 2006.

Paris, Roland. *At War's End*. Cambridge: Cambridge University Press, 2004.

Patrick, Erin. Intent to Destroy: The Genocidal Impact of Forced Migration in Darfur Sudan, *Journal of Refugee Studies*, 18, no. 4 (2005): 410–429.

Peddle, Nancy, Calinda Monteiro, Vello Guluma, and Thomas E.A. Macaulay. Trauma, Loss, and Resilience in Africa: A Psychosocial Community Based Approach to Culturally Sensitive Healing In *Honoring Differences: Cultural Issues in the Treatment of Trauma and Loss*, edited by Kathleen Nader, Nancy Dubrow, and B.H. Stamm, 121–149. Phildelphia, PA: Brunner/Mazel, 1999.

Peifer, Douglas. Commemoration of Mutiny, Rebellion, and Resistance in Postwar Germany: Public Memory, History, and the Formation of Memory Beacons, *Journal of Military History* 65 no. 4 (2001): 1013–1052.

Peifer, Douglas. Genocide and Air Power, *Strategic Studies Quarterly* 2, no. 2 (2008): 93–124.

Percy, Sarah. Mercenaries: Strong Norm, Weak Law, *International Organization*, 61 (Spring 2007): 367–397.

Percy, Sarah. Morality and Regulation In *From Mercenaries to Market: The Rise and Regulation of Private Military Companies*, edited by Simon Chesterman & Chia Lehnardt. New York, NY: Oxford University Publishers, 2007.

Perrin, Benjamin. Promoting Compliance of Private Security and Military Companies with International Humanitarian Law, *International Review of the Red Cross* 88, no. 863 (2006): 613–636.

Petition. "Danger of a Genocidal and Nuclear Iran: The Responsibility to Prevent." Petition signed by leading jurists, genocide experts and survivors. http://www.irwincotler.parl.gc.ca/documents/081209_petition.pdf (Accessed June 4, 2009).

Pfanner, Toni. Interview with Andrew Bearpark, *International Review of the Red Cross*, 863 (2006): 449–557.

Pham, Phuong N., Harvey M. Weinstein, and Timothy Longman. Trauma and PTSD Symptoms in Rwanda: Implications for Attitudes Toward Justice and Reconciliation, *JAMA: Journal of the American Medical Association* 292, no. 5 (2004): 602–612.

Phipps, William E. *William Sheppard: Congo's African American Livingstone*. Louisville, KY: Geneva Press, 2002.

Piiparinen, Touko. Reconsidering the Silence over the Ultimate Crime: A Functional Shift in Crisis Management from the Rwandan Genocide to Darfur, *Journal of Genocide Research* 9, no. 1 (2007): 71–91.

Polgreen, Lydia. Scorched-Earth Strategy Returns to Darfur. *The New York Times*, March 2, 2008.

Potter, David. The International Mercenary Market in the Sixteenth Century: Anglo-French Competition in Germany, 1543–1550, *The English Historical Review* 111, no. 440 (1996): 24–58.

Powell, Steve, Rita Rosner, Willi Butollo, Richard G. Tedeschi, and Lawrence G. Calhoun . Posttraumatic Growth After War: A Study with Former Refugees and Displaced People in Sarajevo, *Journal of Clinical Psychology* 59, no. 1 (2003): 71–83.

Power, Samantha. *A Problem from Hell: America and the Age of Genocide*. New York, NY: Basic Books, 2002.

Power, Samantha. Bystanders to Genocide, *Atlantic Monthly* 288, no. 2 (2001): 84–108.

Power, Samantha. Never Again: The World's Most Unfulfilled Promise. *Frontline*, http://www.pbs.org/wgbh/pages/frontline/shows/karadzic/genocide/neveragain.html

Pramono, Siswo. An Account of the Theory of Genocide. 2002. Refereed paper presented to the Jubilee conference of the Australasian Political Studies Association, 1–22 http://arts.anu.edu.au/sss/apsa/Papers/pramonotheory.pdf.

Princeton University Program in Law and Public Affairs *The Princeton Principles on Universal Jurisdiction*, 28 (2001): 1–50. http://lapa.princeton.edu/hosteddocs/unive_jur.pdf.

Prosecutor of the International Criminal Court, Sixth Report to the Security Council pursuant to UNSC 1593 (2005) http://www.icc-cpi.int/NR/rdonlyres/D084A825-A985-4068-8320-5724AA894430/277791/OTPRP20071205UNSCENG.pdf.

Prosecutor v. Ahmad Muhammad Harun and Ali Muhammad Ali Abd-Al-Rahman, International Criminal Court, Warrant of Arrest for Ali Kushayb, International Criminal Court, ICC-02/05-01/07-3 (April 27, 2007), 1–17. http://www.icc-cpi.int/Menus/ICC/Situations+and+Cases/Situations/Situation+ICC+0205/Related+Cases/ICC+0205+0107/Court+Records/Chambers/Pre+Trial+Chamber+I/WARRANT+OF+ARREST+FOR+ALI+KUSHAYB.htm (Accessed June 12, 2009).

Prosecutor v. Niyitegaka, Case No. ICTR-96-14-A, (July 9, 2004).

Prosecutor v. Stakic, Case No. IT-97-24-T, Judgment (July 31, 2003).

Prunier, Gérard Ecologie, structures ethniques et conflits politiques au Dar Fur In *Sudan: History, Ideology, Identity*, edited by Hervé Bleuchot, Christian Delmet and Derek Hopwood, 85–103. Oxford: Ithaca Press, 1991.

Prunier, Gérard. Chad: Between Sudan's Blitzkrieg and Darfur's War. In *OpenDemocracy.net*, February 19, 2008). http://www.opendemocracy.net/article/democracy_power/africa/chad_sudan_darfur (Accessed June 9, 2009).

Prunier, Gérard *Darfur: the Ambiguous Genocide*. London/New York, NY: Hurst/Cornell University Press, 2005.

Rabil, Robert G. Operation 'Termination of Traitors': The Iraqi Regime through Its Documents, *Middle East Review of International Affairs* 6, no. 4 (2002): 14–21.

Ranger, Terrence. *Revolt in Southern Rhodesia, 1896–1897*. London: Heineman, 1967.

Rawson, Claude. *God, Gulliver and Genocide: Barbarism and the European Imagination, 1492–1945*. Oxford: Oxford University Press, 2001.

Reagan, Ronald. Message to the House of Representatives Returning Without Approval a Bill Concerning Apartheid in South Africa. *The Public Papers of President Ronald W. Reagan*, Ronald Reagan Presidential Library (September 26, 1986). http://www.reagan.utexas.edu/archives/speeches/1986/092686 h.htm (Accessed June 12, 2009).

Reisman, W. Michael. Legal Responses to Genocide and Other Massive Violations of Human Rights, *Law and Contemporary Problems* 59, no. 4 (1996): 75–80.

Reporters Without Borders "Côte d'Ivoire – Annual Report 2005." Reporters Without Borders, May 3, 2005. http://www.rsf.org/article.php3?id_article=13569 (Accessed June 9, 2009).

Research hub: Social Science Research Council. http://mediaresearchhub.ssrc.org/the-media-s-role-in-peace-building-asset-or-liability/resource_view (Accessed June 10, 2009).

Reyntjens, Filip. Rwanda Ten Years On: From Genocide to Dictatorship, *African Affairs* 103 (2004): 177–210.

Rieff, David. The Precarious Triumph of Human Rights. *New York Times Magazine*, August 8, 1999.

Robben, Antonious C.G.M. and Marcelo M. Suarez-Orozco. "Interdisciplinary Perspectives on Violence and Trauma In *Cultures under Siege: Collective Violence and Trauma*, edited by Antonious C.G.M. Robben and Marcelo M. Suarez-Orozco, 1–43. Cambridge: Cambridge University Press, 2000.

Robinson, Randall. The Obligation to Rescue I, *Social Research* 62, no. 1 (1995): 67–75.

Rohrlich, Ruby. *Resisting the Holocaust*. New York, NY: Berg Publishers, 1998.

Rome Statute of the International Criminal Court, July 1, 2002. http://www.icc-cpi.int/library/about/officialjournal/Rome_Statute_English.pdf. (Accessed June 9, 2009)

Rome Statute of the International Criminal Court. U.N. Doc. A/CONF.183/9, 1998.

Rosoux, Valérie The Figure of the Righteous Individual in Rwanda, *International Social Science Journal* 58, no. 189 (2006): 491–499.

Rowley, Charles Dunford *The Destruction of Aboriginal Society*. Canberra, ACT: Australian National University Press, 1970.

Rubenstein, Richard L. and John K. Roth. *Approaches to Auschwitz: The Holocaust and its Legacy*. Louisville, KY: Westminster John Knox Press, 2003.

Rubenstein, Richard L. and John K. Roth. Genocide and Civilization In *Genocide and the Modern Age*, edited by I. Wallimann and M. Dobkowski, 283–298. Syracuse: Syracuse University Press, 2000.

Rutembesa, Faustin, Josias Semujanga, and Shyaka Anastase., eds. *Rwanda: Identité et citoyenneté*. Butare: Editions de l'Université Nationale du Rwanda, 2003.

Rwabuhungu, Digne. Synthèse Du Colloque: 'Les Justes Face Au Génocide: Réflexion Sur Une Attitude Héroïque.' Organisé Par La Communauté Rwandaise De Belgique, 2008.

Saltzman, Ann L. The Role of the Obedience Experiments in Holocaust Studies: The Case for Renewed Visibility In *Obedience to Authority: Current Perspectives on the Milgram Paradigm* edited by T. Blass, 125–143 New Jersey: Erlbaum (2000).

Sansani, Inbal. The Pinochet Precedent in Africa: Prosecution of Hissene Habre, *Human Rights Brief* 8, no. 2 (2001): 32–34.

Sarkin, Jeremy. The Tension Between Justice and Reconciliation in Rwanda: Politics, Human Rights, Due Process and the Role of the Gacaca Courts in Dealing with Genocide, *Journal of African Law*, 45, (2001) 143–174.

Satterwhite, James. Forestalling War in Kosovo: Opportunities Missed, *Peace & Change 27*, no. 4 (2002): 600–611.

Schabas, William A. Genocide, Crimes Against Humanity, and Darfur: the Commission of Inquiry's Findings on Genocide, *Cardozo Law Review* 27, no. 4 (February 2006): 1703–1722.

Scheffer, David. Genocide and Atrocity Crimes, *Genocide Studies and Prevention* 1, no. 3 (2006): 229–50.

Scheffer, David. The Merits of Unifying Terms: 'Atrocity Crimes' and 'Atrocity Law', *Genocide Studies and Prevention* 2, no. 1 (2007): 91–95.

Scheffer, David. 50th Anniversary of the Entering into Force of the Genocide Convention. Address to the United Nations, United Nations Headquarters, New York City, New York, June 13, 2001.

Schneiderman, Harry. Review of the Year 5693. American Jewish Year Book 35, (1932–1933).

Schnoring, Katharina. Deserters in the Federal Republic of Yugoslavia, *International Journal of Refugee Law* 13, no. 1_ and_ 2 (2001): 153–73.

Schulze, Rainer. Keeping Very Clear of Any 'Kuh-Handel': The British Foreign Office and the Rescue of Jews from Bergen-Belsen Holocaust, *Genocide Studies* 19, no. 2 (2005): 226–251.

Sennitt, Andy. Replacing Hate with Hope in Kenya: Hate Radio Fans the Flames of Violence, *Radio Nederland Wereldomroep*, January 31, 2008. http://www.radionetherlands.nl/features/media/080131-kenya-hate-radio (Accessed June 9, 2009).

Shannon, Vaughn. Judge and Executioner: The Politics of Responding to Ethnic Cleansing in the Balkans, *Journal of Genocide Research* 7, no. 1 (2005): 47–66.

Sharp, Dustin N. Prosecutions, Development, and Justice: The Trial of Hissene Habre, *Harvard Human Rights Journal* 16 (2003): 147–177.

Shearer, David. *Adelphi Paper 316: Private Armies and Military Intervention*. London: Oxford University Press, 1998.

Shelton, Dinah. Normative Hierarchy in International Law, *American Journal of International Law* 100 (2006): 291–323.

Sheppard, William H. *Presbyterian Pioneers in Congo*. Richmond, VA: Presbyterian Committee of Publication, 1917.

Sherif, Musharraf Superordinate Goals in the Reduction of Intergroup Conflict, *The American Journal of Sociology* 63, no. 4 (1958): 349–356.

Shklar, Judith. N. *Legalism: Law, Morals, and Political Trials*. Cambridge, MA: Harvard, 1986.

Sibomana, Andre. *Hope for Rwanda: Conversations with Laure Guilbert and Hervé Deguine*. London: Pluto Press, 1999.

Siekmann, Robert. The Fall of Srebrenica and the Attitude of Dutchbat from an International Legal Perspective, *Yearbook of International Humanitarian Law* 1, (1998): 301–312.

Singer, Peter W. Humanitarian Principles, Private Military Agents: Some Implications of the Privatized Military Industry for the Humanitarian Community In *Resetting the Rules of Engagement: Trends and Issues in Military-Humanitarian Relations*, In edited by Victoria Wheeler and Adele Harmer Humanitarian Policy Group Report 21. London: Overseas Development Institute, 2006.

Singer, Peter W. Peacekeepers Inc. In *Policy Review*, No. 119 (June/July 2003), http://www.hoover.org/publications/policy%20review/3448831.html (Accessed June 15, 2009).

Singer, Peter W. War, Profits, and the Vacuum of Law: Privatized Military Firms and International Law, *Columbia Journal of Transnational Law* 12 (2004): 521–547.

Singer, Peter W. *Corporate Warriors: The Rise of the Privatized Military Industry*. Ithaca, NY: Cornell University Press, 2003.

Singleton-Gates, Peter and Maurice, Girodias *The Black Diaries: An Account of Roger Casement's Life and Times with a Collection of his Diaries and Public Writings*. New York, NY: Grove, 1959.

Sixth Report of the Prosecutor of the International Criminal Court, to the Security Council pursuant to UNSCR 1593 (2005).

Sniderman, Andrew. 'If Lives Matter, Then You Use the Private Industry': Blackwater USA and the Genocide Intervention Fund November 12, 2005, unpublished paper.

Special Committee on Hate Propaganda in Canada *Report of the Special Committee on Hate Propaganda in Canada*. Minister of Justice, Canada. Ottawa, ON: Queen's Printer, 1966.

Spicer, Tim. *An Unorthodox Soldier: Peace and War and the Sandline Affair*. Edinburgh: Mainstream Publishing, 1999. Quoted in Andrew Clapham. Human Rights Obligations of Non-State Actors in Conflict Situations. *International Review of the Red Cross*, no. 863, (2006): 491–523.

SS Lotus Case (France v. Turkey), P.C.I.J. Series A, no 10 (1927).

Stanton, Gregory. The Eight Stages of Genocide. First Working Paper (GS 01), Yale Program in Genocide Studies, 1998. http://www.genocidewatch.org/8stages1996.htm (Accessed June 4, 2009).

Staub, Ervin. The Psychology of Bystanders, Perpetrators, and Heroic Helpers, *Understanding Genocide: The Social Psychology of the Holocaust*. Oxford, UK: Oxford University Press, (2002): 11–42.

Staub, Ervin. Genocide and Mass Killing: Origins, Prevention, Healing and Reconciliation, *Political Psychology*, 21, no. 2 (June, 2000): 367–382.

Staub, Ervin. Reconciliation After Genocide, Mass Killing, or Intractable Conflict: Understanding the Roots of Violence, Psychological Recovery, and Steps Toward a General Theory, *Political Psychology* 27, no.6 (2006): 867–894.

Staub, Ervin. *The Roots of Evil: The Origins of Genocide and Other Group Violence*. Cambridge: Cambridge University Press, 1989.

Steinberg, Maxime. *La Persécution Des Juifs En Belgique* (1940–1945). Editions Complexe , 2004.

Stohl, Michael. Outside of a Small Circle of Friends: States, Genocide, Mass Killing and the Role of Bystanders, *Journal of Peace Research* 24, no. 2 (1987): 151.

Stolleis, Michael. *The Law under the Swastika: Studies on Legal History in Nazi Germany*. Chicago: University of Chicago Press, 1998.

Stoltzfus, Nathan. Protest and Silence: Resistance Histories in Post-War Germany: The Missing Case of Intermarried Germans In *Resisting the Holocaust*, edited by Michael Marrus, 151–78. New York, NY: Berg, 1998.

Straus, Scott. *The Order of Genocide*. Ithica, NY: Cornell University Press, 2006.

Sudan Divestment Task Force Divestment Statistics: Figures for States, Universities, Cities, International & Religious Organizations and Countries. Sudan Divestment Task Force. http://www.sudandivestment.org/statistics.asp (Accessed June 8, 2009).

Sudan Divestment Task Force Task Force Model for Targeted Divestment. Sudan Divestment Task Force. http://www.sudandivestment.org/position.asp#model (Accessed June 8, 2009).

Suedfeld, Peter, and Stefanie de Best. Value Hierarchies of Holocaust Rescuers and Resistance Fighters, *Genocide Studies and Prevention* 3, no. 1 (2008): 31–42.

Suedfeld, Peter. Cognitive Managers and Their Critics, *Political Psychology* 13, no. 3 (1992): 435–453.

Suedfeld, Peter. Reactions to Societal Trauma: Distress and/or Eustress, *Political Psychology* 18, no. 4 (1997): 849–861.

Summerfield, Derek. A Critique of Seven Assumptions Behind Psychological Trauma Programmes in War-Affected Areas., *Social Science & Medicine* 48, no.10 (1999): 1449–1462.

Sykes, Gresham M, and David Matza. Techniques of Neutralization: A Theory of Delinquency, *American Sociological Review* 22, no. 6 (1957): 664–70.

Szita, Szabolcs. *Trading in Lives?: Operations of the Jewish Relief and Rescue Committee in Budapest, 1944–1945*. Central European University Press, 2005.

Taylor, Charles. The Politics of Recognition In Chap. 2 *Multiculturalism*. Princeton, NJ: Princeton University Press, 1994.

Taylor, Christopher. *Sacrifice as Terror: The Rwandan Genocide of 1994*. Birmingham: Berg Publishers, 1999.

Tec, Nechama. Jewish Resistance in Belorussian Forests: Fighting and the Rescue of Jews by Jews In *Resisting the Holocaust*, edited by Ruby Rohrlich, 77, Oxford, UK: University of Nebraska Press, 1998.

Tedeschi, Richard G., and Lawrence G. Calhoun. Special Issue: Editorial Note, *Traumatology* 11, no. 4 (2005): 207–208.

Tedeschi, Richard G., and Lawrence G. Calhoun. The Posttraumatic Growth Inventory: Measuring the Positive Legacy of Trauma, *Journal of Traumatic Stress* 9, no. 3 (July 1996): 455–471.

Tedeschi, Richard G., Crystal L. Park, and Lawrence G. Calhoun, Posttraumatic Growth: Conceptual Issues In *Posttraumatic Growth: Positive Changes in the Aftermath of Crisis*, In edited by Richard G. Tedeschi, Crystal L. Park, and Lawrence G. Calhoun, 1–22. Hillsdale, NJ: Erlbaum, 1998.

Teitelbaum, Joshua. *What Iranian Leaders Really Say About Doing Away with Israel*. Jerusalem: Jerusalem Center for Public Affairs, 2008.

Territorial Dispute (Libyan Arab Jamahiririya/Chad). Judgment, International Court of Justice Reports, 1994.

The Prosecutor v. Eliezer Niyitegeka, Case No. ICTR-96-14-A, Appeal Chamber Judgment, (July 9 2004).

The Prosecutor v. Elizaphan and Gérard Ntakirutimana, Case Nos. ICTR-96-10 & ICRT-96-17-T, Judgment, (February 21, 2003).

The Prosecutor v. Kajelijeli, Case No. ICTR-98-44A-A, Appeals Judgement, (May 23, 2005).

The Prosecutor v. Joseph Nzabirinda, Case No. ICTR-2001-77-T, Sentencing Judgment, (Feb 23, 2007).

The Prosecutor v. Juvénal Kajelijeli, Case No. ICTR-98-44A-T, Judgment and Sentence, (Dec 1, 2003).

The Prosecutor v. Tihomir Blaskic, Case No. IT-95-14-T, Judgment, (March 3, 2000).

Thomas, Gerry S. *Mercenary Troops in Modern Africa*. Boulder, CO: Westview Press, 1986.

Thompson, Mark. *Forging War: The Media in Serbia, Croatia, Bosnia and Herzegovina*. Luton and London: Article 19 & the University of Luton, 1999.

Thomson, Janice E. *Mercenaries, Pirates and Sovereigns: State-Building and Extraterritorial Violence in Early Modern Europe*. Ewing: Princeton University Press, 1994.

Tiemessen, Alana E. After Arusha: Gacaca Justice in Post-Genocide Rwanda, *African Studies Quarterly* 8, no. 1 (2004): 57–76.

Tóibín, Colm and Diarmaid, Ferriter. *The Irish Famine: A Documentary*. New York, NY: St. Martins, 2001.

Totten, Samuel. The Intervention and Prevention of Genocide: Sisyphean or Doable?, *Journal of Genocide Research* 6, no. 2 (2004): 229–247.

Totten, Samuel, Paul Robert Bartrop, and Steven L. Jacobs *Dictionary of Genocide*. London: Greenwood Publishing Group, 2008.

Tripodi, Paolo. Peacekeepers, Moral Autonomy and the Use of Force, *Journal of Military Ethics* 5, no. 3 (2006): 214–232.

Tripodi, Paolo. When Peacekeepers Fail Thousands Are Going to Die. The Eto in Rwanda: A Story of Deception, *Small Wars & Insurgencies* 17, no. 2 (2006): 221–36.

Tzur, Eli. From Moral Rejection to Armed Resistance: The Youth Movement in the Ghetto In *Resisting the Holocaust*, 39–58. New York, NY: Berg Publishers, 1998.

U.S. Congress. House *MEJA Expansion and Enforcement Act 2007*, HR 2740, 110th Cong., 2007.

United Kingdom, Foreign and Commonwealth Office (UK), "Private Military Companies: Options for Regulation," (February 12, 2002), http://www.fco.gov.uk/Files/kfile/mercenaries,0.pdf (Accessed June 11, 2009).

United Nations ESCOR, 53rd Sess., UN Doc. E/CN.4/1997/24, February 20, 1997.

United Nations General Assembly Resolution 2200A (XXI) *International Covenant on Civil and Political Rights*, 21 U.N. GAOR Supp. (No. 16) at 52, U.N. Doc. A/6316 (1966), 999 U.N.T.S. 171, *entered into force* Mar. 23, 1976.

United Nations General Assembly Resolution 260 (III) *Convention on the Prevention and Punishment of the Crime of Genocide*. December 9, 1948.

United Nations General Assembly Resolution 260 (III). *Convention on the Prevention and Punishment of the Crime of Genocide*. December 9, 1948.

United Nations General Assembly, 49th Session., UN Doc. A/49/362 (1993).

United Nations General Assembly, Res. 1761 (XVII), U.N. Doc. A/1761 (November 6, 1962).

United Nations General Assembly, Res. 3068 (XXVIII), *International Convention on the Suppression and Punishment of the Crime of Apartheid*, July 18, 1976.

United Nations General Assembly *2005 World Summit Outcome*, UN Doc. A/60/L1, September 15, 2005. http://daccessdds.un.org/doc/UNDOC/GEN/N05/487/60/PDF/N0548760.pdf?OpenElement (Accessed June 10, 2009).

United Nations Secretary-General Kofi Annan SECRETARY-GENERAL: First of all, I don't know how one makes a distinction between respectable mercenaries and non-respectable mercenaries. Transcript of Press Conference by at UN Headquarters, SG/SM/6255. June 12, 1997. http://www.un.org/news/Press/docs/1997/19970612.sgsm6255.html (Accessed June 11, 2009).

United Nations Secretary-General Secretary-General Welcomes Adoption of Security Council Resolution Referring Situation in Darfur, Sudan, to International Criminal Court Prosecutor. SG/SM/9797, AFR/1132, April 1, 2005. http://www.un.org/News/Press/docs/2005/sgsm9797.doc.htm (Accessed June 12, 2009).

United Nations Security Council, Res. 1564, U.N. Doc. S/RES/1564 (January 25, 2005).
United Nations Security Council, Res. 1593, U.N. Doc. S/Res/1593, (March 31, 2005).
United Nations Security Council, Res. 161, UN Doc. S/4741, (February 21, 1961).
United Nations Security Council, Res. 1679, U.N. Doc. S/RES/1679 (May 16, 2006).
United Nations Security Council, Res. 169, UN Doc. S/5002, November 24, 1961.
United Nations Security Council, Res. 418, U.N. Doc. S/RES/418 (November 4, 1977).
United Nations Security Council, Res. 591, U.N. Doc. S/RES/591 (November 28, 1986).
United Nations Security Council, Res. 661, U.N. Doc. S/RES/661 (August 6, 1990).
United Nations Security Council, Res. 687, U.N. Doc. S/RES/687 (April 8, 1991).
United Nations Security Council, Res. 706, U.N. Doc. S/RES/706 (August 15, 1991).
United Nations Security Council, Res. 712, U.N. Doc. S/RES/712 (September 19, 1991).
United Nations Security Council, Res. 819, 3199th meeting, April 16, 1993, U.N. Doc. S/RES/819 (1993), 2.
United Nations Security Council, Res. 836, 3228th meeting, June 4, 1993, U.N. Doc. S/RES/836 (1993), 2–3.
United Nations Security Council, Res. 872, 3288th meeting, October 5, 1993, U.N. Doc. S/RES/872 (1993).
United Nations Security Council, Res. 986, U.N. Doc. S/RES.986 (April 14, 1995).
United Nations Security Council, Res.743, 47 UN SCOR at 42, 3055th meeting, February 21, 1992, U.N. Doc. S/RES/742 (1992).
United Nations *A More Secure World: Our Shared Responsibility*. Report of the Secretary-General's High Level Panel on Threats, Challenges and Changes. New York, NY: United Nations Publications, 2004.
United Nations Economic and Social Council. *Report of the Representative of the Secretary-General on Internally Displaced Persons, Mr. Francis Deng, submitted pursuant to Commission on Human Rights Resolution 2002/56.* E/CN.4/2003/86/Add.5, November 27, 2003.
United Nations *Human Rights Compilation of International Instruments*. Office of the High Commissioner for Human Rights. ST/HR/1/Rev.6 (Vol.I/Part 2). New York and Geneva, 1994.
United Nations Office of the High Commissioner for Human Rights. The Core International Human Rights Treaties. New York, NY: United Nations, 2006.
United Nations *Report of the International Commission of Inquiry on Darfur to the Secretary-General of the United Nations*. Geneva, January 25, 2005, http://www.un.org/News/dh/sudan/com_inq_darfur.pdf (Accessed June 12, 2009).
United States National Security Council *The National Security Strategy of the United States of America 2002*, Part IV(C)(4) (Washington D.C.: September 2002), http://slomanson.tjsl.edu/NSS.pdf (Accessed June 9, 2009).
United States National Security Council *The National Security Strategy of the United States of America 2002*, Part III. Washington D.C., September 2002. http://merln.ndu.edu/whitepapers/USnss2002.pdf (Accessed June 9, 2009).
United Nations Security Council, Res. 181, U.N. Doc. S/RES/181 (August 7, 1963).
UNSC 1593 (2005), December 5, 2007. Accessed June 9, 2009, http://www.icc-cpi.int/library/organs/otp/OTP-RP-20071205-UNSC-ENG.pdf.
Update of Communications received by the Office of the Prosecutor of the ICC. February 10, 2006; Annexes: Iraq response and Venezuela response. Accessed June 9, 2009, http://www.icc-cpi.int/organs/otp/otp_com.html.
Van Shaack, Beth. The Crime of Political Genocide: Repairing the Genocide Convention's Blind Spot, *The Yale Law Journal*, 106, no. 7 (May, 1997): 2259–2291.
Vangroenweghe, Daniel. *Du sang sur les lianes: Léopold II et son Congo*. Bruxelles: Didier Hatier, 1986.
Veridrama, Guglichmo. The Genocide Definition in the Jurisprudence of the ad hoc Tribunals, *The International and Comparative Law Quarterly*, 49, no. 3 (July, 2000): 578–595.

Verwimp, Philip. Death and Survival During the 1994 Genocide in Rwanda, *Population Studies* 58, no. 2 (2004): 233–245.

Vetlesen, Arne Johan. Genocide: A Case for the Responsibility of the Bystander, *Journal of Peace Research* 37, no. 4 (2000): 519.

Vidal, Claudine. Les Commémorations Du Génocide Au Rwanda, *Les temps modernes* 613 (2001): 1–46.

Villiers-Tuthill, Kathleen. *Patient Endurance: The Great Famine in Connemara*. Dublin: Connemara Girl Publications, 1997.

Volkan, Vamik. *Bloodlines: From Ethnic Pride to Ethnic Terrorism*. Colorado: Westview Books, 1998.

Wagner, Michele D. All the Bourgmestre's Men: Making Sense of Genocide in Rwanda, *Africa Today* 45, no. 1 (1998): 25–36.

Waldron, Jeremy. Boutique Faith. *London Review of Books*. July 20, 2006.

Walliman, Isidor, and Michael Dobkowski. Introduction In *Genocide and the Modern Age: Etiology and Case Studies of Mass Death*, In edited by.Isidor Walliman and Michael Dobkowski. Syracuse, NY: Syracuse University Press, 2000. Quoted in George J. Andreopoulos. *Genocide: Conceptual and Historical Dimensions*, edited by George. J. Andreopoulos. Philadelphia, PA: University of Pennsylvania Press, 1997.

Walzer, Michael. Mercenary Impulse: Is there an Ethics that Justifies Blackwater?, *The New Republic*, March 12, 2008.

Weber, Max. Politics as a Vocation In *From Max Weber: Essays in Sociology*, edited by H.H. Gerth and C. Wright Mills, 77–128. New York, NY: Oxford University Press, 1946.

Wei, Zhao. About the Identification Process of the 55 Minority Nationalities, *Ethnic Unity* (March 1999), 52.

Weisberg, Richard H. *Vichy Law and the Holocaust in France*. New York, NY: Routledge, 1996.

Weitz, Eric D. *A Century of Genocide: Utopias of Race and Nation*. Princeton, NJ: Princeton University Press, 2003.

Welch, Steven R. 'Harsh but Just'? German Military Justice in the Second World War: A Comparative Study of the Court-Martialling of German and Us Deserters, *German History* 17, no. 3 (1999): 369–99.

Wenqi, Zhu. The Trigger Mechanism of the International Criminal Court and the Reaction of USA, *Henan Social Science* 11, no. 5 (September 2003).

Werner, Emmy E. *A Conspiracy of Decency: The Rescue of the Danish Jews During World War II*. Boulder, CO: Westview Press, 2002.

Wiebes, Wiebes. *Intelligence en de oorlog in Bosnië1992–1995*. In *De rol van de inlichtingen- en veiligheidsdiensten* (Intelligence and the war in Bosnia 1992–1995. The role of the intelligence and security services). Amsterdam: LIT Verlag Berlin-Hamburg-Münster, 2002.

Williams , George Washington *History of the Negro Race in America from 1619 to 1880*. In *Negroes as Slaves, as Soldiers, and as Citizens, Together with a Preliminary Consideration of the Unity of the Human Family and Historical Sketch of Africa and an Account of the Negro Governments of Sierra Leone and Liberia*. New York, NY: G.P. Putnam's Sons, 1883.

Williams, Sharon A. Commentary on the Rome Statute of the International Criminal Court In edited by Otto Triffterer, 336–338. Germany: Nomos Verlagsgesellschaft, Baden-Baden, 1999.

Wimmer, Andreas. The Making and Unmaking of Ethnic Boundaries: A Multilevel Process Theory, *American Journal of Sociology* 113, no. 4 (2008): 970–1022.

Wittmann , Rebecca Elizabeth Indicting Auschwitz? The Paradox of the Frankfurt Auschwitz Trial, *German History* 21, no. 4 (2003): 505.

Woocher, Laurence. Developing a Strategy, Methods and Tools for Genocide Early Warning. *Paper Prepared for the Office of the Special Adviser to the UN*

Secretary-General on the Prevention of Genocide, Center for International Conflict Resolution. Columbia University, September 26, 2006.
Wood, William B. Geographic Aspects of Genocide: A Comparison of Bosnia and Rwanda, *Transactions of British Geographics*, New Series, 26, no. 1 (2001): 57–75.
Woodham-Smith, Cecil *The Great Hunger*. New York, NY: Harper & Row, 1962.
Xinyu, Leng. *On the Universal Jurisdiction.* Doctoral diss., Renmin University of China (April 2007).
Young, Iris Marion Responsibility and Global Labor Justice, *The Journal of Political Philosophy* 12, no.4 (2004): 365–388.
Zarate, Juan Carlos The Emergence of a New Dog of War: Private International Security Companies, in International Law, and the New World Disorder, *Stanford Journal of International Law* 34.75 (1998): 75–162.

Index

B

D

T